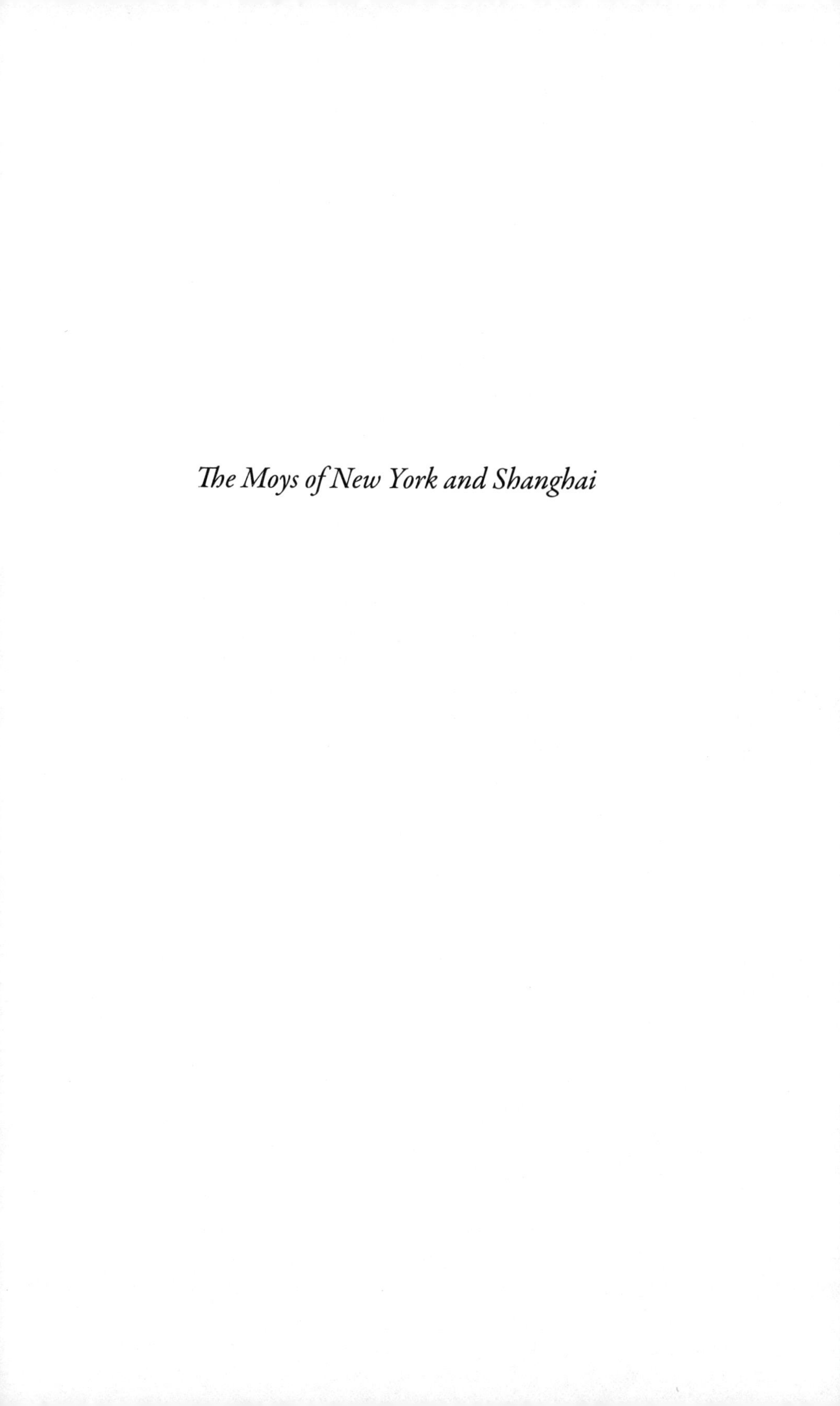

The Moys of New York and Shanghai

A

Philip E. Lilienthal

BOOK

The Philip E. Lilienthal imprint
honors special books
in commemoration of a man whose work
at University of California Press from 1954 to 1979
was marked by dedication to young authors
and to high standards in the field of Asian Studies.
Friends, family, authors, and foundations have together
endowed the Lilienthal Fund, which enables UC Press
to publish under this imprint selected books
in a way that reflects the taste and judgment
of a great and beloved editor.

The Moys of New York and Shanghai

ONE FAMILY'S EXTRAORDINARY JOURNEY THROUGH WAR AND REVOLUTION

Charlotte Brooks

Foreword by Helen Zia

UNIVERSITY OF CALIFORNIA PRESS

University of California Press
Oakland, California

Back jacket photos, clockwise from top left:
Ming Tai, Kay, their older children, and Harry the chauffeur, ca. 1921. Courtesy of Jolly Young King.
Alfred, Alson, and Alice Lee studio portrait, ca. 1936. Courtesy of Douglas A. Lee.
Ernest in Suzhou, 1928. William and May Moy Photo Collection.
Alice and Alfred with Alson, 1935. Courtesy of Douglas A. Lee.
Mei Lanfang, Ruth, and C. C. Chang, 1930. Courtesy of the children of Loring and Moyra Moy.
Loring, Ernest, and Ken at Moy Sing and Han Ying's gravesite in Shanghai, fall 1945. Family photograph, courtesy of Douglas J. Chu, Museum of Chinese in America (MOCA) Collection.
Adelaide and Alice posing on a Chinese wheelbarrow, 1936. Courtesy of Douglas A. Lee.
Helen, Alice, Bill, and baby Herbert (in stroller), 1912. William and May Moy Photo Collection.
Mary Appleton Wood, Yvonne Chevalier, Mei Lanfang, Maurice Chevalier, Mary Pickford, C. C. Chang, Dolores Del Rio, Ruth Moy, and Louis Bromfield (partly hidden), 1930. Courtesy of the children of Loring and Moyra Moy.
Helen in her AWVS uniform with Donald, ca. 1942. Family photograph, courtesy of Douglas J. Chu, Museum of Chinese in America (MOCA) Collection.

Library of Congress Cataloging-in-Publication Data

Names: Brooks, Charlotte, author. | Zia, Helen, writer of foreword.
Title: The Moys of New York and Shanghai : one family's extraordinary journey through war and revolution / Charlotte Brooks ; foreword by Helen Zia.
Description: Oakland, California : University of California Press, [2026] | Includes bibliographical references and index.
Identifiers: LCCN 2025030738 (print) | LCCN 2025030739 (ebook) | ISBN 9780520409552 (cloth) | ISBN 9780520409569 (ebook)
Subjects: LCSH: Moy (Family : approximately 1883– : New York, N.Y.) | Mei family. | Chinese Americans—New York (State)—New York—Biography. | Children of immigrants—United States—Biography. | Chinese Americans—History—20th century. | Chinese Americans—China—Shanghai.
Classification: LCC CT274 (print) | LCC CT274 (ebook)
LC record available at https://lccn.loc.gov/2025030738
LC ebook record available at https://lccn.loc.gov/2025030739

Manufactured in the United States of America

GPSR Authorized Representative: Easy Access System Europe, Mustamäe tee 50, 10621 Tallinn, Estonia, gpsr.requests@easproject.com

35 34 33 32 31 30 29 28 27 26
10 9 8 7 6 5 4 3 2 1

The publisher and the University of California Press Foundation gratefully acknowledge the generous support of the Philip E. Lilienthal Imprint in Asian Studies, established by a major gift from Sally Lilienthal.

For Pam

CONTENTS

PART TWO
WAR

PART THREE
REVOLUTION

Illustrations follow pages 38 and 166.

EDITOR'S NOTE

This is the story of six siblings and their spouses, the most extraordinary family you've never heard of. They include a revolutionary, a "Rosie the Riveter," an engineer who helped put the first man on the moon, and a radio announcer who broadcast for the Nazis. One of the couples owned the most famous restaurant in 1920s New York; another won Medals of Freedom for their service during World War II. Separately and together, they lived astonishing lives, yet almost no one today knows anything about them.

That's because the Moys were a Chinese American family at a time when the United States excluded most Chinese immigrants and barred all of them from citizenship. Unlike their parents, Kay, Ernest, Helen, Alice, Bill, and Herbert Moy were "birthright citizens"—American citizens because they were born on US soil—yet this created few opportunities for them. Instead, American law and tradition cast them as inherently alien and undesirable simply because of their race. They faced discrimination in almost every facet of life, from education to jobs to housing.

The Moys' story is both individually incredible and strangely representative. Part of the first sizable Chinese American citizen generation, they and many of their peers were urbane, sophisticated, and self-consciously modern, and they challenged not just what Chinese could do in America but how other people saw Chinese Americans. Complicated and flawed individuals, the Moys were not hypertraditional stereotypes of imagined Chineseness, either. Like so many American families, they experienced infidelity, divorce, bankruptcy, and suicide. Among the six siblings, there was one arranged marriage—and two divorces, a white mistress, a secretly adopted son, a much younger lover, and an abandoned wife.

The Moy siblings navigated these challenges not just in the land of their birth but also in China. Half the Chinese Americans of this period, including four of these extraordinary siblings, moved to their parents' homeland to escape the racism they encountered almost everywhere in America. But in China they grappled with new cultural and legal barriers to full acceptance. The Moys and their spouses who lived in China's most developed and Westernized city in the 1930s and 1940s were part of a large but almost wholly forgotten Chinese American community there. When the Japanese invaded China, each of the siblings and their families made a different choice about where to go and how much to accommodate the occupiers. The Communist victory in the Chinese Civil War once again forced the Moys and thousands of other Chinese Americans in China to decide whether to leave the country for good.

Almost no one has explored this aspect of the Chinese American experience, which requires doing research in Chinese and questioning the powerful myth that immigrants' children could always expect better lives in America. One of the extraordinary achievements of this engaging and illuminating book is Charlotte Brooks's meticulous research, which reflects a decade's worth of work in archives across the United States, mainland China, and Hong Kong. Using a wide variety of sources, from letters and diaries to FBI files, family archives, and Chinese-language newspapers, Brooks explores the often messy choices that the Moys and their spouses made, flouting tradition in their relationships and resisting racist limitations on their careers and social lives. She has written a bibliographic essay at the end of this book to explain how she came to find this family, the kinds of sources she is using, and how she uncovered them.

Not only has Brooks found a multigenerational Chinese American family whose transnational story covers the long history of Chinese immigration to the United States from the late nineteenth century to the close present, but her use of such disparate sources is testament to her unique ability to tell histories few others can. As Erika Lee writes, Brooks "deepens and personalizes threads of Chinese American history that we have known only superficially. This first generation of Chinese Americans have usually been eclipsed by the Chinese exclusion story. But, as this book shows, this generation played an outsized role in defining and testing the possibilities of citizenship. Brooks opens up new worlds and demonstrates new ways of doing and writing history."

This book can be read as an example of how war can shape a family's destiny by the choices made under stressful conditions. It also exemplifies how families choose to handle the decisions made by other family members; how immigrant families choose to express their American patriotism while still maintaining ties to their country of origin; and how American society treats those who do not fit into a particular idea of what an American is or who can be considered an American, especially in a time of war.

This is also a story of a family that was surprisingly ahead of its time. World War II is often seen as the watershed in American history when women and ethnic minorities of this era were able to finally find jobs and gain admission to certain schools or live outside of their ethnic enclaves. Here, however, we see these trends take hold for the Moy family a generation earlier—and they may not be completely unique in this regard. As Scott Wong writes,

> this is by far the most detailed study of a single family in Chinese American history. They were atypical due to their eventual celebrity status in certain circles. Few other families, Chinese or not, had access to both in the US and China; at that time, few Chinese families could enroll their children in well-known boarding schools and colleges, and few had the means to travel across the Pacific as often as various members of the Moy family did. However, I tend to believe that there were more families like the Moys than we know of during this time period. Aside from San Francisco and New York City, there were long-standing Chinatowns in Chicago, Detroit, Philadelphia, and Boston and there were probably families there that also had trans-Pacific connections.

The Moys of New York and Shanghai is a tour de force, an epic biography of a fascinating multigenerational Chinese American family whose relative social and economic privilege during the height of anti-Chinese racism and violence afforded some family members a charmed life of influence and success, while plaguing others with a life of frustration, despair, and chronic failure. In the end, neither the United States nor China recognized Chinese Americans of this era as fully legitimate, loyal, and desirable citizens. So the siblings and their peers faced the excruciating task of trying to build decent and meaningful lives in nations that simultaneously claimed and rejected them. The Moys' incredible story thus offers a kaleidoscopic view of an entire generation's poignant struggle to navigate war, revolution, social transformation, and discrimination in two nations over a tumultuous half century.

FOREWORD

The first time I heard about the Moy family of New York and Shanghai, I was in a coffee shop with Charlotte Brooks. She tangentially mentioned the Moys. Though it was a brief aside, I felt an instant familiarity with this New York Chinatown family that lived generations before my time.

With this engrossing book, *The Moys of New York and Shanghai*, Professor Brooks takes us deep into the lives of this Exclusion-era family, providing detailed accounts with their photos, drawn from correspondence, journals, and public and private records. We get to see their children grow into complex human beings with their own hopes and dreams, messy lives and loves, making hard choices in extraordinary times.

The more I learned of these Moys of a century ago, the more I recognized the threads of their lives throughout the story of Chinese and Asians in America, intertwined with the broad, diverse American narrative.

In 1883, a man named Moy Sing left Taishan in the Pearl River Delta to enter the US at the port of San Francisco. Despite virulent anti-Chinese policies such as the 1882 Chinese Exclusion Act and the violent white mobs hell-bent on driving out people like Moy, he was admitted into the US, possibly because he was literate and may have been categorized as a merchant, exempt from exclusion.

Perhaps that special status made it possible for him to bring his wife, Han Ying, from China to join him ten years later, at a time when Chinese women were largely barred from America, because they were all presumed to be prostitutes (and vermin). Keeping Chinese women out of the US also ensured that the Chinese in America would remain bachelor societies, unable to put down roots with families and children.

But that's exactly what Moy Sing and Han Ying did. Their first child, a girl, was born when they lived in Chicago. Their son came two years later when they were living in Philadelphia. In search of better opportunities, they moved to New York City's Chinatown and had four more children, as well as a number who didn't survive beyond infancy.

Like so many of his Taishan brethren who built and filled America's Chinatowns, Moy was an enterprising businessman, successful enough to send his six kids to school. The eldest son took it upon himself to give "American names" to himself and all his siblings. As a Chinese *American* family, the children had distinct trajectories, talents, aspirations, idiosyncrasies, and dilemmas that shaped their individual journeys, separate from and sometimes in conflict with the family collective.

Kay, the eldest daughter, had to end her schooling after the eighth grade because further education for a girl was deemed unnecessary. Her parents set her up to be married at seventeen, though they let her choose between two preapproved candidates. Her selection was an entrepreneur like her father, a path for many Asians in America shut out of other employment. Kay and her husband created a home in the nearby New Jersey suburbs for her several children and, occasionally, her younger siblings. In time, she became the steady anchor and matriarch of the extended Moy family.

The eldest son was an idealist. Studious and athletic, he named himself Ernest—and he was. In his early teens he joined pro-China groups and went to hear Dr. Sun Yat-sen, a revolutionary and "the father of modern China," at a rally in Chatham Square. During a private session afterward, Sun asked the boy why he had joined a revolutionary party. The teen replied that he wanted to bring freedom to the land of his parents, just as patriots had done for his country—America. Ernest envisioned a future for himself beyond the restaurants and laundries, as "a personage of greater consequence." But he could not break through the stereotypes that limited him. Instead, he used his American English to become a publicist for Chinese businesses and found his way to China to seek his fortune and build a life of consequence as part of Sun Yat-sen's republican revolution in China. There, he believed he could advance by using his talent and skills, without the stigma of anti-Asian racism of America.

Helen, the third child, was saddled with the household chores at the age of eight after her elder sister Kay got married. Athletic and outwardly focused, she did not want to get steered into marriage while just a teen. Instead, she gravitated toward the Young China Society and other groups that had attracted her elder brother Ernest. In an era when women were denied the right to vote, Helen joined the Daughters of China, where she met politically active American-born Chinese girls who were suffragists. Unlike her sister Kay, she attended college to become a PE teacher, putting off marriage until she was an "old maid" at the age of twenty-six, when she married a fellow ABC who hailed from the hinterlands of Brooklyn, where the young couple made their home.

Alice, the vivacious, fashionable, pampered fourth child, loved to socialize. She tagged along with Helen to meetings of the service organizations, but her real interest was New York's party circuit for young ethnic Chinese. As an attractive American-born Chinese girl, she was especially popular among the China-born college students who congregated at Columbia's International House. When one of them proposed to her, she impulsively said yes—losing her US citizenship in the process because she married a foreign-born Chinese man, by federal law deemed "ineligible for citizenship" in those Exclusion years. She moved to Shanghai with him, but when his career and business prospects plummeted, she divorced him and married another suitor who could lavish her with the lifestyle she loved—in Shanghai.

William, the fifth sibling, a quiet and serious young man who studied engineering, couldn't find work because of his Chinese face. After the US economy tanked in 1929, the elder siblings decided that their parents would be better off in China, where they could have a higher standard of living than in the US. Eldest brother Ernest promised the two youngest sons that he could get them good jobs in Shanghai at a time when no work was available in the US due to the Depression. Hence, Bill and his younger brother headed to China, bringing their parents to live in Shanghai. When Bill returned to the US, he continued his engineering education and later became part of a NASA team that designed the lunar module's radar, helping put Neil Armstrong and Buzz Aldrin on the moon—where they planted the American flag.

Herbert, the sixth child, was the youngest. Outgoing and charismatic, he was also spoiled and undisciplined, getting into trouble at school and arrested at fifteen for gambling. His elder sisters were so worried about his future, they managed to arrange his admission to Mt. Hermon, a boarding school for boys in western Massachusetts that accepted Chinese. Young Herbert eloped with an equally young white woman whose parents were so enraged by this interracial relationship that they filed charges with their town's racist police to arrest him. Skipping town for Shanghai offered Herbert a convenient escape.

Predictably, the good jobs that Ernest overpromised never materialized and the two younger brothers scrounged for work using their American educations as news reporters and as publicists in the international sector. The charismatic Herbert was able to find success and celebrity as an English-language radio announcer in wartime Shanghai. During the Japanese occupation of the city, he cast his lot with the enemy, using his American accent to become the Shanghai equivalent of Tokyo Rose—even as his brother Ernest was working for America's ally, Chiang Kai-shek.

The two eldest Moy sisters, Kay and Helen, stayed close to Chinatown, holding down the home front through the Depression years, World War II and McCarthyism. The other four siblings—Ernest, Alice, Bill, and Herbert—had left New York, America's most cosmopolitan city, to seek better opportunities in Shanghai, China's great metropolis. It may not have been a huge culture shock for these savvy international urbanites to become expats in the Westernized international sections of Shanghai, but their timing was extraordinary, as Professor Brooks describes their experiences and historical context in vivid detail. The Moys, in particular Ernest and Alice, were witnesses to China's most tectonic period of social and economic change: the rise of warring political parties and revolutionary movements, the growth of capitalist industries and global trade, Japan's merciless war against China that included the occupation of Shanghai, followed by a full-blown civil war, and then a communist revolution. The Moy family saga is both familiar and extraordinary.

• • •

These stories begin in the late 1800s and early 1900s, the decades just after the violent anti-Chinese agitation of the Exclusion period. To some, those long-ago times may seem ancient and unrelatable to our new millennium. In many ways, though, these stories are hauntingly similar to those of Asian Americans today.

For example, the reverse migration to China made by four of the Moy siblings: Many generations of Asian Americans, including some today, have looked East toward their ancestral lands, for the opportunity to become a "personage of greater consequence," as Ernest wished for himself, in search of a career or a life where their racialized features wouldn't count against them.

Asian Americans today are still fighting for the recognition and acceptance of their full humanity and full participation in America—against the image of the perpetual foreign invader who can never be trusted as an American, or the don't-make-waves doormat of the "model minority" who craves to be an honorary white. In between these stereotypes lies perpetual invisibility.

For example, in my own immediate family of six kids—four boys and two girls—three of us went to study or work in China, Taiwan, and Hong Kong in our early adulthood. As the daughter of immigrants from China, born in New Jersey, I was constantly asked, "Where are you *really* from?"—as though "New Jersey" defied belief. More aggressively, I was told to "go back where you came from" so many times that I wondered if I should go to China, a place I had never been, because my status as a native-born American citizen was so suspect.

Over the years, many other Asian Americans have told me they also went "back" to the place they had never been, to see if—like the Moys—they might do better in a place where they could possibly blend in and find belonging, where their aspirations to be personages of greater consequence wouldn't be thwarted by a barbed fence of prejudice and racism.

In his memoir *Turning Japanese*, the novelist David Mura explores his experience in Japan as a *sansei*, a third-generation Japanese American. He questions what makes him American, and what seems to make him Japanese. On my own first trip to China, I found that locals would instantly peg me as a foreigner. It didn't matter that I had a face like theirs; I was rightly seen as an outsider who didn't belong there. I had to go to China to learn how truly American I am.

Nevertheless, by the 1990s, the constant refrain emanating from Washington operatives and the news media portrayed all Asian Americans as likely China spies, invasive foreigners intent on corrupting the White House. That recurrent theme has direct roots in the anti-Chinese hysteria and "driving out" period of the late 1800s—around the time that the Moys' eldest daughter Kay was born. As a counterpoint to that toxic anti-Asian drumbeat in the 1990s, I wrote my first book, *Asian American Dreams: The Emergence of an American People*, in order to highlight the resistance, resilience, and civil rights contributions that Americans of Asian descent have brought to this democracy.

In our current time, more than two decades after I wrote that book, the population of Asians in America has more than doubled to exceed twenty-four million Asian Americans and Pacific Islanders (AAPIs), and continues to increase as America's fastest-growing racial population. The growing numbers of Asian Americans have brought greater diversity and visibility, and even prominence to the role that AAPIs play in education, culture, government, business, technology, media—indeed, every sphere of American life.

However, simultaneous with these domestic developments, international trends indicate, according to some scholars and pundits, that we are entering the Pacific Century (as opposed to the previous Atlantic centuries) or even the Chinese Century. This narrative has led to a political consensus that considers China an existential threat to the United States and its role as the global superpower.

Sadly for Asian Americans, newer iterations of anti-Chinese and anti-Asian tropes have come to dominate the public discourse in America. During the COVID-19 pandemic, the name-calling and blaming of the "China virus" and "Kung flu" contributed to a pandemic of hate and violence toward all who "look Chinese." Policies such as the so-called "China Initiative" have assumed that every ethnic Chinese scientist, international student, or waiter in a Chinese restaurant poses a national security risk. Modern-day "alien land laws" have been advanced in several states, harking back to the 1800s of the Moy family's time; these harsh updated versions aim to prohibit non-US-citizen Chinese from owning property such as homes, farms, and businesses. Proposals and orders to restrict birthright citizenship threaten Americans whose families include those born outside this "nation of immigrants." Any peeling away of birthright citizenship will have a devastating impact on AAPIs, the one racialized group with the highest proportion of foreign-born persons. Moreover, this fundamental piece of American history is inextricably linked to Asian Americans, because it was San Francisco–born Wong Kim Ark who fought his case for birthright citizenship all the way to the Supreme Court in 1898. He won, reaffirming the 14th Amendment of the Constitution.

All these efforts to roll back settled law and policies are creating an increasingly dangerous climate for Asian Americans, reminiscent of the social and political times that drove the American-born Moy siblings to seek a better life in China more than a century ago.

It must also be noted that the Moy siblings didn't "turn Chinese," in the way of David Mura in Japan. They used their very American English and New York know-how to survive in China. There, they were able to live at a higher standard of living than in America. The Moys, like many other Chinese Americans before, during, and after their time, realized that US dollars could buy a lot more elder care in China than in America—leading the siblings to bring their aging parents from the US to stay with them in Shanghai.

But their quest to make a place for themselves in their ancestral "homeland" came at a price. Ernest, Alice, Bill, and Herbert found themselves buffeted by China's political chaos and had to make compromises at every step. No matter how hard they tried, they were never really accepted as Chinese—indeed, they were expatriates living the expat life. Eventually, as the Chinese Communist revolution approached, there was no place for American Chinese to be part of the New China. The Moys made their way back to the States, where their own children would make their lives as Americans.

This, too, is why the Moys' stories seem so familiar. Amid ever-shifting global geopolitics, traveling to China as a Chinese American—or elsewhere in Asia as an Asian American—demands extra caution and awareness. Asian Americans can find themselves caught between the politically driven narratives of both the Chinese and American governments.

The story of the Moys of New York and Shanghai shows how six sisters and brothers of the past century tried their best to navigate their tumultuous times. It remains to be seen how present and future Asian Americans (as well as others) will navigate these cataclysmic times, ideally toward beloved communities that embrace diversity, equity, inclusion, and belonging so that all may become "personages of greater consequence."

Helen Zia

MOY FAMILY
TREE

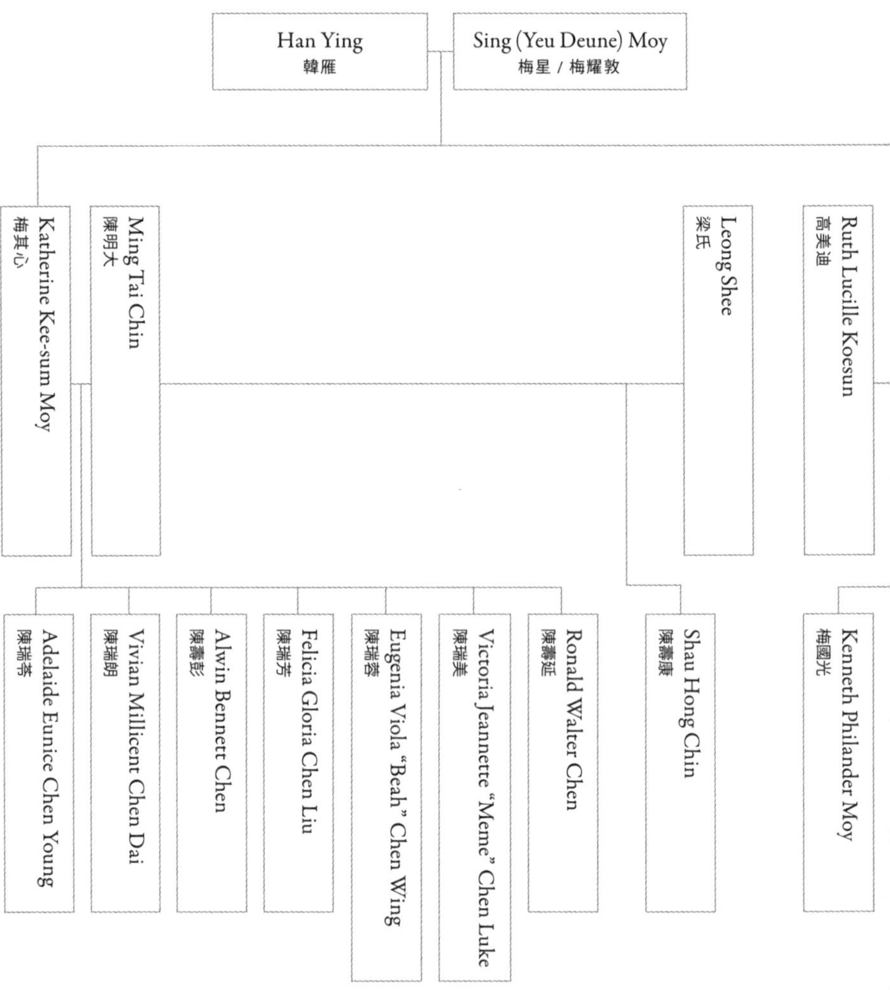

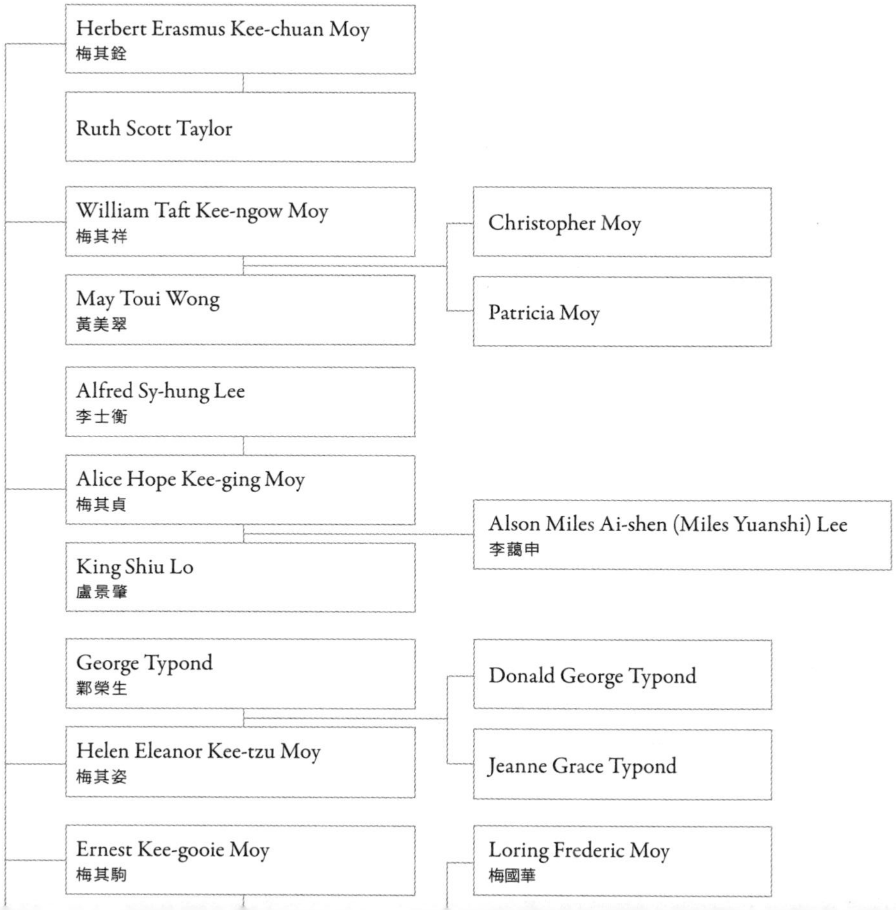

Herbert Erasmus Kee-chuan Moy
梅其銓

Ruth Scott Taylor

William Taft Kee-ngow Moy
梅其祥

May Toui Wong
黃美翠

Christopher Moy

Patricia Moy

Alfred Sy-hung Lee
李士衡

Alice Hope Kee-ging Moy
梅其貞

King Shiu Lo
盧景肇

Alson Miles Ai-shen (Miles Yuanshi) Lee
李藹申

George Typond
鄭榮生

Helen Eleanor Kee-tzu Moy
梅其姿

Donald George Typond

Jeanne Grace Typond

Ernest Kee-gooie Moy
梅其駒

Loring Frederic Moy
梅國華

MOY FAMILY & WORLD EVENTS
TIMELINE

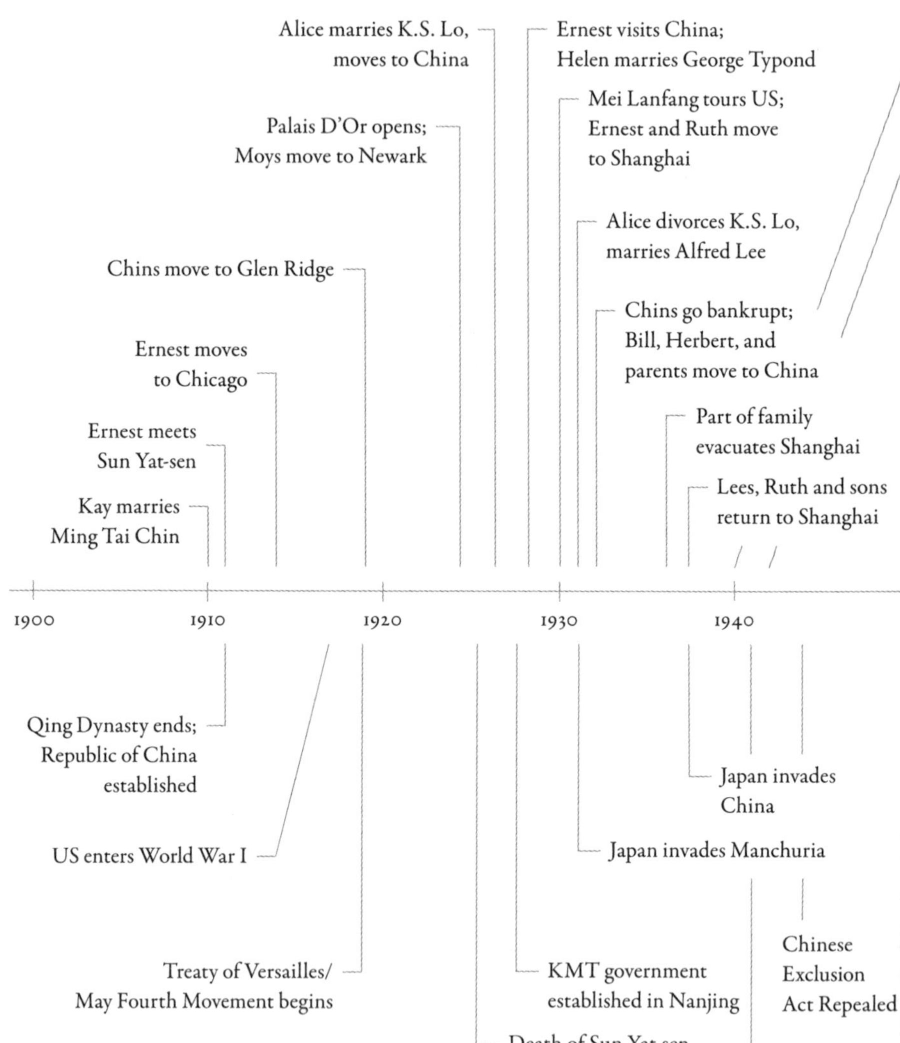

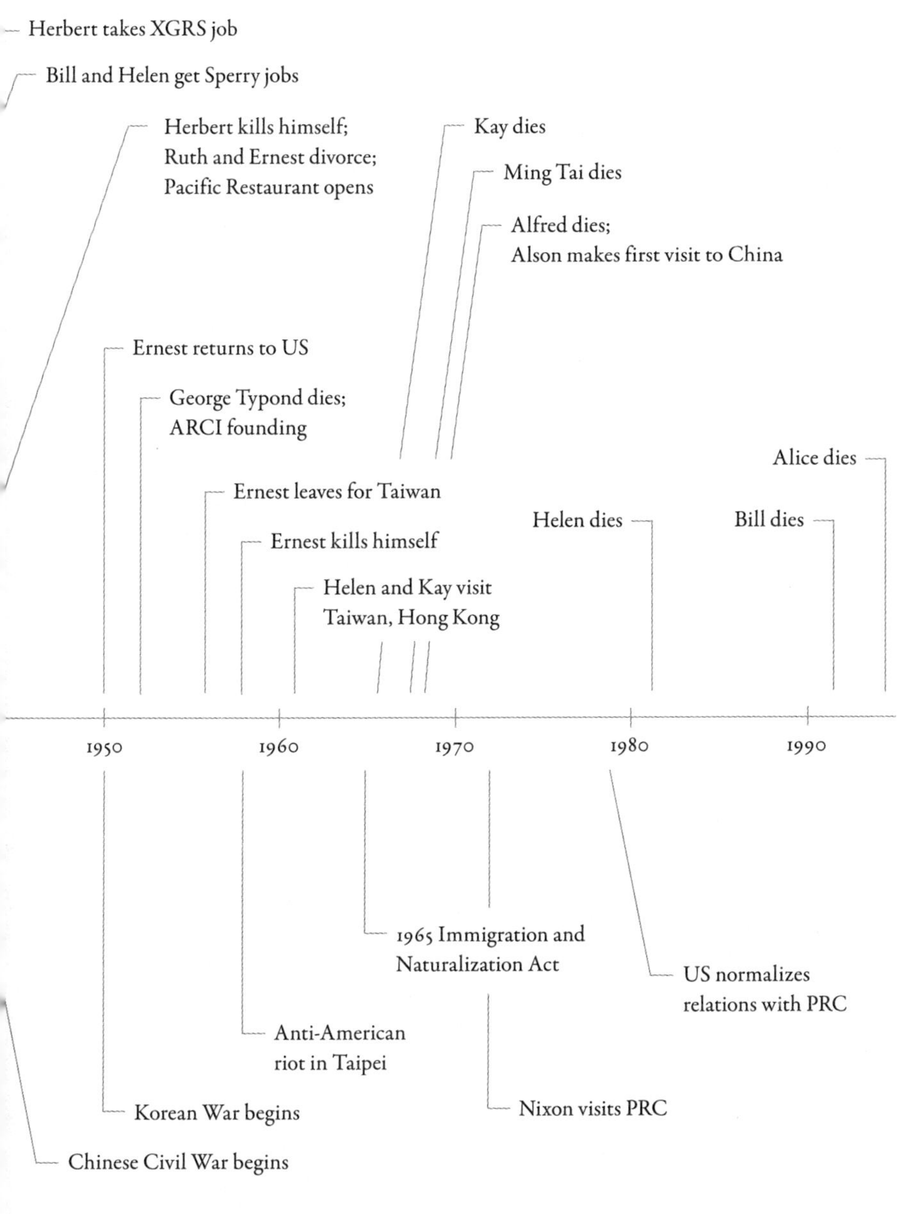
Herbert takes XGRS job
Bill and Helen get Sperry jobs
Herbert kills himself;
Ruth and Ernest divorce;
Pacific Restaurant opens
Kay dies
Ming Tai dies
Alfred dies;
Alson makes first visit to China
Ernest returns to US
George Typond dies;
ARCI founding
Alice dies
Ernest leaves for Taiwan
Helen dies
Bill dies
Ernest kills himself
Helen and Kay visit
Taiwan, Hong Kong
1950
1960
1970
1980
1990
1965 Immigration and
Naturalization Act
US normalizes
relations with PRC
Anti-American
riot in Taipei
Nixon visits PRC
Korean War begins
Chinese Civil War begins

Prologue

IN THE LATE NINETEENTH CENTURY, the failing Chinese Empire's biggest export was people. The vast majority of these people came from the south, especially the province of Guangdong, which Westerners often called Canton. Social unrest, economic instability, and a shortage of good farmland prompted hundreds of thousands of Cantonese men to seek work overseas. Most departed from nearby Hong Kong and traveled to one of scores of ports across the world, usually selecting their destinations on the basis of where previous emigrants from their region or village had settled. So the Kingdom of Hawai'i attracted throngs of Chinese from Zhongshan, Chaozhou people flocked to Siam, and half the Chinese in the United States came from Toisan, an area of Guangdong's Pearl River Delta. If those Toisanese were surnamed Moy, they invariably hailed from one of the villages of Duanfen, a subdistrict of Toisan.[1]

When Moy Sing turned twenty-five, he too left Duanfen for America. Following a route two of his brothers had already traveled, he took a passage boat to Hong Kong, where he joined hundreds of other Pearl River Delta men boarding a steamship for San Francisco. Like his fellow steerage passengers, Moy Sing knew the city only by its Cantonese name: Gau Gum Sang, or "Old Gold Mountain," a moniker dating to the California gold rush. Yet this was no golden age for Chinese immigrants. By the 1860s, violent anti-Chinese agitation had become central to the politics of the Pacific Coast. White workingmen's groups rioted against Chinese across the West, and city and state governments created discriminatory laws to make life intolerable for them. In 1882, Congress passed what eventually became known as the Chinese Exclusion Act; it halted further immigration of Chinese laborers and codified court rulings that prevented Chinese immigrants from becoming US citizens because of their race. The law still allowed

Chinese merchants to enter the country, but by the late 1880s, officials began to turn back many of the men who tried to claim merchant status.[2]

Moy Sing arrived in San Francisco around 1883, when a literate Chinese man with reasonably soft hands could still enter without too much difficulty. Though not a real merchant, he was not a laborer either. During his years in America, he earned a living by selling his literacy to the laborers who needed it: He carved signature "chops," painted store signs, ran gambling rooms and lotteries, and managed clubhouses. But he did none of this work in San Francisco, because he quickly headed to Chicago, his intended destination all along.[3]

By the 1880s, Chicago had become a magnet for Moys. A decade earlier, three Duanfen brothers—Moy Dong Hoy, Moy Dong Chow, and Moy Dong Yee—came to the Windy City from the West Coast and liked Chicago so much that they encouraged kinsmen to make the trip as well. At first, most of the new arrivals were refugees from the Pacific Coast, but within a few years Moy relatives were emigrating directly from subtropical Toisan to icy Chicago. There they worked in laundries, groceries, restaurants, and the other businesses that their relatives owned and underwrote.[4]

Shortly after arriving in Chicago, Moy Sing found a job running one of the gambling rooms that served this growing, heavily male population. Chinese tradition discouraged female emigration, since a daughter-in-law's foremost duty was to care for her husband's parents under their roof. Bringing wives to the United States also cost far more than most Chinese immigrants could afford, while US authorities found many ways to discourage Chinese women from attempting to enter the country: The courts interpreted the Chinese Exclusion Act as barring not just Chinese laborers but also their wives, and officials routinely treated all Chinese women like potential prostitutes. So only a handful of Chinese women lived in Chicago in the 1880s, and they tended to be concubines rather than primary wives.[5]

Because Moy Sing's first wife had died without bearing children, his parents married him to fourteen-year-old Han Ying right before his departure for the United States. He did not leave her pregnant, which heightened tensions between her and Moy Sing's mother—a woman so difficult that her other daughters-in-law refused to live with her, despite the village gossip this provoked. Unlike many sons, Moy Sing sided with his wife, whose unusual literacy allowed her to communicate her unhappiness directly; still, he never made enough money in Chicago to pay her passage. But when his father died suddenly in 1891, Moy Sing used his entire inheritance to bring Han Ying to America at last. She arrived the next year.[6]

• • •

After a few months in Chicago, Han Ying became pregnant. Moy Sing hoped desperately for a son, a desire he shared with almost every Chinese man of his generation. Giving birth to sons was both a cultural preference and a duty: boys grew into men who continued the family line, worshipped their ancestors, and supported aging parents, while daughters simply cost money until they married into another family. So Moy Sing was deeply disappointed when Han Ying gave birth in July 1893 to twin girls Kee Sum and Kee Luey. During the next long and miserable winter, Kee Luey died, probably of pneumonia. After city police began raiding Chinese gambling establishments the next summer, Moy Sing decided to accept a kinsman's offer of a job managing a fraternal lodge in Philadelphia. His wife was pregnant again, and he hoped their luck would change.[7]

A few months after the family arrived in their new home, Han Ying gave birth to a healthy baby boy, delighting her husband and making him the envy of his friends. When the infant was a month old, Moy Sing hosted the traditional naming celebration, something he had not done for the twin girls. Excited to show off his son and heir, Moy Sing reserved two separate restaurants in Philadelphia's Chinatown to accommodate all the friends and kinsmen he invited. He had decided to name the boy Kee Gooie, a combination that included a generation character (Kee, which the infant shared with his sister Kee Sum) and a second unique part (Gooie), meaning "colt" and reflecting his father's excitement about this male child.[8]

The day of the festivities, Han Ying dressed the baby in a bright red and orange silk jacket and a black cap, then handed the boy to her husband; naming ceremonies were only for men. At both restaurants, Moy Sing designated friends to receive gifts and tributes from well-wishers, who crowded into the dining rooms to drink toasts and eat delicacies. When Moy Sing passed the boy around, many of the men dandled and cooed at the child, thinking about their own little ones across the Pacific. Others nodded in vigorous agreement each time the proud father pointed out that his son had inherited the Moy family nose. A *Philadelphia Times* reporter who caught wind of the unusual celebration—the city had even fewer Chinese women than Chicago—described the ceremony and gifts with equal parts exoticism, condescension, and admiration: “A pair of beautifully ornamented gold bracelets, a hammered gold ornament for the front of the boy’s cap, rings and a large and miscellaneous assortment of silver coins . . . were among the treasures which were brought for the new scion of the house of Moy.”[9]

The house of Moy was soon on the move again. In late 1895, legislators began probing police corruption in Philadelphia, where officers routinely took bribes to ignore the presence of gambling and prostitution in Chinatown. Now on the spot, the police started to raid known gaming establishments. This time, the Moys moved one hundred miles northeast to New York City, where they settled for good.[10]

. . .

In the mid-1890s, the Chinese population of New York City was growing rapidly, with refugees from the violent politics of the Western states flowing in. A deep national depression made life hard for many new arrivals, including the Moys, who initially struggled to gain an economic foothold. To help make ends meet, Moy Sing toured around summer carnivals playing an “Oriental fortuneteller,” while his wife took in sewing, tailored clothes, and made Chinese buttons.[11]

For Han Ying, the family’s first decade in Manhattan was a blur of pregnancy, exhaustion, and despair. In November 1896, she gave birth to a sickly baby boy who died shortly afterward. She became pregnant again almost immediately, and in February 1899, the couple’s third son arrived. The city endured subzero temperatures that winter, and the new infant grew ill and died within weeks. The next summer, Han Ying was pregnant again, and again her infant son perished shortly after his birth. By this point, Han Ying had given birth to six children, only two of whom had survived more than a few months.[12]

When Han Ying became pregnant again, Moy Sing decided to take a chance on a Western-trained “woman doctor.” Physician Esther Bok could not change the fact that Han Ying’s body was tremendously depleted: The physical toll of so many pregnancies so close together made each one riskier and each new infant likelier to be sickly. Still, under Dr. Bok’s care, the seventh Moy child, Kee Tzu, was born plump and healthy in August 1902. Though the Moys’ eighth child and fourth daughter died weeks after her birth in early 1904, Kee Ging, an infant girl who arrived in 1905, managed to thrive.[13]

. . .

Dr. Bok also encouraged the Moys to send their children to Chinatown's new kindergarten, recently organized by Reverend Fung Mow of the Morning Star Mission on Doyers Street. The Moys soon enrolled both Kee Sum and Kee Gooie, who learned their first words of English there. Once the two moved on to Public School 23, they also mingled for the first time with non-Chinese kids, most of them the offspring of the neighborhood's Italian immigrants.[14]

When classes ended for the day, Kee Gooie liked to play baseball with his friends, ducking the policeman who shooed them out of the fenced grass of Mulberry Bend Park. On rainy or snowy days, he spent time at the library reading books or magazines. As a girl, Kee Sum did not get to play with her friends after school, but instead went straight home to do chores—and, when she finished those, more chores. Cooking dinner, sewing, minding her siblings, or washing the family's clothes took up all her free time, especially with Han Ying pregnant so often. Kee Tzu, who almost worshipped her big sister, could not help seeing the unfairness of it all, especially when Kee Gooie moved on to Dewitt Clinton High School while Kee Sum had to leave school after eighth grade. Neither Han Ying nor Moy Sing thought the young woman needed anything more than that for her future as a wife and mother.[15]

Kee Sum never rebelled against these old ideas, but like many immigrants' children, she and her siblings created their own identities for the parts of their lives their parents did not control. At school, the Moy children adopted English names that they used not just there, but with each other. Now Kee Sum became "Katie," lengthened on legal documents to the more regal-sounding "Katherine" or shortened to simply "Kay" by her brothers and sisters. Kee Gooie became "Ernest," a reflection of his earnestness and idealism, and he chose new names for his younger siblings too. After Helen Keller published her autobiography, he named little Kee Tzu "Helen." Before Kee Ging was old enough to venture an opinion, Ernest dubbed her "Alice," after the volatile, charismatic daughter of President Theodore Roosevelt. Like her namesake, charming Alice Moy liked admiration and attention and was generally able to get it. And in 1909, Ernest named his newest brother William Taft Moy, in honor of the president inaugurated days before the child's birth.

PART ONE

Family

1910–1929

MOY SING AND HAN YING emigrated from a faltering empire that faced numerous existential challenges. In the nineteenth century, natural disasters and widespread rebellions weakened China's ruling Qing dynasty, while aggressive Western and eventually Japanese encroachment eroded imperial sovereignty. In 1842, China lost the First Opium War to Great Britain and had to cede the island of Hong Kong to the British, as well as open several ports to foreign trade. During the next decades, the foreign powers provoked other wars, made further demands, and wrenched additional reparations from the flagging dynasty. In 1900, desperate Qing leaders threw in their lot with North China's antiforeign Boxer movement, hoping it could evict the foreigners once and for all. That summer, the Boxers laid siege to Beijing's foreign legation quarter for fifty-five days, until a multinational military expedition crushed them and sacked the capital.[1]

No one was more aware of China's weakness than the Chinese abroad. Traveling across the world, they saw up close the immense power and wealth of the industrialized West and rapidly developing Japan. They knew as well that supporting the Boxers—who claimed that their martial arts moves stopped bullets—was extraordinarily foolish. Little wonder that the Chinese overseas were often enthusiastic supporters of movements for political and social change in China.[2]

Debates about China's future divided these communities between reformers and revolutionaries. The former envisioned a constitutional monarchy for China, while the latter, led by a Western-trained doctor named Sun Yat-sen, argued for more violent and wholesale change. In 1911, a revolution ended China's last dynasty, but the fragile republic that replaced it soon disintegrated. After 1916, warlords and different political factions controlled various parts of the country. At the same time, a growing number of China-born students streamed into American universities; delighted Chinese American youths found these newcomers more broadminded and far less traditional than their own immigrant parents.[3]

The Chinese students also represented an alternative for the many second-generation people who wanted to escape the racism and discrimination they faced in America. Not only did the Chinese Exclusion Act continue to operate until World War II, but legislators and the courts reaffirmed it and extended its impact, part of the wider anti-immigrant politics of the 1920s. The Supreme Court denied Chinese American citizens the right to bring China-born spouses to the United States. When Congress allowed the renaturalization of American women who had lost their US citizenship by marrying foreign-citizen men, it denied this privilege to one specific group: Asian Americans. In addition to official discrimination, routine and widespread racism narrowed Chinese Americans' access to jobs, housing, education, and basic civil rights. The bleak situation inspired thousands of them to emigrate to China in the hope of finding greater opportunities there.[4]

ONE

Kay

NEW YORK, 1910–1911

KAY WOKE BEFORE DAWN to the sound of rain rattling the windows. She rose, washed her face, and was just getting dressed when she heard a gentle rap on the apartment door. Han Ying had invited a matronly friend—selected because of her happy marriage and large family—to comb Kay's hair from girlhood braids into a married woman's bun. It was the first ritual of Kay's wedding day, November 21, 1910.[1]

Earlier that year, Moy Sing and Han Ying had decided to find their oldest daughter a husband. They waited until Kay turned seventeen but saw no reason for further delay. After all, Kay was already three years older than Han Ying had been at the time of her own marriage. So Moy Sing asked local merchant Lee Weenom, an amateur matchmaker, to find Kay a suitable mate. The task was formidable, but not because of Moy Sing's lack of wealth or social prominence. In 1910, fewer than forty single or widowed adult Chinese women lived in New York City, compared to about fifteen hundred single or widowed adult Chinese men. The matchmaker spent weeks winnowing down the large number of proposals he received. That fall, Lee selected his top three candidates and, in the accepted fashion, sent an acquaintance's wife to deliver the proposals to the Moy family.[2]

After the woman left, Moy Sing and Han Ying discussed each candidate's merits in detail. The first offer came from Chin Gin Hay, a prosperous local merchant. Seeing the man's name, Moy Sing shook his head and wondered what Lee Weenom could have been thinking. Around Chinatown, people whispered that Chin Gin Hay was dating a white woman who taught piano in the neighborhood. That made his proposal not just questionable but dangerous. Only a year earlier, New York City police had discovered the body of a murdered white missionary, Elsie Sigel, stuffed into a trunk in the apartment of a Chinese man named Leon Ling. When the cops uncovered a trove of love letters from Sigel to Ling, racist white civic leaders and journalists whipped up a storm of anti-Chinese feeling. And though the police never caught Ling, they spent months harassing young Chinese men, like the Moys' son Ernest.[3]

Chin Gin Hay was trouble, no matter how much money he had. Moy Sing tossed the proposal aside, and he and Han Ying turned to the other two candidates. Thankfully, both were much better, especially Chin Shiu Wing, who seemed like an excellent prospect. He was a China-born youth just about Kay's age—they had briefly attended Public School 23 together—and his father was the managing partner of a thriving store down the street. Chin Ming Tai was slightly less suitable, since he was a widower fourteen years older than Kay. His first wife had died in China just a year or two earlier, and their son, a boy named Chin Shau Hong, now lived in Hong Kong. Ming Tai did have one major advantage, though: He was reputed to be rich, since he owned shares in at least two local factories and a dry goods shop.[4]

After comparing the proposals again, Han Ying and Moy Sing made an unusual decision: They would let their daughter choose which of the two men she wanted to marry. To strangers, Kay seemed demure, diffident, even shy, an impression her youthful appearance helped create. But her family knew better. Kay had definite opinions about what she wanted, what she liked, and what she would not tolerate. Her parents understood this, and they also trusted her judgment.[5]

Kay had long assumed that when she grew up, she would marry and have a family of her own. From what she observed of her parents' generation, that was the only option open to a virtuous woman. She did not object to this future, but she did not relish living the way her mother had. After all, Kay had spent her girlhood minding a growing brood of siblings in a series of small Chinatown apartments with a father whose income could not always sustain a family in much comfort. So while Moy Sing and Han Ying assumed Kay would choose Chin Shiu Wing, she surprised them by selecting Chin Ming Tai instead.[6]

Kay's choice was not merely, or even mostly, about money. To begin with, Shiu Wing lived with his parents, and she had heard plenty of stories, including from Han Ying, about domineering mothers-in-law. Besides, Kay had passed Chin Ming Tai in the street more than once, and he had made a good impression on her. He was not much taller than she, slight of build, and rather youthful looking. He kept his hair cut short and brushed back, had removed his queue, and usually wore Western clothes. Ming Tai was not particularly handsome—his small mouth pursed a bit, and when he smiled, she could see his crooked teeth—but he looked kind. And it was true that Kay also noticed his well-tailored and fashionable suits and heard about his wealth. She was not lazy—she had been cooking, sewing, cleaning, and taking care of her younger siblings as long as she could remember—but she was also tired of the economic insecurity that plagued her family.[7]

Moy Sing informed the matchmaker that he accepted Chin Ming Tai's proposal. Then he consulted a horoscope book to select proper days for the wedding and the prescribed events leading up to it. On the first chosen day, Ming Tai sent over the traditional gifts that signified the engagement, as well as a wholly unexpected one: a diamond solitaire engagement ring, a nod to American wedding practices that delighted Kay. Ming Tai then ordered the customary small cakes to distribute in the neighborhood as a formal announcement of the upcoming wedding. The more cakes a man distributed, the greater his prestige. Locals claimed that Ming Tai ordered almost ten thousand.[8]

· · ·

Chin Ming Tai believed in showing affection by spending money on his family and friends. This was a natural lesson for someone who grew up in a village where almost all the men between sixteen and sixty were absent, working overseas and sending money back home to support the families they rarely saw. Ming Tai's father and uncles, who owned successful businesses in the United States, were no different. Originally, Ming Tai prepared to follow in their footsteps. When he turned seventeen, his family arranged his marriage to a Leong family woman, who in 1899 gave birth to their son Shau Hong. Ming Tai did not meet the boy for years, because he had already left to work abroad.[9]

Sailing to Cuba just months after the Spanish-American War's end, he disembarked at Havana, a major transit point for travelers from China. Smugglers and forgers in the Cuban capital did a brisk trade selling the documents and new identities that enabled Chinese men to claim US citizenship by birth or through US citizen fathers; these "paper sons" could then enter the United States despite Chinese exclusion laws. After purchasing the paperwork he needed to establish his supposed birth in San Francisco, Ming Tai traveled on to New York.[10]

The older Chin men decided that Ming Tai would settle in Manhattan and work for his uncles, merchant Chin Sung Fung and cigar manufacturer Chin Sung Pan. The young man was a quick study, learning the ins and outs of the mercantile and cigar trade and showing a keen business sense. His uncles were duly impressed, and in 1905, when Sung Pan retired to China, Ming Tai took over the older man's shares in two cigar factories and the dry goods store, Kwong Tai Chong.[11]

Despite his success, Ming Tai felt deeply lonely as he read the letters from his loved ones in Toisan and looked at the photos of his wife and rapidly growing son. By the time he made his first trip back to China, he had decided that he did not want to live apart from his family. Before returning to the United States, he told his wife that he planned to bring her and Shau Hong to America soon, but she surprised him by resisting the idea. Though he did not hear from her again after he arrived in New York, he assumed she would come around—and then he received the letter from his mother, by way of a village scribe who wrote notes for the illiterate. As Ming Tai read and reread the news of his wife's death, delivered in a stranger's handwriting, he felt a mix of shock, sorrow, and disappointment. Months later, when his friend Lee Weenom approached him, he was ready.[12]

• • •

After Han Ying's friend finished combing up Kay's hair, she whispered some words of reassurance in the young woman's ear and then slipped out of the apartment. Han Ying had given her daughter a small mirrored vanity for her wedding day—"to reflect everything good," her mother said—and Kay now examined herself, trying to reconcile her round, girlish face with the hairstyle she had seen so many older women wear. Finally, she buttoned herself into the white, high-necked, Western-style dress she had purchased for her wedding, while Han Ying herded the younger Moy children into their best Chinese formal clothing. Suddenly, they heard another rap at the door, which Moy Sing, balancing little Bill on his hip, answered. There stood Ming Tai in a stylish Western suit with a smartly knotted silk tie.[13]

Brushing away tears, Kay tried to smile at her fiancé but could barely meet his eye. He guided her down the stairs and into the street, opening his umbrella to protect her from the rain. The rest of the Moys followed behind: Han Ying tottering slowly down on her bound feet, Ernest taking two steps at a time, and Helen and Alice bouncing off the stairwell walls, much to Moy

Sing's annoyance. Kay and Ming Tai stepped into a waiting cab, while the rest of the family and some friends followed in other cabs hired for the occasion.[14]

A year earlier, New York State started requiring all couples to obtain a marriage license from a city clerk, even if they wed in a religious ceremony. Ming Tai and Kay planned to marry at City Hall that morning before their Chinese wedding later in the day. Neither realized that they were the first Chinese couple in the city to apply for a license under the new ordinance. When Ming Tai, Kay, and their entourage arrived at City Hall, they attracted so many gawkers that police arrived to clear the steps. Two officers finally guided Kay and Ming Tai into the building through the basement to avoid the rowdy throng. In a private office, an alderman wed the couple as their families and friends watched and translated the ceremony for those who did not understand English.[15]

Blushing behind a bouquet of lilies, Kay spoke in an almost inaudible voice, but she smiled reassuringly down at her two sisters, both of whom clutched her skirt folds. Helen wept quietly, believing her world had come to an end, while Alice, always comfortable with attention, cried more lustily. By then, a *New York Tribune* reporter had arrived and was furiously scribbling into his notepad. Within two days, the Moy-Chin nuptials became national news, the sort of story that editors of small-town papers liked to pluck out of the big-city dailies and run alongside items about the oldest living person or the length of the Nile River.[16]

Kay returned to her parents' apartment to dress for what she, Ming Tai, and the Moys all considered her real wedding ceremony. She exchanged her white gown for a red cotton blouse and trouser ensemble and red veil, which in China symbolized happiness and good fortune. When she left her parents' apartment for the second ceremony, she climbed into a waiting horse-drawn wagon with a piece of red fabric tied to it—the closest the Moys could come to the red sedan chairs that carried brides to their new husbands' homes in China. The wagon proceeded slowly down Mott Street as throngs of Chinese and white passersby stopped to watch. Then it made a sharp right onto Bayard Street and immediately stopped, because Ming Tai lived only about five hundred feet from the Moys' apartment.[17]

Dressed in a Chinese black silk coat and a dark blue robe, he stood waiting for Kay outside his apartment building. Using a ceremonial fan, he rapped on the door of the carriage, another Chinese wedding ritual. At the sound of his fan, Kay climbed down to the street and then followed Ming Tai up the stairs to her new home. After he lifted her veil, they burned incense, bowed to each other, and walked back around the corner to their wedding feast at Mon Far Low, where Ming Tai's uncle Chin Sung Fung acted as master of ceremonies.[18]

Local gossips claimed that Chin Ming Tai paid Moy Sing a bride price of $20,000, an astronomical sum for the time. The true amount was probably less, but Ming Tai was a successful businessman, and marriageable Chinese women were incredibly scarce in New York. Whatever the amount, the money brought a new prosperity to the Moy household, and by 1911, Moy Sing believed that another big payoff was within his reach.[19]

TWO

Ernest

NEW YORK, 1910–1914

ERNEST LOOKED LIKE HIS FATHER—everyone said so. They had the same nose, same thin lips, same small chin. But neither of them particularly resembled the moon-faced youth in the photo. Whoever this boy was, he did not take after Kay, Helen, Alice, Bill, or Han Ying, either. Still, Ernest knew better than to mention this to his father. Moy Sing was brimming with confidence, in contrast to Han Ying, who was trying her best to remember the details of the improbable story her husband had concocted.[1]

Two weeks earlier, the moon-faced boy had arrived in Boston and followed the other Chinese passengers into the crumbling Long Wharf immigration shed. Most of them clutched sheaves of documents, attempting to prove their right to enter the United States. But the youth carried a copy of the photo Ernest had seen, together with a far more convincing piece of paper: an embossed New York City birth certificate bearing the name Moy Kee, born at 43 Mott Street to parents Moy Sing and Han Ying. Though immigration officials viewed most Chinese with skepticism, the Boston inspectors treated the birth certificate as solid evidence in this youth's favor—at least initially. Then officials interrogated him, and the boy could not even answer the most basic questions about his father's family, the people he claimed Moy Sing and Han Ying had sent him to China to live with nine years earlier. A skeptical inspector soon contacted his colleagues in New York, and now Ernest, a high school sophomore, found himself cramming for a new kind of exam.[2]

Moy Sing had laid the groundwork years earlier, duly registering with local officials the births of all eleven of the Moys' children, though only five lived past infancy. One son passed away so young that Moy Sing and Han Ying never had the chance to choose a character for him beyond the generational designation "Kee," so his birth certificate bore only the name "Moy Kee." In late 1910, this long-dead son would have turned fourteen, a good age for emigration, and Moy Sing spread the word that he had a birth certificate to sell. The Chinatown men who represented the Hong Kong remittance and immigration firms took note. Very soon Moy Sing had a buyer, a Toisan youth named Chin Jin Gow whose family wanted to send him to the United States.[3]

Moy Sing assumed that the birth certificate was irrefutable evidence and felt little concern when the Immigration Service official demanded to interview not just him and Han Ying, but also Kay and Ernest—both of them older than their imaginary sibling. Since Han Ying was pregnant for the twelfth time and due in July, the interrogations took place at the Moys' Chinatown apartment. After Helen and Alice left for school that morning, Ernest carried little Bill around the corner to Kay and Ming Tai's place and then walked home, mentally reviewing the details of the skeletal story Moy Sing had provided.

The immigration inspector, his stenographer, and their Chinese interpreter soon arrived and informed the Moys that everyone needed to give their testimony privately and separately. Han Ying went first, answering the inspector's questions through the interpreter while her husband sat in one bedroom and her oldest son in another. Waiting his turn, Ernest grew increasingly jittery, pressing his ear to the door, fidgeting with his tie, and dabbing the sweat from his forehead. What could possibly be taking so long? Finally, the inspector called him into the front room of the apartment and questioned him directly in English.[4]

As Ernest fumbled through the man's queries, he fervently wished his father had done more to prepare him for the interrogation. Sensing the boy's uncertainty, the inspector began to spit out his questions in rapid time: Why did Ernest mention only one brother in China, when his parents said there were two? (Moy Sing had not told his son that he planned to sell a second birth certificate.) Had Ernest and Kay attended school with Moy Kee? (Han Ying and Moy Sing said no, Ernest said yes.) By the end of the interview, Ernest was blushing and sputtering. The whole situation reminded him of the way the police had treated him and his friends in the months after Elsie Sigel's murder, stopping them on the street to question them in the same contemptuous, impatient way.[5]

The next day, the inspector and his stenographer visited the Chins' apartment around the corner, since Kay, too, was pregnant. By the time she gave her testimony, she had heard all about the previous day's disaster from her parents and Ernest. Prepped by Ming Tai, who had far more experience with immigration interrogations than Moy Sing, Kay answered her questions with much greater confidence and specificity than Ernest or her parents. Still, it was not enough. The Immigration Service deported "Moy Kee" a few days later, and a chastened Moy Sing never tried to sell the other birth certificates.[6]

• • •

True to his English name, Ernest was earnest, a born idealist with grandiose dreams and lofty principles. When the local Chinese Students Club (CSC) organized Chinatown's first Boy Scout troop, he immediately joined the group whose ideals seemed to match his own. He dutifully studied American flag etiquette and learned the Scout Oath and Law by heart, and when he won the high jump at the citywide Boy Scout track meet, he tried mightily to stay humble. Yet he also struggled with the contradictions that characterized so much of his life and his community. He felt slightly ill when lying to the immigration inspector about Moy Kee, since like any good Scout, he had pledged to "do my duty to God and my country." At other times, he wondered if he had violated his pledge to be "morally straight," since his father supported the family by working in Chinatown's gambling industry.[7]

By his mid-teens, Ernest was also beginning to lose his faith in the America of his schoolbooks, with their empty platitudes about equality. He noticed that his white classmates did not face police harassment after Elsie Sigel's murder. Their fathers did not have to carry documents proving their right to be in the United States, and sightseeing guides did not come to their neighborhoods and tell gaggles of tourists that their mothers and sisters were prostitutes or "slave girls."[8]

These lies made Ernest's blood boil, and he itched to do something, anything, to change the way other people treated the Chinese. In early 1911, as Moy Sing shopped Moy Kee's birth certificate around, Ernest screwed up the courage to approach the half brother of his friends Henry and Nom. Just twenty-five, Chu Su Gunn was the community's most well-known revolutionary; he served as treasurer of the New York Tongmenghui, a group known in English as the "Young China Society." Its founder was the famous revolutionary Sun Yat-sen, upon whose head the Qing government was rumored to have put a massive price. Even this far from China, most of the local members kept their involvement a secret, which made the group seem particularly exciting to Ernest. He appreciated how it was trying to strengthen China so that no one would treat people like him with contempt anymore. And best of all, he could see nothing contradictory or hypocritical about Sun's revolution, whose aims and ideals seemed as clear and lofty as Ernest's own.[9]

In spring 1911, Sun Yat-sen toured the United States to whip up support and raise money for the Tongmenghui. He visited Manhattan in early April, giving a rousing speech at the Chinese Theatre on Chatham Square. The large, enthusiastic audience roared in approval, tired of the empty promises and half measures of the flagging dynasty and its reformist supporters. Buoyed by the crowd, Ernest and his friends finally declared themselves, sitting proudly in the section reserved for Young China Society members. Afterward, Sun met with them in a supporter's apartment on Bayard Street.[10]

Ernest treasured the memory of that night for the rest of his life. Chu Su Gunn introduced him to Sun, explaining that the boy was the Tongmenghui's youngest New York City member. Sun smiled and spoke to Ernest in standard Cantonese, to which the young man could only stammer a halting reply. How humiliating! He was far more comfortable using his parents' Toisan dialect but knew that it had a reputation as a peasant tongue. Sensing Ernest's embarrassment, Sun quickly switched to English. Why, Sun asked, had Ernest joined the revolutionary party? The boy replied, "I want to bring freedom and independence to the country of my parents, just as the American patriots won liberty for my native land!" Years later, he fondly recalled that "after listening to Dr. Sun that night I was ready to do or die in any undertaking that promised the freedom" of China.[11]

His first "undertaking" was not death but an essay that, unsurprisingly, exuded idealism. Titled "The Meaning of Chinese Reform," it lashed China's moderates and proclaimed that "the blood of patriots is the price of liberty." Ernest submitted it to William Randolph Hearst's *New York American*, where reporters smiled at the youth's audacity. Hearst's papers were scathingly and notoriously anti-Asian, yet an editor agreed to publish the piece anyway, and a number of other Hearst journals even reprinted it. It was Ernest's first foray into journalism.[12]

· · ·

A few months later, in October 1911, a revolutionary uprising began in the Chinese city of Wuchang. Several companies of Qing troops mutinied instead of fighting the rebels, and the revolt spread quickly through Central China. News of it created a frenzy of excitement in New York; Young China Society members were used to hearing about this or that uprising, but they sensed something different in this growing conflict. Older Chinatown residents disagreed; many of them, including Moy Sing, had been born during or immediately after the destructive Taiping Rebellion. Against the odds, the Manchus had—after more than a decade—managed to defeat that movement, which at its height controlled more than a third of China. This time, they declared, would be no different.[13]

Ignoring the skeptics, Ernest reveled in the excitement of the moment and basked in the attention he received. As the rebellion grew, local reporters flocked to the Tongmenghui clubhouse to interview New York party members about the aims and course of the revolution. Chu Su Gunn usually spoke for the group, but when he was away, Ernest eagerly stepped in, assuring reporters that he was a "personal friend of Dr. Sun." This was not precisely the truth, but it sounded impressive and gave greater weight to the words of a high school student.[14]

In late October, two of Sun's deputies held a mass meeting in Chinatown to call for the establishment of a republic. Almost two thousand Chinese and Chinese Americans attended, cheering wildly for each speaker. Ernest proudly sat among the Tongmenghui members, who leapt to their feet to yell "Long live Dr. Sun and the Republic!" at the best parts of all the speeches. Ernest's comrades even voted to send him to Detroit to take flying lessons in preparation for fighting the Qing army. These plans quickly dissolved with the dynasty itself. Ernest never went to flying school because in early 1912, two thousand years of imperial rule ended, and China became a republic.[15]

The new government made almost no impact on Chinese New Yorkers, though. The police still harassed the Chinese, and the tour guides still told their lies. The main change was literally cosmetic: Men who wore queues, a sign of submission to the Manchus, now cut off the braids. A queueless Moy Sing suddenly noticed his own receding hairline and took to wearing a flat cap to hide it. As for Ernest, he watched enviously as his older comrades from the New York branch of the Tongmenghui—which soon became the Kuomintang (KMT), or Chinese Nationalist Party—left for China to take part in the new government. If only he were old enough to follow![16]

Within a year, many returned. Lacking military power, Sun Yat-sen quickly resigned from the presidency in favor of the former Qing official and general Yuan Shikai, who took a dim view of democracy, shared governance, and the new parliament. In 1913, KMT-aligned governors in several provinces revolted against Yuan, who easily snuffed out this "Second Revolution." Sun Yat-sen and other KMT leaders fled China once again, Yuan dissolved the parliament for good, and China's brief experiment with limited democratic government soon ended. So did Ernest's dream of traveling to his parents' homeland to serve the KMT, though he did not know what to do with himself instead.[17]

· · ·

Moy Sing had always indulged his oldest son, so he supported Ernest's revolutionary enthusiasm, just as he tolerated the boy's decision to manage and play for the Chinatown baseball team. But he was also a practical man, and when Ernest left high school, he pushed the boy to get a job of some kind. Otherwise, he implied, how would he ever find Ernest a suitable marriage partner?

Ernest shuddered at his father's intimations. He knew only what he *didn't* want to be: like most of the other Chinese men in New York. The foreign-born ones almost all worked in hand laundries and restaurants and often spent their spare time gambling away money they couldn't afford to lose. Most of the "merchants" owned just enough shares in a partnership to skirt the exclusion laws or, like Moy Sing, ran illicit lotteries and gambling rooms. Though Ernest loved his father, he could never forget that the Chinese Boy Scout leaders condemned gambling as a blight on Chinatown and a humiliation to its decent residents.[18]

Being a US citizen did not give Ernest many more options, though. Several of his old PS 23 classmates worked for their fathers as store clerks or restaurant managers. A handful of the others acted as immigration interpreters or as the public face of the tongs that controlled the local vice trade. When they hit twenty, their parents usually bundled them off to the old country for a year to marry women who, because of exclusion laws, would probably never set foot in the United States. Ernest wanted desperately to go to China, but not that way.[19]

The people Ernest really idolized were the CSC men who had helped organize the Scouts. They seemed incredibly urbane, polished, and modern, and their educational credentials would certainly open doors for them when they returned to China. Ernest modeled himself after the CSC members in his dress, his speech, and even his haircut. He wanted to be like them in every way, to wield a valuable degree from a prestigious school and travel to China to help build a new nation. But since he had lost interest in high school after the 1911 revolution, he had not even earned his diploma before leaving. It was just one more contradiction with which to grapple.[20]

One day, Ernest saw a small but arresting advertisement. "Chiropractic: The New Science," it announced. "This intensely interesting book should be read by every man and woman who is looking towards a professional career.... [I]t suggests possibilities in a new field of human endeavor.... [F]or a limited time, we will send a copy free upon request." Each phrase drew Ernest in: a professional career, a new field—and a free book that would explain it all.[21]

Practicing medicine appealed to him for many reasons. Not only was Sun Yat-sen a Western-trained doctor, but medicine seemed both a legitimate and very *modern* profession. Ernest immediately wrote to the National School of Chiropractic in Chicago to get his free book, which promised that learning chiropractic would help him "become a personage of greater consequence, both financially and socially." Not just a person, but a personage! The best part was that the National School was mainly a correspondence school, offering a "three-year course" of fifty-four lessons that students could actually complete in less than a year. After that, they received a "degree of diplomat." If they spent three months' "residency" at the school's Chicago campus, they could transform the "degree of diplomat" into a "degree of chiropractic doctor."[22]

The cost of the correspondence course was $40, a seemingly immense sum. Still, the pamphlet promised a yearly income of $3,000 to $5,000, and the chance to begin practicing even before the end of the course. If Moy Sing would not give him the money, perhaps Ernest could borrow $40 from Ming Tai. By late 1914, the young man had scraped together enough cash to enroll in the Chicago correspondence school, and he quickly completed the course. When a state census taker visited the Moys that winter, Ernest informed the man that he, though just twenty years old, was a doctor. A few months later, he packed his suitcase and boarded a train for Chicago, determined to complete his "residency" and set up his own practice.[23]

THREE

Alice

NEW YORK, 1914–1918

AT KAY'S WEDDING, ALICE AND HELEN clung to the folds of their big sister's dress, weeping and distraught at the idea of her moving out. As Alice grew older, she suspected there might have been more to Helen's reaction than just her attachment to Kay. Their mother compared their oldest sister's marriage to "losing my right arm" and apparently expected her middle daughter to act as her new limb. Eight-year-old Helen now spent most of her free time cooking, cleaning, and minding her younger siblings, while Ernest played baseball with his friends or talked politics at the Young China Society headquarters. In mid-1911, Han Ying gave birth for the twelfth and last time; she and Moy Sing named the healthy baby boy Kee Chuan. Ernest pulled out his high school philosophy textbook to select the moniker that appeared on the child's official birth certificate—Herbert Erasmus Moy—but that was the extent of his duties. Though Helen said nothing about the unfairness of the situation, Alice could read her sister's face easily enough. And suddenly she realized that she, too, might someday have to become her mother's new limb. It was not a welcome prospect.[1]

Born three years apart, Alice and Helen had personalities as different as night and day. Helen was kind, quiet, and hardworking, while Alice was fun-loving, free-spirited, and a little selfish. Perpetually rumpled, Helen loved to run and jump as much as Ernest did but soon noticed that no one encouraged girls to be athletic. As a teenager, she also learned to suppress her toothy grin, because older people kept telling her it was unfeminine. No one ever criticized Alice for lacking femininity. She had high cheekbones, expressive brows, a Mona Lisa smile, and an innate fashion sense, accessorizing her outfits while still in primary school.[2]

Though dissimilar, Alice and Helen were almost inseparable. They skipped down the street together to visit Kay and Ming Tai's apartment, walked to PS 23 together each morning, and strolled home together every afternoon. Alice even tagged along with Helen to the local evening and weekend Chinese school, run by earnest Young China Society members. Neither learned much in the stuffy room full of squirming, restless tweens, but Helen was always happy to get a break from her chores and little Alice smart enough to figure out that Han Ying might draft her instead if she stayed home.[3]

As Alice grew older, she learned to deploy her charm to avoid the worst of the household drudgery. Fortunately, Han Ying had mellowed over the years; Kay's bride price provided the family with some financial stability, while Ernest's departure for Chicago gave everyone a little more space. Meanwhile, Kay actively intervened, inviting her younger siblings along when she, Ming Tai, and their growing family visited Long Branch and Asbury Park on the Jersey Shore, or Bear Mountain upstate. She also gave her sisters her stylish hand-me-downs, as well as occasional pocket money.[4]

The Chinese Presbyterian Church, run by the walrus-mustachioed minister Huie Kin, provided the two girls with another escape. The Moy parents did not share Helen's budding interest in Christianity—Han Ying was a Buddhist, while Moy Sing had, at most, a passing faith in good luck charms—but they appreciated Reverend Huie's Sunday School, where churchwomen supervised Helen and Alice and kept them out of trouble. The Moys even let the two girls attend high school after noticing how many of the other Sunday School daughters were doing the same.[5]

At the church, Alice and Helen discovered a community they had only briefly glimpsed at the Morning Star kindergarten. None of the older women in the congregation seemed anything like Han Ying. Mrs. Thom let her daughter make public speeches to raise money for missionary work and was planning to send the girl to Barnard. Mrs. Typond, though married with two young sons, lobbied for suffrage and better education for Chinese women. As for Reverend Huie's daughters, they radiated an energy and warmth that entranced Helen, who listened in awe as they talked about suffrage or their educational aspirations. Helen particularly worshipped Alice Huie, a member of the Barnard hockey and track teams. Alice (Moy) paid more attention to the Huies' fashionable frocks and hairdos, so different from the black trousers and tight buns that Han Ying and other Chinese women favored.[6]

Helen and Alice also discovered that the Huies and their friends cared as passionately about China as any Young China Society member. In January 1915, the Japanese government secretly presented Yuan Shikai with the "Twenty-one Demands," a power grab meant to give Japan control over large parts of China's economy, government, territory, and military. Once word leaked to the press, Chinese inside and outside of China deluged Yuan with outraged telegrams and letters. The New York CSC and its umbrella organization, the Chinese Students Alliance of the United States, both fired off protests to the Chinese government. The four oldest Huie girls, all active members of the CSC, threw themselves into one of the club's most important jobs: informing the American public about Japan's pressure campaign.[7]

The moment Helen entered high school, she joined the CSC too, bringing Alice along to its picnics and outings. The younger girl was not as interested in the club's patriotic activities, but spending time with Helen and her friends made her feel more grown-up. By the time Alice entered high school herself, she already knew most of the city's Chinese and Chinese American students through the CSC. In fact, that's where she met Sy-hung Lee.

• • •

Alice made a far deeper impression on Sy-hung than he did on her. A round-faced, bespectacled youth, Alfred, as he told her to call him, was one of the seven children of a merchant named Lee Chong and a concubine. Born and raised in San Francisco, the boy barely remembered his father, who had died in 1906 while visiting China. Lee Chong's death left Alfred, his mother, and his local brothers and sisters in dire financial straits, and the great earthquake that year made matters worse. When anti-Chinese discrimination in San Francisco threatened the boy's educational goals, he left home to live with his brother in Manhattan and prepare for college.[8]

Alfred Lee quickly became part of Alice and Helen's life, spending much of his free time with the siblings. Chatty and outgoing, the young man joined every club he could and thought nothing of making an impassioned speech at the big bond rally in Chinatown, where he and other Boy Scouts urged residents to contribute to the nation's war effort. Yet Alfred was often tongue-tied around Alice, something Helen had seen time and again with other boys. Her sister possessed a natural magnetism and an effortless charm that made her the center of attention at most CSC gatherings. Helen liked Alfred well enough but felt an amused pity for the poor boy, whose infatuation was so obvious and so obviously unrequited.[9]

Anyway, Helen had weightier matters on her mind these days. Now that America had entered the Great War, she and her friends threw themselves into their work with the New York Daughters of China, their version of the

Boy Scouts. The members spent many hours knitting socks for American soldiers at the front, and of course Alice came along to help. At the Daughters' meetings, needles flew as the young women talked over the world and their worries. Almost all of them feared an arranged marriage and wondered if their parents were plotting to tie them to some boy they had never met. The young women deplored the practice as backward and conservative. Didn't all the China-born CSC students say so?[10]

The Daughters of China members kept returning to an article by Mabel Lee, who had gained fame riding on horseback in the giant 1913 New York suffrage parade. Lee had just graduated from Barnard and was now working on an economics PhD at Columbia, the first Chinese woman to do so. In her article, she argued that marriage partners should be intellectually compatible and strive for equal companionship. Most of the girls in the knitting circle had seen copies of Lee's piece, and they all agreed with it. But they could only imagine what their parents would say about such ideas.[11]

Helen did not know how to talk to her mother about her marriage concerns. Culture, language, and generation had created a wide gulf between the Moy siblings and their parents, an experience most of their friends shared. Helen was acutely aware that the Moys had arranged Kay's marriage the moment her big sister turned seventeen, and she now hoped that Han Ying would just be too distracted to notice her middle daughter's impending birthday. Fearful of losing her closest sister—and the rest of her own free time—Alice hoped so too.[12]

FOUR

Kay and Ming Tai

NEW YORK AND GLEN RIDGE, 1918–1919

THE INFLUENZA THAT SWEPT THROUGH New York in fall 1918 killed thousands of people in the most crowded areas of Manhattan. On the streets, residents took to wearing gauze over their faces for protection, and soon, the Daughters of China switched from knitting socks for soldiers to sewing masks for the Red Cross. The flu did not kill anyone in Kay's family, but it made her start questioning the wisdom of raising her children in such a crowded neighborhood. Then the family's doctor delivered the bad news: Adelaide had asthma. What the girl needed, he said, was some fresh country air. Don't we all, Kay thought to herself. The family's apartment had seemed so modern and spacious in 1912, when Kay, Ming Tai, and little Adelaide first moved in. But Kay had given birth to three more children since then, and now the place was impossibly cramped.[1]

After hearing the doctor's recommendation, Ming Tai agreed that they needed to leave the city. Still, he wanted to be close to Manhattan, since he was now the managing partner of his uncle's old dry goods company. A number of Westchester and New Jersey suburbs fit the bill, and money was not a problem, either: Under Ming Tai, Kwong Tai Chong's profits had grown quickly. The real issue was race. Sellers and agents refused to show homes in nicer neighborhoods to "colored," which frequently but not always included Chinese. White residents often banded together to keep out people of color, too, signing legally binding agreements to discriminate.[2]

To clear these hurdles, Ming Tai enlisted the help of James Storey, a legend in Chinatown. Storey was a white customs broker with a sideline helping Chinese merchants navigate the US immigration system. He was so well regarded locally that gifts from grateful Chinese clients filled Storeyland, his summer home; old Lee Kee had even named his son after Storey (though everyone called the boy Shavey, not James). A number of Kwong Tai Chong partners used Storey's help entering the United States, so Ming Tai was on good terms with the broker.[3]

He now explained his problem to Storey, who offered a possible solution: His boss knew someone with a house to sell in Glen Ridge, New Jersey, an affluent, all-white suburb near Newark. The home had been empty for almost a year, and the owner was eager to unload it—so eager, in fact, that he was willing to sell to a Chinese family. Intrigued, Ming Tai and Kay took the train to Glen Ridge, just a half hour away from Manhattan. Since the owner lived near the house, the Chins dressed carefully to show what a well-off, Americanized couple they were.[4]

The realty company's agent was waiting in front of 190 Linden Avenue, a Victorian set back from the street on a half acre of land. The Chins admired the home's wide, shaded front porch, punctuated by round Tuscan columns and turned wood railings. Entering the foyer, they inspected the living room, looked out its large bay windows, and then peered into the high-ceilinged formal dining room. A skilled cook, Kay immediately liked the kitchen, with its large butler's pantry and space for a huge icebox. The agent then shepherded the Chins up the stairs, where they counted four generous-sized bedrooms, multiple walk-in closets, and two well-appointed full bathrooms. Finally, they ascended to the attic level, which featured two more bedrooms and another bathroom. To Kay, the rambling Victorian seemed like a mansion.[5]

Not everyone was so excited. When Helen heard that the Chins had bought the Glen Ridge house, she felt almost as distraught as when the couple wed years earlier. Kay's old apartment had been a welcome refuge for her sisters, and as Helen neared seventeen, she continued to worry about her parents' plans for her. She dreamed of attending college to become a physical education teacher, though she doubted Moy Sing and Han Ying would approve. At least, she hoped, they would allow her to complete her senior year of high school—but with Kay no longer down the street, who would convince their parents?

Then Ming Tai and Kay invited her to move along with them. She could help with the kids, have her own room, and finish high school in Glen Ridge. Helen said yes without a second's hesitation, and now it was Alice's turn to be distraught.[6]

• • •

Kay decorated their new home with Chinese paintings, Oriental rugs, and the heavy, intricately carved wood furniture popular at the time. Ming Tai gave her free rein to choose whatever she liked and took great pleasure in her enjoyment of the process. He also jumped into suburban homeownership himself by taking driving lessons, buying a new car, hiring a contractor to build a driveway, and laying out a garden behind the grand Victorian.[7]

Still, he spent relatively little time at home. A month after his family's move, he formed a business partnership with his close friend J. S. Sem, a flamboyant San Franciscan with an impressive mustache and an impeccable sense of style. They called their new company Leeng Nom, an ancient term for South China and the modern Chinese name of the Guangzhou school both their sons attended. The Leeng Nom Corporation immediately bought 28–32 Pell Street, the Chinatown building that housed Kwong Tai Chong and where Ming Tai and Kay had previously lived. Now the partners became a rarity: Chinese American property owners in Chinatown, whose landlords were largely white outsiders.[8]

When Ming Tai wasn't going over numbers with J. S. Sem or at Kwong Tai Chong, he was busy strategizing with his attorney to bring Shau Hong, his son by his first wife, to the United States. Ming Tai's claim of birth in San Francisco made Shau Hong a "derivative citizen," meaning the young man could supposedly apply for entry to the US as a citizen himself. But of course Ming Tai had not really been born in the US, and he was starting to worry that some enterprising junior immigration agent might dig up enough old records to expose him. Ming Tai had let his guard down only once, but he had never stopped regretting it.

In early 1908, he agreed to testify on behalf of his uncle Sung Fung, who was returning from a visit to China. Ming Tai had never acted as a witness for someone else's immigration case, and he found himself stumbling over unexpected questions about his own status. Without thinking, he made a rookie mistake, blurting out the truth: that he had been born in Toisan, not San Francisco, as he had claimed when he arrived from Cuba a decade earlier. Fortunately, Ming Tai was merely testifying on someone else's behalf, and his statement was not attached to his own Immigration Bureau record. But a few months later, when he traveled back to China for the first and only time, he started thinking about the error he had made. A decade later, as he prepared to bring Shau Hong to the United States, he worried that his mistake would catch up with him, and with his son.[9]

Under the circumstances, Ming Tai's attorney decided that the safest way for Shau Hong to enter the United States was on a student visa. The boy fit the bill in every way: He was not only studying English but also completing a college prep course at Canton Christian College (Leengnom/Lingnan University), a Guangzhou institution founded by US missionaries and popular with Chinese abroad. Ming Tai wrote to his son and briefed him on the plan, which went off without a hitch. At the Guangzhou US consulate, the handsome, well-dressed young man suitably impressed staff members with his fluent English, school transcript and recommendation letters, and claims about his father Ming Tai Chin, a "wealthy merchant exporter and importer" living in Guangzhou. Student visa in hand, Shau Hong settled into his first-class ship cabin, bound for the United States.[10]

But he was not alone. Staying just down the hall, also in first class, was Shau Hong's fiancée, Chau Chai Ching, a sixteen-year-old girl whose English language name was Daisy Chow. Ming Tai had arranged the marriage to further cement his relationship with J. S. Sem, whose full name was really Jew Shuck Sem. Shuck, as his friends called him, used "J. S. Sem" only when dealing with non-Chinese. His actual surname was Jew, the Cantonese pronunciation of which could also be romanized as Joe, Chau, or Chow, and he was Daisy's half brother.[11]

Shuck had known Ming Tai for years, their sons in China were school friends, and the older men were now business partners, too. Arranging a marriage between their two families was a natural next step, yet one that also revealed how Ming Tai divided his world. He never tried to arrange marriages for his American-born children or interfere in their personal lives, especially once they reached adulthood. By contrast, Ming Tai parented his firstborn son in a more traditionally Chinese manner, right down to choosing the young man's future wife.[12]

Neither Shau Hong nor Daisy mentioned this to the consular officials in Guangzhou, however. Chinese sex traffickers in the United States had imported hundreds if not thousands of Chinese women to work as prostitutes in the mid-nineteenth century. Such days were long past, yet US immigration officials still looked with particular suspicion at unmarried Chinese women who claimed to be entering the country for marriage. Instead, Daisy Chow applied for a student visa herself, though the consular officer who interviewed her quickly realized that she spoke little English. Still, since she obviously had money, and a letter of reference from an American missionary, he gave her the visa she sought.[13]

In August 1921, the two youths arrived in Glen Ridge. Shau Hong moved into one of the bedrooms in the spacious Linden Avenue house and registered for classes at Columbia. Meanwhile, Shuck placed Daisy in a nearby boarding school for young women, where she set to work studying English and home economics. At sixteen, she was far older than her classmates, but she was sweet, hardworking, and determined to hide her homesickness. She had grown up understanding that Shuck and her mother, his late father's second wife, would arrange a marriage for her, and she accepted their choice without complaint.[14]

Kay did not complain either, but she felt the awkwardness of the new situation. Though she had always known about Shau Hong, for years the boy was so far away that he was more of an abstraction than an actual person. Now, he became part of the Chins' everyday life, and she quickly concluded that he was a rather pampered youth. Though Kay and Shau Hong navigated around each other with formal politeness, there was little actual warmth in their relationship. Kay did not protest when Ming Tai lavished money on the boy, but she did not approve, either. Meanwhile, Shau Hong came to feel that Kay saw him as almost a threat to her own children's position because of his status as the oldest son.[15]

In spring 1923, Daisy graduated from eighth grade. That summer, just two months before her eighteenth birthday, she married Shau Hong at Huie Kin's church in Manhattan. The couple honeymooned in Atlantic City, after which Daisy formally moved into the Glen Ridge house, where she never felt completely at home. In a different world, she and Kay might have become good friends—hardworking Daisy was secretly inclined to agree that her new husband was rather spoiled—but she also sensed her new mother-in-law's discomfort with Shau Hong and, by extension, with her.[16]

FIVE

Ernest

CHICAGO AND NEW YORK, 1915–1922

THE BUILDING HAD NO VISIBLE signage. Could this really be the place? After arriving in Chicago, Ernest rented a tiny, cheap apartment near Lincoln Park, an El ride and a transfer away from his school. From a street map, he could see that the campus must share a train stop with the Cook County Hospital, but when he stepped off the El, he realized that his destination was several blocks in the opposite direction. And now here he was, staring up at a low-slung office building with at least a dozen tenants on the nameplate. Not only did the grand-sounding "National School of Chiropractic" lack a campus, it did not even have its own building! Ernest tried not to feel disheartened, but little about his three-month stint at the National School proved encouraging. All the classes met at night, the professors seemed scarcely more educated than their students, and after he received his diploma from the "Post Graduate School of Chicago," Illinois began requiring a special exam for chiropractors. Medical reformers not only labeled chiropractic a "cult," but a state official publicly dismissed schools like Ernest's as "cheap and worthless money grabbing medical institutions."[1]

Still, he could not bear to crawl back to New York with nothing to show for all his big plans and even bigger talk. So he studied hard, passed the new exam, and then looked for some kind of job that would allow him to save enough money to go into private practice. Fortunately, Chicago was booming as a result of the Great War overseas, which had largely cut off immigration from Europe. For the first time ever, some businesses were willing to hire Chinese Americans and other people of color. By 1916, thousands of African Americans from the South were arriving each week to work in Chicago's factories—the beginning of what became known as the Great Migration. But Ernest wanted an office job, and soon he found a position as an assistant section manager at Marshall Field's, the famous department store downtown. After he began to put away a little money each week for his future practice, he finally felt his luck starting to change.[2]

So when the US entered World War I, Ernest was torn. He admired President Woodrow Wilson and favored the Allies, but he had little interest in leaving his job to serve in the army. Twenty-two and single, he duly registered for the draft but claimed on his form that he was the sole support for his mother and three of his siblings. New York was far away, and how would anyone in Chicago ever learn about his living, breathing, and occasionally working father? Though Ernest received a deferment in the first call-up, the city's draft boards soon grew stricter. When he read that a man could earn a strong deferment through government service, he quickly presented himself to the Illinois State Council of Defense. By spring 1918, Ernest had become secretary of the new state Farm Labor Administration (FLA), which helped farmers find workers despite the wartime labor shortage.[3]

Ernest had no agricultural experience at all, but his FLA boss, on loan from the US Department of Agriculture, just needed someone who could run the Chicago office. Detail-oriented and precise, Ernest showed a talent for such work, though nothing about it fit his idealized self-image. Years later, he claimed that he had personally organized the FLA and served as its "executive secretary"—a nonexistent post but one that sounded extra important. The reality was far more prosaic: Ernest took care of routine forms and correspondence, organized farm labor applications, and answered press inquiries when his boss was unavailable. Most weeks, he completed his tasks after leaving Field's each night, since he earned nothing for his voluntary service. Still, when Ernest's lids grew heavy and he began to confuse Rockford, Rockton, and Rock Island, he remembered his ironclad draft deferment and brewed another cup of coffee.[4]

When the war ended and the FLA closed, Ernest finally quit his job at Field's and used his savings to rent a small office in the Otis Building, an imposing high-rise in the Loop. His tiny cell was on the thirteenth floor, a bargain location because superstitious tenants avoided it. Soon, though, Otis landlords began to cut deals on other floors. With the war over, the national economic boom turned into a slump. It was a bad time for anyone to go into business, but it was an even worse one for Ernest, who faced skepticism not just for being a chiropractor but for being a *Chinese* chiropractor.[5]

Initially he found some consolation in politics, because the outlook for China finally seemed brighter. The year before, President Wilson had explained America's war aims to Congress in his famous "Fourteen Points" speech, which rejected secret treaties and affirmed the need to protect the "political independence and territorial integrity [of] great and small states alike." For seventy-five years, the Western powers and then Japan had scrambled to grab pieces of Chinese territory, but now Wilson seemed to be calling for an end to colonialism itself. Asian nationalists celebrated, beatified Wilson, and eagerly anticipated the end of the war and the founding of what became known as the League of Nations. Ernest felt sure that Wilson would stand up to the Japanese at the treaty talks in Versailles and defend China's sovereignty.[6]

Excited about China's future, Ernest took the El up to Evanston one cold winter evening for the "grand social" of the new Northwestern University Chinese Students Alliance. He rarely attended such functions, since China-born students often looked down their noses at his correspondence-school degree. Still, he wanted to hear the featured speaker, who promised to deliver a rousing address about the evils of Japanese aggression in China. At least that was Ernest's excuse. He also knew that Northwestern was coed, and perhaps some of the CSA's female students might attend the social. As a modern-minded KMT member, he opposed old customs such as arranged marriage—yet, like most young Chinese Americans, he also had no dating experience.[7]

The night was not a disappointment, not by a long shot. During the social hour, Ernest met Paul Koesun, a medical student and the Northwestern club secretary. A slightly built man, Paul had sloping shoulders, thick glasses, and a suit that seemed several sizes too large. Like Ernest, he was American-born, and the two men quickly bonded over their shared backgrounds and enthusiasm for tennis. That night, Paul introduced Ernest to a number of other club members, as well as to a tall, serious woman named Ruth. She was Paul's sister, though Ernest never would have guessed it from seeing the two of them together.[8]

. . .

Ruth Koesun was not a Northwestern student but a recent graduate of Kentucky's Berea College. Since returning to Chicago the previous year, she had been staying in a dormitory on the near West Side and training in the Frances Willard Temperance Hospital's three-year graduate nursing program. Her brother Paul still lived at home, sharing an apartment in the emerging Chinatown section of the South Side with their mother; their siblings Louis, Margaret, Anna, and William Koesun; their half brothers Albert and Robert Chan; and, at times, their stepfather, a man named Chan Jack Lem. As Ernest soon found out, Chan was a national leader in the On Leong Tong; though not well educated, he was intelligent, charismatic, fearless, and, many people whispered, completely ruthless.[9]

Rumors swirled in Chinatown about the Chans and the Koesuns. Ruth's mother had come to the United States as a girl in the early 1880s, almost certainly trafficked as a sex worker. Around 1890, when she was about fifteen, she married a much older man named Go Sun. The Gos lived briefly in Chicago, where Paul was born, and then moved to the small railroad town of Belvidere in north-central Illinois. There, Go Sun ran a laundry, and Annie Go Sun, as she called herself in those days, gave birth to William in 1894 and Anna in 1901. The Go Suns eventually collected affidavits from white Chicago and Belvidere residents attesting to the American births of Paul, William, and Anna, since none of them had birth certificates.[10]

No such documentation existed for Ruth. None of the Belvidere neighbors mentioned her in their affidavits, and the local paper did not announce her birth, though it noted the arrivals of William and Anna. Indeed, Ruth herself seemed unsure of where or when she was born: Sometimes she gave her birthplace as Belvidere and other times as Chicago. Over the course of her life, a host of census takers, immigration officials, and county clerks wrote down the date as 1889, 1895, 1900, 1901, or 1910. Her gravestone bears the year 1898, though she completed school so much earlier than Paul that she might have been older than he. Whatever the case, people whispered what they believed to be the truth: that Ruth, whom her mother originally called Lucy, was only half Chinese, the daughter of Annie and a white man, a Dutch sailor. That's why she was much taller than her siblings and looked so different, resembling a young Eleanor Roosevelt.[11]

In 1902, Go Sun abruptly left for Chicago, forcing his family to rely for a time on local charity. After some months, he finally sent for them, and they moved into an apartment in the South Loop. But after 1910, Chicago's white leaders began pushing Chinese residents and businesses out of the area, claiming they were detrimental to the central city's economic development and general moral tone. The On Leong Tong, of which Chan Jack Lem was an increasingly important member, scouted for locations and helped develop a new Chinatown on the near South Side, around Cermak, Wentworth, and Archer Avenues. During this period, Chan, who already had a wife and children in China, met Annie, and she left Go Sun for him, taking her sons and daughters with her. Go seems not to have challenged his wife's decision, instead boarding a train west and never coming back. But after he passed away in Seattle a few years later, his friends claimed he had died of a broken heart.[12]

As a respite from their troubled home life, Paul and Lucy, who now called herself Ruth Lucille Koesun, threw themselves into their studies, though Annie was even less supportive of her daughter's ambitions than of her son's. Paul was almost twenty-five when he finally graduated from high school, while Annie tried to pull Ruth out of grade school until local truancy officers intervened. After that, Ruth decided to use education as her ticket to independence, winning a scholarship to Berea and then admission to the Willard program. She was just finishing her second year there when she met Ernest.[13]

. . .

All through spring 1919, Ernest's practice continued to lose money, while the news from the negotiating table at Versailles left him increasingly horrified. He began to realize that President Wilson had never meant to include colonial Asia or Africa in the places that deserved independence. The worst moment came when the Allies formally recognized Japan's claim to Germany's former concession in China. On May 4, 1919, news of the Treaty of Versailles provisions reached Beijing, causing students there to rally in protest and then attack the homes of government officials known to be pro-Japanese. The incident marked the beginning of the May Fourth Movement, a literary, cultural, political, and nationalist movement that led to the revival of the flagging KMT and the creation of its eventual ally and later rival, the Chinese Communist Party. It was, in essence, the birth of the modern Chinese nation, but Ernest had no way of knowing it at the time. Still, the treaty details did not plunge him into despair, because by then he was falling in love with Ruth Koesun, whom he married in a small ceremony that June.[14]

A few weeks later, a white man killed a Black youth for transgressing an imagined racial boundary at one of Chicago's beaches. The murder triggered a week-long race riot in which vicious white mobs attacked the segregated "Black Belt," looting and burning residents' homes and shooting and beating Black Chicagoans. Almost forty people, most of them Black, died in the violence, and hundreds more were injured. Ernest and Ruth, not knowing how white mobs might treat people like them, hunkered down in their Lincoln Park apartment. Though the couple emerged safely, the riot was the last straw for Ernest. He was done with Chicago, and with his useless chiropractic degree too.[15]

Promising to send for Ruth as soon as he could, he returned to New York and moved back in with his parents, Alice, and two little brothers, who barely remembered him. No longer toddlers who spoke only Chinese, Bill and Herbert now attended PS 23, chattered away in English, and were enthusiastic members of Ernest's old Boy Scout troop. Their scoutmaster was none other than Alfred Lee, frenetically busy as always between his clubs, his part-time job, and his classes at Columbia and NYU. Despite this, Helen warned Ernest, Alfred was still "hanging around" the Moy apartment, because he remained completely smitten with Alice.[16]

It was true, yet Ernest did not mind. The two became fast friends, and at Alfred's invitation, Ernest attended a meeting of the Chinese-American Citizens Alliance (CACA), one of the young man's many clubs. The group was a fairly new local affiliate of an older San Francisco civil rights and civic leadership organization; New Yorkers had formed their CACA in 1915 in response to politicians' inflammatory claims about "hyphenated Americanism" during the Great War. The organization's focus on politics and patriotism interested Ernest, who not only joined the local group but quickly set out to convince Lee Du, its president, that his association needed a publicist. How else could it draw attention to the patriotism and loyalty of its members and sway public opinion about China at the same time?[17]

Lee Du was a savvy businessman who liked to throw his weight around in Chinatown. At the same time, he felt self-conscious about his lack of education and poor grasp of English, and he was also an On Leong Tong member who knew exactly whose stepdaughter Ernest had married. The younger man understood that a publicist's first and most important client is himself, and he easily bowled Lee Du over with self-confidence, résumé inflation, and some multisyllabic words. By the end of their conversation, Lee Du agreed to bankroll the publicist plan for a year. In January 1920, the New York CACA distributed the inaugural edition of a newsletter called *The Alliance Advocate*, with Ernest as editor and Alfred as one of his assistant editors. The venture allowed Ernest to earn just enough to rent a furnished room in a building in northern Manhattan, where Ruth soon joined him.[18]

Lee Du cut off the venture's funding in 1921, after learning of Chicago On Leong members' growing disenchantment with Chan Jack Lem, but by then Ernest had come up with a new plan. Chinese warlord Chen Jiongming was on the march toward Guangzhou and had invited Sun Yat-sen to form a "true" national government there. Ernest thought back to the 1911 revolution, when so many of his Tongmenghui friends left New York to join the cause. He had been too young to make the trip then, but why not go now? As a longtime KMT member, he felt sure he could find some kind of job with the new regime. Ruth agreed, though she was pregnant and far enough along that they decided to delay their departure until after she gave birth. Kenneth Philander Moy—named in part after pro-China senator Philander Knox—arrived on January 3, 1921.[19]

A steady stream of visitors now descended on Ernest and Ruth's uptown apartment, bearing gifts, food, and congratulations for the couple and their new son. Most of the well-wishers were close friends and relatives, so Ernest was surprised to see Ma Soo when he opened the door one day. Alfred had introduced the two men a year earlier at a CACA function where Ma was a featured speaker. A scholar and prominent KMT journalist, Ma had fled China in 1913 after the failure of the Second Revolution and was what Ernest long claimed to be: a personal friend of Sun Yat-sen.[20]

Ma offered his congratulations but then shifted gears. Already Sun Yat-sen's representative in the United States, he had just received a new assignment: to act as the "Trade Commissioner of South China" in the US. The Congress was considering legislation that eventually became the China Trade Act of 1922, and Sun and other KMT officials hoped that their Guangzhou-based regime could benefit in some way. Ma said Ernest should come work for him and direct the trade promotion side of his expanding portfolio. When Ernest explained that he and Ruth planned to travel to Guangzhou, Ma urged him to reconsider: Staying in New York would be the best way for Ernest to serve the KMT, Dr. Sun, and China.[21]

Ernest was flattered and even a little relieved, since his job prospects in China were hazy at best. After accepting Ma's offer, Ernest threw himself into his new position, and within a month, he had launched a new magazine called *China Trade*. Later that year, it became the more robust *China Review*, which covered trade issues while actively promoting Sun Yat-sen's newest Guangdong-based regime. The publication also lobbied hard for the southern government's inclusion in the 1921 Washington Conference, which considered several key questions of influence and sovereignty in China. Ernest even organized a massive demonstration at which almost two thousand Chinese and non-Chinese New Yorkers rallied for Sun's government. Best of all, he began to receive frequent invitations to speak about China at organizations and clubs across the metro area—one of his favorite parts of the job.[22]

Ernest still longed to see China and even to move there, but he felt he had made the right choice in accepting Ma Soo's offer. He was building a solid reputation in public relations work and meeting most of the important Chinese businesspeople who visited New York. Even better, he had forged a strong relationship with a powerful mentor and knew that when he eventually did go to China, his track record and Ma Soo's connections would ensure that all doors opened for him.

Kay in the 1920s. (Family photograph, courtesy of Douglas J. Chu, Museum of Chinese in America [MOCA] Collection)

Bill, Alice, and Helen, ca. 1911. (Family photograph, courtesy of Douglas J. Chu, MOCA Collection)

Ernest, ca. 1912. (Family photograph, courtesy of Douglas J. Chu, MOCA Collection)

Ruth ice skating with Bill and Herbert at Van Cortlandt Park in the Bronx, New York, January 1922. (William and May Moy Photo Collection)

Helen, Alice, and Bill with baby Herbert in his stroller, 1912. (William and May Moy Photo Collection)

A page from Helen's scrapbook, including photos of her CSA and Savage School friends and their offspring; Alice; Kay, Ming Tai, and their children; and newlyweds Ernest and Ruth. (Family photographs, courtesy of Douglas J. Chu, MOCA Collection)

The Chin family with their limousine, ca. 1921. Front row, left to right: Ming Tai, Vivian, Alwin, Gloria, Adelaide, and Kay. Harry the chauffeur is in the driver's seat. (Courtesy of Jolly Young King)

Ernest in Suzhou during his 1928 visit to China. (William and May Moy Photo Collection)

Newlyweds K.S. and Alice Lo at the Chins' home in Glen Ridge, New Jersey, May 1926. (Family photograph, courtesy of Douglas J. Chu, MOCA Collection)

Newlyweds George and Helen Typond at the Chins' home in Glen Ridge, New Jersey, May 1928. (Family photograph, courtesy of Douglas J. Chu, MOCA Collection)

Adelaide and Herbert in Glen Ridge, New Jersey, May 1928. (Family photograph, courtesy of Douglas J. Chu, MOCA Collection)

Ruth with C.C. Chang, May 1930. (Courtesy of the children of Loring and Moyra Moy)

Ruth, Mei Lanfang, and Ernest at Douglas Fairbanks and Mary Pickford's "Fairford" beach house in Santa Monica, California, May 1930. (Courtesy of the children of Loring and Moyra Moy)

SIX

Alice

NEW YORK, 1920–1924

ALICE MISSED HELEN EVERY DAY—especially while sweeping the Moys' apartment, shopping for the family's meals, or washing their clothes. After Kay's marriage, Helen had become Han Ying's new helper, but with Helen in Glen Ridge, the job now fell to Alice. She understood her mother's attitude, of course. Han Ying had given birth twelve times, buried six infants, raised most of the others with her feet bound, and these days tired easily and suffered from leg pain. Still, Alice took on so much of the family housework that she had to attend East Side Evening High School to make time for it all.[1]

Helen could not help feeling a bit guilty about the situation. Some weekends when the Moys did not go out to Glen Ridge, she dropped by their apartment to check up on everyone, especially her younger brothers. Bill, a once cheerful and smiley boy, had grown into a quiet, even somber adolescent, and though Herbert had charm and charisma to spare, Moy Sing and Han Ying were obviously spoiling him. Fortunately, Helen could stop by more easily these days. With Kay and Ming Tai's support, she enrolled in the Savage School for Physical Education, a two-year training college for physical education teachers near Columbus Circle, just a subway ride from Chinatown.[2]

Alice was excited to see Helen more often, though she struggled to feign interest in the Savage curriculum. Her sister had always loved to run, jump, and play sports, activities Alice knew girls were not supposed to like so much. Helen had also sensed this and learned to stay quiet about her passions—until now. At Savage, she palled around with a group of likeminded women, immigrants' daughters all, who shared her dream of becoming a PE teacher in the city school system. Helen, Masao, Tiny, Mugsy, and Caroline spent hours each week working on and talking through gymnastics routines and PE exercises, activities Alice found beyond tedious.[3]

She preferred gossiping about the Chinese Students Alliance meetings she and Helen still attended together, or about their plans for the CSA Eastern Section's annual convention. The yearly event always took place in September on some leafy college campus. Helen entered the women's athletic events and also competed for a part in the convention's dramatic productions, while Alice, having served on a committee one year, learned to keep her time free for the parties and socials, where she inevitably attracted a throng of male admirers. When the CSA met at Haverford, the Andover soccer stars Tom Chan and Dick Tseng vied for Alice's attention; when the CSA convened at Princeton, a UPenn student named Irving Lee followed her around like a lovesick puppy. Helen had become so accustomed to this that she paid attention only to those young men who did *not* fall for her sister. One was George Typond, an engineering student whose mother Helen knew from church. He didn't seem even to notice Alice, and Helen liked him all the more for it.[4]

Poor Alfred Lee—he rarely attended CSA functions, probably because he couldn't stand watching other young men clamor for Alice's attention. Silently devoted to her, he was determined to prove himself in his career before declaring his love. In early 1924, he moved one step closer to his goal when he got a plum job at the Manhattan branch of the Nanyang Brothers Tobacco Company. To take the position, he had to drop out of school for good, but he did so willingly. At a time when college-educated Chinese Americans struggled to find decent work in the United States, getting this job was like winning the lottery. Even better, Nanyang Brothers had offices in China's major cities and throughout Southeast Asia, giving Alfred options for the future. Luckily, Alice had just turned eighteen, so Alfred knew he still had time to save up enough money to show that he was a serious suitor.[5]

In late spring 1923, Alice and Helen received their respective diplomas from East Side High and Savage. Perhaps Kay had spoken to Moy Sing and Han Ying, or maybe the Moys had just mellowed, because there was no more talk of arranged marriages, at least for the time being. Instead, Helen enrolled at Columbia Teachers College to finish her PE teacher training, while Alice—well, Alice didn't really do anything for a while, besides the family's housework. She envied Helen's sense of purpose, though she dreaded spending the next two years hearing about the relative difficulty of rings versus pommel horse. Maybe, Alice thought, she should take a course in shorthand and typing at a business college, like so many of her East Side classmates. But what would she really do with a business certificate? She had never met a Chinese American secretary, and she was not all that sure she wanted to find a job anyway.[6]

So Alice spent her precious free time at Helen's place, itself an unimaginable concept just a year or two earlier. In something of a miracle, Helen had convinced Han Ying and Moy Sing to let her share an apartment with a few other Columbia students up in Washington Heights. Maybe Kay had intervened again, or perhaps Ernest and Ruth were to thank, since they lived just around the corner from Helen's new place and promised to keep an eye on her. Whatever the case, Alice happily made the long trek from Chinatown whenever she needed a break from chores and younger brothers.[7]

Helen's place soon became a sort of clubhouse, not just for Alice but for Ruth's siblings. The first one to arrive was Anna Koesun, who moved from Chicago in 1922. Though neither Helen nor Alice had ever really warmed to Ruth, they became fast friends with her little sister. Anna was short and petite, with a long, solemn face that belied an impish sense of humor. She soon joined Alice, Helen, and their friends on camping trips, hikes along the Palisades, and CSA gatherings. Anna and Alice got along particularly well because neither had really decided what they wanted to do with their lives. All Anna knew was that she planned to stay in New York for the long term and, apparently, so did her brother Paul. He arrived in summer 1924 to work at the city health department and crash on Ruth and Ernest's couch. Helen and Alice both wondered why the Koesuns had fled Chicago, though asking seemed impolite. Only later did they understand, after the papers reported that the siblings' stepfather Chan Jack Lem, pushed out of the On Leong Tong, had joined the rival Hip Sings, igniting a bloody conflict between the two groups.[8]

• • •

The Chan Jack Lem fiasco worsened an already difficult year for Chinese New Yorkers, whom local police and federal agents began to target in earnest in 1924. Everyone knew that the local cops refused to enforce Prohibition and instead rounded up Chinese to prove they were cracking down on "vice." Meanwhile, federal officials started zealously administering new laws against narcotics and opium, using the opportunity to arrest and deport Chinese who were in the country unlawfully. Moy Sing had seen versions of this cycle play out over and over, and he had learned to keep his head down and wait for the storm to pass. When business resumed, he went back to pulling the numbers and running the games.[9]

A few years earlier, Moy Sing would have kept the family afloat by doing carpentry or making signs for a while. But his fading eyesight rendered such work difficult, and he could no longer stand for long periods. He'd lost most of his teeth years earlier and tended to clamp his lips together in a pinched frown, a grimace accentuated by owlish glasses—almost the opposite of the rotund, smiling god of wealth that reminded gamblers to stay in the game. To help with his aches, he occasionally smoked opium, an increasingly risky habit. Newark was emerging as a new, laxer destination for Chinese gamblers. Why not move where business was better and easier? Rent would certainly be cheaper, too. Ming Tai had recently invested in a building in Newark's small but growing Chinatown and wanted someone he could trust to keep an eye on it.[10]

Han Ying bore the news stoically, but Bill and Herbert were obviously upset. They had never lived anywhere but Manhattan, and moving meant leaving not just their home but their circle of friends. Alice was no happier. Newark was closer to Glen Ridge and the Chins, but her social life revolved around her Chinatown friends and the CSA. Helen was the most surprised of all. Her parents pointed out that Ernest and Ruth were expecting another baby and looking for a larger and cheaper apartment. How could her big brother keep an eye on her if he was no longer nearby? Helen reluctantly left Teachers College and never returned.

In late spring 1924, the Moys moved into "The Victoria," the grandiosely named building that Ming Tai and his partners owned. The apartment was nice enough—Kay had seen to that—but neither Alice nor Helen ever felt at home there. When Alice walked to her classes at Drake Business College, just a few blocks from the apartment, she pointedly avoided the throngs of Chinese men from across the metro area who came to Newark on their days off to gamble and socialize. Now that she could no longer flee to Helen's place, she had to find something to occupy her time.[11]

As for Helen, she looked for work somewhere, anywhere, outside the neighborhood, and eventually landed a temporary gig at a local furniture store's model home. Wearing a cheongsam, she posed as "Kai-tsi Moy, Chinese historical expert" and explained the features of the "Chinese room" to a stream of sightseers—many of whom spoke to her in the pidgin English they assumed she would understand.[12]

Eventually, both sisters gave up looking for jobs, having concluded that no one would hire them for anything besides waiting tables or running the cash register at a Chinese restaurant. Helen instead threw herself into her church activities and volunteer work in Manhattan. Sometimes Alice tagged along to her sister's Chinese Students' Christian Association excursions or picnics in the city, but she increasingly found Helen's crowd a little dull, preferring to pal around with her friend Lenore Chin, another young Chinese American woman marooned in Newark. But then Lenore met Billy Chang, a Chinese graduate student at Wharton, and they became serious. Alice envied her, envied Helen, envied even her sister's boring Christian friends. They all seemed to have a purpose, while Alice just felt adrift.[13]

SEVEN

Kay and Ming Tai

NEW YORK, 1924–1927

MORE THAN FIVE HUNDRED PEOPLE poured through the doors of the Palais D'Or that evening, eager to ring in 1925. As the orchestra played the old year's biggest hits, scores of couples swayed in the bluish half-light of the velvet-draped chandeliers. Throughout the night, a stream of white-jacketed Chinese waiters descended from the upstairs kitchen to deliver plates of egg foo yung, chop suey, and filet mignon to hungry diners at the booths and tables ringing the dance floor. Stopping by to check in, Ming Tai glanced around and nodded at his two managers, who looked like the silent movie actors Buster Keaton and Fatty Arbuckle. The Palais had been open just three months, and already it was the hottest ticket in town.[1]

A large card in the middle of each table warned patrons against drinking alcohol on the premises, and for good reason. Until May 1924, the Palais D'Or had been the Palais Royal, a well-known cabaret that had violated Prohibition laws one too many times. Finally a judge closed the place, making it the latest casualty of the 18th Amendment. All around Times Square, the Volstead Act had shuttered the most popular nightspots, and savvy Chinese American investors were starting to snap up the best spaces at bargain prices. They usually reopened quickly as large restaurants with orchestras, dance floors, Chinese food, and tea in place of liquor. Unimpressed, guide books and society reporters dubbed the new spots "chop-suey-and-dancing joints" and sniffed that "none is, in the least, fashionable."[2]

Ming Tai had changed that when he assembled a group of Chinese investors to bid for the vacant Palais Royal space. The judge who had padlocked the old cabaret needed to approve the deal, so Ming Tai invited Keaton and Arbuckle—whose names were actually C. M. Joe and William Hong—to serve as the "head partners." Hong and Joe were young laundrymen with little money and even less restaurant experience. However, Joe was one of Shuck's cousins, and both he and Hong were US citizens, army veterans, and fluent English speakers. The judge was impressed enough to award them the lease—especially once they promised to rename the business and post a large bond guaranteeing they would serve no alcohol.[3]

The "Palais D'Or" moniker was Ming Tai's idea. Chop suey had a reputation for being cheap, and the names of Times Square's other Chinese restaurants left no doubt about their cuisine: Yoeng's, Sam Toy, Joy Yoeng, the Far East Restaurant, Chin Lee. By contrast, "Palais D'Or" suggested luxury and opulence and tied the new place to the popular old Palais Royal. Even better, it saved the partners time and money: Workmen quickly replaced "Royal" with "D'Or" on the huge electric marquee that shone over Broadway. Inside the restaurant, Ming Tai and his partners decided not to fix what wasn't broken, so they preserved the cabaret ambience and the moody, romantic lighting. There would be no dragons or pagodas in this space.[4]

The one big change they made was to move the orchestra to the front of the dance floor, because the partners knew that the restaurant's success depended on its band. After scouring Broadway, they finally hired Charles Strickland's orchestra, which had gained local prominence after a new radio station, WHN, broadcast its Jersey Shore summer concerts. Before the advent of national networks, stations low on cash but hungry for content offered an often random mix of programs. Strickland's competitors in 1924 included amateur singing groups, the occasional harpist, and lectures like "Progress in Industrial Disease Prevention," "Youthful Skin and How to Keep It," and "Seasonal Hay Fever." When Strickland's concerts were a hit, WHN made the band part of its fall lineup.[5]

Ming Tai was more than happy to accommodate this expansion. The house bands at some of the other Broadway Chinese restaurants had done live broadcasts, but only once or twice as a novelty. By contrast, Strickland's renamed "Palais D'Or Orchestra" earned a weekly spot, making the restaurant the first in the city to have its own regular radio show. Every Tuesday morning, WHN's engineers set up their equipment around the orchestra stage, ready for when Strickland went on at 12:30 p.m. Thousands of listeners across the Northeast tuned in to hear the band's half-hour broadcast, giving the Palais the kind of publicity Ming Tai and his partners could not have bought at any price—yet it was all completely free. Now, when the bridge-and-tunnel crowd visited Manhattan, they knew exactly where they wanted to eat.[6]

No wonder the Palais was buzzing at lunch and thronged from dinner to closing. On a typical night, scores of couples came in for pre- and post-theater meals or for the floor show, checking their hats and coats downstairs before ascending to the dining room. There they encountered the host stand, where members of the Louis Heyman Friendship League, the Tau Gamma Phi sorority, or another big group were inevitably vying for one of the larger side tables. While dancers whirled at the room's center, diners on its edges ordered from the "Chinese" and "American" menus and waiters circulated with teapots and spare plates. Weaving through it all, Hong and Joe charmed patrons and cracked wise as they steered couples and groups to their seats.[7]

Though the restaurant's lineup changed, its cachet did not. When Strickland moved on, Ming Tai and his partners signed bandleader B. A. Rolfe, whose sweet, high cornet solos and swinging tempo became a sensation, helped along by radio's startlingly swift evolution. The orchestra soon switched from a weekly set on WHN to a daily show on the larger WEAF, which had just become one of the two flagships of the new National Broadcasting Corporation, or NBC—the first national radio network. In 1924, thousands of people across the tristate area listened regularly to Strickland's program. Now, millions of Americans across the country tuned into Rolfe's shows during the orchestra's daily lunchtime broadcasts and its primetime Saturday-night show.[8]

The press took to calling the restaurant the "famous" Palais D'Or, or as *Harper's* put it, "the latest thing in town." Across the country, Americans snapped up copies of the Rolfe band's recordings, and when artist Howard Thain painted his series of iconic 1920s New York places, he chose Grand Central Station, Times Square, and the moody blue dusk of the Palais D'Or dance floor. Even the company that sold coffee to the restaurant jumped on the bandwagon. "When in New York you wish to revel in luxury for a night, go to Palais D'Or," its ads proclaimed, promising that those who bought its coffee could relive that feeling. Through savvy marketing and the magic of radio, Ming Tai's place had become the best-known Chinese restaurant in America.[9]

• • •

When journalists asked who owned the Palais D'Or, the managers often winkingly credited a mysterious "Mr. D'Or." It was their own little joke, but Ming Tai did seem to have the golden touch as he sank his part of the Palais's profits into real estate and other restaurants. More quietly, he bought additional shares in gambling houses, expanding his Manhattan holdings and putting money in Newark, too. The practice was not unusual for a successful Chinese merchant, and certainly Kay had no objections.[10]

She did try to say as little as possible to the children about this side of the business, or the fact that Ming Tai himself liked to gamble occasionally. The older kids had read enough lurid newspaper and detective stories to get the occasional nightmare about tong men chasing their father, himself a nonfighting senior On Leong member. In the end, Ming Tai foiled Kay's best efforts when he scored the winning numbers at bak-kep-pai one night; he returned home and, despite the late hour, roused all the children to distribute good-luck money to each of them. Kay could only smile and shake her head the next evening when, after losing every last penny of his previous day's haul, Ming Tai told the children to return their share, too.[11]

She did not begrudge her husband the need for a little recreation. After all, his hard work and shrewd investments had brought a new level of wealth to their already prosperous household. By mid-decade, the Chins were living in a style that sometimes made Kay pinch herself. She could never forget the way Han Ying, exhausted from constant pregnancy, had sewed late into the night to help Moy Sing pay the rent on the family's cramped Chinatown apartment. Now, Kay and Ming Tai slept in a veritable mansion crammed to the roof with fine paintings, valuable rugs, expensive china, fashionable clothes, and every modern convenience she could imagine, from a massive console radio to a Victrola phonograph. After school and homework, the children shot marbles under the dining-room table, played hide-and-seek in the wide halls and deep closets, ran their electric train in the parlor, practiced piano in the living room, grabbed treats from the big glass cookie jar in the kitchen, read volumes of the *Book of Knowledge* on the window seats upstairs, roller skated on the sidewalk, and climbed the trees in the backyard. The family took vacations to the Jersey Shore, and Kay and Ming Tai bought the kids a pony and a puppy, enrolled them in music lessons, sent them to summer camp, and treated them to lavish Christmases, epic Fourth of July fireworks displays, and festive Easter egg rolls.[12]

As a girl, Kay had spent most of her waking hours doing chores, but now she had a housekeeper to clean the mansion, a gardener to tend to the yard, and nursemaids to help with each new baby. And of course there was Harry: the broad-shouldered, cleft-chinned chauffeur who ferried Kay and the children around town in the family's Cadillac limousine. He made a particular impression on Han Ying. Perhaps her initial misunderstanding was linguistic; ever since the Chins' move to otherwise all-white Glen Ridge, the oldest kids had lost their childhood Chinese, and the younger ones never learned much of it at all. So while Han Ying knew that Ming Tai had hired a driver, she did not realize that Harry was a white man until he pulled up in the massive car. For Han Ying's entire time in America, white people had been the masters and Chinese the servants. Now her daughter had white servants! Han Ying never quite got over her surprise, or her satisfaction.[13]

. . .

Though having a housekeeper, a driver, and a nursemaid helped Kay stay sane, she occasionally felt the throb of a headache from all of the children and their noise. Sometimes she applied Tiger Balm to her temples and pinched her nose to alleviate the pain; other days, she sent Harry to Newark to pick up Helen, who always did her best to give Kay a break from all the children. The sisters still laughed about the time Helen had set the Chins' formal dining table with the family's best dishes, made her nieces and nephew wear their nicest clothes, and tried to instruct them on the finer points of table manners. By the end of the lesson, she had to admit defeat; there were just too many children for one instructor to handle.[14]

Helen had laughed a lot less since Herbert started at Barringer High School, though. Unlike quiet, studious Bill, Kay and Helen's baby brother seemed uninterested in his classes and unmotivated, and Alice's recent elopement had made the situation even worse. Weeks after she and her husband sailed for China, the police arrested fourteen-year-old Herbert just down the street from the Moys' apartment. He had been gambling, the officers claimed, and Herbert didn't deny it. His own father ran numbers, and so did his friends' fathers. Newark's Chinatown was built on gambling, so what was the big deal? After Herbert paid a $10 fine, the police released him.[15]

Both Kay and Helen were initially relieved when their baby brother seemed to develop a real interest in school during his sophomore year. Then Helen heard about the uproar at Barringer over Herbert and Ruth Taylor, a freshman girl with wavy hair, light blue eyes, and a shy smile. Ruth's parents were furious when they found out about their daughter's Chinese boyfriend, but to her credit, she refused to break up with him. So the Taylors pulled her out of school for good, and the principal suggested that it might be in everyone's best interest if Herbert left for a while, too. Bill was quietly livid, but

Herbert just seemed deflated. With Ruth gone, he needed little encouragement to drop out. By early 1927, he was working as a waiter at a Chinese restaurant downtown.[16]

Helen and Kay agreed that Herbert was wasting his time and his talents, and they worried that like Alice, he would become bored and eventually drift if he stayed in Newark. Late that summer, they convinced their little brother to enroll at Mount Hermon, a Christian, all-boys boarding academy in rural north-central Massachusetts. Though a prep school, it had a history of admitting lower-income Chinese American youths, including a good number from New York's Chinatown.[17]

Knowing that her parents cared less about Herbert's education than she did, Helen completed the Mount Hermon application herself. Some of the blanks were simple enough to fill out—she had no problem describing her brother's restaurant job or his grades at Barringer, for example. The question "Has he any bad habits?" was more difficult. "No," she eventually wrote. True, the Newark police had arrested Herbert for gambling, and he had left school because of his entanglement with Ruth Taylor. But if Mount Hermon helped Herbert turn over a new leaf, these past issues would resolve themselves. The question "Why do you wish to send him to this school?" was easier. "Spiritual inspiration; association with good companions; and the good atmosphere for industrious work," Helen replied. She then got a promise of financial aid from a clergyman friend and started rounding up the required letters of recommendation. Herbert's old English teacher lauded his writing skills, but the boy also needed the backing of "some business man." Helen typed up a testimonial and gave it to Kay, who had Ming Tai sign it. The school didn't need to know that he was Herbert's brother-in-law.[18]

In September 1927, Helen packed Herbert off to Massachusetts, hoping he could charm his way into Mount Hermon despite the fact that the semester had already begun; whatever his faults, Herbert was definitely charismatic and persuasive. To her tremendous relief, school officials thought Herbert and his application impressive enough to merit immediate admission. Finally, Helen and Kay could breathe a little easier. Their baby brother would not end up drifting as Alice had.[19]

EIGHT

Ernest and Ruth

NEW YORK AND SHANGHAI, 1925–1928

COLUMBIA'S NEW INTERNATIONAL HOUSE AUDITORIUM was built to hold five hundred people, but more than a thousand squeezed in that day for the Sun Yat-sen memorial. Before Sun's March 1925 death, his alliance with the Soviets had alienated most of his former supporters in New York. Even Ernest's boss and mentor Ma Soo stepped down as Sun's US representative, closing the *China Review* and the China Trade Bureau and leaving Ernest without a job. Now, though, Ernest saw some of the same people who had recently cursed Sun's name standing in the audience, choking back tears. Looking at the crowd, Ernest suddenly knew just what his next career move would be. It was right there in front of him.[1]

Until the memorial, Ernest had been floundering. Ma's resignation could not have come at a worse time: Shortly after Ernest got the news, Ruth gave birth to their second child. They named the infant Loring after their friend Loring Black, a Brooklyn congressman who supported the Nationalist cause. But given the KMT's left turn, Ernest could not figure out how to support that cause himself anymore. As he packed up his old office, he tried to see the silver lining: At least he would have plenty of time to spend with his infant son.[2]

Still, he had no idea what he would do for a living until he attended the Sun memorial. For almost four years he had edited a journal that represented Sun's regime to the American public. Why shouldn't he now try to speak for the laundrymen, cooks, waiters, merchants, and other Chinese Americans who squeezed into the hall that day? Inspired by the idea, he used all of his and Ruth's savings to found the *China Monitor*, a semimonthly journal aimed at Chinese Americans. Ernest felt that most of its articles should be in Chinese, the language his readers understood best, so he special-ordered type from China. Until it arrived, Ernest mimeographed the paper and recruited a Chinese student with excellent handwriting to make the stencils. The first number of the *China Monitor* appeared in October 1925, and it was such a flop that Ernest closed it for good in December, after just a few issues. Several months later, the Chinese typecases finally arrived—the world's most expensive paperweights.[3]

Ruth had taken great pride in Ernest's *China Review* work, never complaining about his small salary and the penny pinching it required. Most of the Chinese in New York—in America!—worked in restaurants, laundries, or Chinese groceries, but her husband was a journalist contributing to China's future. However, losing all their savings made Ruth anxious and tense, as did having no dependable source of income. Her brow seemed to be permanently furrowed, and the couple quarreled so easily that Ernest took pains to avoid contentious topics altogether and did not press her to spend more time with his siblings or take the children to see his parents in Newark. He knew that Ruth had been hoping for a girl instead of a boy and said nothing when she dressed Loring in feminine clothes and let the toddler's hair grow long. Though Ruth was legendarily strong-willed, Ernest figured she would eventually have to accept that she could not make Loring into the daughter she wanted.[4]

To support his family, Ernest now served as the official US correspondent for two or three of China's English-language newspapers—the ones that paid the worst, he assumed. He also tried to interest stateside publishers in China-related articles. One of the few takers was a magazine editor who hired him to review a book about mahjong, the hottest trend in New York. The man apparently assumed that as a Chinese, Ernest would be an expert at the game. In reality, most Chinese Americans first encountered mahjong when it became a fad in the 1920s. Ernest learned to play from the book he was reviewing.[5]

To raise his profile as a China expert, Ernest also gave lectures for anyone who asked, from fraternal orders to church groups. Some had strange names, like the 12:45 Club or the Entre Nous Club, but even the Rotarians and Exchange men served the same mediocre fare at their meetings: wilted lettuce with Russian dressing, creamed corn, and oven-toughened fowl they liked to call squab or poulet. It was always just chicken, regardless. Still, Ernest relished the chance to speak in front of an audience. The moment he started talking about China, the disdain he often faced because of his race vanished. Just looking at him, listeners assumed an extraordinary expertise, and he never let on that he had not actually visited China himself.[6]

Increasingly, though, he wondered if he ever would—especially if the Kuomintang succeeded in establishing a national government. By now, he knew he was deeply tainted by his association with Ma Soo, a party "rightist" in an organization dominated by the leftists who had formed a "United Front" with the Chinese Communist Party. Once privy to inner-party information, Ernest found out about the KMT's "Northern Expedition" from the *New York Times*. In mid-1926, the party's National Revolutionary Army (NRA) began a campaign to unify China by defeating or co-opting the northern warlords. Launched from Guangzhou, the Northern Expedition achieved some early successes, but Ernest felt deep ambivalence about the whole thing. The leader of the NRA troops was a little-known officer named Chiang Kai-shek, whom some journalists called the "Red General." Soviet advisors helped Chiang train his army, and the general described his movement as "part of a world revolution." Ernest wanted to see a unified China, but he feared the leadership of leftists like Chiang.[7]

So he was surprised in late 1926 when one of the party higher-ups reached out to him with a job offer. Poised to control much of China, the KMT needed a better public relations setup in the United States. Since the party had little money and few personnel to spare, the man hoped to recruit someone already in New York. Would Ernest be interested? Despite his misgivings about KMT leftism, he jumped at the chance to serve the party again—and to earn a regular salary.[8]

• • •

In the late 1920s, the top firms were all leasing space in Midtown, so Ernest looked downtown for bargains. He eventually rented a cheap room on Broad Street, just a block from the ferry terminals and freight piers. The area was the opposite of fashionable: Elevated trains clattered by at all hours, disgorging commuters bound for Brooklyn and Staten Island. On warmer days, the grandly named Centennial Building smelled more like a bicentennial building, and Ernest's neighbors in its warren of tiny rooms were a mix of chemical exporters and stock cheats. Still, he was excited to be back at work serving China, and he was deeply relieved that the tension with Ruth had finally dissipated. His new job barely paid enough to support the four of them, but having a dependable income again made a world of difference.[9]

In mid-March 1927, Ernest officially launched the US branch of the Kuo Min News Agency, which he called the "semi-official organ of the Nationalist

Party." This strange description reflected the factionalized and fractured nature of the Nationalist regime. Supposedly Kuo Min acted as the mouthpiece only of the Ministry of Foreign Affairs, led by party leftist Eugene Chen. As for the "news agency" moniker, it was not particularly accurate either. Ernest's job was not really to gather information but to transmit and monitor it. Much of this work involved lightly rewriting the KMT's communiques for dissemination to the American press. He also kept a close eye on how journalists reported news from China, sometimes complaining to their publishers about coverage he found unfair. The final part of his job was a familiar one: giving talks about the China situation to interested American audiences.[10]

Early on, Ernest stumbled in his attempts to represent a fractured political movement in the midst of a volatile military campaign. Days after he opened Kuo Min, NRA troops in Nanjing killed several foreign residents, looted their homes, attacked their consulates, and shelled evacuation ships. A few days later, Ernest spoke at a meeting of the Brooklyn Independent Order Brith Sholom, whose members had invited him before the Nanjing story broke. Now it was all over the news, and Ernest had barely finished his lukewarm coffee before he faced a barrage of questions about the incident and Eugene Chen's statement on it: that shelling from US and British ships had killed a hundred Chinese. Ernest knew his audience didn't care if Chen's words were true or not, so he blamed partial and garbled reports from China for a "misunderstanding." But he might as well have been describing his own lack of clarity. All he had were confusing reports from dueling factions and provocative comments from Chen.[11]

In late March 1927, labor unions tied to KMT leftists and communists succeeded in gaining control of the Chinese areas of Shanghai, which NRA troops then entered with ease. At the same time, the party's internal divisions were increasingly impossible to hide. Relying on official communiques, Ernest informed US news outlets that reports about intraparty friction were overblown. Days later, Chiang Kai-shek and his loyalists in Shanghai suddenly turned on the unions and the leftists, violently purging and killing thousands of known communists and their allies across the city and much of the country. US journalists now reported the astounding news that red Chiang had never been red at all: He had merely been biding his time.[12]

From New York, Ernest watched the purge and the intraparty struggle with a mix of confusion and concern. By summer, the rightists in Nanjing, Chiang's chosen capital, seemed to have the upper hand; Eugene Chen and many of the other leftists now fled to the Soviet Union. Thinking about the party, Ernest felt profoundly relieved, since he identified far more with the rightists than the leftists. Personally, though, he worried about his job and the possibility that the new leadership would tie him to Eugene Chen. Each new cable and letter from China left a knot in his stomach. Finally, he received word that the Nanjing foreign ministry wanted him to stay on as Kuo Min's New York representative.

Now Ernest grew antsy for other reasons. All that fall, he did his best to seem interested in his family's dramas: Helen's engagement to George Typond, Kay's latest pregnancy, Herbert's life at Mount Hermon. But he was preoccupied with his hope that the new government would call him to China, at least for a visit. When he got home from work each night, Ruth searched his face for some clue about whether a summons had come. One evening in early December, Ernest threw open the door and flashed a broad, toothy grin. He was on his way at last.

• • •

On a foggy day in early 1928, the SS *President Pierce* chugged down the Huangpu River toward Shanghai. Ernest stood on deck, alternately peering into the fog and wiping the mist from his glasses. He had been writing, thinking about, and serving China since he was a teenager, but only now, at thirty-two, was he arriving in the country for the first time. Finally, he saw the outline of Shanghai's famous Bund begin to rise up on the starboard side, and he felt his heart start to pound.[13]

The fog was lifting by the time the *President Pierce*'s tenders set out for the jetty. Though Ernest had lived both in New York and Chicago, he gaped like a hayseed at the skyscrapers that lined the Bund and marveled at the sheer number and variety of passenger liners, foreign naval vessels, small junks, coastal steamers, and tiny boats competing for space in the muddy Huangpu. Debarking on the city side of the river, Ernest was assaulted by a torrent of sounds and smells—auto exhaust, horns honking, sewage, the scent of dried fish, incomprehensible snatches of Shanghai dialect, babies crying, sweat, garbage. Riding to his hotel, he gasped as rickshaw pullers darted in between the cars and trams, and he stared in wonder at the heaving crowds of shoppers, businesspeople, vendors, students, and beggars crowding the sidewalks.

Ernest had come to this throbbing metropolis to report to the Chinese Foreign Ministry's propaganda department, familiarize himself with the new regime, and confer with other party "news agency" operatives from around the world. By January 1928, the Nationalists directly controlled much of Central China and nominally governed several other areas, including Beijing, through allied warlords. Who really led the party itself remained an open question, but Chiang Kai-shek was emerging as the first among equals. Most of the foreign powers had yet to recognize the KMT as the legitimate government of China, but that step seemed likely in the near future. Once it occurred, the Nationalists planned to press the foreign powers to revise the unequal treaties that undermined China's sovereignty. Ernest was excited to participate in the great Nationalist endeavor and thrilled to finally see China for himself—even if the experience initially overwhelmed him.[14]

Ernest stayed in China for almost five months, visiting ministries, meeting officials, and attending a dizzying number of meetings. But he also made time to catch up with old friends now living in Shanghai. Ernest was particularly happy to see Alfred Lee, whose business acumen had kept the *China Review* solvent for so long. In those days, Alfred's real job had been secretary of the Nanyang Brothers Tobacco Company branch in Manhattan. When it closed, there was nothing left to hold him in New York—especially once Alice married another man. Ernest felt grateful that her letter announcing the birth of her son arrived after Alfred's departure for Shanghai. The poor man would have been devastated all over again.

In any case, he was delighted to see that his friend was thriving. These days, Alfred worked for an American leaf tobacco company that was trying to break into the China market. From the cut of the younger man's suit, Ernest guessed that his old friend was making a nice living. Then Alfred mentioned his address, and Ernest was certain of it. Genial and outgoing as ever, Alfred already counted many friends in the city and had even stood up in one of the major "society" weddings that year. Casual acquaintances wondered why such an eligible bachelor was himself still single, but it seemed rude to ask.[15]

NINE

Alice and K.S.

SHANGHAI, 1925–1929

ALICE ALWAYS LOOKED FORWARD to the Sunday *China Press,* with its breathless coverage of Shanghai's garden parties, country club outings, fancy weddings, and the chicly dressed people who attended them. Once upon a time, she had imagined being one of those people, but now she just lived vicariously through the newspaper. Pulling out the society section one morning in April 1928, Alice flipped through its pages: a wedding at the Union Church, a wedding at the Holy Trinity Cathedral, a children's dance group—then a photo caught her eye and she suddenly felt her insides twist up. "The wedding of Miss Annie Ying Tong . . . [was] solemnized at the Majestic Hotel. . . . Mr. Alfred S. H. Lee was best man." She looked at the tall, tuxedoed young man standing with the bride and groom. Apparently, her old friend—the one who had been in love with her forever—now lived in Shanghai, too.[1]

When Alice was growing up, she constantly heard that China-born women made much better wives than Chinese American women. Her father's friends and other immigrant men supported this claim with a litany of *toos:* Chinese American women were too Americanized, too opinionated, too fast, too interested in dances and parties. And worst of all, they were too fond of luxuries, like restaurant meals, fashionable clothes, movie tickets, jewelry, and fancy apartments. Alice had not grown up with many of these things, but she was indeed fond of all of them and not ashamed to admit it. So the willingness—no, the *eagerness*—of China-born college men to date and even marry Chinese American women was refreshing, to say the least.[2]

One of these eager young men was King Shiu Lo, who came into Alice's life in 1925. She first met "K.S." at Columbia's International House, the de facto social club for Chinese students in New York. Alice's friends Dorothy Wong and Lenore Chin knew everyone in the tristate area, but they didn't recognize the young man in the gray suit. They could tell he was from out of town by the cut of his jacket, which looked like he had bought it at some Midwestern general store, next to the pickle barrel. As Alice would later learn, this was basically true: K.S. had earned his degree in leather chemistry from Iowa State College in tiny Ames and purchased his wide-lapeled, double-breasted suit at Jacobs-Valentine on Main Street. The salesman lied, saying it would make his shoulders look broad. K.S. kept the suit when he moved east, and he wore it when he came down to New York from Worcester, where he worked at a tannery. Like many Chinese students, he was trying to gain practical experience before returning to China, where he hoped to open his own leather factory.[3]

Alice kept running into K.S. at International House, though they seldom attended the same events. He was serious and rarely smiled, unlike lively and free-spirited Alice, but by summer he had fallen hard for her. This was nothing new; young men had been chasing Alice since she was in her teens, and she enjoyed the attention. But she was older now, and restless, bored in Newark, unsure about her future, and envious of friends like Lenore, with serious boyfriends and big plans. When K.S. stammered out a proposal, Alice imagined leaving drab Newark behind for an exciting, adventurous future in China. She found herself saying yes.[4]

They had taken the subway right down to City Hall that day and tied the knot. They didn't even tell their friends, so the city clerk had to flag down two of his colleagues in the hall to act as witnesses. Alice felt particularly guilty about Helen's absence, but her closest sister was up at Syracuse for the CSA convention that weekend. How surprised she and everyone else would be to hear the news! Alice's siblings and friends often described her as pampered, even spoiled; by eloping with penniless K.S., she was showing them all how little she cared about material things.[5]

Instead, they thought her decision impulsive, though she insisted it was completely romantic. She had married for love and chosen a man with almost no money of his own. And anyway, they would not be poor forever, because K.S. came from a good family, and he and his friend C. Y. Lin had big plans to open a tannery in China and contribute to the nation's industrial development. When Alice saw Ernest in Shanghai a few years later, she hoped he could not tell just how miserable she was. Even now, she would have died rather than admit that her friends and family had been right.[6]

• • •

Alice and K.S. arrived in Hong Kong in summer 1926. She initially felt overwhelmed by the smells and sounds of the famous port, a steamy, humid city of collonaded buildings that crept from the waterfront up the green sides of Victoria Peak. After a brief stay in the British colony, K.S. arranged for them to continue upriver to his native village in the Shuntak district northwest of Hong Kong and south of Guangzhou. He had not seen his mother since leaving for the United States in 1920, and he wanted to introduce her to Alice before the couple moved to Shanghai.[7]

Shuntak was famous for its silk production, and mulberry trees covered the low hills on both sides of the river. This was the China Alice's parents had described, with tiled farmhouses, bounded green fields, and the occasional whiff of what everyone euphemistically called "nightsoil." But as the boat chugged upstream, Alice also realized that the crewmen were carrying weapons and watching the boat's passengers and neighboring sampans with equal suspicion. The seemingly sleepy district was in fact a tumultuous place; pirates menaced passenger boats, and bandits frequently kidnapped people for ransom. Often these brigands targeted the families of the Chinese who migrated overseas for work and sent money home.[8]

The large number of returned "old overseas" workers in Shuntak had created a market for foreign goods, or at least that's what everyone claimed. Still, Alice was dubious. When she craved butter and other Western foods, K.S. tried to please her by sending one of the servants to scour the markets for foreign delicacies, but they were always hard to find. And even though K.S.'s family compound was comfortable enough by the standards of rural South China, those were not Alice's standards. The Lo home lacked an indoor toilet, electricity, and running water. No electricity meant no light bulbs and no powered fans to move the air during the desperately humid days and nights. Instead, kerosene lanterns provided light, maids carried buckets of water for cooking and baths, and people fanned themselves frantically to keep perspiration and mosquitos at bay. To Alice, K.S.'s village seemed completely removed from the modern world.[9]

After several months in Shuntak, K.S. and Alice bade his mother farewell and returned to Hong Kong, where they boarded a ship for Shanghai. Though Alice tried not to show it, she was overjoyed to be escaping from her husband's backwater village, and just in time, too. She knew she was pregnant, and she had no desire to give birth in Shuntak.[10]

C. Y. Lin had arrived in Shanghai a few months earlier, and he immediately set about convincing friends and relatives to purchase shares in the factory that he and K.S. had planned in their student days. When those close to him could not provide enough funding, C.Y. sold additional shares to a handful of large investors in exchange for giving them control of the company's operations. The new Da Nan (Great Southern) tannery opened with a president and director the big investors had chosen and with K.S. and C.Y. as its chief engineers.[11]

Initially, business seemed promising, and K.S.'s salary of Ch$300 per month—a decent amount for an American-trained professional man—enabled the Los to rent a foreign-style apartment. In early 1927, however, the Northern Expedition paralyzed the city's economy. Labor unrest and strikes by KMT-affiliated unions mainly affected foreign-owned factories, but the larger battle for the lower Yangzi hurt business conditions for everyone. The big investors in the tannery panicked and demanded that K.S. and C.Y. slash expenditures and take drastic pay cuts.[12]

By the time Alice gave birth to their son, she and K.S. were trying to get by on Ch$50 a month, a salary far more comparable to a laborer's pay than an engineer's. To make ends meet, K.S. took a second job as an adjunct chemistry instructor at Fudan University, yet they still had to look for a much cheaper apartment and watch every penny. K.S. promised Alice that life would get better once the factory's business improved, but Da Nan closed just a few weeks later. Heavily in debt, C.Y. spent decades repaying his friends and family, while the big shareholders' final demands left K.S. completely broke. When Alice saw Ernest in Shanghai, the Los were trying to live wholly on K.S.'s tiny teaching salary.[13]

Alice's romantic ideas about her future had evaporated as quickly as K.S.'s savings. She loved little Miles deeply, but she had come to regret her hasty marriage to the boy's father. Their financial struggles not only strained their relationship but also magnified their differences. K.S. felt like a failure and avoided friends and colleagues, while Alice longed to go to parties and restaurants and the movies, none of which they could afford anymore. Except for her old pal Lenore, who was now married to Billy Chang, Alice initially knew no one else in Shanghai. Not only was she lonely and deeply homesick, but she also realized that she cared about material things far more than she had ever admitted to herself.[14]

Yet she could see no way out. She could not take Miles back home, because she had lost her US citizenship by marrying a Chinese, and American immigration laws defined her as racially ineligible for naturalization despite her birth in New York City. She could enter the United States temporarily to visit her family, but only if she had enough money to both qualify for a visa and purchase a steamship ticket. Of course, she had neither. Nor did she have any way of supporting herself and her son in Shanghai if she left K.S. Looking at Alfred's photo in the paper, she couldn't help but wonder how differently her life might have turned out had she ever encouraged his feelings. But it was too late now.[15]

TEN

Kay and Ming Tai

NEW YORK, 1928–1929

AS KAY, MING TAI, and the children rounded the corner, they spotted nervous, tuxedoed George Typond chain-smoking in front of the church. Kay smiled reassuringly at him as the Chins climbed the stairs and entered the nave. Scanning the room, she spied her two youngest brothers sitting with her parents on what she assumed must be the bride's side. Kay could see that seventeen-year-old Bill had started pomading and parting his hair like Rudolph Valentino, though he had yet to master the actor's alluring pout. Herbert, back from Mount Hermon for the occasion, grinned at his sister, while Moy Sing just pursed his lips, his best three-piece suit hanging as loosely as always from his gaunt frame. Han Ying disliked Western clothing, but even she had gamely paired her finest Chinese silk jacket and trousers with a Western-style hat, perched uneasily atop her head.[1]

Everything about this wedding screamed proper, correct, *dependable*. Even the invitation seemed calculated to erase the memory of Alice's elopement. Printed on heavy cotton cardstock with raised, swirling type, it used Moy Sing's formal name to proclaim: "Mr. and Mrs. Yeu-Deune Moy request the honour of your presence at the marriage of their daughter Helen E. Kai-Tze to Mr. George Yip Typond." Though officially retired, Rev. Huie Kin was officiating at the wedding, and rather than anonymous City Hall clerks, George's brother Jim and Helen's niece Adelaide signed the marriage license. But really, did anyone expect Helen to dash off to China with a young man she had just met?[2]

George entered the church and took his place at the altar, after which the organist began to play. As the audience stood, Kay saw Herbert glance over at her and then look again in surprise. Well, he was not the only one. Firstborn Adelaide was about to finish high school and youngest child

Victoria had just started first grade, yet late the previous fall, Kay had sensed that she was pregnant. The doctor confirmed her suspicions, telling her she was due in early summer 1928—just around the time Ernest planned to return from China. After giving the matter some thought, Helen decided on a March wedding date anyway. She would miss her older brother, but she knew her wedding would not feel complete without Kay.[3]

• • •

Helen's siblings liked her fiancé well enough. A whip-smart, intense civil engineer, George Typond rarely spoke, but he seemed to adore Helen—and thank goodness: She was about to turn twenty-six, in danger of becoming an old maid. (George was twenty-eight, but of course no one whispered such things about him.) Still, the Moys could not help but notice just how *Brooklyn* George was. Born in the borough, he attended grade school and high school within a two-block radius of his family's apartment in Park Slope. To be fair, he had branched out for college, enrolling at the Polytechnic Institute—in downtown Brooklyn. At least George now worked in midtown Manhattan, one of the only college-educated Chinese Americans in the city who held a secure, white-collar position in his chosen profession. Still, he was looking for a better job, by which he meant a position in Brooklyn. George even sounded the part, at least in English, though he probably had a Brooklyn accent in Chinese, too.[4]

Of course, none of them had heard George speak it. Though Moy Sing and Han Ying both understood some English, all of the Moy siblings grew up speaking Cantonese and Toisanese, the dialect their parents were most comfortable using. These days, Kay and Ming Tai still used Cantonese together, especially when the children were eavesdropping. But Grace and Yip Typond usually spoke English to their sons and often to each other, and unlike other parents, they never dressed their sons in Chinese clothing, even for photos. Instead, George and Jim's childhood pictures featured them in an array of sailor suits. Even in college, George avoided Chinese community activities. He sang in the Poly glee club and was a member of the Civil Engineering Society, but he never bothered joining the CSA and rarely attended the group's conventions.[5]

So Kay noticed with some amusement the very Chinese situation into which Helen had gotten herself. Years earlier, Kay had accepted Ming Tai's proposal in part because she knew she would never have to live with his mother. George might see himself as all-American, but he and Jim had just bought a home to share with their parents—in Flatbush, Brooklyn, of course. Luckily, Helen liked Grace, and hopefully she would like Brooklyn, too. The Typonds would not be dislodged from the borough, it seemed.

. . .

Kay gave birth to the Chins' seventh child at home in Glen Ridge on the day before Mother's Day, 1928. Ming Tai named the infant Shau Yin, using the Chins' male generation character, but Kay selected the baby's English name herself. After some thought, she settled on Ronald because her favorite movie star was the dashing Ronald Colman. Ernest, who had given the rest of the Chin children their English names, would probably not have approved, but he was in Shanghai and in no position to interfere.[6]

Assuming they had weeks to spare, Kay and Ming Tai had planned a Mother's Day party in Glen Ridge, a family tradition and a sort of welcome for George Typond. Even after Ronald crashed the festivities, Kay refused to consider canceling. She loved these get-togethers and the central role her home played in the lives of her siblings. She was so much older than most of them that they had grown up viewing their nieces and nephews as if they were all just cousins. Alice, Bill, and Herbert had particularly fond memories of riding the Chins' pony, playing in the spacious Glen Ridge backyard, and taking trips with Kay, Adelaide, Vivian, and Alwin to the shore or the Roton Point amusement park.[7]

From the upstairs window, Kay smiled down at the large group of chattering teens, parents, and children, all in their Sunday best. Even Herbert was there, having surprised them all by coming down from Mount Hermon again to announce his plan to reenroll in Barringer that fall. Alwin walked around snapping photos of everyone—Herbert and Adelaide, George with little Victoria and Beah. Helen grinned as her new husband plopped down on the grass to roughhouse with her little nieces, oblivious to his three-piece suit. If only Alice could be there too.[8]

. . .

Helen did not notice another absence. During Kay's pregnancy, Ming Tai had moved Shau Hong, Daisy, and their three daughters from Glen Ridge to the building he owned on Pell Street in Manhattan's Chinatown. With another baby on the way, he claimed that everyone needed more space, but he also hoped to ease the tension between his wife and oldest son. Daisy did not mind leaving, even though that meant she could no longer rely on the Chin family nurses and maids. In fact, she relished the chance to manage her own home as she chose and to finally meet some other Chinese women who were not related to her in-laws.[9]

Despite Kay's skepticism, Ming Tai had also given Shau Hong a chance to help run a new restaurant that he and his partners opened in late 1927. The "Jardin Royal" sat directly across the street from the Palais D'Or and used the same formula: reasonably priced Chinese food, a fake French name, and a snappy dance orchestra. Ming Tai put Shau Hong to work at the place with instructions to learn from C. M. Joe, the popular Palais D'Or manager who shifted to the Jardin to get it up and running. Unaware that the same group of partners owned both places, the white-owned entertainment sheets put a racist spin on the move, speculating that the Jardin had poached C.M. and that competition between the two places would spark a tong war. Ming Tai, who had always avoided the spotlight, was dismayed to discover that Shau Hong relished the reporters' interest in what they began calling the "Chin syndicate." The older man tried to ignore the silly tidbits his son fed the press, like Shau Hong's boast that the company running the Jardin was the American representative of seventeen different governments. Ming Tai had no idea where that came from. Maybe it was the number of warlords claiming to be China's official government, though he could never keep track—that was Ernest's department.[10]

Regardless of Shau Hong's careless words, C. M. Joe initially seemed to have broken the space's curse. Over the previous few years, the place had operated as Rector's, the Cinderella Ballroom, the Club New Yorker, and Paul Whiteman's Club, but even that famous bandleader couldn't make a profit from it. Now, though, *Variety* gushed about the way the Jardin's management had created an "atmosphere of warmth and life" in an immense space that seated nine hundred. Ming Tai and C.M. decorated the room with immense swags of blue and gold, accented by huge crystal chandeliers and massive hanging plants with cascading vines. They also signed the well-known Paul Specht Orchestra, giving the Jardin a regular spot on the CBS radio network.[11]

Ming Tai had long known that C.M. wanted to visit his family in China, so, after the manager's departure in spring 1928, Shau Hong succeeded him. But it quickly became obvious that Shau Hong lacked both C.M.'s easy charm and, more importantly, his work ethic. Within six months, the Jardin Royal went bankrupt. When it closed in late December 1928, Ming Tai told his son to go back to Columbia and finish his business degree, and he promised his partners that he would take no more leaps of faith.[12]

At least the Palais D'Or remained profitable and popular. In fact, it was so successful that Ming Tai decided to open a larger branch of it just a few blocks north. In the summer of 1929, he signed a $2 million lease on an entire floor of a new building between 51st and 52nd Streets. The planned restaurant, which he named the Palais Royal—no judge could bar the use of the old cabaret's name in a different space—was twenty thousand square feet and could seat up to two thousand diners. Ming Tai scheduled the grand opening for early December 1929, just in time for what was shaping up to be a roaring holiday season.[13]

ELEVEN

Ernest and Ruth

NEW YORK AND SHANGHAI, 1928–1930

WHEN ERNEST RETURNED HOME that summer, the United States was close to officially recognizing the Nationalist regime as China's legitimate government. This would certainly mean more work for him in the fall, so he took the opportunity to slip away, while he still could, for some much-needed family time. One hot July morning, Ruth packed a picnic lunch, and they took Ken and Loring up the Hudson for the day. Spreading their towels on the riverbank, the four of them rushed into the water, seeking relief from the sizzling heat. Ernest splashed in the shallows with his sons and marveled at how quickly they were growing. So much had changed during his five months in China that Ruth struggled to update him on all of it, especially the family baby boom. Kay and Ming Tai had named their new infant after some movie star rather than waiting for Ernest to make a more appropriate choice. Married and living in Brooklyn, Helen was pregnant and due in early 1929. In Chicago, Paul and Mary Koesun had named their new baby Ruth Ann after Paul's two favorite sisters. And, in the most stunning news of all, Shau Hong's wife Daisy was *not* pregnant for the first time since their marriage. Riding home on the train that night, Ernest smiled at his sunburned and sleepy family and then thought excitedly about all his ideas for promoting China to the American public. Kuo Min News Agency's New York branch needed to expand, and fast.[1]

Instead, the Shanghai Kuo Min leadership used American recognition as an excuse to deeply slash the budget for US operations. Lacking funds, Ernest closed his Broad Street office and began to run Kuo Min from his family's apartment far uptown. At a tiny desk, he rewrote communiques from Nanjing and then worked the phones, trying to convince US newspapers to publish his items, a far harder sell after the end of the Northern Expedition.[2]

Soon Ernest grew bored with his shrinking job, which no longer seemed central to the goals of the new regime. And while he still enjoyed invitations to speak about China, he yearned to return there and actually take part in the events he described to distracted diners at a Brooklyn oyster roast or the Essex County College Women's Club. But when Ruth fell ill and required surgery, he tried to reconcile himself to his work. The family needed a stable income, despite his restlessness.[3]

Still, a steady stream of houseguests and visitors from China reminded Ernest over and over of his own thwarted ambitions. The most memorable was Jennie Chen, whom they met through friends of Ma Soo and helped comfort after her husband, Chiang Kai-shek, disavowed her to marry the politically connected and American-educated Song Meiling. Then, the prominent YMCA leader John Y. Lee, whom they had known since his Chicago student days, dropped by, followed by their old friend Frank W. Lee, who now served as the Nationalists' special diplomatic envoy to the United States. A New York–born KMT leader of mixed ancestry, he was the son of a notorious On Leong Tong leader, so he and Ruth got along particularly well. Ernest liked him too, but he envied Lee even more.[4]

· · ·

All that fall, Ernest's frustrations mounted, but he saw no way out of his dull job. Then he got a call from Chih Meng, head of New York's new China Institute, offering him an unbelievable opportunity. The institute promoted Chinese culture in the United States and was assisting Chinese opera singer Mei Lanfang with his upcoming American tour. A performer in the traditional Beijing style, Mei always played girls or women and enjoyed celebrity status in China for his sensitive, enthralling interpretations. The China Institute had agreed to help arrange and publicize Mei's performances in major cities across the country. Since Ernest had recently joined the institute's board, Meng asked him to manage the tour's publicity once it left Broadway.[5]

Mei arrived in Manhattan in February 1930 and, despite linguistic and cultural barriers, became a smash hit. Each night, Chinese American actress Soo Yong introduced and explained in English the evening's different numbers, after which Mei performed them. Theater critics gushed about his genius, and though he extended his stay from two to five weeks, scalpers still sold tickets to his performances for three times their face value. The only people who complained were local Chinese Americans, who preferred Cantonese opera and groused about the cost of Mei's shows.[6]

When Ruth's health fully returned, she helped her husband manage various aspects of Mei's tour. Ernest called reporters and wrote up press releases for planned shows in other cities, while Ruth shepherded members of the tour's entourage to an endless string of New York City receptions, parties, and banquets thrown in Mei's honor. During those weeks, she became very friendly with the company and especially with the tour's two coordinators, a Chinese opera expert named Chi Ju-shan and the tour's young general manager, Chia-chu "C.C." Chang.[7]

When Mei's New York run finally ended, both Ernest and Ruth joined the tour's entourage, leaving their sons behind with Anna and her husband, Harry. By then, the Moys had concluded that now was the time to move to Shanghai. Mei Lanfang's triumphant American visit made headlines not just in the United States but also in China, and Ernest was certain he could use his role in the tour to land a publicity job with the KMT government. He and Ruth decided that she would accompany the tour to Hawaii and travel directly from there to Shanghai, while Ernest would return to New York to pack up the family apartment. Then he and the boys would join Ruth in China.

• • •

On the train ride to Chicago, where Mei was scheduled to do a week of shows, Ruth sat alone by the window, watching the passing scenery. Suddenly she felt someone's eyes on her and looked up to see C. C. Chang standing in the aisle. He took the seat next to her and, as the landscape flew by, they fell into easy conversation about anything and everything—poetry, movies, popular music, the funniest episodes in the New York part of the tour. After that day, he teasingly began to call her "Midi," her Chinese name, which she almost never used with anyone.[8]

In Chicago, Mei's entourage stayed at the mammoth new Stevens Hotel on Michigan Avenue across from Grant Park. Taking advantage of the unusually warm April weather, Ruth and C.C. strolled to the new Buckingham fountain and up to the Art Institute. Their conversations became more frequent and more intimate, too. Ruth shared childhood memories of Chicago, while C.C. told her about living in the shadow of his famous relatives. One of his older brothers was head of the Bank of China, and another was a well-known politician. And of course, everyone knew that C.C.'s close friend and former brother-in-law was the famous poet Xu Zhimou, who had scandalized their social circle by divorcing C.C.'s sister. At the end of Mei's week in the Windy City, Ruth found herself in C.C.'s room, the console radio softly playing crooner Rudy Vallee's hit song "Deep Night." They were falling in love, and she was more surprised than anyone.[9]

After all, her marriage seemed solid enough, and Ernest was an affectionate husband and father. Of course, they had drifted apart a bit during the last few years, maybe because of his travels or their money woes. Nor could she always overlook the way he exaggerated his education and accomplishments, occasionally veering into self-aggrandizement. He had even begun to let people think he had organized the entire tour! She understood his puffery; if he didn't talk himself up, no one else would—certainly not the white people who assumed he was just another laundryman or chop suey cook. Yet his exaggerations had started to wear her down.[10]

Ruth was not always adept at playing the adoring wife, or pretending that her educational achievements did not surpass Ernest's. While their marriage was not a bad one, it was not always a good one, either—something Ruth had not fully realized until C.C. came into her life. Now, this wealthy, handsome, and cultured young man openly admired her—the daughter of a prostitute and an unknown white man, who had made her way almost entirely through her own effort. Ruth hoped that no one else could see C.C.'s ardor—or if they did, how she returned it in spite of her best efforts to suppress her feelings.

Fortunately, Ernest was far too caught up in the work and glamour of the tour to notice what was happening right under his nose. After a stop in San Francisco, where demand for tickets to Mei's show led the theater to extend it an additional week, the group finally arrived in Los Angeles. Most of Mei's entourage stayed at the Ambassador Hotel on Wilshire Boulevard, but movie star couple Douglas Fairbanks and Mary Pickford put Mei himself up at "Fairford," their Santa Monica beach house. Fairbanks and Pickford had befriended Mei during an earlier trip to Beijing and insisted on entertaining much of his entourage both at Fairford and at "Pickfair," their legendary Beverly Hills estate.[11]

Ruth and Ernest never forgot those days in Los Angeles, though for very different reasons. As a Chinese American, Ernest was accustomed to both small slights and outright discrimination, but now he was hobnobbing with some of the most famous people in America, including Irving Berlin and Mack Sennet, and they were treating him like an old friend and a celebrity.

The day after Mei's entourage arrived in Los Angeles, "Doug and Mary" invited Ernest, Ruth, C.C., and Mei to a special lunch in their honor and introduced them to movie stars Dolores Del Rio and Maurice Chevalier. Ernest himself was the guest of honor at another lunch at the Biltmore, making a speech that prompted *Los Angeles Times* reporter Alma Whitaker to gush about "his voice, his manner of delivery, his exquisite English." At Pomona College, which awarded Mei an honorary doctorate, administrators heaped praise on the acceptance speech that Ernest translated for the crowd.[12]

Ernest could tell that Ruth was also having the time of her life, smiling more than he had seen her do for months, if not years. She appeared to be enjoying the glamour and luxury of Hollywood as much as he was, from swimming at the Fairford pool to sunning herself on the Santa Monica beach. True, she seemed a bit distracted, admitting at one point that she had gotten a parking ticket for waiting in an alley near the theater where Mei was performing. (She did not mention that C.C. was in the car with her.) So Ernest was a bit relieved when she decided to rest and not accompany the remainder of the group on a day trip to Catalina Island, nor did he suspect a thing when C.C. offered to stay behind and keep her company. The lovers spent the day together touring the city. In Pasadena, they stopped to explore an orange grove, taking advantage of the cover that the leafy, fruit-laden trees provided; for years afterward, "juicy oranges" was part of the flirtatious code they shared. Then they went to see a showing of *Song o' My Heart*, holding hands in the darkness and enjoying one of the first "talkies" either had ever seen.[13]

Ernest felt a bit guilty when Mei extended his stay in Los Angeles, just as he had everywhere else. The delay meant that C.C. and Ruth would need to go on to Honolulu in advance of the rest of the group to prepare for the shows there. Fortunately, Ruth accepted her assignment without complaint, kissing her husband goodbye and promising to meet his boat in Shanghai. Then she and C.C. boarded the train to San Francisco to catch the NYK line's Tatsuta Maru, the ship they were taking to Hawaii.[14]

NYK ran frequent steamers between San Francisco and Shanghai, with stops at Honolulu, Yokohama, and Kobe, so a traveler could easily debark at any of these points and spend a few days ashore before boarding another liner to continue the trip. Ruth and C.C. took full advantage of this, leaving one ship at Honolulu, completing the last publicity and logistical tasks for the Mei tour, then lingering at the Moana Surfrider Hotel on Waikiki Beach before sailing for Japan. When their ship reached Kobe, they debarked again for a sightseeing trip that took them to the hot springs of Sansuirou, the historical sites of Nikko, and the quiet shrines of Nara. From Tokyo's luxurious Imperial Hotel to the intimate Miyako in Kyoto, they basked in the anonymity of being just another well-heeled Chinese couple on their honeymoon.[15]

The fantasy ended in Shanghai, where both knew far too many people to expect anonymity. As tempting as a future with C.C. seemed, Ruth was unwilling to lose her sons or subject them to the kind of embarrassment and even humiliation that had marked her own childhood in Chicago. And though deeply in love, C.C. knew that his family would probably never accept Ruth, given her marriage, children, and mixed ancestry. Yet the two could not fully break off their affair. Their romantic relationship continued, on and off, for almost two decades, and their friendship persisted until Ruth's death.

• • •

Unaware of Ruth's slow boat to China, Ernest arrived back in New York to tie up loose ends and retrieve his sons. The head Kuo Min office wanted to keep its New York branch open, so Ernest told his bosses that he was simply making an "inspection tour" of conditions in China. In fact, he had already decided to ask Herbert to take over the agency's Manhattan work permanently. His baby brother had been running Kuo Min in Ernest's absence, having agreed to fill in during the Mei Lanfang tour. To do so, Herbert had taken spring term off from Barringer, where he was so popular that he had been elected junior class president the year before. Still, he was more than willing to drop out for good; he wanted to be a journalist, and diploma or not, he already sensed that he would never even get his foot in the door at a white-run paper or wire service.[16]

Ernest reasoned that he could negotiate Herbert's position with the head office once he got to Shanghai. The pay was dismal, but at least Kuo Min was a job, and those were scarcer with each passing month. Certainly, the position was better than Herbert's other option: waiting tables at a Chinese restaurant. In mid-1930, the young man assumed the title of New York Kuo Min's "associate director" and jumped into the work with enthusiasm. Herbert loved seeing his name in print when he convinced a paper to run a story, and like Ernest, he relished the invitations he received from local groups interested in hearing him speak about China.[17]

With the Kuo Min issue settled, Ernest and his sons boarded the through train to Vancouver, where they caught a China-bound ship. When the steamer dropped anchor in Honolulu, Ernest jumped at the chance to take his sons into the city for the day. The three walked down the gangplank, where friends and family greeted travelers with orchid leis. Suddenly, Ernest heard a familiar voice calling his name. From down the wharf, a smiling woman with an armful of leis waved at him. He was stunned to see his sister Alice.[18]

TWELVE

Alice

SHANGHAI, HONOLULU, AND NEW YORK, 1930

ALICE DRAPED LEIS AROUND the necks of Ernest, Ken, and Loring, all while clutching a squirming Miles. Though Ernest grinned at his sister, he was still in shock. To qualify for a visa to visit the United States, a woman like Alice needed to show a certain amount of ready funds, and that was *before* she purchased steamship tickets and posted the required $500 bond for herself and a second one for Miles. Had K. S. Lo's fortunes changed so quickly? Ernest was dying to know but stopped himself from asking. Not only was the wharf crawling with Immigration Service officials, but a clutch of well-dressed Chinese stood nearby, openly watching the sibling reunion.[1]

Suddenly, Alice turned and started introducing the spectators to Ernest and his boys. Apparently, she knew the entire group—and in fact, she and Miles had been staying with one of the couples, Ella and Luke Young, since arriving in Hawaii a few days before. Alice had originally met the Youngs earlier that year when they visited China, but because the world of second-generation Chinese Americans was so small, the three already knew *of* each other: Ella's brother, a doctor in Shanghai, had done his internship in New York, while Luke's brother, who owned Shanghai's only Nash auto dealership, had studied at Columbia. Alice and the Youngs got along so well that when she decided to take Miles to the United States, Luke and Ella helped arrange the required immigration bonds in Honolulu. Ernest knew how charming Alice could be. Perhaps these new friends had lent her money for her passage? Once the siblings had a moment alone, Alice told Ernest the whole story—and as it turned out, he had played an inadvertent role.[2]

Two years earlier, Ernest had seen Alice in Shanghai and sensed just how unhappy she was. She would not admit it, of course, but Ernest knew his sister well enough. Looking around her apartment, he could also tell that the

Los were struggling financially. Ernest visited Alfred right around the same time, though scheduling had been difficult that spring because his old friend was taking part in one of Shanghai's biggest society weddings. Had Ernest mentioned this to Alice? He could not recall, but he might have. Back in New York, Alice had never really paid much attention to Alfred. Round-faced, bespectacled, a little pudgy, he was not her idea of dashing or romantic. Supposedly he exuded charm around others, but she had never noticed it; in front of her, he was tongue-tied. But when she saw a photo of the wedding in the *China Press*, she could barely take her eyes off the tall, tuxedoed figure in the back.[3]

Ernest almost certainly did say something to Alfred, because the younger man began to discreetly ask old friends like Lenore Chang about Alice's situation. And what he heard made him seek her out and finally confess his love, offering her a way out of her unhappy marriage. Alice did not need to give Alfred's proposal (for that's what it was) much thought. Since her arrival in China, she had come to accept that she cared more about material goods than she had previously acknowledged to herself or anyone else. But Alfred's familiarity appealed to her as much as his financial success. Several years earlier, she had impulsively eloped with a man she hardly knew and moved to a country that she found surprisingly foreign; now, living so far from home, she finally understood the appeal of a kind old friend who appreciated her for who she was, from her love of luxury to her very American ideas and tastes.

• • •

While Alfred quietly reached out to Alice, K. S. Lo found a new job with a British chemical company. The pay wasn't great, but the experience would be valuable in the future, and at least the Los would have some income besides his small teaching salary. K.S. felt sure that the news would make his wife happy, so he was blindsided when she asked for a divorce. Alice's lightheartedness and free-spirited nature had attracted K.S. when they first met, but he now realized that they had almost nothing in common except for Miles. Maybe the best way to fix things was to let her go, though he was stunned when she said she wanted to take their son with her.[4]

In asking for full custody of Miles, Alice was gambling on the inherent decency and kindness of a man she no longer loved but still trusted. Finally, and reluctantly, K.S. agreed that Miles would be better off with his mother. She promised she would take the boy to the United States to see her family, an act that would shield her from immediate scandal and would protect what remained of K.S.'s pride. No one needed to know that Alice and Miles were leaving K.S. for good, and he could tell all their nosy neighbors that he was moving to the YMCA because a married man could not be expected to manage his own household when his wife was away. Listening to Alice's plan, K.S. felt deflated, and he could not bring himself to ask where Alice would get the money to make such an expensive trip. Deep down, he already knew.[5]

• • •

By spring 1930, Alice and Miles had relocated to a furnished apartment for which Alfred paid. He spent as much time as possible with them, though his dying mother and favorite sister Nellie had moved from San Francisco to Shanghai earlier that year. In late May, he came by on a Sunday afternoon to give some documents to Alice, since she was about to apply for a visa to enter the United States. Paperwork was not all Alfred brought, however. He also had a porter carry in a large crate, which he opened to reveal a shiny new pedal car for Miles's third birthday. That date was two months away, but by then Alice and Miles would be bound for America. The little boy climbed into the driver's seat of the auto and squealed with delight. Though Alice almost chided Alfred for spoiling her son, she knew she would do the same if she could—and that he wanted to create a bond with the child he planned to adopt someday.[6]

On the first Monday in June, Alice visited the municipal public safety bureau and presented the bankbook that Alfred had given her to show she had enough money to qualify for the "huchao," a guarantee Chinese citizens needed to obtain before traveling abroad. Then she trekked out to the colonnaded US consulate building on Whangpoo Road, wrinkling her nose at the stench from nearby Suchow Creek. How strange it felt to need permission to enter the country of her birth! But having lost her citizenship for marrying a Chinese alien, she had no choice but to go from office to office, submitting forms and adding to her stack of stamped and endorsed documents. After a week of this, Alice finally sat for her interview at the American Consulate. The man she spoke with turned out to be not the clerk she anticipated but the actual consul general, who was easy to charm and very impressed with her recommendation letters—including a sterling one from the well-respected businessman Alfred Lee. Visa finally in hand, Alice moved on to the NYK office on the Bund and purchased a steamship ticket to San Francisco using money that Alfred had provided. Two months later, she and her son arrived in Hawaii.[7]

. . .

Ernest could be rather judgmental, so Alice held her breath as she and her big brother watched his boys swinging little Miles between them. But after hearing his sister's explanation, Ernest simply wished her a safe trip to New York. Though he found Alice's revelations troubling, in the end he cared more about her happiness and Alfred's. He also loathed the racism of the US laws that deprived her of her citizenship forever, simply for marrying a Chinese alien. Had she wed an immigrant from any part of Europe, she would have remained an American citizen under the law—and could have returned to the United States with Miles when her marriage failed. So, before he bade his sister farewell and reboarded his own ship that evening, he found himself offering her and Miles a place to stay when the two returned to Shanghai before her divorce and remarriage. Ernest knew that Ruth did not care much for his baby sister and that any whiff of infidelity might offend his wife, but Alice was still family, after all.

Two weeks later, Alfred and his own sister Nellie arrived in Honolulu. Both were fairly subdued—their mother had died just a few weeks earlier—but Alfred's mood visibly improved when he saw Alice and Miles waiting at the wharf with their stateroom baggage. Away from Shanghai, there was no need to hide, so the two boarded Alfred's ship for the rest of the voyage to San Francisco. Once back home, Nellie said her goodbyes, and now Alfred, Alice, and Miles took the the express train to New York.[8]

To Alice, Penn Station in Manhattan felt gloriously familiar, the light pouring through the glass atrium and the crowds of travelers gathered in the waiting area. Alfred hailed a porter and supervised as the man loaded all of Alice and Miles's luggage onto a hand truck. Giving the redcap a generous tip, Alfred waved goodbye and plunged into the crowd. As he walked away, he heard a familiar voice calling Alice's name and knew it was Kay, whom they had cabled from San Francisco. Alfred did not stop—Alice planned to break the news about K. S. Lo by herself—but he did let himself glance back just once at the sisters' reunion.

Now he had a train to catch. George Monk, his boss at A. C. Monk's Shanghai branch, valued Alfred so highly that he offered to subsidize the younger man's trip as part of the expected "home leave" package, as all expatriates called it. In return, Alfred promised to visit the company headquarters in eastern North Carolina to learn how Monk cured and graded its leaf product, but he did not look forward to the trip; from the map and timetable, he could tell he would be on the train for another five hours at least.[9]

And then there was the racial question. At Union Station in Washington, DC, he grabbed a quick meal and looked for his gate. As he boarded his train, he encountered for the first time a sign indicating that the frontmost car, notorious for catching the locomotive smoke, was for "colored." Alfred knew about the South and its Jim Crow system, but only in the vague and belittling way common to so many in his circle. Chinese and Chinese American students occasionally performed blackface minstrel shows at college events and "returned student" gatherings. Of course, as a Chinese American in San Francisco, Alfred had grown up with segregation limiting every aspect of his own life: the "Oriental School," with its broken windows and restricted offerings; the jobs not open to him; the fact that Chinese could live nowhere but Chinatown. Still, what did "colored" mean in Washington? A passing white conductor, sensing the reason for Alfred's hesitation, pointed back toward the white cars. Breathing a sigh of relief, he walked through several cars and found a seat, ignoring the occasionally bewildered stare.[10]

. . .

Alice and Miles settled easily into the Chins' big Victorian, a place she had always loved. Little Ronnie, Kay and Ming Tai's youngest child, quickly took a shine to his only slightly older cousin, and the two spent hours together on the floor of the attic playroom. Alice had brought a little silk Chinese jacket and trouser ensemble as a gift for Ronnie and a baby-sized robe for Helen and George's new daughter, Jeanne. Victoria and Eugenia, whom everyone called Meme and Beah, delighted in dressing the smaller kids up like dolls. That first afternoon, while the little children napped, Alice told her sisters about her separation from K. S. Lo and plans to marry Alfred. It was definitely a topic that called for using Cantonese, since several of the older kids were within earshot. Though initially shocked, Kay and Helen actually seemed relieved in the end. Both had seen the hasty marriage as a mistake, while Helen knew that it had broken Alfred's heart.[11]

Alfred returned to New York just in time for Thanksgiving, which the entire family spent in Glen Ridge eating an enormous turkey and gorging on Kay's delectable pies. As usual, she insisted on making the entire meal herself, chasing even her sisters out of the kitchen until it was time to set out the whole spread on the massive buffet in the dining room. Over dinner, the siblings chatted with Alfred just as they always had, and even Helen was only a little scandalized to hear her old friend call Alice "darling" in front of everyone.[12]

• • •

Alice, Alfred, and Miles returned to Shanghai in mid-December, traveling together in Alfred's cabin—though, for the sake of propriety, he had purchased two steerage tickets for Alice and Miles. The three arrived in Honolulu on Christmas Day but opted to stay on board and eat in the ship's dining room. The next morning, Alfred woke early and flagged down the Chinese interpreter tasked with compiling a list of all ethnic Chinese on the ship, regardless of citizenship. When no one was looking, he whispered in the man's ear and slipped him a few bills in exchange for a promise to leave Alice's, Miles's, and Alfred's names off the Shanghai manifest. Journalists with the city's two main English-language papers generally copied arriving ships' passenger lists and published them so that readers would know who among their friends had returned from home leaves and vacations. Though Alfred generally enjoyed the social calls that inevitably resulted, this time he was determined to protect Alice from any gossip.[13]

Once back in Shanghai, he immediately got to work, hiring the Columbia-educated attorney Hua Chuan "H.C." Mei to draw up divorce papers for Alice. San Francisco–born H.C. was Alfred's close friend and, by virtue of his surname, a Moy "cousin" as well. Helen and Alice had also known H.C.'s wife Anna since her CSA days at Barnard. H.C. was surprised but relieved when K.S. Lo willingly relinquished all parental rights, despite Chinese tradition's emphasis on the importance of a son to carry on the family line. In mid-February, Alice and her first husband met for the last time at H.C.'s office to initial their divorce agreement. K.S. looked pale and downcast, and his hand shook a little as he signed the document in both English and Chinese, as H.C. instructed. Once the divorce was final, Alice publicly donned the engagement ring Alfred had chosen for her: a jewel-encrusted bauble that cost far more than K.S.'s annual salary even in the best of times.[14]

In late March, Alfred and Alice went to the American Consulate, where a judge from the US Court for China married them. One of the legacies of the system of extraterritoriality, the court dealt with cases involving American citizens living in China, so H.C. soon made another visit there to file a petition legalizing Alfred's adoption of Miles. Under US law, Alice remained a Chinese citizen, despite her marriage to Alfred, and the adoption did not change Miles's Chinese citizenship either. But Alfred didn't care; he was now Miles's father, and he wanted to ensure as much legal recognition and protection as possible for his new son.[15]

. . .

When K. S. Lo left H.C.'s office, he walked out of Alice's and Miles's lives forever. Neither ever saw him again, and though Alice was initially relieved at the finality of their split, decades later she regretted that Miles never got to know his birth father. By that time, though, it was much too late. When the Sino-Japanese War broke out in 1937, the Nationalist government asked C. Y. Lin to oversee the relocation of Chinese factories to "Free China." Naturally, he recruited K.S. to help, so his old friend moved to Liuzhou, a small, remote city in Guizhou, to manage a tannery. The Japanese relentlessly bombed the town and, in 1944, finally overran it. By the time the war finally ended, K. S. Lo was dead.[16]

PART TWO

War

1930–1945

IN LATE 1929, THE UNITED STATES was plunged into the Great Depression. Within two years, more than a quarter of working-age Americans were jobless, while many others suffered deep wage cuts. New York City's growing throngs of unemployed, homeless, and hungry joined breadlines, begged for change, and squatted in makeshift encampments, including one in Central Park. Throughout the United States, the economic catastrophe hit people of color hardest. Most already earned much less than white Americans and had far fewer opportunities even in the best of times.[1]

The Depression touched almost every part of the world, but for a while, China's decision to remain on the silver standard created unusual economic prosperity in Shanghai. Money flowed into the city, prompting a real estate boom and loose credit. After 1934, however, the Depression began to affect China deeply. KMT policies also provoked growing popular unrest there, especially after Japan's 1931 invasion of Manchuria. Patriotic Chinese, particularly students, criticized Chiang Kai-shek's decision to use his military to fight the Chinese Communists rather than standing up to the Japanese. Only in early 1937 did the Nationalists and Communists finally forge an uneasy "Second United Front" against Japan.[2]

Barely aware of China's political tensions, many Chinese Americans who could not find jobs in the United States moved to Shanghai in the interwar years. It had been a divided city since the 1840s, when Qing officials set aside areas for exclusive foreign settlement. They initially saw the division as way to minimize foreigners and their influence in the city; instead, in the years that followed, Chinese refugees from internal unrest poured in, and they soon made up an overwhelming majority of "foreign concession" residents. Still, foreigners wielded authority over what came to be known as the French

Concession (an area governed by the French consul-general and a municipal council) and the International Settlement (run by an elected body, the Shanghai Municipal Council, which excluded Chinese for most of its history).[3]

In 1937, when war broke out between China and Japan, the Nationalist-governed areas of Shanghai became the scene of ferocious urban combat. After three months of tenacious, costly fighting, Chiang Kai-shek's forces finally withdrew up the Yangzi, retreating deep into the interior. Over the next year, they lost most of China's heartland to the invaders, finally establishing their wartime capital in Chongqing. In 1941, the American Volunteer Group, or "Flying Tigers," under General Claire Lee Chennault, began flying against the Japanese from the southwestern city of Kunming. After Pearl Harbor, Kunming became the main base of the US 14th Air Force, also under Chennault's command.[4]

In occupied China, the Japanese set up puppet governments—in 1940, Chiang Kai-shek's old rival Wang Jingwei agreed to head the collaborationist regime in the lower Yangzi—but few Chinese had any doubt who was really in charge. Until 1941, the Japanese claimed to recognize the independence of Shanghai's foreign areas, but they simultaneously worked to exert power and influence over these places. After the fall of France in 1940, Vichy collaborators governed the French Concession in cooperation with the Japanese. Following Pearl Harbor, the Japanese marched into the International Settlement as well. This effectively cut off Shanghai's American residents from both unoccupied China and the United States.[5]

THIRTEEN

Kay and Ming Tai

GLEN RIDGE AND NEWARK, 1930–1932

IN THE FLUSH 1920S, the Chin family's chauffeur spent much of his time ferrying the children to music lessons and various gatherings. But with Adelaide in college and most of the other children nearly grown, did the family really *need* a driver anymore? So Ming Tai laid off Harry, and eventually Kay let the housemaid go—anything to trim the family's lavish spending. In September 1929, Ming Tai had signed an extremely expensive lease for a prime piece of Broadway real estate, investing tens of thousands of dollars to renovate a space that the press called the "largest Chinese restaurant in the world." Less than two months later, the New York Stock Exchange began the free fall that marked the end of the seemingly endless boom—and the beginning of the Great Depression, though no one knew it yet. After a sluggish holiday season, Ming Tai began questioning the wisdom of operating a restaurant that seated twenty-five hundred people.[1]

By 1930, Ming Tai increasingly struggled to replicate the factors that had made his other restaurants so successful. He offered bandleader B. A. Rolfe a stake in the new Palais Royal, but the cornetist strung him along for weeks and then left for good; Rolfe had used the extra time to negotiate a lucrative contract for his own radio show. Even worse, he proved irreplaceable, since other top musicians were following his lead. Broadcasters had finally figured out how to make money by selling advertisements and even whole time slots to sponsors, who paid for shows like "B. A. Rolfe and his Lucky Strike Dance Orchestra." Stations did not need to fill hours of time with house bands, and the hottest orchestras now avoided restaurant gigs.[2]

Ming Tai had always been willing to pay top dollar for the best location, the best band, and the best dancers, but by late 1930 he had to scale back everywhere. When the original Palais D'Or lease expired, he gave up the old space and made the Palais Royal the new Palais D'Or. After another truly anemic holiday season, he cut even deeper, breaking the restaurant's contract with its new bandleader, hiring a cheaper orchestra, and reintroducing an inexpensive version of the floor show the Palais had featured years earlier. None of it worked. By late 1931, the Palais was hemorrhaging money.[3]

Even worse, to buy time for a recovery that never came, Ming Tai loaded his other companies with debt, borrowed thousands of dollars from the bank, and delayed payment of outstanding invoices. Now, those bills came due, one after another, and by early 1932 the Chins were facing financial catastrophe. That January, Kwong Tai Chong—the dry goods firm Ming Tai's uncle had founded in 1891—went bankrupt. Not only had Ming Tai channeled Palais debt through the company, but Kwong Tai Chong also struggled to collect outstanding invoices from other restaurants that were themselves floundering. Adding insult to injury, Ming Tai owned shares in some of these same eateries.[4]

Finally, he swallowed his pride and reached out to his brother-in-law George Typond for help. George quickly put in a call to his brother Jim, the only person anyone knew who was actually doing well these days. A New York University (NYU) business graduate, Jim had forged ties to Tammany Hall and the Brooklyn Democratic machine and could speak Cantonese as well as English. Before the crash, he used these talents and connections to start a service firm that sold insurance and helped Chinese restaurants and laundries get the licenses they needed from the city. Now, he spent most of his time liquidating the same companies for a commission.[5]

The Chins provided plenty of work for Jim that year. Just two weeks after Kwong Tai Chong failed, the Palais D'Or closed its doors for good. With some clever restructuring, Jim was able to help Ming Tai and his partners hold on to their Pell Street and Newark apartment buildings, but his wizardry could not save the Chins' spacious Glen Ridge home. To spare the family as much embarrassment as possible, Jim convinced local authorities to publish the required notice in the *Newark Jewish Chronicle*, to which few in WASPy Glen Ridge and no one in Chinatown subscribed. In April 1932, the county sheriff brought down the hammer and auctioned off the stately Victorian. The Chins now moved to their Newark Chinatown building, sharing it with tenants who included waiters, laundrymen, the family of their old matchmaker Lee Weenom, and Kay's parents and younger siblings.[6]

The Typonds helped the Chins pack their boxes but could offer no real financial assistance. Helen and her husband still lived in the Flatbush house that George and Jim had bought with their parents a few years earlier. Of course, Jim's career was flourishing, while George had been fortunate enough to keep his engineering job despite the economy's nosedive. Still, finances at the Typonds' were tighter than they had ever been. The brothers now paid all their parents' bills, since the Depression had forced Yip Typond to retire from his laundry supply business.[7]

. . .

Ming Tai loved spending money on his family, but now bankruptcy forced him into a series of difficult conversations with the beneficiaries of his largesse. To Kay's satisfaction, her husband finally told thirty-year-old Shau Hong to support Daisy and their daughters on his own—which meant moving out of the 30 Pell Street building the Chins still partially owned. Kay felt far less gratified when Ming Tai hinted that he could no longer afford to let her parents live rent-free in the Newark Chinatown building. Still, she reasoned, she had three adult brothers whose first duty was to support Moy Sing and Han Ying.[8]

Bill and Herbert tried to carry the load on their own but struggled in the dreadful economy. Hoping to find work, Bill dropped out of the Newark College of Engineering after a year, but jobs were scarce, and his Chinese face didn't help. In 1931, he finally went into what had become the de facto family business, accepting a tiny salary to help Herbert run the New York Kuo Min News Agency during the busy months after the Japanese invaded Manchuria. But late the next spring, Shanghai headquarters closed the Manhattan Kuo Min branch for good, leaving both brothers jobless. The young men and their parents now depended entirely on Moy Sing's shares in a few Newark Chinatown gambling rooms, which paid less and less each month. A couple years earlier, local and federal authorities had declared war on narcotics and gambling in Newark Chinatown, and they seemed equally intent on driving Chinese as a whole out of the city. With the family income dwindling, something had to change—and fast.[9]

After much back and forth, the US- and China-based siblings finally came up with a plan. Shanghai was still booming, so Bill and Herbert decided to move there with their parents. Ernest promised to find his brothers jobs and to help support Han Ying and Moy Sing. Shau Hong, stung by his father's ultimatum, announced that he would take Daisy and their five daughters to Guangzhou, where he had once attended prep school and now assumed he could find work. Shau Hong, Daisy, and their girls would accompany the four Moys as far as Hong Kong, and everyone agreed on an early November departure to allow time to tie up loose ends and get necessary immigration paperwork.[10]

Within weeks, though, the tidy plan began to unravel. Shau Hong and Daisy dropped out completely after doctors hospitalized one of their children with nephritis, and Bill began to waver, too. He had started dating the sister of his best friend, George Wong. May shared Bill's interest in photography and wore impossibly chic outfits that she sewed herself. Because of the economy, she had just dropped out of Parsons Art School to work on one of the big steamships that ferried passengers from New York to Europe, but Bill managed to see her every time she returned to town. Unwilling to part, the two decided to marry, though May agreed to stay behind in New York until Bill could support both of them in China. Their ceremony took place at the same church where Helen had wed George six years earlier, but this time Herbert missed the event. He had left for Shanghai ahead of Bill, their parents, and the law.[11]

. . .

Herbert had never really gotten over Ruth Taylor, his girlfriend at Barringer High School, and he still bristled at how much her parents hated the idea of their daughter being with a Chinese boy. After pulling her out of school, they pressured her into marrying a salesman named Ed Niles—sure, he was twenty-nine and still lived with his mother in her Syracuse boarding house, but at least he was white. Poor Ruth wanted so much to please them that she agreed to the union, even though she was only sixteen. But the marriage made her so miserable that the moment she turned eighteen, she left Niles (and his mother) and sought an annulment.[12]

Her letter arrived at the Moys' Newark apartment shortly before the family's scheduled departure for Shanghai. Herbert recognized the handwriting and tore open the envelope, eagerly reading the note and its declaration of love. He rushed over to the rooming house where Ruth was staying while she contemplated how to tell her parents about her annulment. When she finally dared, the Taylors were stunned, especially when she informed them that she and Herbert were back together. When the Taylors demanded she end that relationship, a despondent Ruth took poison and phoned Herbert to say goodbye.[13]

In a panic, he drove back to the rooming house and got her to the hospital just in time; yet, rather than feeling grateful, Ruth's parents blamed him for the near catastrophe. A day or two later, the cops showed up at the Moys' apartment and arrested Herbert as a "material witness" to some vague crime they refused to specify. He could easily tell that the Taylors had asked the police to scare him away, and of course the Newark authorities were happy to oblige—any chance to go after a Chinese. Then he and Ruth showed everyone, eloping in Manhattan after he posted bail and she slipped out of her parents' home. Two days later, traveling alone, he crossed into Canada, took a train to Vancouver, and boarded a Shanghai-bound steamship. He needed to get out of Newark and away from the cops, but he promised Ruth that they would find a way to be together soon.[14]

. . .

Kay felt a tremendous sense of relief when her parents and brothers finally left for China. She and Ming Tai had more than enough mouths to feed without the Moys to support as well. Adelaide had returned home after a year of college, and now all seven Chin children lived in the cramped Newark flat. Though Adelaide adored her family, she did not feel the same about Newark, so she made sporadic attempts to escape the city. First she signed up to be a counselor at a summer camp in New Hampshire, and then she took a job as a lounge waitress on the same trans-Atlantic ocean liner that hired May. But when May left the ship after marrying Bill, Kay and Ming Tai made their daughter quit, too.[15]

Adelaide reluctantly agreed, mainly because she was waiting expectantly for her boyfriend's return from China. Though born in Hawaii, Jack Young had grown up mainly in Central China, and during leaves from his journalism studies at NYU, he became well known for guiding wealthy foreign adventurers and hunters in Sichuan and Tibet. When the sons of late president Theodore Roosevelt visited China to search for pandas, they recruited Jack to serve as their guide, and he even helped shoot and kill the first giant panda sold to an American museum. In fall 1931, he accepted an invitation to guide an expedition to northern Tibet, so he took another leave from NYU—but not from his budding relationship with Adelaide.[16]

Ming Tai and Kay liked Jack well enough, and he definitely wanted to impress them. The young man knew a number of rich, well-connected people because of his guide work; when Adelaide told him about Ming Tai's business problems, Jack approached his wealthy contacts to ask about a loan. Still, Kay and Ming Tai worried about what Adelaide called Jack's adventurous spirit and what they considered his recklessness. They also wondered about his ability to provide a stable home for their oldest daughter. When Jack departed for China, they breathed a sigh of relief.[17]

Yet Kay could hardly blame her daughter for wanting to get out of the house. The apartment felt horribly cramped and noisy, especially after spacious, leafy Glen Ridge. Kay disliked walking through the streets of Newark's gritty, treeless Chinatown, and she hated the way the police randomly hassled Chinese men there. When Herbert told her about his experience with the cops after he saved Ruth Taylor's life, she knew he was not exaggerating. It had gotten so bad that many longtime Chinatown residents, including some of Ming Tai's tenants, were planning to move over to New York or down to Philadelphia.[18]

Ming Tai hoped to get his own family back to Manhattan as soon as he could stabilize their finances. He had never expected to live in his investment building in Newark, and he had no illusions about the local Chinatown's character. Some of his family's income came from gambling-house revenues, but he did not want to raise his children in a gambling mecca—even one that the police were slowly suffocating.

FOURTEEN

Ernest and Ruth

SHANGHAI, 1931–1932

SPYING ERNEST AND THE BOYS on the ship's deck, Ruth waved her handkerchief until they caught sight of her. Once the three debarked and collected their bags, the family took a taxi to the French Concession apartment Ruth had found for them after her own arrival in Shanghai two months earlier. Though she treasured the memories of her trip with C. C. Chang, she resolved to put the affair behind her. Settling into her new life in Shanghai, she focused on mundane tasks like finding new schools for the boys and setting up their flat in the Savoy Apartments. But Ruth could not resist opening and responding to the letters C.C. posted from Sichuan, where he now worked as assistant manager of the Bank of China. She blushed when reading his plea to tell him what she wanted for her heart and body, and she thanked her lucky stars that Ernest was too caught up in his job search to notice.[1]

He had looked forward to joining the Nationalist regime's information division, certain that his reputation and the Mei Lanfang tour would open doors there. When he saw Alice in Honolulu, he had been not just optimistic about the future, but positively giddy. Now, after two months in China, he was increasingly disheartened. Though he haunted government offices in Shanghai and Nanjing, he gained no traction with the men in power, even though he had been a member of the KMT longer than almost all of them. Chiang Kai-shek and his backers showed no interest in Ernest, an "overseas Chinese" without the right ties to the party's most powerful cliques.[2]

Sensing the way things now worked, Ernest scrambled to use the few connections he did have. He remembered Judge Paul Linebarger, a KMT advisor he had known in New York, and sent him an almost desperate letter. "It would go a long way to facilitate matters if you wrote to such men as Dr. C. T. Wang, and Dr. Sun Fo, and to Dr. H. H. Kung whose ministries are most concerned with foreign publicity," Ernest pleaded. But Linebarger declined to intervene, or even respond. And though Ma Soo was happy to hear from his old friend, he had not only fallen out of favor in the party, but seemed alarmingly frail. To Ernest's dismay, his old mentor died just a few months later.[3]

Ernest finally formed a partnership with S. D. Wang, a Shanghai stockbroker who wanted to start a government bond division. Ernest had no financial industry experience, but Wang needed an English-speaking partner with some Nationalist credibility. Ernest fit the bill well enough and was a skilled administrator. Although he took complete credit for "organizing" the bond department at S. D. Wang & Co., his main job was producing English-language reports for foreign investors interested in buying Chinese government bonds. This was not the kind of exciting, colorful service he had hoped to perform, but it was a living.[4]

At least his social life got off to a roaring star. When Douglas Fairbanks stopped in China on his way to hunt big game in Southeast Asia, Ernest and Ruth hosted a tea and reception for the film star at Shanghai's glitzy Cathay Hotel on the Bund. The party was the hottest ticket in town. When sending out invitations, the Moys asked for RSVPs only from those who did *not* plan to attend. That afternoon, more than two hundred guests, mainly US-educated Chinese, Chinese Americans, and white Americans, crowded into the Cathay's ballroom. In the United States, the mainstream papers ignored Chinese American trendsetters and social elites, but Shanghai was different. Reporters breathlessly recounted the guest list and the fashions—including the "ultra-chic afternoon black chiffon velvet suit" that Ruth donned as she "so charmingly assisted Mr. Moy in receiving the several hundred guests."[5]

• • •

As Ernest plugged away at his bond reports, his career frustrations merged with his concerns about the KMT's direction. In early 1931, Wang Jingwei and other alienated Nationalist leaders formed a separatist regime in Guangdong in response to Chiang Kai-shek's authoritarianism. Ernest was horrified at the prospect that the country could plunge into civil war, especially when the consequences of Nationalist disunity became clear. In September 1931, a group of renegade Japanese officers took advantage of the Chinese government's divisions, secretly dynamiting a section of railroad tracks belonging to the Japanese-owned South Manchurian Railway. As the plotters hoped, Japanese leaders publicly blamed nearby Chinese troops for the minor explosion and used this "provocation" to launch a wholesale invasion of Manchuria.[6]

Across urban China, angry citizens took to the streets to protest the government's divisions and weak response to Japanese encroachment. As protests swelled in Shanghai, Japanese army leaders demanded the demilitarization of Chinese areas of Shanghai and the suppression of all anti-Japanese activism in the city. In late January 1932, the Japanese landed ground forces in Shanghai and shelled areas with concentrations of Chinese troops. To the surprise of Japanese commanders, these soldiers—most famously the Cantonese 19th Route Army under General Cai Tingkai—fought back tenaciously. Their resistance galvanized the nation but came at a very high cost. What became known as the "Shanghai Incident" lasted until March and resulted in ten thousand Chinese and twenty-five hundred Japanese deaths.[7]

As the situation spiraled out of control, Ernest released a public statement titled "Has the Kuomintang Collapsed?" With the nation in crisis, Chiang Kai-shek and Wang Jingwei finally agreed to patch up their differences and form a new government in Nanjing, but Ernest saw the KMT dithering as too little, too late. Noting his long party membership and service, he criticized leaders for the infighting and factionalism that had made the country so vulnerable to Japanese aggression. "The immediate fate of the country rests with these very men who cannot agree!" he exclaimed, calling for real unity. Party leaders and the Chinese papers completely ignored him.[8]

As Ernest watched from the sidelines, the brief war gave Ruth new purpose and unusual prominence. During the fighting, local Chinese doctors rushed to set up makeshift hospitals wherever they could find space, and the Chinese Red Cross and other charitable groups pleaded with the public for donations to help the wounded and homeless. Fired by patriotism, Ruth joined about twenty other women to form the Ladies' Aid for Chinese Soldiers (LACS). The organization provided an outlet for Ruth's tremendous energy and gave her something to divert her thoughts from C.C.[9]

Initially she sewed sheets and pajamas with the other LACS women, but then she and another former nurse in the group decided to tour one of the ad hoc field hospitals. The "No. 5 Emergency Hospital" was a cluster of jury-rigged buildings with tin roofs and almost no furniture or supplies. Wounded soldiers, still dressed in their dirty, tattered uniforms, lay sprawled across the dirt floors. Patriotic high school and college students with no nursing experience attended the patients and sometimes did more harm than good, while the doctors who ran the place frantically tended to the constant stream of wounded arriving at all hours. Surveying the place, Ruth was appalled.[10]

She immediately asked to speak with the head doctor, C.Y. Yue. After dealing with yet another wounded soldier, a harried Dr. Yue stepped outside to talk to the very serious-looking visitor who insisted he meet with her. A foreign busybody . . . or was she Chinese? He could not tell, but he could feel himself tense up at the thought of all the time he was wasting on this. Then Ruth introduced herself, described her nursing background, and offered to train the volunteers. She could even speak Cantonese, the dialect that most of the soldiers but few of the doctors understood. Yue's defensiveness evaporated, and he gratefully accepted Ruth's offer.[11]

She leaped right into the work, reorganizing the entire hospital and bringing in desperately needed beds, sheets, and pajamas. Within days, Ruth also gave the LACS sewing group detailed instructions for nurses' uniforms and masks, and soon the volunteer staff wore far more sanitary clothing. Ruth still thought about C.C., but tending to the wounded and checking on the nurses' work kept her frantically busy and gave her a tremendous sense of purpose. As for Dr. Yue, he was delighted by Ruth's efforts. "She transformed the place so thoroughly and with such efficiency; and was so cheerful in all the things she did, that she quickly endeared herself to both the staff and the patients," he recalled. "I dare say that the patients of no other emergency military hospital in Shanghai at that time could have been happier than those in our hospital as well as its staff."[12]

• • •

Each morning during the Shanghai conflict, Ernest watched Ruth put on her nurse's uniform and leave their apartment with her purposeful stride, off to tend to suffering patients. He felt both proud and jealous—or was it embarrassed? Ernest could do little himself except watch the conflict from the relative safety of the French Concession. Sometimes he took foreigners to see Ruth's hospital, determined that they understand the results of Japanese aggression. But those visits also left him keenly aware that unlike his wife, he had little to offer these heroic soldiers. Once again, he felt like an onlooker rather than a participant in China's great patriotic struggle.[13]

Then the newspaper owner T.B. Chang threw him a lifeline. Chang owned the city's Shun Shih News Agency and needed someone with administrative skills to help expand the company's newspapers and network of correspondents. Chang simply wanted a good manager, but Ernest saw the offer as his chance to get off the sidelines. By September 1932, having successfully reorganized Shun Shih, he convinced Chang to place him in a more frontline newspaper position: editor of the city's *China Press*.[14]

Ernest coveted the position for its promise of action and involvement in current affairs, but there was another upside, too. Despite a flood of letters from New York, he could not bring himself to invite Han Ying, Moy Sing, or his brothers to move in with his own family. Still, pressed by Kay and Helen, he finally offered to find jobs in Shanghai for Bill and Herbert. It was a tall order; Ernest himself had struggled to land a decent position when he first arrived. And though his brothers spoke Toisanese and Cantonese, neither could read or write Chinese all that well or understand Shanghai dialect, let alone Mandarin. Many of the Western-educated Chinese on the job market could do all of these things and had college or even graduate degrees, too, while Bill possessed only a high school diploma and Herbert not even that. As for job experience, both had none except for a year or so at the New York Kuo Min News Agency. But once T. B. Chang agreed to let Ernest run the *China Press*—a paper published in English—he finally wrote to New York and told his brothers to come to Shanghai. He would hire them himself.[15]

FIFTEEN

Alice and Alfred

SHANGHAI, 1932–1934

OF COURSE PEOPLE TALKED, but Alice didn't care, and neither did Alfred. He was over the moon, and anyway, she was not the only divorced woman in Shanghai, not by a long shot. Her friend Ann Summers Chen had arrived from the United States with one Chinese student, moved on to her current husband, and was rumored to have been married to a completely different man in New York. Perhaps Ann was a little shameless, but everyone knew you could reinvent yourself in Shanghai.[1]

Alice did sometimes wonder if her prim and proper sister-in-law whispered about her behind her back. Ruth was probably just jealous of Alfred's stability. Ernest always wanted the kinds of positions he could not get or was never really qualified for in the first place. He excelled at organization and administration, yet he quickly grew bored with such work. Ever since arriving in Shanghai, he had moved from job to job: from Kuo Min to S. D. Wang to Shun Shih. At some point he started talking about running a dairy on Great Western Road, and then he became the editor of the *China Press*. That position had only lasted three months, and now he was on the board of a realty company. Who knew how long he would stay there?[2]

The big problem was that Ernest had promised his brothers jobs at the *China Press*. Herbert arrived in late November, while Bill and their parents debarked in Shanghai right before Christmas. They were all still living out of suitcases at Alice and Alfred's place when Ernest broke the news: He and T.B. Chang, the owner of the paper, had mutually agreed that he should resign. Publicly, the two men claimed this had always been the plan, but Bill and Herbert knew better. Fortunately, Alfred put a word in with prominent local banker Percy Chu, a friend from his NYU days. Now head of the University of Shanghai's new Downtown School of Commerce, Chu invited

Ernest and Herbert to jointly teach a journalism class for a semester. That bought Herbert some time, but Bill was beside himself. He had only come to Shanghai because a job supposedly awaited him, and now he had to write to May and explain the situation.[3]

Thankfully, Alfred was reliable, unlike Ernest. Alice had come to love her second husband for the very thing she had once disliked about him: his utter dependability. As a younger woman, she had seen this trait as dull and unromantic, but now she appreciated it. Of course, Alice knew why others thought she found Alfred attractive. Vivian, Kay's daughter, reported the consensus to a friend: "I hear that Auntie's second marriage is a very happy one and also that Alfred is making out quite well financially. That always helps the situation for Alice craves a luxurious life." It was true that after four years with K.S. Lo, Alice particularly enjoyed Alfred's financial shrewdness and his success. But she also loved that he valued her spontaneity and carefree nature, and she appreciated his chatty, social side. Indeed, he seemed to know at least half of the city's foreign businessmen, whether through the Amity Lodge Masons, the American University Club, or one of the other sash-wearing, speech-making organizations to which he belonged. And he seemed to belong to all of them. Alice never complained about the endless social obligations this created, because she thoroughly enjoyed them.[4]

During her marriage to K.S., she had envied the groups of well-dressed men and women whose photos dotted the social pages of the city's English-language press. Alice could not read Chinese well enough to bother with the papers K.S. took, a divide that seemed to extend to their social life. Almost all of his friends, often engineers or other teachers at Fudan, were born in China. Most spoke passable English, but when they got together, they quickly fell into some dialect of Chinese that Alice could barely follow. Growing up in New York, she had always assumed she was inherently Chinese, but among K.S.'s friends, she felt completely American.

These days, Alice sometimes spotted her own face in the social pages, and many weeks she and Alfred spent more evenings out than at home. One night they were attending a formal ball at the French Club, the next having a casual meal with friends at Jimmy's Kitchen. The Nationalists' new campaign to push Chinese to reject Western "decadence," from fur coats to swing dancing to permanent waves, made little impact on the Lees; all their overseas Chinese friends claimed to support the "New Life Movement," but no one wanted to give up American movies or chic evening gowns. And since they lived inside the foreign-controlled areas, they did not have to.[5]

Alice relied on her servants to help juggle the Lees' many social obligations, especially after Alfred and Tzse Pun opened an import-export sideline company in addition to their work at A. C. Monk. Fortunately, many of Shanghai's top merchants had roots in Guangdong, so Cantonese-speaking servants were easy to hire in the city. Many nights, Alfred brought the car around while Alice told the cook what to make Miles for dinner and instructed the amah on when to put the boy to bed. Servants made her own tea parties and get togethers so much smoother, too, especially since she disliked cooking so much.[6]

After all, Alice had her own social obligations, part of the job of being a successful businessman's wife in Shanghai. In the months after her marriage to Alfred, Alice had joined the same groups as Ruth, fearful that people might look down on her as a divorcee. She quickly realized that few cared very much, especially because Alfred was so popular. Within a year, she had largely detached herself from Ruth's orbit—who really wanted to be in the Women's Christian Temperance Union anyway?—and made her own set of friends in Shanghai. Most of them resembled the men with whom Alfred worked and socialized: a mix of white American businessmen's wives, "overseas Chinese" from the US, Canada, and Australia, and China-born women who had attended college in the United States and whom she sometimes remembered from her CSA days. Alice's closest friend remained Lenore Chang, her old pal from Newark; the two had a standing mahjong date each week, while their children played together under the watchful eye of the Changs' amah.[7]

• • •

Alfred traveled frequently for work and brought Alice along whenever possible. Sometimes they took Miles, too, as in January 1934 when they visited the Philippines. While Alfred called on clients and attended a Masonic event, Alice and Alson enjoyed the tropical sunshine, a welcome break from the damp cold of Shanghai. The only downside was that Chinese exclusion functioned everywhere in America, so Alfred had to arrange visas for his noncitizen wife and son to enter the US colony.[8]

During the voyage home, Alice and Alfred began to talk about how Miles could move more comfortably in their world. Although Alfred was a citizen, the visit had been yet another reminder of the hurdles that all people of Chinese ancestry faced on US soil. Alfred and Alice decided that Miles needed to attend a school where he could become fully bilingual. Only then would he be at home in the kinds of places where his parents lived and worked, especially Shanghai's foreign-controlled areas. Alfred saw these gray zones of overlapping sovereignty as the best places for people like them—places where their biculturality served as an advantage, and where they could avoid the worst indignities of American racism while still enjoying some US protection.

Not all of their friends felt the same about schooling. H.C. and Anna Mei's children and Ruth and Ernest's oldest boy attended the Shanghai American School, where they were usually the only ethnic Chinese in their classes. Lenore and Billy enrolled their children in the school attached to their church, St. Francis Xavier. Their catechism was excellent, but Alice wondered about their Chinese. So Alice and Alfred chose the Lingnan School north of the city, where Miles could study English and Chinese and befriend other children with roots in South China and ties to the diaspora.[9]

As the boy started to learn his first Chinese characters, Alice and Alfred realized that he would soon have an awkward question for his parents. Alice wanted to wait until Miles was much older to tell him about his birth father, but long before then, he would learn to write his Chinese name and ask why his parents had chosen it. The truth was that K.S. had done that—which is why Miles's Chinese name included a character from K.S.'s own "courtesy" name, which he had taken when he reached adulthood. In other words, Miles's name contained a direct reference to the man his mother had divorced and never told him about.[10]

Alice and Alfred solved the problem by giving their son a whole new identity. When he turned seven and entered school, they arranged for the minister at the American Community Church to baptize him, with H.C. and Anna acting as his godparents. Miles Yuanshi Lee became Alson Miles Lee. His new Chinese name was Aishen, while his English name tied the boy directly to the two parents he knew about. Even as an adult, Alson Miles Lee never realized that he had been born with a Chinese name meant to connect him to the birth father he could not remember.[11]

SIXTEEN

Kay and Ming Tai

NEWARK AND NEW YORK, 1933–1934

ADELAIDE MARRIED JACK YOUNG three months after he returned from China. Kay and Ming Tai accepted their daughter's choice and tactfully said nothing about their earlier concerns. After all, Jack obviously loved their daughter, and her feelings for him had not diminished during their year and a half apart. Given the Chins' finances, Kay and Ming Tai also appreciated the young couple's decision to have a very small wedding in Newark. It made sense—all but one of Kay's siblings were now in China, as were Jack's parents—though deep down, Ming Tai wished he could give Adelaide something fancier and larger.[1]

Ten days after the wedding, the newlyweds left for China on what they called their honeymoon. Jack had received support from the American Museum of Natural History to make another expedition to Tibet, and Adelaide intended to accompany him the whole way. Kay wondered how her oldest daughter would fare in rugged, mountainous Tibet, chasing the storied panda bears that almost no one had ever seen before. True, she had been a summer camp counselor in New Hampshire, but somehow Kay doubted that three months at Camp Interlaken had completely prepared Adelaide for what was to come. Once again, though, she said nothing. It was her daughter's choice.[2]

While the Chin family was close, the older children seemed keen to follow Adelaide's example by trying to escape from their cramped Newark apartment. Gloria planned to apply to be a counselor at Camp Interlaken, while Alwin buried himself in engineering textbooks and won admission to Cooper Union, which offered every student a full-tuition scholarship. He would nominally live at home, but the Chins knew that he would probably spend all his time on campus. As for Vivian, she got a clerical position at the Chicago "Century of Progress" fair during the summer of 1934 and headed west. By early July, she confessed that she was bored to death at work but enjoying a robust social life in the Windy City. Kay was not surprised when her daughter quit the original job and took a temporary position assisting a sociology student from China. Bingham Dai was finishing his PhD at the University of Chicago when he met Vivian through mutual friends in the city. By the time the summer ended, the two were in love, and Kay guessed that there would be another family wedding very soon. Both she and Ming Tai were tickled that their two oldest daughters seemed destined for lives in China.[3]

While the older Chins began departing on their own, Kay helped her younger children escape Newark by taking them to visit the Typonds in Brooklyn. Soon they adopted Jeanne as their new favorite toy, and since Newark's Chinatown had few trees and almost no play space, they also appreciated the vastness of nearby Prospect Park. The Typonds offered other comforts, too. Each July, George and Helen leased a modest bungalow in Bradley Beach, the one Jersey Shore town that welcomed Chinese American renters. Kay and the younger kids came down sometimes to join them and to escape the oppressive summer heat. Helen enjoyed those days and appreciated the extra help with Jeanne now that she was pregnant again.[4]

She could tell that George was excited, though she also began to worry about her quiet, intense husband. These days, he worked for Gifford Construction, a Queens-based infrastructure firm that specialized in sewers and roads. Federal New Deal money was beginning to flow into the New York metro area through public works projects, and Gifford successfully bid on a number of contracts. Conscientious George now spent long hours over his drafting board and visiting company sites on western Long Island. He never forgot that he was the only Chinese engineer at the company, a realization that inspired pride but also fear and insecurity.[5]

Though George rarely spoke of the pressure he felt, Helen could see it plainly in his heavy smoking, the bags under his eyes, and the weekends he spent at work instead of at home. Leafing through photos, Helen noticed just how much older George looked than he had just five or six years earlier. His brother Jim's energy seemed to flow out in handshakes and laughter and schmoozing, but George was the opposite: He kept everything inside.[6]

• • •

Ming Tai did not join his wife and children on their excursions to the Typonds' Bradley Beach rental. Instead, he worked on ways to get his family out of Newark and back to financial stability. By mid-decade, most of their income came from the buildings in which Ming Tai still had a stake. The Pell Street one that he and his Manhattan partners had bought back in 1919 remained valuable, but the Victoria in Newark was increasingly a losing proposition. The Depression devasted the income of Newark's Chinese waiters and laundrymen, while others fled the city to avoid police harassment. The shrinking Chinatown also sat on a racial fault line between heavily Black neighborhoods to the west and segregated, almost wholly white areas to the north and south. Tensions existed between Black and Chinese Newark residents as well; shared experiences with white racism failed to create any real affinities. So Ming Tai and his partners finally put the Victoria on the market, and he began to look around for a reasonably spacious but inexpensive Manhattan apartment for his family to rent.[7]

He also had another difficult talk with his oldest son. Shau Hong's daughter had at last recovered after spending months in the hospital. His wife Daisy was now pregnant for the sixth time, because Shau Hong wanted a son so desperately. And though he had given up his plans to move back to China, he had a new idea: He would open a movie theater in New York to play imported films for Chinese audiences. Although generally indulgent, Ming Tai had neither the funds nor the patience this time. He told his son to either start paying rent on his apartment in the Pell Street building or look for another place for his family. Ming Tai needed to get the full benefit of his shares, rather than forfeiting Shau Hong's rent each month. Though upset, Shau Hong agreed to move in early 1935, after his wife gave birth to the baby he was sure would be a son.[8]

• • •

The young woman waiting on the platform at Newark's Market Street station always kept her eye out for the Chins. She knew they lived nearby, and she had no interest in sharing the trip to Manhattan with them, especially since she was usually going there to see George Finnie, her new fiancé. When she and Herbert originally eloped, he promised that he would send for her soon, but then his letters stopped coming. Once in Shanghai, the thrill and romance of his hasty marriage wore off, and he decided he did not really want a wife after all. Years later, Ruth Taylor Finnie read about Herbert's fate in the newspapers with a mix of sadness and relief.

SEVENTEEN

Ernest and Ruth

SHANGHAI AND NEW YORK, 1933–1934

RUTH BLUSHED WHEN SHE SAW the parking ticket. A few months after her arrival in Shanghai, C. C. Chang sent the Moys a scrapbook with photos and ephemera from the Mei Lanfang tour and its aftermath. Ernest examined the album with interest, beaming at the photos of himself with Maurice Chevalier, Douglas Fairbanks, and Mei. Ruth, on the other hand, could not avoid seeing how carefully and subtly C.C. had woven their affair into the pictures and souvenirs he chose. In addition to numerous snapshots of her in a swimsuit or clutching C.C.'s arm, he had included photos of her in a Pasadena citrus grove, a reminder of his flirtatious references to her "juicy oranges." She noticed as well the two pictures snapped on a boat in San Francisco: In the first, she sat on a capstan with Ernest, smiling gamely for the camera, while in the second, she and C.C. perched in exactly the same place, her smile larger and less reserved. Still, Ruth could not believe he had kept the ticket, which a churlish traffic cop gave her after she and C.C. parked too long in an alley off Spring Street. Ruth remembered the two of them giggling like naughty schoolchildren as they finally drove away from the "scene of the crime."[1]

Looking at the scrapbook, Ernest initially seemed oblivious to its subtext, or so Ruth assumed. But now she began to wonder. In early 1933, after months of heavy bleeding and exhaustion, she consulted one of Shanghai's leading gynecologists and decided to have a hysterectomy. Lying in her room at the Country Hospital a day or two later, Ruth picked up a slice of toast and flipped through the latest edition of the *China Press*. That's when she spotted the headline: "Successful Operation Performed on Mrs. Moy." The piece did not spell out the particular procedure, but it did name the surgeon, a prominent gynecologist whose patients included half of the foreign women in Shanghai. Perhaps this was Ernest's passive-aggressive revenge.[2]

Not only that, but the same edition of the paper carried a front-page article about Ernest's departure from the *China Press*, complete with the flimsy claim that he had never intended to stay beyond a few months and that her illness had helped prompt his decision to leave at that time. Ruth was accustomed to Ernest's occasional self-aggrandizement and embroidering of his resume. She was not innocent of this tendency herself, having spent much of her life concealing the parts of her own story that she found distasteful, right down to her birth year. But Ernest's defensiveness about his departure from the paper now collided with her desire for privacy, and the result did not feel good.[3]

Maybe Ernest would finally settle down at the Nan Mow Land Company, whose board made him managing partner when he agreed to produce the kinds of bond reports he had once churned out at S. D. Wang. Instead, in late May, Ernest parted ways with the company. As usual, he assured Ruth that he had lined up something better. This time, he and a group of other Chinese Americans began to organize their own venture, the Overseas Trust Company, to help returning Chinese from the United States find places in China to invest their capital.[4]

If only she and Ernest had any capital themselves! Shanghai seemed to cost far more than New York, at least if you wanted to live in a Western-style apartment with one or two servants. Ruth was picky about cleanliness, so she also shopped only at the places she completely trusted. That inevitably cost more, as did the American foods she, Ernest, and the boys could not live without. Then there were school fees: Ruth had enrolled Loring at the Marist Brothers Junior School, while Ken attended the Shanghai American School. At both, the quarterly tuition seemed reasonable, until she remembered that children attended classes for three-quarters of the year.[5]

But Ernest's restlessness was the main reason for the family's financial insecurity. He had not stayed at any single job long enough to accumulate a nest egg. This bothered Ruth less when they were younger, for she believed in supporting her husband's ambitions. After fifteen years of marriage, though, she hated that they still needed to pinch every penny. It had become exhausting. Well, maybe this Overseas Trust idea would pan out.

The firm was the brainchild of Thomas P. Chan, a recent arrival who until 1932 had published the independent *Chinese Journal* in Manhattan. Then Chan defaulted on the *Journal*'s debts and hopped the next boat to Shanghai, though Ernest did not know this. To him, Chan seemed to project an air of success: He was charismatic, worldly, and confident in his claims about Chinese Americans' reserves of capital.[6]

Chan, Ernest, and their other partners launched their venture in grand style, with a banquet for leading businessmen at the Mary Garden Restaurant that June. They formally opened for business on July 4, 1933, a date meant to remind investors of their American ties. To further reaffirm the link, the China-born Chan eventually suggested making Ernest president, a move that also played on the American's vanity. What Ernest did not grasp were the US policy shifts on silver that culminated in Congress's passage of the 1934 Silver Purchase Act. These changes helped drive up the price of silver worldwide; in China, the outflow of silver caused a financial panic and pulled the country firmly into the global depression. By early summer 1934, the Overseas Trust Company teetered on the verge of collapse.[7]

Desperate to save the firm, Ernest proposed using some of its remaining assets to bankroll a temporary trip to the United States to raise more capital. He told Ruth that they could think of it as a second honeymoon, a chance to repair a marriage that had grown tense and distant. One of Ernest's partners, C. Y. Cheng, agreed to accompany the Moys, while Thomas Chan said he would look after the company's affairs in Shanghai. Cheng and the Moys set out in June, visiting Honolulu, Los Angeles, and San Francisco. Out of conviction, and to draw more people to their pitch meetings, the two men cloaked their roadshow as a mission to lobby for Chinese exclusion law reform.[8]

But in the middle of the Depression, no one had money to sink into their company. By the time the travelers reached Chicago, they were desperately trying any way they could think of to pull in potential investors. In addition to announcing their mission to lobby for immigration changes, Ernest took out ads in the local Chinese-language paper inviting "old friends" to visit him at the hotel where he and Ruth were staying. Kay's daughter Vivian and her boyfriend Bingham Dai stopped in, as did Ruth's mother, her brother Paul, and his family. However, the only other people who dropped by the hotel were some of Ernest's old KMT comrades, none of whom had money to invest in the Overseas Trust Company. The story was the same in New York, Ernest's last hope; he could not raise any capital there, either.[9]

That fall, the Moys returned to Shanghai from what Ernest now publicly called a "pleasure trip." The Overseas Trust had closed for good the previous month, so Ernest was out of a job just as Shanghai's economy hit rock bottom. Even worse, three days after Ernest and Ruth's return, local authorities brought charges against Thomas Chan for misappropriation of company funds. Chan was convicted late that year, and though no one suggested that

Ernest had broken the law, he felt deeply embarrassed for having trusted Chan.[10]

Ernest still had a financial interest in the Standard Dairy, one of the Overseas Trust investments, but the Moys could not survive on milk alone. So Ernest was right back where he had been in 1930—knocking on doors, talking to friends, trying anything to find a job. Finally Alfred and Billy stepped in. They knew most of the well-connected men in Shanghai, and in spring 1936, Billy put a word in with his friend Loy Chang, a Chinese Hawaiian graduate of Harvard who held a number of high positions in the Finance Ministry. As a favor to Billy and Alfred, Chang offered Ernest a deanship at the Shanghai Customs College, a sort of vocational school that trained young Chinese for the various departments of the Chinese Maritime Customs Service (CMCS).[11]

Ernest's job was mainly administrative and, once again, did not quite reflect his idealistic, heroic view of his place in the Nationalist revolution, because the CMCS was largely foreign run. Founded during the Taiping Uprising, its initial purpose was to enable foreign merchants to pay the required customs duties in the midst of that upheaval. A series of British citizens had led the CMCS since its inception, and foreigners continued to serve throughout its bureaucracy. Still, Ernest enjoyed the prestige of working at a college and the assumptions others made about him as a result.[12]

By 1936, then, Ernest had reinvented himself in Shanghai not just once but three times. He arrived as a journalist and publicist, transformed himself into a financier, and was now a college dean. Almost no one knew he possessed only a correspondence-school chiropractic degree, and he intended to make sure that no one found out, either. In 1933, he had joined the American University Club as a life member, citing a year of study at the University of Chicago and a 1915 "M.D." from the Jenner Medical College, two institutions he had not actually attended. By the 1930s, Jenner had been closed for almost two decades and, conveniently, counted no other Shanghai graduates. Ruth, who had earned an actual college degree, said nothing about Ernest's deception. She was trying to learn to be satisfied in her marriage and was simply relieved that her husband had a real job again. Maybe they could even save up a little money in case of a rainy day.[13]

EIGHTEEN

Alice and Alfred

SHANGHAI, 1934–1936

DAYS AFTER ALSON'S BAPTISM, Jack and Adelaide Young returned from Tibet. The Lees, who had just moved into a new place in the swanky section of Yu Yuen Road, invited the young couple to stay in the guest bedroom until they found a place of their own. While in Tibet, Adelaide had learned to shoot, track, and climb, and she had also wired or posted a series of expedition-related articles to the *China Press*. Now she and Jack received a hero's welcome and invitations to speak at every civic club and scholarly organization in foreign-run Shanghai. After the hubbub died down, they rented their own small apartment, while Jack went to work at his uncle's Shanghai auto dealership. Even on the best days he found the job tedious, and he soon told a reporter that "when I get restless, I am going off again." Though supportive, Adelaide seemed less excited about making another trip, at least "until there's an airplane service to Tatsienlu." In summer 1935, when Jack found a backer for another Tibet expedition, Adelaide decided to wait for him in Shanghai.[1]

Alice felt sorry for her niece, alone in the sweltering, empty city. Much of the foreign community left town during the torrid summer months, when temperatures and humidity routinely lingered in the 90s. The Lees certainly had no plans to stick around. When H.C. and Anna Mei invited them to Mokanshan, Alice jumped at the chance to vacation among Shanghai's social elite. Anna and the children usually left in early June for the famed mountain resort town, while H.C. joined them when he could get away. Alice and Alson planned to spend a large part of the summer in Mokanshan too, and they easily persuaded Adelaide to join them. Alfred drove the three down in the Lees' big Ford, promising to return as soon as he could steal some time away from work.[2]

The trip from Shanghai was much faster than it had been just a few years earlier, before the government built the new motor road connecting Mokanshan to the Shanghai-Hangzhou-Nanjing highway. Some locals complained that officials took the land for all of these roads from poor farmers who received no compensation, but few people dared say such things out loud. It was too easy to attract the government's attention and become another target of its never-ending campaign against Communists. Only a handful of the foreigners who made Mokanshan their playground paid much attention to the controversy. Most of the Westernized and overseas Chinese businesspeople and professionals who vacationed there did not care much, either.[3]

Years later, Alice and Alfred remembered those summer days at Mokanshan with particular fondness. Alson, the Mei kids, and their friends ran wild, exploring the winding mountain paths, swimming in the local pools, and riding at the stables. Energetic Anna somehow managed to corral all the kids to practice for the weekly children's concert that the summer people loved. Alice preferred to spend her time on the verandah of the "Meisonnette," the Meis' gracious, foreign-style summer home, or visiting other Shanghai friends in the neighborhood. Lenore Chang and her children usually stayed through August, so she and Alice often played mahjong or tennis. If Alfred or Billy was there, the four took leisurely strolls through the legendary bamboo groves.[4]

Even Han Ying and Moy Sing spent part of the summer at Mokanshan that year, not just to escape steamy Shanghai, but also to give their middle son some privacy. May had finally arrived from the United States and was now living in the Kiaochow Road flat with Bill, Herbert, and their parents. The place was not large enough for five adults, so they had begun searching for a bigger apartment. Of course, Bill and May dreamed of having their own home, but Ernest seemed disinclined to invite the older Moys to live with *his* family. In theory, Moy Sing and Han Ying could have moved in with Alice, but with three adult sons, why should they rely on a son-in-law?[5]

Ernest's attitude created tensions on both sides of the Pacific. In September, newlyweds Vivian and Bingham Dai also stayed with Alice and Alfred on their way from New York to Beijing, where Bingham had just taken a job. In preparation for their arrival, Vivian briefed her new husband on the assorted relatives he was about to meet. After describing everyone else, she wrote, "Lastly are my Uncle Ernest and Aunt Ruth who were in Chicago [last] summer. All the rest of the relatives hate these two because of their superficiality and insincerity."[6]

Vivian did not explain exactly what she meant by this, but no one had forgotten Ernest's broken promises—whether about jobs for his brothers or the degree of financial support he planned to provide his parents. Bill and May certainly remembered. For the first two years of their marriage, she waitressed at various Chinese restaurants in New York and Newark to earn money for her steamship ticket, while he looked for some kind of steady work. He finally took a tedious job writing financial reports, since the position provided enough money to help his parents and contribute a little extra to May's ticket fund. But he wondered if he would spend his entire life doing jobs he hated, just to make ends meet.[7]

• • •

Ernest's broken promises affected Herbert, too. After the men's temporary journalism-teaching gig ended, Ernest seemed to assume that his baby brother would find something else on his own. Herbert applied to the *China Press* for a staff position, citing his Kuo Min experience, but the editor decided against hiring him after reading the sample article he produced. In Manhattan, Herbert's experience involved rewriting Nationalist communiques for local distribution. Now he simply put together a brief piece on Mei Lanfang's trip to the United States that described the way the star's unnamed "publicity men" harnessed the "power of ballyhoo" to convince theatergoers of the actor's brilliance. Herbert's essay seemed both a tribute to and a swipe at his oldest brother, but either way, he showed no interest in hustling for stories.[8]

Thank goodness he did not have a wife to support. Herbert felt some regret about his treatment of Ruth Taylor, until he heard that she had married again. Had she gotten another annulment, or did she ask a judge for a divorce based on desertion? Maybe she had not bothered with the paperwork, instead assuming he would stay in China forever. Now Herbert really had no reason to go back to New York, where there were never any decent jobs for people like him anyway. At least in Shanghai, he could reinvent himself into whatever he wanted, just like Alice and Ernest had done. Herbert possessed Alice's easy charm and more polish than Ernest, having absorbed a kind of prep school, Ivy League air from his wealthier Mount Hermon classmates. Bill could slog away at his financial reports if he wanted to, but Herbert decided that *he* deserved something better.[9]

In the meantime, he became a regular at the best-known Shanghai nightclubs, and his siblings could not keep track of his newest girlfriend any given week. Much of the rest of the time, he palled around with the hard-drinking reporters who staffed the city's English-language paper. *China Press* writer and occasional theater promoter Hal Mills was one of his most frequent drinking buddies. Mills was initially impressed by Herbert's charisma, as well as the Harvard degree the young man claimed to have. The two friends soon formed the Commercial News Agency, a public relations firm meant to trade on Mills's show-business and news connections and Herbert's Kuo Min experience. When Mills realized that Herbert had no real idea of the kind of work required to run a PR company, they dissolved their partnership, though they continued to go out drinking together. In fact, Herbert spent much more time socializing with his friends than doing any sort of substantive work during his first two years in Shanghai. By 1935, Alice was concerned enough to ask her husband to try to find a job for Herbert that he would actually do.[10]

Alfred immediately thought of his own most recent project. He and some of his businessmen friends were organizing what they called the International Club of Shanghai. Through the 1920s, social life in the city had often taken place in spots like the American Club, the Casa d'Italia, and the Japanese Club, as well as in even more specific, nationally oriented groups, from Den Danske Tennisklub (the Danish Tennis Club) to the Deutscher Garten Klub (German Garden Club). Many of the groups excluded Chinese and people of mixed ancestry, so Alfred and a number of his Chinese, European, and white American friends hoped to create a social club open to all men who could pay the dues. They had leased space for it but needed a manager to run the place.[11]

Herbert agreed to take the job after Alfred assured him that he would be an equal member of the organizing committee, not a mere employee. The chance to book shows, bands, and entertainment for the club appealed to him. That December, Herbert threw himself into preparations for the inaugural tea dance and cocktail party, sending invitations to fifteen hundred of the most prominent people in the city. He followed it up with a successful New Year's Eve party and, the next spring, launched a weekly tea dance series. Herbert's greatest triumph occurred when famed Chinese American actress Anna May Wong attended the 1936 season's first dance as guest of honor. Everyone who was anyone in Shanghai clamored to get in, including the mayor. Yet the mundane aspects of running the club bored Herbert, and by the end of the summer he was looking for an excuse to quit.[12]

• • •

That fall, his friend Earle Chang offered him one. Chang was a Chinese Canadian radio enthusiast who had come to Shanghai in early 1929 to work for the Nationalists' new Radio Bureau—which did not hire him. He cobbled together other jobs until radio broadcasting took off in Shanghai and then started his own radio station, XMHC, with his brother-in-law Hugh Kwong Lowe. The men called it the Overseas Broadcasting Company, a reference to their status as "overseas Chinese," and it won a large audience by broadcasting in English, Shanghainese, and Cantonese. After Chang and Lowe heard Herbert emcee at the International Club, they invited him to come work at the station as a full partner.[13]

The two Canadians thought Herbert had talent, but in late 1936, they cared more about his passport. The Nationalist government had begun to crack down on radio stations in Shanghai, arguing that the dozens of low-powered, poor-quality broadcasters there were jamming up the airwaves. The larger purpose of the Nationalist campaign was censorship: Authorities banned several popular forms of entertainment from all broadcasts made between 1 and 10 p.m., and they also insisted that every station submit announcements, skit scripts, and other material for official preapproval. Foreign-owned radio stations resisted complying, and they used their location in the concessions and consular registration to thwart KMT enforcers.[14]

Earle Chang and Hugh Lowe knew that the Chinese government's censorship drive imperiled XMHC's lineup and popularity, and foreign ownership did not necessarily offer it protection. The Canada-born Lowe and Chang were British subjects, but when Chang attempted to register with the British consulate, officials turned him away on the basis of his race. Herbert's status offered stronger protection for XMHC. As a US citizen, he could register a company with the US consulate if necessary and claim some kind of protection for the firm.[15]

In late 1936, Herbert quit the International Club and began working full time for XMHC. He started by arranging radio plays and booking entertainers, but soon he debuted as an English-language announcer. By early 1937, Herbert and Earle Chang's live broadcast from the Saturday night fights at the French Concession auditorium became a staple of many a Shanghai resident's weekend. Alice realized that she had never seen her brother working as hard as he was at Overseas Broadcasting. Herbert had an obvious talent for radio, but even better, he seemed to love the job. She felt a wave of relief that he had finally found something that suited him and in which he obviously had a bright future.[16]

NINETEEN

Kay and Ming Tai

NEW YORK, 1935–1937

KAY FELT TREMENDOUSLY RELIEVED when they finally returned to Manhattan. If she couldn't live in Glen Ridge, she didn't want to live in New Jersey at all. Thankfully, in spring 1935, she and Ming Tai found a relatively roomy and inexpensive apartment on a block in West Harlem right behind the St. Regis Convent. Days earlier, he and his partners signed off on the sale of their building in Newark's Chinatown, joining the general exodus of Chinese from the city. After years of harassing Chinese American residents, Newark's police had succeeded in almost completely eliminating Chinatown.[1]

The disposal of the Newark shares helped Kay and Ming Tai's financial position, though it remained precarious. They and the other shareholders in the Pell Street building made a little money from rents; however, New York's continued economic malaise meant broken leases, shrinking profits, and tenant demands for better terms. A tailor and a tiny eatery occupied the ground floor, and though a single restaurant would have worked better in the space, no one could afford to go into business now. Places were failing everywhere. The Palais D'Or had been one of the first big Broadway chop suey and dancing spots to go bankrupt, but others followed in quick succession, even the smaller and cheaper places. Recently, Ming Tai had heard that Yoeng's had finally gone belly up, while the place out in Coney Island opened by former Palais D'Or manager C. M. Joe was struggling.[2]

Until more people started going to restaurants again, the Chins would have to figure out other ways to get by. For now, most of the family's income came from Ming Tai's share of the Pell Street building gambling rooms' profits, which changed like the weather. To bring in some extra cash, Kay began to do beading for hire. As a girl, she had learned the skill from Han Ying, who took in beadwork because Moy Sing could not make ends meet on his own. Ming Tai appreciated Kay's efforts, but they pained him at the same time. So much had changed for them in just a few short years.[3]

The move to Manhattan created some new problems for the family, too. The neighborhood boys ganged up on Ronald, who had to learn to use his fists to defend himself. Meanwhile, teens Beah and Meme began to quarrel over the smallest matters. In Glen Ridge they could have retreated to different parts of the house, while in Newark they might have taken refuge with friends in the building. Kay now felt lucky that her children hated to cook, since she could at least hide in her kitchen to get some peace.[4]

. . .

Shortly after the Chins moved to Harlem, May's father, Wong Soon, relocated his own family to a nearby block. Always kindly, he even talked his new landlord into renting a flat to Shau Hong, Daisy, and their children. Wong, who owned a Chinese restaurant, also hired Shau Hong as an occasional waiter, though the younger man insisted to Ming Tai that the work was only temporary. He would quit when he was able to open his dream movie theater in Manhattan for imported Chinese films.[5]

Ming Tai tried not to encourage his son. Shau Hong needed to get his head out of the clouds and start supporting his large and growing family. Daisy had given birth the previous year, but since Diana was not the son Shau Hong so desperately wanted, he and his poor wife would almost certainly try again. Donald George Typond had arrived less than two weeks before Diana, and suddenly Helen, who had always been especially kind to Daisy, felt slightly awkward around her.[6]

Shortly after Donald's birth, his uncle Jim moved out of the family home to marry his girlfriend, Hazel Wong. Their relationship scandalized more than a few of Grace Typond's church friends. Hazel, a dancer whom everyone called Lonnie, was the daughter of a Fall River Chinese restaurant owner and his Irish immigrant wife. Jim met Lonnie when she arrived in New York with the other members of the Chinese Whoopee Revue after a stint in Paris. The group played venues across Manhattan and Brooklyn, and Jim soon became a stage-door Johnny at Loew's Metropolitan Theatre in downtown Brooklyn.[7]

Of course, Jim could not bear to leave Brooklyn, so he and Lonnie moved into a building on Parkside Avenue, less than a mile away from his parents. The newlyweds still dropped by the Flatbush house all the time to see the older Typonds, though Helen could tell that the doting uncle also missed his niece and nephew. As for Lonnie, Helen didn't judge. Ming Tai's old Palais D'Or had featured a floor show with dancers, and anyway, the young woman seemed a good match for garrulous, back-slapping Jim. Both moved effortlessly between their Chinese friends and family and their largely white, Catholic neighbors.[8]

Helen soon grew fond of her sister-in-law, whose free-spirited nature reminded her of Alice. She made a point of helping Lonnie navigate the neighborhood, especially now that Jim worked in Manhattan. He had previously used the Brooklyn office of Edward S. Moran Jr., an old school friend who also served in the State Assembly. Initially, the arrangement seemed ideal: Jim loved politics, and the two men could talk for hours about the fortunes of the New York Democrats. Moran even hired Lonnie's little brother Clifford as an errand boy, and since Lonnie and Cliff's mother was a Moran too, they joked about being part of the same big Irish-Chinese family. In 1936, though, Jim went into business with another old pal, Shavey Lee, and the men leased an office on Mott Street in Chinatown. Perhaps Jim had already guessed that Moran was crooked, but he just said that he needed to be where his customers were.[9]

When Lonnie became pregnant, Jim was ecstatic, and George and Helen were excited as well. Kay's youngest son was a year older than Jeanne, while the rest of the Chins would be in college by the time Donald entered primary school. Bill and May were expecting their first baby, as were Jack and Adelaide Young, but they and most of Helen's family now lived in China and seemed likely to stay there for the foreseeable future. The arrival of little Carole Typond was almost like a Christmas present for Donald, who finally got a playmate and cousin close to his own age.

When Donald turned two, Jim also convinced George and Helen to enter the boy in the Chinatown baby contest, since Carole was still too young for it. Organizers hoped the June competition would draw more tourists to the neighborhood, and though a Brooklynite at heart, Jim had become quite a Chinatown booster. Helen gamely dressed up her little boy and took him across the bridge to Columbus Park, but in the end, another toddler edged out Donald to win the title of baby king of Chinatown—a grave miscarriage of justice, according to Jim and George.[10]

• • •

By July 1937, the city was suffocating under an almost unbearable heat wave that killed at least a dozen people in a few short days. Seeking relief, Kay took

Ronald to shady Riverside Park and wondered if Gloria, now in her second summer as an Interlaken counselor, was any cooler up in New Hampshire. Helen, George, and the kids headed to Bradley Beach for their annual vacation but found only a little relief at the shore. Helen did not envy poor Lonnie, nursing her infant in a sweltering city apartment.[11]

One July evening, Helen and George were buying the children ice cream on the boardwalk when they noticed the headline in the late edition of the *Asbury Park Evening Press:* "Chinese Defy Jap Ultimatum; Defend Old Walled City Against 1,000 After Midnight Clash." Helen was a devoted *Brooklyn Eagle* reader but handed three cents to the newsboy anyway. The story offered little detail besides the worrying fact that Chinese and Japanese soldiers had clashed near Beijing, an event that later became known as the Marco Polo Bridge Incident.[12]

Kay heard about the incident on the radio that same night and felt a spasm of fear. Vivian and Bingham lived in the old capital, and Jack and Adelaide were staying with the Dais. Ad had just given birth to baby Jacqueline at the Peking Union Medical Center (PUMC), where Bingham worked. Now pregnant herself, Vivian joked in one of her newsy letters about getting a discount at PUMC; she said nothing about the possibility of war. Kay pushed her concerns to the back of her mind. Something of this sort was always happening in China, and anyway, the announcer noted that troops had withdrawn to avoid further conflict.[13]

A few days later, Ming Tai saw a crowd gathered around the local Chinese newspaper's wall billboard next to Jim Typond's Chinatown office. According to the headlines, the Nanjing government had dispatched troops to the north and was preparing for war. Ming Tai felt his stomach knot, for like Kay, he thought of his two daughters and his new granddaughter in North China.[14]

Over the next few weeks, the atmosphere in Chinatown changed almost daily. Sometimes the news said all-out war was imminent, while other reports assured nervous residents that peace negotiations were underway. People milled around on the street in small groups, talking over the latest bulletins and expressing profound ambivalence about what might happen. No one wanted more death, more bloodshed, but the majority hoped the government would finally stand up to the Japanese. If it did, though, could it prevail? No one was sure about that, either, or what the cost would be to their families in China.[15]

TWENTY

Ernest and Ruth

SHANGHAI, 1937

FOR YEARS, CHIANG KAI-SHEK FOCUSED on wiping out the Communists, whom he considered a greater threat to China than Japanese imperialism. But as Japan grabbed more and more Chinese territory, patriotic Chinese increasingly demanded that the Nationalist government resist. Even KMT loyalist Ernest spoke up, in thinly veiled language, to single out Japan as the major threat to China: "It is impossible to believe that those at the head of China's National Government are willfully indifferent to the task which confronts them of preserving the sovereign integrity of the country," he wrote in 1932. "The very existence of China as an independent and sovereign state is at stake!" As public discontent grew, Chiang Kai-shek and his allies suppressed anti-Japanese protests with increasing brutality. In late 1936, however, Marshall Zhang Xueliang kidnapped Chiang during the leader's visit to the northern city of Xi'an and pushed him to change course. Zhang acted on his own, not knowing that the Communist leadership had been secretly negotiating with Chiang to create a united front against Japan. In any case, the "Xi'an Incident" not only galvanized the nation but ended with Chiang's release, Zhang's imprisonment, and a major policy shift: The KMT government finally stopped its anti-Communist campaigns and slowly began to push back against Japan. That's why the Marco Polo Bridge Incident and its aftermath sent shudders through Shanghai. Many residents felt that Japanese forces in the north had intentionally created a crisis to justify moving against an increasingly resolute and united China.[1]

Ernest and Bill worked at opposite ends of Shanghai's foreign-controlled area, but as each man walked to his office in early August, they noticed the growing stream of fearful Chinese entering the concession areas for safety. They were not the only ones on the move: Japan was evacuating its nationals from many ports on the Yangzi. In the International Settlement, foreign Shanghai Volunteer Corps (SVC) members stood guard, having traded their business suits for uniforms. The newspapers reported that Chinese and Japanese troops were pouring into the metropolitan area, and Japanese warships and gunboats suddenly clogged the harbor. Shanghai remained peaceful, but no one believed that would last. They were right: War broke out on August 13.[2]

• • •

Bill and May never forgot the war's first terrible days. By early 1937, they had settled into married life in Shanghai and felt increasingly optimistic about their future there. The previous year, Bill met Darwin Utter, whose company distributed and showed American-made films in Shanghai. Recognizing Bill's intelligence and mechanical ability, Utter initially offered him a job as a projectionist, then promoted the young man to company accountant and secretary in late 1936, shortly before May discovered she was pregnant.[3]

She went into the hospital two weeks after the Marco Polo Bridge Incident. The Moys' apartment was close to the Country Hospital, which was in Chinese territory, just outside the French Concession. Bill already had a bad feeling about how events were shaping up in the north, so he took May to the International Institute for Women and Children on Rue Chapsal instead. The institute was deep inside the French Concession and close to Ernest and Ruth's apartment, though he and May rarely went there. Still, if there was trouble, it might offer a refuge.[4]

May gave birth to Patricia Ann Moy on August 4. The next day, Bill brought a box of his favorite cigars to his office at the Capitol Theatre and handed them out to Utter and the other men. All feigned a cheerfulness they did not feel; from their building, they could see that the stream of fearful Chinese had become a flood, packing the Soochow Creek bridges into the International Settlement. Bill also tried not to show his unease when he visited May and the baby at the hospital each night. Nor did he mention to his wife the phone call he had received from the district director of the American Emergency Committee (AEC), a hastily formed organization of leading citizens and consular officials. When the man asked about his dependents, Bill mentioned newborn Patricia, prompting the rushed volunteer to offer his congratulations before hanging up. The Battle of Shanghai began soon after May and the baby came home, and within two days the kindly volunteer called once again: American officials had just urged all US citizen women and children to evacuate immediately.[5]

Now Bill and May had an excruciating choice to make. Neither was willing to be separated again, especially since Patricia's arrival, but buying ship tickets to the United States would take their entire savings. That meant their decision would be final; they could not afford to return to Shanghai if the war ended soon, and the career Bill was finally building in China would be over for good. Even worse, he knew what awaited him in New York: some kind of menial job, probably waiting tables at a chop suey joint—the type of work he had moved to China to escape.[6]

Yet Bill and May began to realize they might not be able to salvage much by staying, either. Most of the city's amusement spots, including its movie palaces, were closed due to a lack of patrons. Darwin Utter sent everyone home for the time being, since there was no work to do. Banks had shuttered, gas was almost impossible to get, and food had grown both scarcer and more expensive. SVC members now manned a sandbagged bunker at the end of the Moys' street, while the sound of artillery and gunfire punctuated the days and nights.[7]

Bill was also haunted by what he had witnessed since the outbreak of the war. From the windows of Utter's suite, he saw great gray clouds of smoke billowing up from the devastated Chinese neighborhoods across Soochow Creek. Inside the foreign-controlled areas, ragtag refugee camps were sprouting everywhere, their shabby, stunned inhabitants radiating misery and begging for food and money on the sidewalks. The day after the war began, Chinese planes accidentally dropped bombs on busy Nanking Road, the International Settlement's main shopping street; hundreds died and thousands more were injured on "Bloody Sunday." Walking to his office the next morning, Bill passed the smoldering ruins and noticed that cleaning crews had poured sand on the sidewalks to cover the sticky blood still coating them. He could not get the smell of death out of his nose for days.[8]

Just after dawn on August 20, Bill snapped a final photo of his wife and daughter sitting on a suitcase outside their building. Then the three left their home on Route Sayzoong to join a thousand other Americans evacuating on the SS *President Hoover*. All had received instructions to gather at the Customs Jetty by 7:30 a.m. to take a tender to the ship, and May held Patricia close in the crush of waiting people. She finally located her younger brother Sunny, who was evacuating with them; her older brother George planned to stay in Shanghai, since he could not easily bring his China-born wife back to the United States.[9]

It seemed to take hours for all of them to board the *Hoover*, but at last they were underway. As the ship slowly chugged out of the harbor, Bill and May watched the Shanghai skyline grow smaller and smaller until it completely disappeared. They never returned to China.

. . .

Each morning, Ruth walked briskly through the rubble-strewn streets to the Number 17 Red Cross Hospital. After war broke out in Shanghai, she immediately volunteered to help, becoming a valuable member of the hospital staff just as she had in 1932. Still, as the fighting grew worse, she and her husband had much the same conversation as Bill and May. Ernest was adamant that he would not leave China in its moment of need, but he and Ruth agreed that she, Ken, and Loring would be far safer in the United States. They could stay in New York with her sister Anna and brother-in-law Harry, at least for the time being. To Ruth's dismay, though, Ernest admitted that he could not afford steamship tickets for her and the boys, nor did he wish to ask Alfred for a loan. Fortunately, he told Ruth, the State Department was providing funds to "destitute" Americans wishing to evacuate, so all she needed to do was to apply to the American Emergency Committee for approval.[10]

In other words, Ruth realized, *she* needed to swallow her pride and go ask for the money so that Ernest would not have to endure such embarrassment himself. That stung, but she decided that getting her sons out of harm's way was more important than her ego. As she suspected, the application experience was a humbling one. Some of the AEC members had attended the Fairbanks reception way back in 1931, when the Moys made such a big splash in Shanghai. Others were friends from yacht parties and clubs, or had children at the Shanghai American School. Now, they knew that she and Ernest were broke, even seven years after their arrival in China. She could hardly believe it herself, nor could the consular official who rejected the AEC's recommendation to provide the needed funds. The staffer relented only after Ernest wrote a letter promising to pay back any loan once he could "proceed safely to Peiping to liquidate some of my assets there."[11]

Ruth had no idea what assets he meant but felt tremendous relief when she finally received a check from the US Consulate. She and the boys would just make the next sailing of the *Hoover*. The steamer had returned from Manila to pick up another load of American evacuees and was scheduled to sail back to the Philippines on August 31. Gritting her teeth, Ruth purchased three third-class berths, all the loan would cover; in 1934, she and Ernest had booked second-class berths on the same ship, which felt like a comedown from her first-class trip to China in 1930 with C. C. Chang. She and the boys took their luggage down to the pier in preparation for the *Hoover*'s arrival. Hours later, a Chinese bomber plane accidentally dropped an aerial explosive on the ship's stern deck, spraying it with shrapnel and injuring several crew members. The captain turned around and headed to Kobe, leaving the expectant passengers stranded in Shanghai.[12]

The consulate and the AEC scrambled to come up with an alternative, finally arranging for the US Navy to ferry evacuees to British Hong Kong, where they could board ships bound for America. The AEC instructed Ruth and her sons to take the small gunboat USS *Sacramento* on September 13, so she rushed to the consulate to finalize their documents. There, she met with J. B. Pilcher, a Brylcreemed, baby-faced consul who looked her up and down and then claimed that her name was not on the *Sacramento* list. He explained that the ship had only fifteen women's berths, all of which were occupied, and advised her to use some of her loan money to buy berths on an Italian liner bound for Hong Kong.[13]

Ruth pointed out that doing so would leave her and the boys short of what they needed to get home. She had another objection to taking the Italian ship, though she did not confess it: Ernest's sister Alice and her son Alson had booked a comfortable cabin on it, and Ruth felt humiliated at the idea of traveling in steerage on the same boat. Pilcher shrugged and ended their discussion, saying he had other business. A frustrated Ruth returned to the AEC, where committee representatives told her that she and the boys were definitely on the list for the *Sacramento*. Given the contradictory information, she decided against trying to depart.[14]

Ruth's gut feeling about Pilcher was validated in later press coverage of the *Sacramento*. After it left for Hong Kong, a local newspaper reported that "every effort has been made by the AEC to find 40 American citizens who were willing to leave Shanghai" on the ship, but "they were only able to find 23." Just nine were girls or women. Ernest was livid and Ruth even more so. She clearly remembered Pilcher's contemptuous look and dismissive attitude, and reading the list of passengers, she now realized that all of them were white except for two very young mixed-race children. Whether by consular or naval insistence, the *Sacramento* evacuation was for whites only.[15]

Over the next two months, Ernest waged a public and private war of words against the consulate, whose officers demanded to know why Ruth and the boys were still in the city. Ernest wrote anonymous, accusatory letters to the *Shanghai Evening Post and Mercury* and sent pointed, signed complaints to the Department of State. The consul-general responded with deflections, demurrals, and counteraccusations, as well as veiled references to possible legal action. Finally, the consulate offered Ruth and the boys berths on the far larger transport *Chaumont*, which eventually carried about forty passengers—including several Chinese Americans and Filipinos—to Hong Kong.[16]

The proposal defused the situation and allowed both sides to save face. Ernest felt completely vindicated, but Ruth had grown weary of the ordeal. She could not help thinking that she could have avoided the entire ugly episode, had Ernest ever managed to save any money or stay at one job for more than a brief time. After all, Bill had lived in Shanghai for just a few years, and he could afford to pay for return passage for his family. Ruth also resented Ernest's eagerness to tangle from afar with the consulate, since she was the one who had to deal in person with the targets of his letters.

What broke her was learning that she would need to pay additional small sums for food on the *Chaumont* trip and for a hotel and meals in Hong Kong. The extras added up to just $37.50, but she did not even have that much cash. Ernest told Ruth to ask for help at the consulate, where a smirking Pilcher informed her that she could sign promissory notes with the other "destitute" passengers. Ruth agreed—what choice did she have?—but she never forgot the humiliation.[17]

TWENTY-ONE

Alice and Alfred

SHANGHAI AND NEW YORK, 1937

ALSON (WHOM EVERYONE STILL CALLED Miles) had started horseback riding with Alice when he was six. In 1937, the year he turned ten, H.C. and Anna Mei gave him a horse of his own, a white stallion he kept at Alfred and Alice's country home. The Lees had built the spacious bungalow in the newly developed Lingnan Villa section of suburban Kiangwan, a popular second-home spot for well-to-do Shanghai residents. Alfred equipped the place with a stable, a tennis court, and a shaded pavilion, so his family spent most weekends there. Since it was only fifteen miles and a fairly easy drive from central Shanghai, friends with their own nearby country homes or tee times at the local Seekingjao golf course often dropped by for cocktails.[1]

When Bert Lee arrived in Shanghai that June, he could not help but notice the luxurious style in which his aunt, uncle, and cousin lived. Bert's father, Chiu Hung Lee, was the seventh child in the Lee family, while Alfred (Sy-hung) was the thirteenth, but Bert and Alson were born just two weeks apart. Chiu Hung and his American-born wife, Suey Ping, who ran a well-regarded school in a remote county south of Guangzhou, sent Bert up to spend the summer of 1937 with his Shanghai family. Bert liked Alson immensely, but he quickly noticed that his cousin had a great deal in common with Alice: Both were a little spoiled, and Alson had enough of Alice's charm to get away with considerable mischief.[2]

The boys spent most of June and early July at the Lingnan Villa bungalow, where they rode and groomed Alson's new horse, played with the other children in the neighborhood, and camped outside in a tent Alfred bought for them. But within a week of the Marco Polo Bridge Incident, many of the area's second-home owners began to pack up and return to the city. Though Alfred and Alice hung on a while longer, by late July they had started to reconsider. First the Chinese paramilitary force that patrolled the area began to dig trenches there, and then some locals claimed to have heard machine gun fire nearby. At that point, Alfred and Alice decided the family needed to return as quickly as possible to their apartment in the protected French Concession.[3]

Now they agonized about what to do with Alson's new horse. The mass exodus of residents from Kiangwan meant they could find no one to care for the animal. Lacking a better solution, Alfred and Alice told Alson just to let the horse go free. As the family got into their car, Alson led his stallion out of the fenced area and stroked its mane a final time. The boy felt a catch in his throat as he gazed back at the creature, who was still ambling down the lane when Alfred turned their car onto the main road and out of sight. When the war broke out the next week, Alfred and Alice worried about the fate of their beloved country home. Alson thought about his horse.[4]

. . .

The conflict quickly upended the Lees' privileged life in Shanghai. Alfred and Alice had chosen their apartment in the West Park Mansions development because of its distance from the more congested parts of Shanghai, but the location now became a liability. From their windows, they could see a refugee camp growing in nearby Jessfield Park and a second one sprouting just south of Soochow Creek. They watched British troops, some of them newly arrived from Hong Kong, building sandbag emplacements up the block. Acrid smoke rose in the north and east, and the constant rumble of artillery and gunfire kept them awake at night.[5]

After Bloody Sunday, Alfred visited his office and came home shaken, his usually ruddy face drained of color. He worked on Kiangse Road, less than a block away from where one of the bombs had fallen. Two weeks later, the Japanese obliterated a bridge on the other side of Jessfield Park, just a few blocks from West Park Mansions. Worried about their building's exposure, Alfred, Alice, Alson, and Bert now moved in with Han Ying, Moy Sing, and Herbert, taking over Bill and May's old room. The Moys' flat was smaller and less comfortable than the Lees' home, but it was farther from the active fighting. In any case, the measure was only a temporary one. Alfred and Alice had decided that she and Alson would go back to the United States for a while. They also wired Bert's parents and made plans for Alice to take the boy to Hong Kong and hand him over to his mother.[6]

Unlike Ernest, Alfred had more than enough money in the bank to pay for all their tickets. Skipping the long lines at the steamship office, he phoned the head of the Lloyd Triestino Italian passenger line, a friend from business circles, and reserved three berths to Hong Kong on the SS *Conte Biancamano.* Then he made another call and got Alice and Alson on the next sailing of the SS *President Coolidge* from Hong Kong to San Francisco.[7]

On a rainy morning in mid-September, he stowed their bags in his car's trunk and closely studied a map of the foreign-controlled roads. Rumor had it that Chinese officials were seizing boys and young men for military service and labor, while Japanese soldiers simply shot the youths they caught. To get the two boys safely to the wharf, Alfred told them to lie on the floor of the backseat and then spread a blanket over them. Alice sat with him in the front seat, her hand gripping his arm.[8]

Lloyd Triestino ships usually sailed from the Lower Wharf, but the Japanese had seized it three weeks earlier. Instead, Alfred headed toward the Customs Jetty, trying to take only roads that stayed inside the foreign-controlled areas and praying that he would not run into any barriers or detours. As they neared the waterfront, the crowds grew so thick in the narrow streets that Alfred shifted into neutral, letting the human tide propel his car forward. Finally, the Lees arrived at the jetty, removed the blanket from the backseat, and helped the boys to their feet. Then Alfred pushed Alice, Alson, and Bert through the massive crowd, carrying their bags to one of the tugboats ferrying evacuees to the *Conte Biancamano.* As the three lined up to board the tender, Alfred noticed that the crew had fortified its bridges with sandbags to protect against gunshots or worse. He banished the thought from his head, and as the tender pulled away, he focused instead on finding Alice in the crush of people on the little boat. She raised her arm over her head, and he waved in return, trying his best to smile.[9]

. . .

Over a thousand people shoved their way onto the *Conte Biancamano* that mid-September morning. As the giant liner slowly pulled away from Shanghai, many of those passengers crowded the ship's decks to watch the city recede from view. Some wept audibly, others stared at the smoldering buildings in a sort of shock-induced daze, and more than a few flinched or ducked involuntarily as airplanes roared past. No one had forgotten the accidental bombing of the SS *President Hoover* a few days earlier, or the utter destruction of Bloody Sunday. Alice gripped the ship's railing and watched Shanghai grow smaller and finally disappear. Like many others up on deck, she wondered if she would ever return.[10]

Three days later, the *Conte Biancamano* docked in Hong Kong, a safe haven from the war across the border in China. Alice cabled Alfred, knowing that her husband would be on pins and needles until he heard from her. She kept her message brief, not wanting to worry him, but she could see that conditions in the colony were only slightly less chaotic than in Shanghai. A recent typhoon had smashed through piers and buildings, a cholera epidemic raged, and desperate refugees from all over China packed themselves into the city. Harried colonial officials transformed schools, a race course, and hotel ballrooms into temporary lodging for new arrivals, but there was still a terrible shortage of beds.[11]

Bert's mother met them at the pier, and while her naturally arched eyebrows always gave her face an anxious cast, she looked even more worried than usual. Alice soon realized why: The war had expanded to South China. When Japanese planes bombed Guangzhou, the Nationalist government moved many of the city's schools to outlying districts like the Lees' area. The influx of students and teachers caused a spike in the price of food and sent a ripple of anxiety through the villages, since no one believed that the Japanese would spare the countryside.[12]

Bert's mother had initially planned to retrieve him in Hong Kong and take him home, but her plans quickly changed when the war expanded. Instead, she brought the boy's US passport with her to Hong Kong and told Alice that she and her husband wanted to send Bert to safety in the United States. Now they just needed to get him on the *Coolidge* with his aunt and cousin.[13]

The next few days passed in a blur of lines, crowds, and sore feet. Suey Ping secured a place for the travelers to stay while Alice joined the long queue snaking out of the Pedder Building, the headquarters of Dollar Steamship's local ticket agency. A similar line curled out of the nearby Union Building, where the Canadian Pacific Steamship Line agency was located. Hundreds of Americans from across China had evacuated to Hong Kong and were scrambling for berths to anywhere on the West Coast, or at the very least to Manila or Honolulu.[14]

The Dollar office sat directly across from the Hong Kong branch of Jimmy's Kitchen, and as Alice waited in line, her mind wandered to the many times she and Alfred had eaten at the original Jimmy's in Shanghai. She was not the only one: All along the line, anxious evacuees talked about whether they would ever eat at Jimmy's again, ever dance at the Paramount, ever return to Shanghai. After what seemed like an eternity, Alice finally reached the office, where the agent agreed to let Bert squeeze into the same cabin as his cousin and aunt. While Alice paid the additional fare, she felt particularly thankful that Bert was US-born and that she and Alson had obtained their visas in Shanghai. At Hong Kong's American consulate, the line was the longest of all, with US citizens, many of them ethnic Chinese, waiting anxiously to get the paperwork they needed to buy a ticket to safety. Alice had always enjoyed her trips south with Alfred, but after three long days in refugee-clogged Hong Kong, she had never in her life been happier to leave a place.[15]

. . .

When the SS *President Coolidge* finally docked in San Francisco, Alice prepared herself for one last hurdle. Almost every Chinese American anticipated delays and even harassment at that port, where white supremacy carried a particularly anti-Asian edge. To make matters worse, Alice and her son were not citizens; instead, they traveled on a joint Republic of China passport. Perhaps the incongruity of the Lees' status confused the inspector just enough: two Chinese citizens, Alice and Alson, speaking fluent, American-accented English, traveling with California-born Bert, who despite his US passport understood almost no English at all. Whatever the case, Alice felt tremendous relief when the inspector waved all of them through.[16]

One of Bert's aunts met them at the pier, ready to help with the last part of the plan that Alice and Suey Ping had hatched during those frantic days in Hong Kong. Alice and Alfred still did not know whether or when she and Alson could return to Shanghai, or even if Alfred would eventually have to leave as well. They could not make such decisions right away, yet like Suey Ping and her husband, they worried about the war's impact on their son's education. Alson had missed almost two months of classes, and Bert knew so little English that he would necessarily enter his American grammar school in the lowest grade and still struggle. After discussing the problem, Alice and Suey Ping finally decided to send Alson with Bert to Napa, where the boys could attend the local elementary school together and lean on each other as well.[17]

From afar, the idea had seemed sound enough, but Alice began to have misgivings as she and Bert's aunt made the final arrangements. Bert's widowed grandmother ran a Chinese merchandise store out of her Napa home, a ramshackle building in the tiny Chinatown that abutted the riverbank. Two of Bert's aunts helped around the shop, but the Depression had hurt business so much that they all lived in poverty. Alice was not sure how her pampered boy would fare in such a place, but she vowed to herself that she would retrieve Alson as soon as she possibly could. She only wished she could rescue Bert as well.[18]

TWENTY-TWO

Kay and Ming Tai

NEW YORK, 1937–1939

KAY KNEW EXACTLY WHAT HER baby sister was thinking. Though Alice had heard about Ming Tai's business setbacks, the Chins' new home still shocked her. She had last visited the United States in 1930, when she stayed at the Chins' comfortable Victorian in Glen Ridge, but these days, Ming Tai and Kay shared a four-bedroom walk-up in Harlem with their five unmarried children. During Alice's own tenement girlhood, she would have thought the Chins' apartment comfortable enough, but she and her sisters had known so much better since then. With a twinkle in her eye, Kay then dropped a bombshell on Alice: When the Chins' two oldest daughters and granddaughter arrived from North China, they too would be staying in the apartment. Kay could see the younger woman try not to flinch at the thought of so many people crammed into such a small space. Kay didn't relish the idea either, but she accepted it with her characteristic unflappability. Alice felt oddly envious of her sister's steadiness; if Kay missed her old life of luxury, she refused to mourn for it or feel self-pity.[1]

Instead, she set to work cheering Alice up with good cooking and company. Helen soon pitched in, bringing Jeanne and Donald to Harlem to see and distract their aunt, and Bill and May stopped by with baby Patricia too. The family exchanged news and gossip as well: Weeks after their departure from Beijing, Adelaide, Vivian, and Jacqueline were still making their way across the Pacific; Bill and May had spent almost a month in Manila trying to get on a mainland-bound ship; and Jim Typond had recently gone into business with their old PS 23 friend Shavey Lee. This prompted laughter and speculation about which of the two legendary talkers would get the last word in *that* partnership.[2]

But Helen's face soon grew thoughtful. Twelve years earlier, Alice had lost her US citizenship when she wed K. S. Lo, and Shavey's sister Emily had also lost her US citizenship for marrying a Chinese citizen—in her case, the son of a Hong Kong shipping magnate. In 1931, Congress finally revised the hated law to allow Asian American women born on US soil to regain citizenship lost through marriage. When Emily returned from Hong Kong to help care for her ailing father, she applied for naturalization under the new law and regained her citizenship two months later.[3]

Alice had heard about the legislative change when it happened, but had given it little thought. Apparently, a woman could apply only from the United States, and she and Alfred had no immediate plans to visit the land of their birth. Now she was in New York and had more free time than she knew what to do with. Helen promised to call Jim and start the process, and her brother-in-law did not disappoint: Within days, Alice was standing in front of a judge and taking her citizenship oath. After she signed the form that the judge's clerk handed her, Kay and Helen signed it as her witnesses—and, in a blink of an eye, she was an American citizen again.[4]

Helen tried to be helpful in other ways as well. With Adelaide, Vivian, and little Jacqueline due in New York at any time, Helen invited her younger sister to stay with her in Brooklyn. Alice could hardly imagine a more Siberia-like location than the Typonds' Flatbush home, so when Alfred cabled to tell her he would be in New York by Christmas, she extricated herself from her predicament. As much as she appreciated George and Helen's offer of their spare room, she said, Alfred was on the way and the two could not possibly impose. Instead, Alice took a suite at the comfortable Hotel Marseilles, an Upper West Side hotel about thirty blocks south of the Chins' apartment. She had been eyeing the place for a while and, after a little investigation, discovered that it welcomed Chinese with enough money. Having grown up in New York, she knew that such things were not always guaranteed.[5]

. . .

Kay and Ming Tai felt tremendous relief once their two daughters and granddaughter finally reached New York. When the war broke out, the Chins had told them all to come home immediately, but getting out of wartorn China was no easy feat. In mid-October, consular officials helped Vivian, Adelaide, and Jacqueline leave occupied Beijing for Tianjin and then coastal Qinhuangdao, where they transferred to a US Navy transport. At the Japanese port of Yokohama, the three boarded the SS *President Hoover*, which was packed with evacuating Americans. The travelers stopped at

Honolulu, debarked at San Francisco, and then boarded a train to New York. The trip took almost a month and was exhausting both for Vivian, who was eight months pregnant, and Adelaide, who was still breastfeeding Jacqueline. A few years earlier, the Chins had expressed pleasure at the thought of their daughters marrying men who returned to China for work, but now the widening war changed their minds.[6]

At Christmas, the entire family spent every cent they could afford on new clothes and baby things for Adelaide and Vivian, who had left much of what they owned behind in Beijing. Though the two women did their best to seem cheerful, the rest of the Chins could tell how much both sisters missed and worried about their husbands. Neither couple had any idea when they would see each other again, a reality that weighed heavily on the two women. Bingham Dai was still working at the American-run Peking Union Medical College, where he and Vivian assumed she would eventually return, but both knew he would miss the birth of their first child. Meanwhile, Jack Young had traveled to central China and volunteered his services to General J. L. Huang, the head of the Nationalists' War Area Services Corps, a sort of Chinese Army USO. Though not exactly on the front lines, he was hardly out of danger.[7]

Three days after Christmas, Vivian went into labor before dawn. Kay and Adelaide rushed her to the hospital, and Barbara Katherine Dai arrived the same morning. During Vivian's hospital stay, the Chins, their friends, and Alice and Helen all dropped by to visit and keep the young mother company. She needed cheering desperately, since the comings and goings of so many new fathers made her miss Bingham even more.[8]

• • •

With two infants, a ten-year-old, two teenagers, and six adults living under one roof, the Chins' apartment was rarely quiet in the spring and summer of 1938. An unending stream of other family members and friends came by, while the phone rang at all hours. Some of Bingham's old acquaintances and colleagues brought gifts for the babies, as did members of the Ging Hawk Club, a New York Chinese American women's group to which several of the Chin daughters belonged. One of the most frequent visitors was Bangnee Alfred Liu, a Columbia University graduate student desperately in love with Gloria but also married to a woman in China. "B.A.'s" frequent presence reminded an amused Kay of Alfred twenty years earlier—always hanging around.[9]

Once Adelaide and Vivian settled into their parents' apartment, they insisted on contributing money for rent and expenses. Ming Tai and Kay initially refused but eventually relented; the extra money would help, because as Vivian remarked, financially "we'll never be like we used to be." The West Harlem apartment was no Glen Ridge. Ming Tai and Kay had one bedroom, gave the women and their babies the second one, put Alwin and Ronald in the third, and allocated the fourth to their other daughters, who jokingly called it "the girls' dormitory."[10]

Money troubles also distracted Ming Tai and Kay for much of the year, since they never knew quite how much they would earn in a given month. Now that their restaurants and real estate were largely gone, most of their income came from some gambling rooms in which Ming Tai kept a stake and where he sometimes played himself. But that summer, prosecutors across the metro area cracked down on such places, and Ming Tai and many of his peers temporarily closed their businesses to avoid detection. The Chins' family income plummeted. To help out, Vivian did beadwork; Adelaide got a series of part-time jobs at a restaurant, a store, and the YWCA; and Meme and Beah became counselors at Camp Interlaken.[11]

Kay knew that Adelaide was restless and unhappy in New York but was shocked when Jack Young wrote to his wife and asked her to come back to China. Though it took all her might, Kay held her tongue and did not complain about Jack and the insecure life he had given her daughter. Instead, she and Ming Tai tried to be supportive, even when Adelaide scrambled to book a ship ticket and decided to leave her new baby behind with the Chins. Like Kay, Ming Tai and Vivian opposed the plan yet refrained from saying so. At forty-five, Kay had little desire to mother an infant again, but together with Vivian, she promised to take care of Jacqueline until Adelaide's return.[12]

. . .

Adelaide's departure also meant the end of her contribution to expenses, so to save money, Ming Tai and Kay moved the family to a smaller apartment downstairs. Luckily, Alwin left that fall for graduate school and Gloria for college, so space was less tight than it had been over the summer. Looking forward, Kay hoped she could scrape up enough money to bring the young woman home for Christmas, since otherwise Gloria could not return until the next May.[13]

The remaining siblings sensed a growing tension in Ming Tai's late nights and Kay's uncharacteristic culinary misfires. Even the chortling of Butch, the

Chins' canary, began to get on everyone's nerves. Finally, Ming Tai and Kay explained that they had been working on a plan to achieve a more stable income. The couple was negotiating with a number of different parties over the Pell Street building that Ming Tai had bought back in 1919. The last of their real estate holdings from the flush years, it was encumbered by a mortgage and the claims of former business partners. If the Chins could pay those off and gain full control of the property, they could lease the ground floor to a group of businessmen who wanted to open a large Chinese restaurant there. Late in 1938, the Chins settled with their old partners and worked out a mortgage arrangement using all of their combined funds, plus $4,000 more that Kay had saved over the years. The deal took a bit of finagling, and to make it look right to the bank, Ming Tai had a nephew and Kay herself sign as separate parties. With the building in their hands, they negotiated the lease, which included a share in the restaurant but not in the risk it entailed. Construction began immediately, for the lessees hoped to open what they were calling the "Chinatown Casino Restaurant" by the time the World's Fair began in April 1939.[14]

. . .

The Chins weren't the only ones sharing cramped quarters and counting their pennies that year. After arriving in New York, Bill, May, and their baby moved in with May's parents, whose apartment was just a block from the Chins' place. Kay and Ming Tai had initially thought their daughters' month-long trip from China was a lengthy ordeal, until they learned that Bill, May, and Patricia spent almost two months trying to get back to the United States. The SS *President Hoover* sailed directly from Shanghai to Manila, but the Philippine city was crowded with more than a thousand American evacuees from China. In the end, the Moys were not able to find a berth on a mainland-bound ship until late September. When they finally arrived in Seattle in mid-October, there was yet another delay: May had given birth to Patricia just before the war broke out, so Shanghai authorities never sent her birth certificate to the US consulate. This meant that the Moys had to wait until a Board of Special Inquiry could interrogate Bill and May, whom immigration officials described as Patricia's "alleged" father and mother.[15]

It was a depressing reminder of why they had moved to Shanghai in the first place, and there were even more to come. Back in New York, Bill pounded the pavement looking for work, but no one was hiring, especially if you were Chinese. Finally, he took the only job he could get: waiting tables at his father-in-law's chop suey place, the Kwong Chow Low. Bill hated the work and despised the customers who thought they were being hilarious by talking to him in "pidgin English."[16]

Bill wondered how Shau Hong could stand it. Maybe his head was too far in the clouds to notice the indignities both of them faced as they served diners and bussed tables. True, after the war cut off access to Chinese films, Ming Tai's oldest son finally gave up his dream of opening a movie theater. But even though Shau Hong's family was on some kind of public assistance, he refused to let go of his desire to have a son to carry on the family line. So Daisy was pregnant yet again, and in fact, Bill could not remember a time when she had *not* been pregnant. May was an exceptionally tolerant wife, but in a million years he could not imagine her putting up with that.[17]

As for the Wongs, Bill was fond of his in-laws, but he and May tried to escape the crowded apartment and the restaurant whenever they could, taking refuge in Riverside Park or Central Park. When the World's Fair opened in spring 1939, the Moys found a new destination, hopping the subway to Flushing and sometimes meeting up with Helen, George, and their kids to stroll the fairgrounds. On days like those, Bill felt grateful that his daughter was growing up among her cousins and aunts, but such outings could only distract him for a few hours from his dead-end job.[18]

TWENTY-THREE

Ernest and Ruth

NEW YORK AND SHANGHAI, 1937–1938

THE SS *PRESIDENT COOLIDGE*'S ENGINES rumbled around the clock, vibrating through the bowels of third class and saturating the tiny cabins with the smell of machine oil. Ruth had never traveled like this before. In 1930, she sailed to China in a first-class cabin with a private bed, toilet, and sitting area, sharing meals with C. C. Chang at a table for two in the spacious dining room. Four years later, she and Ernest purchased comfortable second-class berths for the Overseas Trust roadshow. Now she slept in one of the bunks of a shared cabin and tried to block out both the engine noise and the snores of her three female roommates, strangers all. The communal toilet and shower were a cramped walk down the low-ceilinged hallway, and she and her sons—who slept in another shared cabin—dined with the rest of the third-class passengers at long tables. It could have been worse, of course. The US consul had urged them to take the earlier SS *Conte Biancomano* to Hong Kong, and Ruth could only imagine the humiliation of traveling in steerage while Alice enjoyed a cabin upstairs.[1]

In San Francisco, Ruth used some of her tiny stash of cash to cable her brother Paul in Chicago, and he met the three of them—stiff and tired from trying to sleep in their seats—at Union Station there. Ruth had always been close to Paul and could tell right away that something was terribly wrong. When the boys were out of earshot, he told her the bad news: Two weeks earlier, someone had murdered their stepfather, Chan Jack Lem, shooting him point blank on a Chinatown sidewalk before fleeing into the rainy night. The police called it an assassination but had no suspects. Neither Ruth nor Paul felt particularly close to Chan, but they could see that their mother and stepbrothers were still in shock.[2]

Under the circumstances, Ruth decided they would spend Christmas in Chicago, staying with Paul and his family in their apartment over Paul's Chinatown medical office. Ruth's brother was married to a white woman, a former nurse he had met when both were in training years earlier. Despite—or perhaps because of—Ruth's own ambiguous origins, she often had misgivings about interracial relationships. Indeed, she had barely spoken to her younger brother William since the early 1920s, when he scandalized Louisville by marrying a white divorcée. Even worse, Paul's wife, the former Mary Magdelene Mondulick, was a practicing Catholic, and Paul was becoming friendly with the local priests. Though Ruth had put Loring in Shanghai's Marist Brothers school, she felt considerable ambivalence about Catholicism and her brother's growing interest in it.[3]

Still, she had softened on the subject over the years, especially after the Koesuns named their only child Ruth Ann. Now nine years old, the little girl insisted that she was going to be a ballet dancer when she grew up. Though skeptical, Ruth appreciated the way the child's pirouettes around the living room—usually accompanied by the excited barks of the Koesuns' white spitz—amused Ken and Loring. She knew both were homesick, and Paul and Mary could see it too. The Koesuns put extra presents under the tree, and Mary raided the giveaway pile at her church for winter coats for the travelers. Perhaps her sister-in-law's Catholicism wasn't so bad after all, Ruth decided; after so long in Shanghai, she had forgotten just how cold Chicago could be in December.[4]

Once the holidays were over, the three Moys resumed their journeys. Ken headed to Williston Academy in rural Massachusetts, where his mother had wangled a one-term scholarship for him with the help of the baseball coach. Ruth and Loring traveled to New York, moving in with Ruth's sister Anna and her husband, Harry. The Koes had no children of their own, but Anna and Harry adored her sister's offspring and assured Ruth that the Moys could stay as long as they wanted. Their Midtown apartment was small, but the Koes were rarely there anyway. Instead, they spent most of their hours at the Bamboo Garden, a nearby Chinese restaurant they owned and ran. Wedged between a 6th Avenue soda fountain and a hardware store, the place usually stayed open late to feed the crowds leaving the nearby Ziegfield Theatre.[5]

• • •

The Shanghai Customs College did not reopen for months, so Ernest had no job to go to. Bored and lonely, he paced around the family's apartment, chain smoking and listening to the news on the radio. Whenever the phone rang, he rushed to answer it, hoping for word from Ruth and the boys. To save money, the family now communicated mainly through a network of helpful amateur radio stations that spanned the globe. Friendly "ham radio" operators relayed messages from the United States to China and back again, and the Shanghai amateurs usually contacted local recipients by phone.[6]

Ruth and Ernest kept their messages short and businesslike, and not just out of respect for the radio operators' time. Whether Ernest cared to admit it, the evacuation episode had taken a toll on their relationship. In the Moys' battle with the US Consulate, Ernest hid his embarrassment about his financial situation under a blanket of umbrage, but Ruth saw through it. She particularly resented the way he criticized the office and its staff in angry, pseudonymous letters to the local papers—and then sent her alone to face the same men he had skewered.

Two weeks after Ruth and the boys left Shanghai, the Japanese pushed out the last Chinese troops and occupied all of the city except for the International Settlement and the French Concession. Even though the shooting had stopped, Ernest could still see flames rising from the devastated areas, the fires blanketing the city with caustic smoke. So much of Shanghai lay in ruins, while rag-clad refugees seemed to sleep on every sidewalk. And die, too: Each morning, the authorities hauled away dozens of bodies of those who had perished overnight. With winter coming, those numbers were sure to grow. Ernest could scarcely imagine anything worse until mid-December, when reporter friends passed along the first stories of the Japanese atrocities at Nanjing. He was glad his family had some semblance of Christmas that year, since he saw little to celebrate in Shanghai.[7]

Yet within the foreign-controlled areas, early 1938 brought a strange, surreal boom that contrasted with the desolation just outside the concession borders. As the Nationalist government retreated inland, it relocated many of its banks and other institutions to the International Settlement. Chinese factory and business owners did the same, following their customers and fleeing Japanese confiscation as well. The Customs College also reopened in 1938, allowing Ernest to return to work and pay off the cost of his family's passage to the United States.[8]

The war was never all that far away, though. With so much of Shanghai under Japanese control, supporters and opponents of the new regime began to attack each other inside the foreign-controlled areas. In the first months of 1938, Nationalist agents assassinated numerous Chinese suspected of collaborating with the occupiers. Pro-Japanese agents used some of the same tactics but also resorted to broader terrorist methods. In one week in February, they left the severed heads of three Chinese near the Shanghai American School, with notes warning against anti-Japanese activity, threw grenades at the offices of several anti-Japanese newspapers, and sent threatening letters to reporters deemed pro-Nationalist.[9]

Ernest tried to focus on his Customs College tasks, glad to have a salary again, but blocking out the news was an impossible task. He knew too many of the players and targets, whether from his years in China or his previous life in America. When Russell Chen, an old acquaintance from New York, joined the collaborationist government, Ernest felt sick to his stomach; born in Boston, the man had attended college with Alfred and seemed decent enough. Far worse was the death of Dr. Herman Liu, whom Ernest had first met in Chicago during the Great War. In April, pro-Japanese assassins put a bullet in Liu's brain, prompting half of foreign Shanghai (or what was left of it) to turn out for the funeral. Unsurprisingly, there was a run on bulletproof cars, while many prominent Shanghai residents hired bodyguards for protection.[10]

In spite of all this, Ruth still wanted to return with the boys. To her, Shanghai was no worse than Chicago, where someone had assassinated her stepfather right on the street. Ernest missed his sons but worried about his family's safety, as well as the soaring cost of everything in Shanghai—even before factoring in the price of three steamer tickets. Still, he knew he could not openly refuse to bring his wife and sons back to China, not after the embarrassment Ruth had suffered when they left. So he expressed his ambivalence passively, sending his wife clippings about the terror attacks in the city. She responded with a birthday parcel for Ernest and a photo of Loring under the Christmas tree, with "Doesn't he look lonesome?" scribbled on the back. Checkmate. By late July 1938, she and the boys were on a ship bound for Shanghai.[11]

TWENTY-FOUR

Alice and Alfred

NEW YORK AND SHANGHAI, 1937–1938

FOR WEEKS, ALFRED DELAYED LEAVING Shanghai, even as the situation there continued to deteriorate. A.C. Monk sold North Carolina leaf tobacco to local cigarette manufacturers and maintained a godown (warehouse) in an area devastated by the fighting. Though Alfred doubted the facility still stood, he had no plans to go check on it after reading about an American who ventured out and failed to return. Even if the warehouse and its contents had survived, to whom would Alfred sell the tobacco? Bombs and fires had destroyed the warehouses and plants of several big Monk clients, including Nanyang Brothers, Hua Ching, and Great Eastern, and Alfred was not sure about many of the others. What he could easily see was the bleak Monk balance sheet: Sales in September were just 10 percent of what they had been in July.[1]

Alfred postponed his departure not because of any misguided optimism about the war or the business climate but because he hated the idea of returning to the United States. Many of his friends would have been surprised at this, since he seemed to embrace his American identity with gusto. During his years in Shanghai, he helped found a New York University alumni club, planned social events for the American University Men's Club, and even organized a Washington's Birthday tea dance at the International Club. By 1937, Alfred belonged to so many fraternal groups that he would not have been out of place in a small midwestern town. Except, of course, for his race. Growing up in the United States had taught Alfred that almost no one there—especially the white people—would ever consider him anything but Chinese. Shanghai not only gave him opportunities that the United States denied, it also allowed him to be an American.[2]

But in October, Monk made no sales at all, and by early November, Alfred judged the situation so hopeless and dangerous that he decided to return to the United States for a while. The whole voyage back reminded him why he had stayed away. On board the ship, the waiters in the dining room looked through him half the time, and then there was the inevitable hassle at San Francisco: While the white US citizens quickly debarked, Alfred had to wait for a preening functionary to examine his paperwork, simply because of his race. At least he was able to see Alson, who was spending the holidays with Alfred's brother John in San Francisco. But when Alfred finally boarded his train to New York, he vowed to himself that he would return to Shanghai the first moment he possibly could.[3]

. . .

Herbert understood exactly why Alfred hung on so long before evacuating. After all, both men had built careers in Shanghai that they could never replicate in the States. And if Herbert was being honest with himself, he knew that he could not really replicate his career in China, either. His Shanghai was neither China nor the United States, but the gray zone of the concession areas. There, foreign citizenship rights and conflicting regulations created opportunities for people willing to take chances and bend the rules. And Herbert Moy was definitely one of those people.[4]

Herbert and his partners Earle Chang and Hugh Lowe never bothered to obey the increasingly restrictive Chinese broadcasting regulations. You did not have to be a business genius to see that canceling the most popular programs in all the best time slots would hurt your advertising revenue. So when the Ministry of Communications began to enforce the law, working with the International Settlement's Shanghai Municipal Police (SMP) force to nab Chinese broadcasters in the foreign areas, one of their first targets was XMHC, the "Overseas Broadcasting Station."[5]

In July 1937, SMP officers pounded on the door of XMHC and presented Herbert with a warrant giving them the authority to confiscate his transmitter. He cooly informed the policemen that he was an American citizen and that XMHC was about to receive US consular protection. In fact, he had already filed the paperwork, and the officers could check with the US consul general if they had any doubts. This stopped the police dead in their tracks, and the SMP man who followed up confirmed what Herbert had said.[6]

Thwarted, the Ministry of Communications tried to arrest Earle Chang, whose status was less secure than Herbert's because of British laws on race and subjecthood. But the partners anticipated this move, too. Chang had once served in the SMP, and an old friend on the force tipped him off. He quickly left Shanghai for Vancouver, planning to come back after the police lost interest. The outbreak of war in Shanghai ended the government's attempts to shut down XMHC, but also prevented Chang from ever returning to China.[7]

As Chinese and Japanese troops fought to control Shanghai, Herbert worked long hours to keep XMHC on the air. The station's transmitter operated from a building just inside the International Settlement, giving Overseas Broadcasting a degree of safety but also subjecting it to a new kind of censorship. In mid-August, the Shanghai Municipal Council issued an emergency order to all local broadcasters. "Nothing can more easily cause alarm and trouble than misleading reports," the order read, and it warned stations "to take immediate steps to insure that no reports are published unless confirmed by competent authorities." The council threatened to send the police to shut down any broadcaster that failed to comply.[8]

"Published." Really? Herbert read the order, hand delivered by an SMP officer, and shook his head in disbelief. Did the fossils on the council really not know the difference between a newspaper story and a radio bulletin? And everyone understood exactly what the council members meant by "alarm and trouble." The real target of the order was pro-Nationalist propaganda, because, more than anything else, the council feared provoking Japan. For over twenty years, the Japanese had used a series of pretexts and made-up incidents to violate China's sovereignty. The council did not want to give the invaders any justification for seizing the Settlement too.[9]

Desperate for revenue as Shanghai businesses stayed closed, Herbert tested the limits of the emergency order while trying to shield his station from punishment. In late September, he sold XMHC's Sunday evening slot to the China Information Service (CIS), a pro-Nationalist organization. The CIS spent the first weeks of the war compiling reports with titles like "Japanese Massacre of Chinese Civilians," and its unvarnished take on the war rattled SMP monitors. The police, with the blessing of the US consul general, visited Herbert yet again, this time warning him that he was responsible for *everything* the station broadcast, even if he did not create it. Herbert pivoted, professing ignorance and innocence and promising to abide by the council's order in the future. Having wrangled with XMHC several times now, the jaded SMP officer assigned to the station described Herbert not as a zealous Chinese patriot but as a savvy opportunist.[10]

Whatever the case, Herbert struggled in Earle Chang's absence to run Overseas Broadcasting alone and to protect himself from the Japanese, who openly threatened independent broadcasters. In May 1938, he finally sold XMHC to the *Shanghai Evening Post and Mercury*, a newspaper whose American owners wanted to expand into radio—and had sufficient capital and close enough ties to the US consulate to protect their investment. Even better, as part of the deal, they hired Herbert as their business manager and occasional announcer. But the new sense of security he got from the sale evaporated almost immediately. A few weeks after he signed the papers, pro-Japanese agents targeted the owners of several radio stations within the French Concession and the International Settlement. Among other places, they lobbed grenades at a home they mistakenly thought was Herbert's. The incident left him deeply shaken; the attack, clumsy as it was, showed that he was no safer than when he had owned XMHC himself.[11]

• • •

While Herbert grappled with Shanghai's growing violence, Alfred arrived in New York unsure of what the future held for him and his family. Monk's profits were in the toilet, but he desperately wanted to return to China anyway. Then he received the Christmas gift of his dreams: a return ticket to Shanghai and a better job. As the war moved up the Yangzi, Shanghai businesses slowly reopened. C. C. Vines, manager of the Carolina Leaf Tobacco Company, telegraphed Alfred in New York and offered him the Shanghai branch's assistant manager position. Not only did it pay more than Alfred's old job, but it came with greater authority. As long as he stayed at Monk, he would always answer to Tsze Pun, who served as the company's comprador—the person who dealt with Chinese clients and staff. It was the most lucrative and senior job a Chinese could achieve at a foreign-owned company, and now, at Carolina Leaf, Alfred had finally landed it.[12]

Alfred accepted the position immediately, sailing for Shanghai in February 1938, the soonest he could buy a ticket. After all, he told Alice, Vines needed him back in China to investigate and file claims for spoiled and stolen hogsheads of leaf tobacco from the war zone. Other evacuees might have balked at the command to return so soon, but Alice knew that Alfred could not wait to go home. And anyway, while Shanghai was not as safe as it had been before the war, Alfred felt it was not *unsafe* for his family. As American citizens, they could always count on the protection of the US Consulate, the security of the foreign concessions, and the cushion their money provided. Everyone knew Japan would never be foolish enough to provoke the United States into war.[13]

Two months later, Alice and Alson embarked for Shanghai, too—and, like Alfred, spent their voyage catching up with the old friends they inevitably discovered on board. So many in the Lees' social circle were returning to Shanghai, determined to continue their lives there despite the war. Alfred and Alice felt the same; by May, they had moved into a new apartment inside the French Concession and rejoined the city's social whirl. Alice did agree to give a talk to her Chinese Women's Club friends about Chinese American fundraising for war refugees, but afterward, she and Alfred tried to put the conflict behind them. They had a sparkling fall season, with Alfred finishing a successful year as American University Club secretary and agreeing to helm the social committee of the NYU club. He was just starting to plan out the group's big reunion dinner and dance when Guangzhou and then Wuhan fell to the Japanese in late October.[14]

Held at the new Winter Garden, the NYU event was one of the highlights of the autumn social season, in large part due to what one paper called the "capable and popular Mr. Alfred S. Lee." Winter Garden owner Jimmy James, who also ran Jimmy's Kitchen, even took out an ad touting the success of the NYU event. Alice couldn't help but smile when she saw the socially prominent men James chose to list: toastmaster Percy Chu, master of ceremonies Percy Kwok, and "Mr. Alfred S. Lee, whom everybody knows and likes." Life in New York could never compete with this.[15]

TWENTY-FIVE

Kay and Ming Tai

NEW YORK, 1939–1940

IT WAS ONLY MID-JUNE, but Columbus Park was already sweltering. Kay, Vivian, Beah, and Meme spread their blanket on the ground and quickly discovered that keeping two toddlers clean and occupied was even harder than catching a cool breeze. One minute the little girls were trying to dig their hands into the sandy dirt, the next they wanted to chase a group of pigeons across the lawn. Thankfully, Helen, George, and their two children arrived at that moment, and sweet Jeanne coaxed her cousins into playing a round of pattycake with Donald. Bill, May, and little Patricia had just shown up when a man with a megaphone called for all entrants in the Chinatown baby contest to report to the recreation building. The adults brushed off the three little girls, put the final touches on their costumes, and retied their bonnets. Barbara managed to pull hers off again, but at least she let Vivian twist on the little lei and grass skirt. As Patricia wiggled in protest, May fastened a hand-lettered sash reading "Miss Shanghai" across the child's torso and plopped a tiny conical straw hat on her head. Only Jacqueline, who had gone as *Snow White*'s Dopey the year before, knew to sit still.[1]

All the judges were white city officials, and they tried unsuccessfully to look serious as they examined each of the fifty-plus squirming children vying for the seven gold-plated trophy cups. At the end of the day, Moy ancestry proved powerful: Jacqueline won "healthiest baby," Patricia "best costumed baby," and Barbara "friendliest baby," and she missed a second trophy for "baby with the best lungs" only because a rival toddler's mother combed his hair down at a particularly strategic moment.[2]

After retrieving their children's prizes, the family lingered a few more minutes to chat and catch up. Alwin had just received his master's degree and was returning to New York to look for work. May's favorite sister, Rosie, planned to get married in just a few weeks. With the recent birth of Robert Richard Chin, Shau Hong finally had the son he wanted, so maybe poor Daisy could get some peace at last. The gossip and the afternoon itself had been a needed distraction for all of them. Bill Moy still waited tables at May's father's restaurant—and still hated it. Jim Typond had just testified in the corruption trial of his former office mate, Assemblyman Ed Moran, and the press coverage deeply mortified Helen and George. Vivian's husband, Bingham, was finally leaving Beijing to join her in the United States, but now she waited anxiously for any word that he had safely arrived in Shanghai, his first stop. Meanwhile, she spent most of her waking hours caring not just for her own toddler, but for Jacqueline as well.[3]

As for Kay, she was trying not to think about what was going on at their building just steps from the park. A few months earlier, she and Ming Tai signed a contract with three men who wanted to open a restaurant in the first-floor space at 30 Pell. The deal required the men to pay Kay and Ming Tai a share of their profits, and the Chins initially believed that the agreement would bring in a dependable stream of income. The lessees seemed competent enough; though none had owned their own place before, all had worked in Chinese restaurants for years.[4]

The renters rushed to finish the restaurant in time for the opening of the World's Fair in late April, expecting a surge of visitors to the neighborhood. Even Ming Tai thought their new two-story vertical neon sign, which screamed "CHINATOWN Casino," seemed tailor-made to reel in the tourists, but the imagined visitors never showed up. Only the restaurants closer to the fairgrounds in Queens seemed to benefit. By summer 1939, the men had stopped paying their contractors and food suppliers, so when the place went bankrupt that fall, the Chins felt lucky that they had none of their own money tied up in it.[5]

After the Casino owners finally settled their debts, Ming Tai and Kay decided to take over the space in partnership with someone they could trust. War had just broken out in Europe, the Roosevelt administration was pushing preparedness, and the economy had finally started to improve. Ming Tai and Kay had only a little savings, but they knew that they might be able to raise some additional capital from their relatives and friends. Ming Tai's nephew Chin Dan Yee had mentioned wanting to get into the restaurant business, and they discussed the possibility that he could manage the place.[6]

Ming Tai mentioned none of this to the immigration inspectors who showed up unannounced at the Pell Street building that summer. As they questioned him, he realized they were probing for evidence that Dan Yee no longer merited merchant status. Ming Tai had seen his nephew just days earlier, but now he shifted into opaque mode. Actually, he told the inspector, he could not really remember when he had last seen Dan Yee. He *thought* his nephew might be somewhere in New York but could not say for sure—and by the way, Dan Yee was not his real nephew but in fact a distant cousin.[7]

Later, Dan Yee told Ming Tai how it had all started. A lawyer from the US attorney's office had spoken with him about a Federal Housing Administration claim involving someone else entirely. Without thinking, Dan Yee told the man that he had been unemployed for several years. Apparently, the US attorney tipped off the immigration office, and days later agents were knocking on his door. Ming Tai shook his head at his nephew's foolishness, then remembered how he had done something similar years earlier when testifying for his own uncle. Immigration officials kept asking different versions of the same set of questions, always hoping to trip up their Chinese targets. Who could blame Dan Yee for eventually getting entangled? At least once the new restaurant opened, he could claim to have a qualifying job.[8]

In late 1940, workmen carefully removed the "Casino" part of the large neon sign and replaced it with "Inn," exactly what thrifty Ming Tai had done at the Palais Royal years earlier. In other ways, though, the Chinatown Inn was a far cry from the Palais. When the restaurant opened its doors on December 7, 1940, it featured neither an orchestra nor a dance floor, and no radio stations broadcast from behind its banquettes. Instead, the focus was squarely on the menu: "Real Cantonese Food at Popular Prices," its advertisement promised. Charley Goon, whose cooking Kay approved of, dished out all the hits: twenty varieties of chow mein, thirty types of chop suey, and ice cream and cookies to finish it all off. The formula of solid dishes at decent prices worked in the space, and the Chinatown Inn soon gained a loyal following. The restaurant's steady success helped stabilize the family's finances for the first time in almost a decade.[9]

So did the war in China, combined with growing American sympathy for that country. No one in the family would have described the conflict in Asia in positive terms, yet it created new opportunities for educated Chinese Americans in New York, including the Chins. All of Ming Tai and Kay's children, except for Ronald, had now graduated from high school. Alwin had a postgraduate degree, and Gloria, Beah, and Meme were attending college part time. Poised, attractive, and far more culturally American than Chinese, they were exactly the combination sought by the organizations trying to make China's case to the American public. Soon, Gloria took a secretarial post with the China Institute, the organization that had once supported Mei Lanfang's American tour, while Meme found work at the United China Relief office. Then Gloria took another job at the new Chinese News Service, the Nationalist regime's publicity organ in the United States. As for Alwin, he found work with Universal Trading, the Chinese government's new procurement office in New York. Kay and Ming Tai got into the act, placing ads for their restaurant in *China Monthly*, a pro-Nationalist magazine with a wide circulation among white Americans interested in Chinese issues. Even little Jaqueline took part when a prominent artist recruited her and Vivian to pose for a China relief poster—at least until the painter decided they looked too happy to be convincing refugees.[10]

· · ·

In July 1940, Jack Young suddenly appeared in New York bearing letters, gifts, and news about Adelaide. The Chins knew that in 1937, he had volunteered for General J.L. Huang's War Area Service Corps—where, among other exploits, he and a small group of officers had loaded the contents of Nanjing's National Museum onto train cars as the Japanese neared the city; in thirty-six hours, they saved much of China's cultural heritage from the invaders. Since then, Jack had also attended a Chinese Army bush warfare training camp and fought the Japanese on the ground. Under the circumstances, Kay and Ming Tai were happy to see him in one piece and in reasonably good health. The previous year, he had been so sick with typhoid fever that he had been delirious and unable to recognize Adelaide as she nursed him back to health.[11]

The Chins privately blamed their son-in-law for dragging their oldest daughter into a war zone but kept their feelings to themselves. Instead, they wanted the latest updates on Adelaide. From her letters, they knew that after joining Jack in Chongqing, she had worked at a guesthouse there. Eventually, she became the secretary for William Langhorne Bond, the Chongqing manager of the China National Aviation Corporation (CNAC), which ran a perilous route between Free China and Hong Kong. Jack now told them that he and Adelaide had both accompanied Bond to the colony in spring 1940. There Jack had boarded his US-bound ship, leaving his wife behind. These days, she lived with his relatives in Kowloon Tong, near Kai Tak Airport and her job at CNAC. Ming Tai and Kay brightened up at this news; if their daughter was in the colony, she was safe from the relentless Japanese bombing raids on Chongqing.[12]

Jack stayed only three weeks before returning to China and his work there. The Chins kept mum about his activities, since his service in a foreign army imperiled his US citizenship. Kay and Ming Tai briefly discussed the possibility of Jack taking Jacqueline to Hong Kong, but eventually he decided against it and left for China alone.[13]

Two or three months later, the Chins received a letter from Adelaide with greetings and news of Jack's safe arrival in Hong Kong and subsequent departure for Chongqing. Fortunately, she remained in the colony to continue her work at CNAC and its partner, Pan Am (Pan American World Airways). Adelaide sent her love to her entire family, but especially to little Jacqueline, whom she had not seen for more than two years. Then she passed along news of a family reunion the Chins had not anticipated. Uncle Ernest had left Shanghai in the middle of the summer, Adelaide wrote, and now he lived just across the road from her in Kowloon Tong, with only a dog and a houseboy for company.[14]

TWENTY-SIX

Ernest and Ruth

SHANGHAI AND HONG KONG, 1939–1941

YEARS LATER, RUTH AND ERNEST blamed the disintegration of their marriage on the global conflict that had forced them to live apart for so long. This narrative served their purposes well: They both cared a great deal about appearances, and lots of couples split up during or after the war. But in reality, Ruth and Ernest's marriage was already crumbling during the last two years they lived together in their French Concession apartment. Their physical separation afterward simply dealt the final blow.[1]

When Ruth and the boys first returned to Shanghai in 1938, she and Ernest tried to return to their old lives, just as Alfred and Alice had been able to do. The Moys enrolled Loring at Shanghai American School (SAS) and attended Ken's SAS track meets and baseball games together. Still, Ernest spent more and more of his evenings at "stag" functions, attending Rotary Club talks and throwing himself into the new Foreign YMCA debate society. The newspapers praised his cleverness during the club's debate over marriage, when he contended that women needed men and would be bored and unfulfilled without them.[2]

After reading her husband's claims in the *China Press*, Ruth rolled her eyes. She was unfulfilled, all right, but not because of Ernest's frequent absences. Many of her American friends had fled Shanghai at the beginning of the war and had not returned. *Her* clubs had curtailed their activities, or worse. Ruth had once poured much of her energy into the Women's Christian Temperance Union, but it ceased functioning after the murder of Dr. Herman Liu, the husband of the group's president.

Meanwhile, Ruth largely avoided the people with whom she and Ernest had once socialized as a couple. She had always felt a little embarrassed about Ernest's tangles—the ill-fated Overseas Trust Company, the judgments for unpaid rent at former apartments and offices—but others' memories of these problems usually faded over time. Now, though, she worried that people might be whispering about how the Moys had applied for a loan as "destitute Americans" in order to evacuate. Ernest seemed unbothered, but Ruth could not share his indifference, so she increasingly spent her evenings at home with her boys, listening to the big console radio behind her favorite armchair.[3]

Occasionally, she heard Herbert on XMHC, but neither she nor Ernest saw him in person very often. He spent most of his free time in bars and nightclubs with one of his many girlfriends or a posse of foreign journalists. Herbert mimicked their bravado, dismissing as trivial the terrorist attack on him the previous summer, but he had grown more and more fearful since pro-Japanese agents tossed a grenade at his door. To keep the anxiety at bay, he often drank heavily, as did most of his friends.[4]

By 1939, many foreign journalists in Shanghai knew they had targets on their backs. Radio announcers were hardly exempt: Outside the foreign concessions, Japanese officials could suppress any newspaper they chose, but they could not as easily silence the broadcasters who reached listeners hundreds and even thousands of miles away. That's why the *Shanghai Evening Post and Mercury* had bought XMHC from Herbert in the first place, and why Carroll Alcott's scathing attacks on the occupiers made his station, XMHA, so popular. Now Japanese and puppet-regime officials started using a mix of threats and actual violence to try to force all stations to report only the "news" that came from Domei, Transocean, and Stefani—the official Japanese, German, and Italian news agencies, respectively.[5]

Those three nations were forging the ties that eventually became the 1940 Axis alliance, and in the midst of China's own war, Shanghai residents began to see the impact of Europe's tensions, too. Chinese loyal to the Nationalist regime in Chongqing read nervously about onetime KMT leader Wang Jingwei's "peace movement" and his praise for the role that Germany and Italy might play in it. Foreigners in Shanghai uneasily followed the European negotiations over the fate of Sudetenland, and many felt horror when Germany seized the rest of Czechoslovakia as well. By 1939, thousands of desperate Austrian and German Jews had also moved to the city, making the European crisis ever more real for Shanghai residents of all backgrounds.[6]

The outbreak of World War II in Europe split foreign Shanghai along national lines. In the months after the German invasion of Poland, many Europeans and Canadians left China to serve in the armed forces of their home countries or scrambled to raise money for the different combatant nations. The tense situation ended many friendships in the foreign community, while neutral nations' citizens treaded carefully between the two sides. Ernest and Ruth found the balance difficult to maintain and stopped bothering after the Japanese placed Wang Jingwei at the head of their puppet regime in Nanjing.[7]

By June 1940, the war in Europe had transformed Shanghai even more directly and ominously. When France surrendered to the Nazis, the collaborationist Vichy government took over the administration and policing of the French Concession. This allowed puppet-regime and Japanese authorities to operate freely in the area, effectively reducing what locals called the *gudao* (isolated island) to just the International Settlement, still under the control of the foreign-elected Shanghai Municipal Council.[8]

. . .

After France fell, the Chongqing government shuttered the Shanghai Customs College on Rue Alfred Magy. When the Wang government took over the institution in August 1940, the new administrators found a mothballed building whose staff consisted of a few caretakers. Most of the other employees refused to serve the puppet regime, a decision that made them potential targets. For his family's safety, Ernest moved out of their home on Rue Lafayette and into the cramped office of Cana-Sino, the nutritional supplement business that was his newest venture.[9]

Although uncomfortable, the tiny space was just his temporary home. Before sunrise on a late August morning, Ernest slipped out of the building and into a waiting car. Sweat trickled down his back, and though he blamed Shanghai's torrid weather, nervousness knotted his stomach, because Wang Jingwei's agents were everywhere. Ernest knew he was small fry, but the puppet government had used threats and violence to try to make everyone join its ranks. When the driver finally reached the jetty, Ernest began to breathe normally again, but his heart stopped pounding only after he was safely on board the American-flagged SS *President Coolidge*.[10]

As the great liner chugged out of the harbor, he could not help but remember his first view of Shanghai back in 1928, when he had felt so hopeful about the future of China, the Kuomintang, and his career and family. Now, like most people who had fled the city since the war began, he wondered if he would ever return to Shanghai, and when he would see his sons again. He and Ruth had agreed that she would stay put with the boys for the time being, and the couple had plenty of good reasons for their decision: Hong Kong was overrun with refugees; finding a new home and schools there would be difficult; and Loring and Ken had moved around enough between 1937 and 1938. By focusing on their sons, Ruth and Ernest avoided stating the obvious: Neither really minded the idea of living apart for a while.

Ernest soon arrived in Hong Kong, where the Nationalists were reopening the Customs College in borrowed space at Hong Kong University. Then the puppet regime caught wind of it and called the school a hoax meant to dupe students. The dispute quickly became even uglier and more public. Since agents of the Japanese and the Wang regime lurked in Hong Kong too, Ernest now bought a dog for protection. The creature also kept him company as he settled into the flat that Adelaide helped him find just down the street from her own place in Kowloon. Fortunately, his apartment was within walking distance of the train to the Star Ferry, since he often went to Hong Kong Island for work or to remit part of his paycheck to his family in Shanghai.[11]

Ernest missed his sons, and he thought often about when and how he might reunite the family. Within days of arriving in Hong Kong, he visited the local Nationalist representative to apply for Republic of China passports for all of them. Nationalist law recognized the Moys as Chinese rather than American because of their ethnicity. Ernest reasoned that if he ever had to leave Hong Kong for unoccupied China, he wanted to smooth the way for his family to join him there.[12]

• • •

Ruth opened the package and stared at the new Nationalist passport, cheaply printed on bright yellow cardstock and hand lettered by the single staff member of the Hong Kong passport office. She wrote Ernest to confirm receipt of the documents, but in reality she could no longer imagine following her husband to Hong Kong, let alone unoccupied China. True, the US-Japanese relationship had deteriorated so quickly that the American consulate had just advised nonessential citizens to leave Shanghai for good. Still, Ruth found Ernest's absence freeing, and though Shanghai had gotten no safer over the previous months, she ventured out more than she had since returning to the city in 1938.[13]

Now that Ernest had left, her embarrassment over the evacuation episode finally dissipated. On pleasant days, she occasionally walked the boys to nearby SAS, where she chatted unselfconsciously with the other parents. Her sons missed their father, but overall they were thriving: Loring was increasingly keen on photography, while Ken, more than a head taller than both Ruth and Ernest, had become such a skilled baseball player that after his junior year, the local Shanghai Amateurs team recruited him to play for them. He was the only high schooler in the bunch, and his pitching clinched their championship that summer. In the fall, he also signed up to be the business manager for the annual SAS school play, and Ruth tried not to laugh when she found out that it was *The Importance of Being Earnest*. Her mirth changed to alarm when an SAS official told her that the school had to apply to the French Concession police for permission to stage the comedy. The Japanese and their allies apparently sought to control everything, even high school drama productions.[14]

With Ernest working in Hong Kong, money was not nearly as tight as it had been just a year or two earlier, since he earned his salary in Hong Kong dollars. The exchange rate on his remittances was so favorable that Ruth decided to splurge on a gift for herself and the boys: a piano. She liked to play and wanted Loring to learn as well. Imported instruments were astronomically expensive, so Ruth decided to buy a Chinese-made piano she had noticed in the window of a Nanking Road music store. One late October day, she saw the boys off to school and then boarded a tram downtown.[15]

Though still the ritziest shopping street in the city, Nanking Road had lost much of its sheen since the beginning of the war. The once grand boulevard seemed almost to have contracted, with familiar landmarks missing and others still bearing scars from bombings in 1937. At the corner of Honan Road, Ruth stepped down from the tram, which was always overcrowded these days. She quickly set off in the direction of the Bund, avoiding eye contact with the beggars whose hands reached out in her direction.[16]

• • •

Ruth and Peter Kim never talked about when and where their relationship had begun. Of course, foreign Shanghai was a small town in many ways, and Loring was good friends with Pete's younger brother Dick. But something definitely shifted the day Ruth shopped for her piano. The S. Moutrie showroom was right next door to Getz Brothers, the large American import firm where Pete worked as the building supplies manager. When they flirted in the store, Ruth realized that she enjoyed his attention, even though she was close to twenty years older than he and still wore a wedding ring. Pete watched with a smile as she ran her fingers over the various keyboards, eventually selecting a moderately priced upright piano and bench. When the salesman started to write out the receipt, he asked for her name, and for the first time since 1919, she replied, "Miss Ruth Koesun."[17]

Ruth began running into Pete quite often near SAS, but she did not mention him to Ernest. In their letters, they mainly stuck to practical matters, such as Ernest's remittances and Ken's college plans. The boy was weighing his options for fall 1941 but had not yet made any decisions. Ruth and Ernest also agreed that Ken should travel to Hong Kong after graduation so that he could spend a little time with his father before heading back to the United States.

Ernest wanted Ken to come south for another reason, too. Since arriving in Hong Kong, he had started attending local baseball and softball games and was now a fan of the South China club, known as the "Nam Hwa" nine. Befriending some of the players, Ernest bragged about his son's pitching prowess and the boy's role in the 1940 Shanghai championship. Nam Hwa's manager wanted to have Ken pitch for his team in the summer of 1941 and was so desperate for hurlers that he asked if Ernest still knew how to throw a fastball. It was not yet Christmas, and Ernest found himself yearning for summer.[18]

At least Ernest felt less alone than he had in his first months in Hong Kong. He now had a roommate, a young Hawaiian clerk whom he had met while playing softball, and he also spent many of his free evenings with Adelaide. Still, he missed his sons terribly, and the holidays that year felt particularly lonely. Unlike Christmas 1937, Ernest was the one who sent gifts to Ruth and the boys, since goods were pricier and scarcer in semi-occupied Shanghai than in Hong Kong. Ken and Loring replied with cheerful cards and newsy letters, which Ernest wanted more than anything they could have bought for him in Shanghai, even before the war.[19]

When Adelaide was busy, Ernest ate dinner in his apartment and then settled into his favorite chair, guard dog at his side, and flipped on his radio for company. If he felt particularly homesick, he could sometimes hear shortwave signals from distant Shanghai, including the stations to which he once had regularly listened. He especially appreciated XMHA and the sarcastic commentary of Carroll Alcott, a harsh critic of the occupation and the target of more than one assassination attempt. Japanese military transmitters so often jammed XMHA that Alcott took to starting his programs with a wry comment about his main advertiser: "This broadcast is brought to you courtesy of the Bakerite Company, Shanghai, leading bakers and makers of better bread. The jam tonight is courtesy of Mr. Suzuki and the Japanese Army."[20]

Constant jamming made XMHA unbearable that Christmas, but another Shanghai English-language station began to reach Hong Kong and points south with little difficulty. The colony's residents quickly figured out why the Japanese did not try to interfere with XGRS. The *X* in its call sign meant it was based in China; *GRS* was an abbreviation for "German radio station." Its announcers praised the Luftwaffe's recent firebombing of London and the sinking of British ships in the North Atlantic. One particularly snide man made scathing remarks about President Roosevelt's pledge to turn the neutral United States into "the great arsenal of democracy." Once Ernest stumbled upon XGRS, he thought that the snide voice sounded strangely familiar. A cold shiver ran down his spine when he heard the announcer's sign-off: "And that, ladies and gentlemen, concludes this edition of the day's news from XGRS in Shanghai, China. Your news announcer is Herbert Moy."[21]

TWENTY-SEVEN

Alice and Alfred

SHANGHAI, 1940–1941

THE SERVANTS BROUGHT THE ENVELOPE into the dining room with the other mail that morning. Stamped "CONFIDENTIAL," it bore the return address of the US Consulate. Alfred was not particularly surprised at what he found inside: an official circular advising all "non-essential" Americans to leave Shanghai as soon as possible. He had heard rumors about such a circular, and he and Alice had already discussed what they would do if it came. Everyone said that ship tickets, even just to Manila, were fully booked into early 1941. Alfred knew that Alice did not fully trust Herbert to care for their aging parents, and anyway, Alson seemed so happy at his school that it would be a pity to pull him out again. The couple did not dwell as long on their larger concerns: What would Alfred do for work if they went back to New York? Wait tables in a restaurant, like Bill? How could pampered Alice move from their luxurious French Concession apartment to a Manhattan walkup? They already knew the answers. They could not possibly leave Shanghai.[1]

Besides, life in the city seemed almost normal in some ways, despite the war news in the papers and the growing tensions between the US and Japan. Of course, Alfred and Alice did not live in a fantasy world. They saw the refugees on the streets, the high prices of goods in the shops, and the arrogant, threatening behavior of police and troops outside the International Settlement. Ernest's hasty and secretive departure that August shook them, too. Regardless, the Lees had returned to as many of their prewar activities as they could, from Alice's weekly mahjong game with Lenore to Alfred's Amity Lodge Masons meetings. The violence that so frightened Herbert and Ernest did not scare them, since Alfred was a businessman, not a journalist or an official. Still, Alice felt grateful that her surname was no longer Moy.

She loved her baby brother, but she could only imagine how his new job was affecting Ruth, Loring, and Ken, who still shared his last name.[2]

. . .

Herbert had not realized how negatively other Americans would view his work at XGRS. Why did it matter so much to everyone? The US was not at war with Germany, so he figured he was not really doing anything wrong. For a while, he mistakenly assumed that one of his first big moves at XGRS had simply rubbed people the wrong way. It involved the British owner of another local station, an older woman whom Herbert had known for years. Mrs. Robertson lived around the corner from him but had no idea that he now worked for XGRS. So he turned on the charm, and she didn't think twice before agreeing to sell him time on her station for what he promised would be a "new type of entertainment." Then he and XGRS manager Charles Flick-Steger used the slot they had bought to broadcast a rabidly anti-British and pro-Nazi program to stunned listeners. Mrs. Robertson was not just horrified but humiliated, and she sent letters to each of the major papers apologizing for the incident. Herbert thought it hilarious and blamed her for being so trusting, but many of his friends weren't laughing. They called him a rat, and unchivalrous to boot.[3]

Then he started to write his own news commentaries for XGRS, and people got even nastier. First he took aim at the British, whom he felt had kept China down for years. Since so many Chinese agreed, he won a large local audience for his well-crafted and slickly produced programs. Listeners also ate up the skits that he and Flick-Steger performed as "Bill and Mack," a wise guy and a dumb sidekick who made fun of Britain's war losses. Soon, the two men started to attack President Roosevelt's support for the British, too. That's when most of Herbert's old drinking buddies began to give him the cold shoulder, even crossing to the other side of the street when they saw him coming. Others called him a sellout. Herbert reasoned that he could not possible be selling out, since he relied for most of his material on the isolationist *Chicago Tribune* and the US senators who criticized the administration's pro-British policies.[4]

He blamed that son of a bitch Carroll Alcott, who used his XMHA programs to attack Herbert. What a self-righteous, patronizing bloviator Alcott was. He fancied himself a champion of the Chinese, but probably the only ones he knew were his servants. Lucky Alcott—*his* bosses hired bodyguards to protect him, and the Settlement's police not only kept a close watch on his home and station but also gave him a bulletproof vest. Herbert had not received such treatment when the Japanese targeted him in 1938. It was easy enough to bait the occupiers when you had enough bodyguards, or knew that you could always cut and run back to a cushy job in the States. When Alcott finally returned to America in September 1941, Herbert doubted that the bull-necked broadcaster was working as a waiter in a chop suey restaurant there.[5]

Anyway, Herbert could not turn down the wad of cash the Germans waved under his nose. At XMHC, he had made Ch$650 a month, an amount squeezed out of the station's owners after heated negotiations. Erwin Wickert, the founder of XGRS, offered Herbert CH$1,500 a month to start. And of course a job with the Germans meant no more threats from puppet-regime or Japanese assassins. Herbert told Wickert he needed a day or two to think it over, but what was there to consider, really? He quickly informed his boss, Frank Burton, that he was leaving for XGRS, and when Burton disgustedly asked why Herbert would take such a job, he replied, "Well, Frank, they are paying me much more than you would ever be able to pay."[6]

Burton's response put Herbert on notice, and he started to make excuses for why he was taking the Nazis' dirty money. When he accepted the job, he told Wickert that he would have turned the Germans down except that his poor old father was an opium addict who was driving the dutiful Herbert into debt. Later, he claimed to one of his last remaining American friends that he had agreed to work for the Germans only to get Ernest off the Japanese blacklist, though in reality his brother had left for Hong Kong weeks earlier. Herbert realized that his excuses had not convinced almost anyone once J. B. Powell of the influential *China Weekly Review* called him "Lord Haw-Haw's Chinese stooge," a reference to the British turncoat who broadcast for the Nazis in Europe. After that, Herbert stopped trying to justify what he had done.[7]

Instead, he doubled down on his ridicule of the administration, not only claiming that Roosevelt was "intent on getting the people of the United States to go to war again in another effort to preserve the decadent British Empire," but also slamming "the Jewish-owned American press." There was no going back now, and when he received the usual biennial notice from the consulate to reregister as a local American citizen, he just ignored it. The consul general quietly telegraphed Washington that this action created "a presumption of expatriation," which meant that Herbert had, in essence, given up his US citizenship. Hal Mills ran into him at a nightclub in fall 1941 and asked him about the rumor that the US Consulate had revoked his passport because of his broadcasts. "I don't give a damn whether my American citizenship is recognized or not," Herbert replied, visibly drunk. "What has America ever done for me?"[8]

. . .

On December 8, 1941, a series of explosions woke Alice and Alfred before dawn. From their apartment, they could see flashes of light coming from the horizon in the direction of the Bund. Alfred switched on the family's radio but heard nothing except static until just after sunrise. When he finally managed to get a signal, he and Alice listened to the announcer reading a prepared statement. A state of war now existed between Japan and the United States, the man said, and "Japanese Army and Navy detachments, as from today, have been despatched to the International Settlement for the suppression of hostile activity and the maintenance of peace and order." British and American subjects should not be alarmed, the man continued, but they must register with the Japanese gendarmerie by December 12.[9]

One of the servants came in and reported that just after dawn, Japanese soldiers had entered the nearby country club and the Shanghai American School. Then he handed Alice a leaflet dropped from a Japanese plane that morning, repeating the statement she and Alfred had heard on the radio: Japan was at war with the United States. Alice glanced over and noticed that the ruddy color had drained from Alfred's face. His quiet alarm worried her. They had received the consular circular more than a year earlier and by now had almost forgotten about it. Of course, many of their friends left, but mainly the white Americans; by contrast, only a handful of Chinese Americans evacuated. Middle-aged professionals like Alfred, they preferred to ride out the storm rather than lose everything they had built in China. None believed they would ever find a decent job in the United States. That's why they had left in the first place.[10]

Now Alfred began to frantically turn the radio dial in a search for any additional scraps of information. On one station, the news announcer reported that the explosions they had heard early that morning came from the HMS *Peterel*, a British gunboat anchored near the Bund. Its commander had refused to surrender it to the Japanese, so the Imperial Navy cruiser *Izumo* opened fire on the ship at point-blank range. By mid-morning, though, none of their usual local stations were still broadcasting; the Japanese had shut all of them down, and shortwave broadcasts were hard to pick up in daytime. Finally, they tuned to XGRS, which, unsurprisingly, remained on the air. The announcer reported that Japanese planes had successfully raided Honolulu after midnight on December 8, or what was the very early morning of December 7 in the Territory of Hawaii.[11]

Alfred told Alice and Alson to stay inside, then made his way to the edge of the International Settlement. He usually preferred to drive his own car, but in recent weeks gas had become almost impossible to buy—yet another sign of the impending conflict, he now realized. At the boundary of the French Concession, Japanese sentries initially turned away those who tried to cross into the Settlement, but in the afternoon they let Alfred enter. When he finally reached the area near the Bund, he could see the overturned *Peterel* still smoking in the water. At the Dollar Building, where the Carolina Leaf Tobacco office was located, Japanese troops seemed to be everywhere. Alfred soon realized that groups of soldiers were going from office to office, interrogating American and European businesspeople. C. C. Vines had left for the United States a month or so earlier, so Alfred answered the soldiers' questions in his place. Then they told him to leave and posted a confiscation notice on the office door.[12]

Alice and Alson were deeply relieved when Alfred returned that evening. Over dinner, he gave them a full account of what he had seen downtown. Eventually the family turned the radio once again to XGRS, whose announcer reported that earlier in the day, the Japanese had also attacked the Philippines, Wake Island, Guam, Malaya, Singapore, and Hong Kong. Alice gasped at the last item: Both Adelaide and Ernest were still living in Kowloon.[13]

Suddenly, a tone chimed and the newsreader announced, "Now, a commentary by Herbert Moy." Alice and Alfred looked at each other with dread. Both had forgotten about Herbert's regular evening spot, but now came the familiar voice: "Ladies and gentlemen, it has happened. The flames of war have roared over the Pacific." Alice closed her eyes and tried not to think about what he was saying, but she could not fully shut out her brother's words. "It is not a new chapter of history that now opens. It is a new book with a new theme. And the theme is the willful destruction of mankind, dictated by Britain and the Jews, whose insidious influence in the White House has brought about the present state of affairs."[14]

The rest of his commentary continued in this vein, including the claim that the United States had forced Japan to make the attack. The next morning, when Alfred joined the long line of British and US nationals waiting to register with the occupiers, many of the people in the queue were heatedly discussing what Herbert had said. Like Alice, Alfred felt relieved that almost no one knew he was related to Herbert Moy. His brother-in-law should watch his back, Alfred thought. Days later, a group of angry Americans saw Herbert at one of his favorite gambling spots and beat him half senseless. The Germans soon hired three burly bodyguards to watch over their star broadcaster.[15]

TWENTY-EIGHT

Kay and Ming Tai

NEW YORK, 1941–1943

THAT CHRISTMAS, THE CHINS TRIED to put on a good show for the sake of four-year-old Jacqueline. All of them struggled to hide the fear they had felt since the first flash report interrupted their Sunday radio program: "The White House announces Japanese attack on Pearl Harbor." All afternoon and evening on December 7, they dialed around the radio searching for more information, every new detail proving worse than the last. When they heard that the Japanese had sunk a British gunboat at Shanghai and taken over the International Settlement, Kay felt her chest constrict. Not only were Herbert, Alice, Alfred, Alson, Loring, and Ruth all stranded there, but the Japanese were making war on Britain, too. And Adelaide and Ernest were in British Hong Kong.[1]

No one slept very well that night. On the morning of December 8, while much of the rest of the country sought more news about the situation in Hawaii, the younger Chins scoured the *Herald-Tribune* for fresh reports from Shanghai and Hong Kong. At midday, the family gathered around the radio to listen to President Roosevelt address Congress and the nation and ask for a declaration of war against Japan. When the president said, "Last night, Japanese forces attacked Hong Kong," Kay stared at the floor and willed herself not to cry.[2]

The same day, newspapers and radio broadcasts carried the first substantive information from the British colony, including a report that Japanese planes had blown up Pan Am's *Hong Kong Clipper*. Kay had no idea what hours Adelaide worked but thought her daughter would not have been at the office on a Sunday. Then she remembered the time difference—the Japanese had bombed Hong Kong on what was a *Monday* morning there. The next day, news reports also noted that the enemy had attacked Kowloon, where both Adelaide and Ernest lived.[3]

By mid-December, Japanese troops had taken the entire peninsula. The only hopeful news Ming Tai and Kay received was a vague report about pilots successfully evacuating many of the employees of Pan Am and CNAC, including four American women. They waited and waited for some kind of confirmation—waited as Hong Kong fell on Christmas Day, as Manila capitulated in January, as the British defense of Singapore collapsed in early February. The letter finally arrived on February 18, bearing a Chongqing return address and familiar handwriting. When Kay saw it in the mailbox, she ripped the envelope open and finally breathed without a catch in her throat. Adelaide was alive. Adelaide was safe.[4]

Dated December 16, the letter had come out on the first run of CNAC's new Chongqing-to-Calcutta route. Adelaide wrote that on the morning of December 8, "I was fussing with my hair getting ready to go to the office" when the Japanese began to bomb and strafe Kowloon. Jack's aunt thought the sounds and roar of planes indicated a drill of some sort, but "with my two years' experience of air raids in Chungking, I KNEW it was the real thing." Her boss called her right away and told her to have her bags ready that evening. After sundown, he drove her to Kai Tak airport, where she got a seat on one of the evacuation planes taking CNAC employees two hundred miles northwest to Namyung, a remote area of northern Guangdong not under Japanese control. From there, pilots eventually ferried the group to Chongqing, where Adelaide reunited with Jack. Now in the relative safety of the wartime capital, she apologized to her parents for her Christmas failures. Adelaide had sent Jacqueline and the rest of the family their holiday presents on the *Hong Kong Clipper*, which the Japanese hit the morning of their first attack. "Well, darlings, the thought was there, anyway," she wrote, then confessed her guilt at having escaped when so many others could not. Adelaide did not know what had happened to Ernest, dashing Kay's hopes of having some good news to report to Ken.[5]

. . .

The Chins' experience was hardly unique. During the first three years that the Japanese occupied South China, Chinese in the United States were still able to travel there and send money to relatives. But the outbreak of war between the US and Japan completely severed communications between Chinese Americans and their families in occupied China. Many Chinese New Yorkers now coped by trying to find a way to contribute to the American war effort, discovering in the process that the conflict could help them get ahead, too. For the first time, the labor shortage forced many local companies to hire women and people of color, however grudgingly. After graduating from high school, Shau Hong and Daisy's oldest daughter, Eleanor, went right to work at an uptown psychiatric hospital that probably would never have hired a Chinese secretary before the war. Janet and Muriel were graduating soon, and though Janet hoped to go to college, both twins were already scouting around for war jobs. The family needed the money, of course, since Daisy had given birth to two more babies since their first son arrived in 1939.[6]

Bill wondered why Shau Hong didn't apply for something himself—he was over forty and had nine children, meaning he had no chance at all of getting drafted. But when Bill ran into Shau Hong in the building, he could tell that his neighbor was not going to or coming from work. Bill often wanted to shake some sense, and responsibility, into the man. He could not imagine how a working-age father could expect his teenage daughters to support him, especially now that prospects were finally improving for Chinese Americans.[7]

Bill had initially been skeptical that the war would change anything. Just before Pearl Harbor, the New York State Governor's Committee on Discrimination in Employment criticized defense contractors for turning away "qualified workers because they [are] Negroes or Jewish, or of Italian or German extraction." Of course, the committee did not even mention Asians, and as Bill guessed, its report opened no doors for anyone, especially not for Blacks and Chinese. Nor did anything change in early 1942, when the federal Fair Employment Practices Committee began nosing around local factories after the NAACP documented their racist practices. But then the military drafted so many men that companies finally began to bend.[8]

As a father over thirty, Bill was deferred for the time being, and in his off hours he had been teaching himself to use a micrometer. He even dug out and reviewed some of his old textbooks from the Newark College of Engineering, while he and May kept a close eye on the want ads. By mid-1942, the same plants that months earlier had demanded an advanced degree and experience were now offering jobs and training to anyone with some technical background. Though Bill knew the color of the "anyones" the companies really hoped to attract, he presented himself at the Sperry Gyroscope office in Brooklyn anyway, filled out an application, and waited for an interview. The recruiter, already startled to see a Chinese, seemed even more surprised to hear him speak perfect English with a New York accent. Days later, Bill returned his apron to Wong Soon. After his first few Sperry paychecks, he, May, and Patricia moved into their own apartment a few blocks away. Bill never waited another table again.[9]

• • •

The spring after Pearl Harbor, Helen joined the Chinese unit of the American Women's Voluntary Services (AWVS) upon the urging of the group's chair, Josephine Moy Hong. Josephine lived just a few minutes' walk from the Typonds in Flatbush, and since she was a Chicago-born Moy, she was technically a relative. Still, Helen doubted they ever would have met without the help of Kay's daughter Gloria, who had worked with Josephine on a United China Relief benefit a few months earlier. After learning that the Hongs had just moved to Brooklyn, Gloria put Josephine in touch with her aunt.[10]

Helen found her new acquaintance rather intimidating. In addition to a withering side-eye, Josephine had a well-connected banker husband, four equally spaced children, a career selling insurance, and a raft of high-powered volunteer commitments, which included leading the local New Life Movement group. Though Adelaide had done talks for the movement in China, Alice usually rolled her eyes when mentioning it. Few could resist Josephine's full-court press, however. Helen and Kay, as well as May and her sister Rosie, soon joined the local New Life organization.[11]

Helen found working in the AWVS far more appealing, and by 1942, she was taking the subway into Manhattan weekly for different group events. Sometimes the Chinatown AWVS organized fundraisers and bond sales, but mainly Helen and the other women ran a breakfast canteen for new enlistees. Operating out of the old Church of the Transfiguration on Mott Street, they served coffee and donuts to groups of Chinese American men departing for training camp. Dressed in her stiff AWVS uniform, with its too-large shoulders, Helen poured refills for the men and smilingly chatted with them in Cantonese, Toisanese, or English—whatever made them most comfortable.[12]

Each time Helen walked from the subway at Canal Street to the AWVS canteen in the church, she could see the changes in the neighborhood where she had grown up. The quarter seemed drained of its young men, many of whom had joined the service so that they could fight the hated Japanese. Kay told her that Ming Tai's restaurant was scrambling to find enough waiters, cooks, and dishwashers, and so was the Mulberry Street restaurant that her brother-in-law Jim Typond had just opened with Shavey Lee. On the rare occasion that Helen spotted a youngish Chinese man, he was inevitably in uniform. Ken was, too: That fall, he sent his aunts a photo of himself in his new uniform, along with the news that he had just dropped out of Georgetown to join the army.[13]

In fact, almost everyone Helen knew seemed to be wearing some kind of uniform these days. Jeanne wore a version for her stints at the AWVS canteen next to her mother, and Donald was so jealous that Helen found a boy's type that she altered to fit him. Jim teasingly asked if Helen wanted to trade her AWVS uniform in for the real thing, as Shavey's sister had done. Emily Lee Shek was the first woman Helen knew to join the Women's Army Auxiliary Corps, though she was so tiny that she had to binge on bananas and drink gallons of water to reach one hundred pounds, the minimum weight for recruits.[14]

Helen laughed at Jim's question and shook her head, but she secretly longed to do more for the war effort than hand out coffee and donuts. The house had seemed lonely since Donald started first grade that fall. Now both he and Jeanne were at school all day. Housework took up considerable time, but not nearly as much as when the children were younger, especially since her mother-in-law Grace insisted on doing so much. And Helen understood, at gut level, why Emily—whose husband and children were trapped in occupied Hong Kong—had enlisted. Helen could not help but worry about her own family in Asia, especially Alice, Alfred, Alson, Herbert, Ruth, and Loring, whom she had not heard from since November 1941.[15]

To her surprise, George readily agreed when Helen asked about getting a war job. He often seemed completely focused on his own work, and with the boom in defense factories on Long Island, Gifford was busier than it had been for years. But Grace Typond had raised him to respect what women could accomplish, and he also noticed Helen's discontent that fall. George worked just a few miles from the new Sperry Gyroscope plant in Lake Success, so he suggested she apply for a job there. The company had started hiring women in significant numbers, and the Typonds knew from Bill's experience that Sperry also had some Chinese American employees. The commute was rather long now that gas rationing made driving so difficult, but Helen still jumped at the chance. By Christmas 1942, she was a Sperry employee and wore a new uniform: a line worker's cap and overalls.[16]

Helen set aside her overalls for the grand reception for Madame Chiang Kai-shek, held in front of Manhattan's City Hall on March 1, 1943. Madame Chiang had come to the United States for medical treatment, and after visiting the White House, she planned to stop in New York City. Jim knew all the big politicians, so he arranged for George and Helen to receive an invitation. Both Typonds took the day off work to stand in City Hall Plaza in the late winter cold with thousands of other attendees. Their invitation meant a closer view of Madame Chiang, though both still had to crane their necks to see her. But a few months later, Helen got the chance to shake the Chinese first lady's hand when she came to the Sperry plant on Long Island. The factory manager gathered together the Chinese American employees for Madame Chiang to meet—one of the highlights of Helen's life. Ernest, she knew, would be jealous, but now that they knew he was alive in Free China, she didn't have to feel bad thinking such a thing.[17]

TWENTY-NINE

Ernest and Ruth

CHINA, 1942–1943

THE SHAPELESS SHIRT AND BAGGY trousers felt alien to Ernest, but the costume saved his life more than once. Just before the Japanese crossed into Kowloon, he discarded his Shanghai-made suits, gave away his dog, destroyed his passport and papers, and left his apartment for the last time. After Hong Kong's surrender, the occupiers rounded up most of the whites who worked for the Customs Service, but many of the ethnic Chinese employees went into hiding—as did Ernest, avoiding anyone who might notify the occupiers of his presence. To protect Elaine Hsieh, his frequent companion during his last months in the colony, he finally stopped seeing her. His final days in Hong Kong were fearful and sleepless, especially after he glimpsed Japanese guards herding scores of captured Canadian, British, and Indian soldiers through the streets of Kowloon. Some onlookers tried to offer the haggard, thirsty prisoners water, until guards threatened the kindhearted observers with bayonets.[1]

Fortunately for Ernest, the occupiers encouraged most Chinese residents to return to their villages on the mainland. Rumor had it that the Japanese hoped to reduce the colony's population, since they had little interest in trying to feed not just Hong Kong's longtime residents, but the recent crowds of war refugees too. All migrants supposedly needed permits to leave the colony, but the Japanese did not enforce this very strictly. So Ernest, some of his friends and their families, and a handful of his Chinese Customs Service colleagues joined the crowds leaving the colony that April. About two dozen in all, they kept their heads down and tried to blend in, and fortunately the Japanese guards simply waved them past.[2]

After crossing into the mainland, Ernest's group followed the roads north and west toward Wuzhou, a city just inside unoccupied Guangxi Province.

In the prewar years, customs employees had joked about this backwater town, one of the worst posts in the entire service; now it was a major destination for Chinese Maritime Customs Service (CMCS) employees escaping the Japanese. Ernest knew that if his group could reach Wuzhou, he could get help traveling to their ultimate destination, Chongqing, where the CMCS had reopened its college.[3]

In peacetime, the trip to Wuzhou was relatively straightforward, involving a comfortable river steamer. But this was not peacetime. Refugees clogged the roads, vying for a place on every bus, boat, and train. Ernest and his party had little money, so they made most of the trip on foot, though the South China monsoon season had already begun. As the rain poured, they walked on mud-rutted roads, their soaked clothes sticking to their skin and their shoes saturated with muck. Whenever the downpours stopped, the humid heat became almost unbearable, and mosquitos buzzed around their faces. As Ernest trudged onward, he felt grateful that he had spent so much time the previous summer playing baseball in the heat. As a young man, he had been an excellent athlete, but years of desk work and cigarettes had taken their toll.[4]

By the time the group crossed into Free China, Ernest was completely spent. When his party reached Luoding, a midsize city in unoccupied northwestern Guangdong, they decided to rest for a few days before heading onward. The town itself was unremarkable, though Ernest admired the thin, storied pagoda nestled in the curve of the river. He was also delighted to discover a sizable Maryknoll Catholic compound where several US priests and nuns ministered to local parishioners and helped feed the thousands of refugees passing through.[5]

The fathers welcomed a fellow American and, even better, had a shortwave radio and war news to share. They told Ernest as much as they could piece together about the situation in Shanghai. One of the American priests admitted that his information about the occupied city came from XGRS, and he lacerated the station's star broadcaster, Herbert Moy. Until that moment, Ernest had been enjoying his chat with the fathers, but now he felt his face getting hot. When he regained his composure, he explained that Herbert was his youngest brother. The assembled priests grew quiet, as well as somewhat embarrassed. Ernest hastily assured them that he, too, felt disgusted by Herbert, but he knew they would not see him quite the same way anymore. He did not visit the compound again and felt relieved when his group continued on.[6]

Family reunion in Honolulu, August 1930. Left to right: Ernest K. Moy, Alice Lo, Miles Lo, Gertrude Young, Kenneth Moy, Loring Moy, Ella Young, and Luke Young. (Courtesy of Douglas A. Lee)

Alice and Miles Lo in Shanghai, May 1930. (Courtesy of Douglas A. Lee)

Alice in Shanghai, a year or two after her marriage to Alfred. (Courtesy of Douglas A. Lee)

Vacation in Hangzhou, China, 1934. Back row: Lenore Chang, Han Ying, and Alice M. Lee. Front row: Alson M. Lee and Leatrice Chang. (Courtesy of Douglas A. Lee)

Moy family photo in Shanghai, 1936. Back row, left to right: Ruth, May, Adelaide, Bill, Alice, Vivian, and Ken. Front row: Han Ying and Alson. (Courtesy of Douglas A. Lee)

Herbert, ca. 1935. (William and May Moy Photo Collection)

Bill, Han Ying, and Moy Sing in Shanghai, ca. 1934. (Family photograph, courtesy of Douglas J. Chu, MOCA Collection)

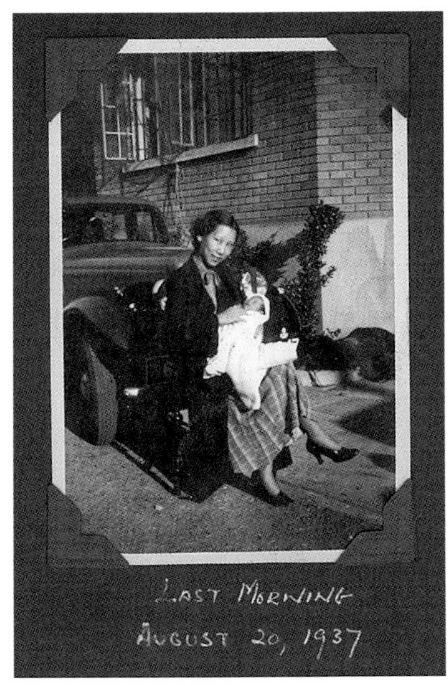

May and newborn Patricia on their last morning in Shanghai, August 20, 1937. (William and May Moy Photo Collection)

Alfred and Alice with their new Dodge sedan after their return to Shanghai, fall 1938. (Courtesy of Douglas A. Lee)

Illustration of the XGRS headquarters from station magazine *Shanghai Calling!*, 1942.

May and Bill in New York shortly after he started his job at Sperry, fall 1942. (William and May Moy Photo Collection)

Loring and Ruth celebrate Ken's birthday in occupied Shanghai, January 1945. (Courtesy of the children of Loring and Moyra Moy)

Ernest working at his office in the Kunming WASC hostel, 1944. (Collection of the author)

Alson with a borrowed army station wagon near the Lees' country home in Kiangwan, fall 1945. (Family photograph, courtesy of Douglas J. Chu, MOCA Collection)

Promotional postcard for the Pacific Restaurant on Pell Street in Chinatown. (Collection of the author)

Ernest on the deck of the USS *Duluth* opposite the Shanghai Bund, with Rear Admiral John H. Carson, an unknown Chinese officer, and Captain William B. Moore, November 1947. (Collection of the author)

Ernest and his CAT boss Claire Lee Chennault offer a toast to attendees at a March 1949 celebration they hosted in Guangzhou to commemorate the sixth anniversary of the organization of the 14th Air Force. (Collection of the author)

Kay and Ming Tai at their daughter Beah's wedding, September 1949. (Family photograph, courtesy of Douglas J. Chu, MOCA Collection)

Ernest and his ex-wife, Ruth Kim, near Point Lobos, California, September 16, 1951. (Courtesy of the children of Loring and Moyra Moy)

Ernest, Helen, Kay, Alice, and Bill at Bill and May's new home in Pompton Plains, New Jersey, June 3, 1952. (Family photograph, courtesy of Douglas J. Chu, MOCA Collection)

Members of the New York Chinese Americans for Eisenhower group in October 1952. Back row, left to right: Ernest Moy, unknown man, Wilbur Pyn, and W.H. Chen. Front row: William T.S. Wu, Henry Lee, Dwight D. Eisenhower, unknown woman, and Huan Yu. (Collection of the author)

The Moy family table at Alson and Lillian's wedding, June 5, 1955. Clockwise from left: Bill, Helen (partly hidden), Jeanne (in hat), Alice, Alfred, Lillian, Alson, Chris, and Patricia (back to camera). (Courtesy of Douglas A. Lee)

President Chiang Kai-shek with Ernest in Taipei, April 30, 1957. (Courtesy of the children of Loring and Moyra Moy)

Kay and Ming Tai's children toast them at their fiftieth wedding anniversary party in New York, November 1960. Left to right: Ronald, Alwin, Meme, Adelaide, Vivian, Gloria, and Beah. (Courtesy of Douglas A. Lee)

Kay and Helen with Ming Tai's niece Mary Hon at the Greenville Amusement Park teahouse, October 1961. (Family photograph, courtesy of Douglas J. Chu, MOCA Collection)

Kay and Helen with newlyweds Loring and Moyra, 1958. (Family photograph, courtesy of Douglas J. Chu, MOCA Collection)

Alice bowling, mid-1970s. (Courtesy of Douglas A. Lee)

In mid-June, the tired travelers finally arrived in Wuzhou, a bustling, low-lying city on a sampan-clogged river. The Wuzhou CMCS staff welcomed them and scrambled to find space for all two dozen in the small customs house. Before they left the next day, Ernest borrowed money from the deputy commissioner to pay for the group's food and travel expenses; the man also helped the party find seats on a bus heading northwest toward Guilin, the next stop on their trip.[7]

When Ernest finally arrived in Chongqing that July, he immediately contacted his family in the United States to let them know he had successfully escaped Hong Kong. He did not mention the physical toll that life in the occupied colony and his arduous overland trip to Free China had taken on him. During the long trek, he had lost a considerable amount of weight, his thinning black hair became streaked with gray, and his back began to ache frequently. But at least he was alive, and that was more than he could say for certain about his wife and younger son, still trapped in occupied Shanghai.[8]

. . .

In the last months before Pearl Harbor, Shanghai had felt edgier, wearier, more *resigned* than even a year earlier. The remaining expatriates there continued to throw parties, dance at the city's nightclubs, and hold tight to the rowdy pleasures of an era that all of them understood was quickly slipping away. Ruth knew more than a few British and American men who had sent wives and children to Hong Kong, Australia, or the Philippines for safety and then embarked on reckless affairs with women who had stayed in Shanghai. Perhaps that same strange heedlessness explained why Ruth let herself get involved with Peter Kim. She liked him, of course, and found his stocky solidity handsome; his love of words and language reminded her of why she had been attracted to Ernest so many years earlier. But she was a married woman almost twenty years Pete's senior. In normal times, she would never have indulged in such an affair.

Despite the giddy abandon that permeated foreign Shanghai in the last months of 1941, she and Pete carefully hid their budding relationship from Loring, their friends, the Moys, and the Lees. Fortunately, the risk of discovery was not all that great, since Ruth and her in-laws did not move in the same circles. As for Ernest, she knew he had no plans to come back—and not just because of the threat from the Japanese and puppet agents. From Ken's letters, Ruth heard all about Ernest's days on the baseball diamond. The other players jokingly called him "Old Folks Moy," but he took it in stride and seemed happier than he had been in years. Hundreds of miles north, she felt the same way and would have been content to continue on as they were indefinitely, except that the Japanese had other plans.[9]

After Pearl Harbor, Ruth queued up with the other Americans who obediently registered with the occupiers, and she and her son took pains to stay within the boundaries of the old foreign areas, as required of enemy aliens. The involuntary idleness was particularly hard on Loring. Now seventeen, he had been one of the few remaining students at the Shanghai American Private School, the successor to the community-supported Shanghai American School that had closed in the summer of 1941 after the US government advised nonessential citizens to leave China. When SAPS shut down after Pearl Harbor, Ruth decided against sending Loring to a Japanese-controlled institution and pulled him out of school for good. She felt lucky that they at least had enough money in the bank to buy food and pay their rent, though coal rationing and a shortage of electricity made Christmas particularly cold that year.[10]

The first time Pete came by after the Japanese takeover, Ruth was surprised to see his bare upper arm. Like other Americans, she and Loring now wore the required "A" armbands to indicate their enemy alien nationality. Of course, many Chinese Americans chose not to wear the bands, which marked them out as foreign and constrained their movements. But Pete was so proudly American that she wondered at this sudden shift. He now confessed to her that he was not the American citizen she had always assumed but had in fact been born in Korea two years after it became a Japanese colony. One of his uncles, a Korean nationalist named Ahn Chang Ho, helped found the Korean National Association in California, and Pete's own parents fled to China in the mid-1910s because of the family's involvement in the anticolonial movement. The Kims eventually traveled to the United States, where Pete's late father attended medical school, so some of his younger siblings were American citizens. As for Pete, he identified as an American, had no Korean name that he knew of, and spoke English better than either Korean or Chinese. He had even served in the American company of the Shanghai Volunteer Corps before the war, but he was actually a naturalized Chinese citizen.[11]

Ahn Chang Ho died in Seoul in 1938, his health destroyed by Japanese prisons and torture, and the occupiers now kept a close watch on his family in Shanghai. Yet Pete was more worried about Ruth's safety. He had expressed this concern ever since they started seeing each other but mentioned it more and more frequently after Pearl Harbor. He wanted to protect her, he said, and though Ruth was almost completely fearless and perfectly capable on her own, she understood the advantages of his presence. In early 1942, he moved into Ruth and Loring's Rue Lafayette apartment.[12]

Pete's strange status now worked in favor of both the Moys and the larger American community. In spring 1942, the American Association began to register US citizens in occupied Shanghai in preparation for possible repatriation to the United States. Washington and Tokyo hoped to swap Americans trapped in Japanese-occupied territories for Japanese citizens stuck in the United States, Canada, and other parts of the Americas. The negotiations between Japan and the United States were both top secret and indirect: US diplomats worked through the neutral Swiss government, while the Japanese used the neutral Spanish government to communicate their demands. Meanwhile, the American Association ran a canteen for destitute US citizens and worked with the local Swiss Consulate, which received US government funds to make subsistence loans to the growing number of Americans who were running out of money. But association leaders struggled to complete such tasks, since the Japanese increasingly restricted their movements.[13]

A few knew about Pete's strange status and asked for his help. Unlike them, Pete could move fairly freely in Shanghai and spoke Chinese quite well. Over the months that followed, Pete took on a growing number of roles for the American Association. First he acted as a general community troubleshooter, before heading the food distribution program that the association established at the old SAS building. By summer 1942, he was working as a liaison for the US servicemen brought from Beijing and Wake Island and imprisoned in Shanghai.[14]

Ruth increasingly worried about Pete and finally admitted to herself how fond she had grown of him, though she also realized that she valued his connections. That spring, when she and Loring ran out of money, they registered with the American Association for a monthly subsistence loan. By that point, the association was digging through hundreds of other applications, so she knew exactly whom to thank when leaders processed hers at record speed. Ruth had also signed up for repatriation, and now she wondered whether she would ever see Pete again once she and Loring left for the United States.[15]

THIRTY

Alice and Alfred

SHANGHAI, 1942–1943

AFTER ALSON'S SCHOOL REOPENED in early 1942, all the British instructors were gone, replaced by Japanese in military uniforms. When the new teachers called a student's name, that boy had to stand and bow deeply and respectfully—otherwise he received a slap or cuff. The instructors used the same method to punish students who botched their recitations. All around the school grounds, as well as on every Shanghai shop window, bus, tram, and utility pole, the Japanese pasted up propaganda posters celebrating their new order in East Asia. Some of the placards used very basic Chinese characters, but most were just pictures, such as a cartoon of handsome Japanese soldiers kicking Uncle Sam in the pants.[1]

Like all US companies in China, Carolina Leaf shut down after Pearl Harbor, and Japanese soldiers soon carted away the last of the tobacco stored in the company godown. With each passing month, Alfred and Alice steadily burned through their savings, withdrawing it from the bank in the small increments the Japanese allowed. By spring, the occupiers not only took over the last enemy-alien-owned companies but also confiscated British and American residents' motor cars. Alfred grudgingly surrendered his beloved 1938 Dodge sedan, originally purchased in the United States to celebrate his new job. A car was no good anyway, since gas could not be purchased at any price.[2]

The occupiers initially allowed most enemy aliens to remain free, but they could not leave the old concession areas. Jobless and idle, many wandered about aimlessly, trading rumors and scraps of information. Some swapped war news picked up from the British and American radio broadcasts to which they secretly listened on clandestine shortwave sets. Others whispered about the prominent US and British businessmen, community leaders, and journalists whom the Japanese had rounded up and placed in the Bridge House Hotel, now a notorious prison. Herbert's former friend Hal Mills and old enemy J. B. Powell had both disappeared into the Bridge House.[3]

On the outside, the Japanese began to ration rice and flour, and eventually they issued ration coupons for coal, butter, and almost everything else worth having. The Lees' servants queued up daily to purchase the limited supplies allocated to the family, though Alfred or Alice quietly bought additional food on the black market. Prices kept going up and up, while the puppet government's currency, which everyone had to use, steadily lost value. Soon the Lees had completely emptied their savings account to pay for food, fuel, and their servants' wages.[4]

Finally, Alfred swallowed his pride and visited the American Association to get a subsistence loan for his family, waiting until the very late spring when the association started its community census. The census, a first step for a possible exchange of nationals with Japan, allowed Alfred to pretend that he was simply visiting the association office to register his family. No one need know that the Lees had finally run out of money, but he saw enough friends at the association's office to realize that his situation was hardly unique. In the weeks after Pearl Harbor, only about two hundred Americans requested loans, but now well over a thousand US citizens depended on them.[5]

In late June, the first repatriation exchange began when the Italian steamship *Conte Verde* arrived at Shanghai to take aboard more than six hundred passengers, including a large group brought from Japan. US negotiators had drawn up a list of repatriates for this first exchange that prioritized diplomats, journalists, missionaries, and certain Canadian and Latin American citizens. After a long, circuitous trip from Shanghai, via Hong Kong and Singapore, the ship was to dock at Lourenço Marques in neutral Portuguese East Africa. There, the passengers would board a Swedish ship called the *Gripsholm* for the voyage to New York, while their Japanese counterparts, who had taken the *Gripsholm* from New York, would leave that ship and board the *Conte Verde*, bound for Yokohama.[6]

The Lees did not make the first repatriation cut, nor did almost any ordinary Shanghai Americans, but they joined the crush of people seeing off the *Conte Verde* anyway. Many of the well-wishers felt sure that they, too, would leave China soon, though the mood turned somber when the Bridge House prisoners boarded the ship, not always under their own power. Stretcher-bearers carried up an emaciated J. B. Powell, his bandaged feet stinking of gangrene; after four months in the Bridge House, he never walked again. Hal

Mills, always thin, looked practically skeletal as he limped up the gangplank, followed by journalist Vic Keene, also much the worse for wear. Such sights left the community shaken, yet most Americans remained optimistic because the American Association and the Swiss consul general, Emile Fontanel, immediately began drawing up lists for two additional exchanges. The next ship, they said, would likely sail in October 1942.[7]

However, negotiations between the United States, Japan, and their neutral representatives soon stalled, and Fontanel learned in early September that the second exchange was suspended for the time being. Still, he said nothing to avoid provoking more anxiety, or acrimony, since the American Association was already objecting to Washington's proposed repatriation scheme. The association argued that US citizens should get automatic priority on the next ship, a sentiment that most members of the community shared. The US State Department ignored this argument, placing a number of Latin American and Canadian citizens in the higher-priority evacuation groups for diplomatic reasons.[8]

Alfred and Alice had registered for repatriation along with almost everyone else they knew, but the wording of the American Association's protest shook them deeply. "Americans should have priority in all cases over non-Americans *regardless of [the] relationship of such non-Americans to American citizens*," the association argued. Its officers drew up their own group of eight categories, including (7) "Americans with alien spouses or dependents entitled to enter the United States" and (8), the lowest priority, "non-Americans entitled to enter the United States." Alson was not an American citizen, so the association's plan would have forced the entire family into the second-lowest category.[9]

Initially, Alfred and Alice were relieved to hear that the US government had rejected the association's scheme. Of course, like other Americans, they felt discouraged when Fontanel finally revealed that the Japanese had indefinitely postponed the second exchange, but they were cheered by the Swiss consul's optimism for a renewal of talks. Then Alfred and Alice discovered that Washington's plan for the stalled second repatriation ship included removing all "mixed families" from it. The second exchange was already postponed, and they would not even be eligible for it! Instead, because their son was a Chinese citizen, they would be relegated to a third and final exchange—if that ever happened.[10]

• • •

Like other Americans in Shanghai, Herbert listened to US and British radio stations, but he did not have to do so in secret. Each program provided rich material for his XGRS commentaries and Bill and Mack sketches. Herbert called President Roosevelt a "hot air merchant extraordinary [*sic*]" and bitingly referred to him as a "self-appointed dictator" whose "burning ambition [is] to rule the world from the White House." He also continued to flay the British and their imperialist record, a tactic that won him more and more fans across China. By 1942, Herbert's voice had become well known throughout much of East and Southeast Asia, too. Even his detractors admitted that his slick, professional broadcasts were incredibly effective. Ever since high school, Herbert had wanted to be a journalist, and now he was much, much more—he was a star.[11]

Of course, his success had not come without effort. He worked incredibly hard at writing and polishing the scripts for his programs, made three or four broadcasts a day, and under various aliases contributed articles to German-sponsored English-language publications in China. The Nazis not only valued him and paid him handsomely but protected him as much as possible from the Japanese, their supposed allies. When the Japanese pulled Herbert's car and gas ration to pressure him to broadcast for Tokyo, XGRS head Klaus Mehnert fell over himself apologizing to the station's top voice.[12]

Herbert pretended to be furious, but in reality he was just scared. In his broadcasts, he read the obligatory Domei dispatches and praised the Axis partnership, but he worried that working for the Japanese would land him in the Bridge House. The occupiers never seemed to get along with their foreign mouthpieces for very long, and anyway, supporting the Japanese overtly might hurt his appeal. After all, many of his fans who hated the British hated Japan equally.[13]

Once, while drunk, he confessed to Alice that he wished he had left China when he still could, rather than taking the German job. After sobering up, he pretended he had never said such a thing, but it was true. He was in over his head, and he could not escape. To steady his nerves, he drank more than he had before and started pouring earlier in the day. Alice worried about Herbert's drinking, though she at least trusted his bodyguards to keep a close eye on him. As for Han Ying and Moy Sing, if they noticed their son coming home drunk, they did not say anything to him, while both appreciated the standard of living that his handsome salary provided.[14]

So, too, did his many girlfriends. Alice noticed one in particular whom he increasingly favored, a white woman with strikingly high cheekbones, large, shrewd eyes, and a long mane of blond hair. Initially, Alice assumed that the woman, whom Herbert eventually introduced as "Mrs. Kwan," was a stateless Russian, like so many of Shanghai's white sex workers. The city was still full of czarist soldiers and their offspring, refugees from the Russian Revolution years earlier. But Marquita Kwan was neither Russian nor a prostitute; instead, she claimed to be British and a divorcée with a Chinese ex-husband in Hong Kong. Alice tactfully avoided asking how she had gotten to Shanghai or what she did for a living. Obviously, Marquita Kwan's "job" was being the girlfriend of powerful men. Since Herbert was fickle, Alice hoped that Marquita Kwan would eventually disappear from their lives, just like all the other women.[15]

• • •

After the postponement of the second exchange ship, Alfred and Alice had dinner with Percy and Mary Kwok and David and Elsie Kwok, two couples with whom they were close friends. As young men, Percy and David's father and uncles had emigrated to Australia, built a business there, and then used their fortune to open the Wing On department store in Hong Kong. Eventually, the company built branches in Guangzhou and on Nanking Road in Shanghai, too. In addition to their department stores, the Kwoks ran the Wing On bank, a steamship line, an insurance company, hotels, and other businesses across Asia and Australia. Alfred had met Percy when both were students at NYU, and they cofounded Shanghai's International Club and NYU alumni club together. David and Alfred were both Amity Lodge Masons, and Alice had become good friends with Elsie and Mary, who were trying to get her to take up their newest passion: bowling.[16]

That night, Alfred and Alice told the Kwoks about the repatriation scheme the US government had laid out. The couples were sympathetic and unsurprised. All had grown up under the racist "White Australia" policy, which Percy and David's father fought before leaving for Shanghai in the 1910s. The two brothers had also personally grappled with America's anti-Chinese immigration system when entering the country for college.[17]

A few days later, Percy called Alfred and invited him to the Wing On building for a chat. Until Pearl Harbor, Percy noted, Wing On had stayed one step ahead of the Japanese. For years, the Kwoks had registered all their companies in Hong Kong, but they had fallen out with the colonial authorities over the lack of protection they received in China after 1937. After that, some of the Kwoks had relocated to the United States and registered their

Chinese businesses as American companies, protecting them from Japanese seizure. Now, however, their luck had run out.[18]

Alfred knew that weeks after Pearl Harbor, someone, perhaps a pro-Nationalist assassin, had shot and killed two people in Wing On and wounded two others. The Japanese held the Kwoks responsible, barricading the area of Nanking Road around the store and not allowing the employees to leave or food to enter. Percy told Alfred that the Kwoks had finally paid half a million dollars to the Japanese to remove the barriers. They also agreed to display pro–Wang Jingwei propaganda and routinely send their employees to the regime's "patriotic" demonstrations. Despite all this, Percy said, the Japanese had demanded more payments and then seized the department store anyway, claiming that it was enemy property because it was registered with the American government.[19]

Percy's family was trying to figure out how to preserve some of the Kwok businesses under the new order. They were particularly desperate to strike a deal to get back their beloved department store, the symbol of their business empire. The family members had always seen themselves as patriots—Percy's father moved the family from Sydney to Shanghai at Sun Yat-sen's invitation—but that did them little good now. Percy's uncle Philip Gock Chin decided that his main duty was to protect his family and its businesses, and he was willing to work with the Japanese. So was Percy's brother Leon, who ran the department store before the occupiers seized it. And it seemed that Percy, too, was willing. If Alfred felt surprise at this admission, he tried not to show it, struggling to hold his poker face as Percy talked. In unsettled times like these, the Kwoks needed not just skilled but utterly dependable men who would be loyal to them and their businesses—not to the Chiang regime, the puppet government, or the Japanese. That's why he wondered if Alfred might be interested in coming to work for Wing On.[20]

Percy understood the implications of his invitation. Enemy aliens were generally forbidden from working, so Alfred could accept the job only if he identified as a Chinese citizen, rather than an American. Of course, the citizenship issue was easy in some ways: Both the Chiang and Wang regimes claimed that all ethnic Chinese, wherever born, were Chinese citizens. Still, the long-term ramifications for Alfred's status were unclear if the United States won the war. Alfred said he needed to talk over a big decision like this with Alice, and Percy agreed to wait.[21]

Back home that night, the Lees discussed the proposal. Even before Percy made his offer, Alice and Alfred had begun to wonder if they should forgo repatriation altogether. To begin with, Alice worried about her parents if Herbert's drinking got worse and she was not around, or if assassins killed her baby brother. But her main concern, and Alfred's, was Alson. Though now fifteen by American understanding, he was sixteen under the traditional Chinese method of counting, and tall for his age. He would almost certainly be seventeen by the time a third repatriation exchange occurred, if it actually ever happened. The puppet administration might very well refuse to let a young, healthy, military-age Chinese citizen leave. If Alice and Alfred stayed in China, maybe they could protect him, but the US government had been very clear about the consequences of refusing possible repatriation: the loss of those subsistence loans that were keeping the Lees afloat.[22]

The next morning, Alfred called Percy and accepted the job at Wing On. After he got his first week's wages, he went down to the American Association, removed his family's name from the repatriation list, and paid back every penny of the loans.[23]

THIRTY-ONE

Kay and Ming Tai

NEW YORK, 1943–1944

ONE JULY EVENING, THE TYPONDS' phone rang just as Helen was cooking dinner. Wiping her hands on her apron, she picked up the receiver and heard an unfamiliar man on the other end of the line. For half a second she wondered if it might be some prankster, but unfortunately the voice sounded fully adult and very serious. Yes, she confirmed, she was Mrs. George Typond. She apologized for not having been home to get his earlier calls, but she worked at the Sperry plant in Queens. Yes, she would absolutely be happy to come down to Foley Square and answer some questions. George had wandered into the kitchen, and now his expression changed from curiosity to alarm. He and Helen both knew that Foley Square was the location of the US Courthouse.[1]

Helen arranged to take the day off from Sperry and presented herself at the FBI office in lower Manhattan. In a small waiting room that smelled like ashtrays and stale coffee, she clutched and unclutched her handbag, adjusted her hat for the tenth time, and tried to tune out the nerve-rattling sounds of jangling telephones and banging typewriters. Finally, a secretary showed her into one of the offices, where Special Agent Clarence Johnson introduced himself and motioned for her to sit down. He needed to ask her a few questions about Herbert Moy, he said.[2]

Helen had long feared this would happen. She and Kay had known about their baby brother's wartime activities for quite a while, ever since Adelaide's days in Hong Kong. Ad had instantly recognized her uncle's voice over the radio—how could she not, since they had grown up sharing pony rides, trips to the shore, and holiday dinners? But Johnson did not need to know any of this.

Keeping a pleasant, vague smile on her face, Helen confirmed to the agent that Herbert was indeed her brother, and then she answered various queries about his education and career choices. Johnson asked why Herbert had gone to China. Helen paused, thinking about how to explain to this buttoned-up white man the way ferocious racial discrimination had thwarted her brother's ambitions. When had Herbert last been in contact? Helen said she had not heard directly from him for years, but then again, he had never been the best letter writer. And of course, since Pearl Harbor, she had received no word from any of her family members trapped in occupied China. Finally, Johnson inquired about Helen's brother Bill and sister Kay—did she think they could offer additional information? Helen took a deep breath. "No," she lied, shaking her head emphatically. To discourage the agent even more, she served up another complete whopper: Kay, Helen said, did not really speak English, so she would be of no assistance at all. When Johnson nodded and wrote down this bit of misinformation, Helen could almost hear the sound of Kay's laughter; maybe she could have mentioned her sister's bound feet, too.[3]

There was not much else to laugh about. In August, the Justice Department indicted, in absentia, eleven Americans in East Asia, charging them with treason for broadcasting for the enemy. The eleven included Herbert, whom the newspapers described as a "New York–born Chinese, mainstay for news and comments on Jap-controlled radio, [who] can easily rate [as] the most brilliant, fluent, and persuasive of the renegade crop."[4]

Herbert's treason indictment added to the burden of fear that the Chins, Moys, and Typonds carried through 1943. Kay and Ming Tai knew that in May, Adelaide had given birth in Chongqing to a healthy baby girl, so when the Japanese bombed the city that summer for the first time in two years, it put the Chins on edge. Meanwhile, they could only hope that their Shanghai family members were alive and safe. By fall, the local papers were printing the names of American civilians due to arrive in New York on the *Gripsholm* in the second prisoner exchange. Kay, Helen, Bill, and their family members eagerly scanned each updated passenger list, but the absence of familiar names—in fact, of seemingly any Chinese names—was even more disappointing this time around than it had been during the *Gripsholm*'s first exchange. Were their loved ones in an internment camp with other Americans, or were they on the outside? Both options sounded awful, with recent repatriates describing great privation and suffering everywhere in Japanese-controlled China.[5]

• • •

In early 1944, the Chins still threw their customary Chinese New Year banquet, since they had a few reasons to celebrate the Year of the Monkey. Gloria was set to graduate from NYU and Beah from Hunter College. Much to Kay's satisfaction, her home also felt full for the first time in several years. Meme was pregnant again, and, since Henry had been drafted, she and their firstborn traveled east from Seattle to stay with the Chins. Even more exciting, Adelaide cabled from Honolulu to say that she and her baby had left Chongqing and would arrive in New York in February. Not only would Kay and Ming Tai meet their new granddaughter, but Jacqueline would get to see her mother for the first time in almost six years.[6]

The New Year banquet was the one family function that Shau Hong, Daisy, and their children routinely attended, but this time they begged off. Shau Hong had a toothache, and anyway, the older girls always seemed to be working, putting in another shift at the war plant to help support their parents and siblings. Ming Tai did not really give their absence another thought until Shau Hong called him a week or two later with some troubling news: The dentist said he did not have a cavity, but rather a potentially cancerous lesion in his mouth. At Bellevue Hospital, a specialist quickly diagnosed stage 4 throat cancer and gave Shau Hong a bleak prognosis. The only way to slow the cancer's growth was with radiation therapy, an extremely painful treatment that kept him hospitalized for weeks and left him with burns all around his throat.[7]

Shau Hong desperately missed his children, since his physicians prohibited any visitors except Daisy. Finally, on the first warm day in May, the doctors let her wheel him out on the hospital's balcony so that he could at least *see* his children, who had gathered on the pavement below. The older ones tried not to reveal their shock at his burnt, bandaged neck and gaunt appearance, but almost all of them began to cry as their father weakly waved from his wheelchair. It was the last time they ever saw him alive. Days later, his doctors moved him to a Bronx hospice that also limited his visitors. Shau Hong passed away in mid-August 1944; his death certificate listed him as a "student," the only occupation in which he had ever been successful.[8]

Daisy had known for months that her husband was dying, yet his actual passing stunned and frightened her. She had never worked outside the home, still struggled with English, and had been married to Shau Hong since she was seventeen. He had left her with significant medical bills, no savings, and seven children under eighteen. Three of them were younger than six. At least the family had not depended on his wages to survive, since he had not worked for years. Instead, they lived off Eleanor's hospital job, Muriel's keypunch position, and whatever part-time work Janet could string together while earning her degree at Hunter.[9]

Fortunately, Ming Tai agreed to pay for Shau Hong's casket and his funeral at a Chinatown mortuary. There, Daisy knew exactly what to do, weeping loudly through the service and the dinner afterward in the way Chinese tradition mandated for widows. Helen understood the display, as did May's parents, who still lived in the same building as Daisy and her children. But the handful of Shau Hong's half brothers and sisters who attended the service seemed baffled. Ming Tai had long kept his Chinese and American lives fairly separate, and the unusual convergence at the funeral showed just how distinct they remained.[10]

In the years that followed, Ming Tai saw his oldest son's family infrequently, sometimes only once a year at the New Year banquet. Usually he would slip Daisy a hundred dollars and tell the children to behave themselves, but other than that he played little role in their lives. For some reason, he could never bring himself to be a real presence for this particular set of grandchildren, and Kay didn't push him. Perhaps Ming Tai saw nothing strange about growing up without a father—he had done so himself sixty years earlier—but whatever the case, Shau Hong's children never completely forgave him.[11]

THIRTY-TWO

Ernest and Ruth

CHONGQING, KUNMING, AND SHANGHAI 1943–1945

ERNEST FELT CHONGQING IN EVERY SINEW of his legs. Free China's wartime capital clung to the cliffs at the confluence of the Yangzi and Jialing Rivers, and its buildings—or what was left of them after years of Japanese air raids—perched awkwardly on slopes that rose at sharp angles from the water. Some foreigners and wealthier Chinese traveled the narrow streets by rickshaw or even in sedan chairs that bearers carried up steeply staired lanes from the riverfront. Unable to afford such luxuries, Ernest walked and walked and walked, painfully aware both of the knots in his calves and of the shrinking value of his Customs College salary. The Nationalist government was simply printing money now, making inflation as much a part of life in the capital as rats, fog, and privation.[1]

US servicemen, diplomats, and journalists in the city constantly disparaged the place, but Ernest had little patience for their endless stream of complaints about Chongqing's foul odors, inedible food, filth and poverty, grasping merchants, beggars and urchins, and incompetent, corrupt officials. After all, white foreigners ate and lived better than almost anyone else in the wartime capital, and their critiques often cast the beleaguered, bombed-out city as a stand-in for China and its people. Still, Ernest hated how much he agreed with some of the criticism, especially as his salary lost value and he struggled to make ends meet. The one silver lining was that he could not afford a radio, so he had few chances to hear his brother's scathing, pro-Axis commentaries on XGRS.[2]

A heavy, protective mist hung over Chongqing during much of the winter and spring, but in the notoriously torrid summer, residents came to fear clear days and the inevitable wail of air raid sirens. The Japanese had finally stopped their relentless bombing after American planes beefed up the Chinese Air

Force, but in late August 1943 the enemy returned for the first time in two years. When the air raid sirens sounded, Ernest and his colleagues rushed into the school's shelter. Though Japanese bombs killed more than twenty people that day, Ernest's niece Adelaide assured him that things had gotten much better since 1939, when bombers routinely pounded the Chongqing into rubble.[3]

Since she had just given birth, Ernest felt too embarrassed to mention how miserable he found life in the "new and improved" Chongqing. He had never known real hunger until his trek from Hong Kong, but earning enough to feed and clothe himself had become a constant struggle in Free China. And Ernest knew he was one of the more fortunate members of the Customs staff, whose morale was extraordinarily low by 1943. Many had already quit.[4]

Then Jack Young came to the rescue. He knew that his old War Area Service Corps (WASC) boss, J. L. Huang, was trying to find someone suitable to run the organization's network of hostels in Kunming, the headquarters of the Flying Tigers' successor, the US 14th Air Force. Under General Huang, a tall, glad-handing Vanderbilt graduate close to Chiang Kai-shek, the WASC arranged housing, food, and recreation, first for the Flying Tigers and later, after Pearl Harbor, for Allied soldiers in China. The WASC was growing quickly, and Huang needed someone bilingual and well organized for the Kunming position. Jack thought his wife's uncle would be perfect for the job.[5]

Shaking General Huang's hand for the first time, Ernest introduced himself as "Dr. Ernest Moy," though he possessed neither a medical degree nor a PhD. Indeed, he had not dared use the doctor title for years, since laws in most of the United States sternly forbade chiropractors from calling themselves "Dr." anything. But General Huang was none the wiser and ate it up, later describing his new "special deputy" as a "highly educated man." Ernest could tell from Jack's briefing that administrative experience would be more valuable at the WASC than a fancy degree. Ernest had the needed skills—though, as usual, he hated to think of himself as a desk jockey; deep down, he dreamed of being a man of action like Jack.[6]

At least he could dress like a man of action. The WASC was part of the National Military Council, making its staff nominally part of the armed forces. Ernest had avoided service in World War I, but he felt a surge of pride the first time he donned his new Chinese Army jacket, with its metal collar bars and WASC forearm patch. As a member of the WASC leadership team, he even held a military rank equivalent to "major general"—the rank of

Flying Tigers commander Claire Lee Chennault. All Ernest lacked was a strip of campaign ribbons.[7]

But when he arrived in Kunming, almost no one saluted him, and he quickly realized that neither Chinese nor US Army personnel saw the WASC staff as *real* officers. Much as Ernest enjoyed wearing his uniform, he soon gave up trying to get others to recognize his rank or putative military status. He envied his nephew, now a second lieutenant in the US Army. American enlisted men and NCOs snapped to attention and saluted when Jack walked by.[8]

Unfortunately, much of Ernest's new job involved frustrating negotiations with US military officials whose attitudes frequently swung between patronizing and condescending. Ernest always responded quickly to their never-ending complaints about poor sanitary conditions and bad food at WASC hostels. In return, he gently suggested that the US government pay the money it owed his organization, or diplomatically reminded Army Air Corps officers of their own responsibilities for items such as "the devising of a system for water purification, the measures required for the safe handling of meat deliveries, the supply of oil for prevention of fly-breeding, the screening of mess hall doors at Hostel No. 10, and the devising of an adequate sewerage system around the mess hall of the tent area referred to in paragraph 7, section B." He tried not to let these tedious details get to him, since he knew he was doing important and valuable work.[9]

• • •

By spring 1944, Ernest and his colleagues in Kunming began to grow anxious about the course of the war. That April, the Japanese launched their largest assault of the conflict, with five hundred thousand soldiers and scores of bombers and fighters. Named Operation Ichigo, it aimed to destroy US air bases in central China, and it caught the Nationalists and their American allies completely off guard. The Japanese moved with deadly swiftness, slicing through famine-devastated areas of Henan, capturing Changsha in June, and occupying Hengyang in August. The campaign revealed both the weakness of the Nationalists' remaining units and the faulty planning and strategy of US military leaders in the China-Burma-India theater. When starving Henan farmers attacked retreating Nationalist soldiers, they also showed just how deeply KMT callousness to the suffering of ordinary citizens had destroyed trust in and loyalty to the government. WASC staff and US units alike read the reports of Japanese victories with growing concern. Might the enemy take Chongqing, or Kunming? Anything seemed possible.[10]

Such anxieties merely added to Ernest's existing concerns about the fate of his family and friends in Shanghai. He worried as well about his son Ken, who had dropped out of Georgetown to join the army in 1943. Since arriving in Free China, Ernest had received sporadic letters from his family in the United States, but military censorship and secrecy kept him from learning very much about Ken's movements and training. He did get personal news, such as a letter announcing Ken's marriage to a woman from Washington, DC, Charlotte Ackerley. Definitely not Chinese, Ernest thought, and wondered what Ruth would say. Given her own background, and her brother Paul's marriage, she might be fine with Ken's choice. Or not, since no woman of any race would ever be good enough for her son. Would she ever find out? Ernest had no way of knowing if Ruth and Loring were still alive, since they were deep in enemy territory.[11]

He could not really imagine Ken married, or in uniform, and still pictured his oldest son as a gangly, grinning teenaged pitching phenom wearing a Nam Hwa uniform and fooling Hong Kong's finest batters. So when the tall, muscled soldier strode into his office in late summer 1944, Ernest could barely believe his eyes. His boy was now a grown man, a second lieutenant and flight navigator with the 14th Air Force. Ken proudly showed Ernest photos of his wife and, in the biggest surprise of all, their newborn infant daughter. Charlotte had given birth that April at her parents' place in Kansas, where she was staying until her husband's return. As Ernest and Ken swapped news and looked at photos of loved ones far away, both struggled to retain their composure.[12]

• • •

Ruth's heart skipped a beat when she tore open the envelope and saw the small, typed note inside. "You are requested to call upon Inspector Tanaka at Room 205, S.M.P. Hdqrs." True, she had applied to the Shanghai Municipal Police for permission to remove her enemy alien armband, and the brief note likely referred to that. But she felt a tingle of fear run up her spine at the possibility that the summons might be for something completely different and far more dangerous. Life in occupied Shanghai was filled with moments like this, though when she arrived at Tanaka's office, he merely checked her documents and issued the oddly named "Permit to Dispense with Armband."[13]

Like most Shanghai residents, Ruth tried to avoid interacting with the occupiers, but she needed the permit for her own safety. In spring 1943, the Japanese began to round up enemy alien civilians and place them in internment camps. Since Japan claimed to support "Asia for the Asiatics," the occupiers focused on white enemy nationals and allowed foreign-citizen Chinese, including Chinese Americans, to remain free. Few of them bothered with their armbands, simply melting into the crowds of ordinary Shanghai residents and moving about the city undetected. Ruth wanted to do the same, but she knew that others sometimes perceived her mixed ancestry. If one of them was a Japanese soldier, the consequences might be dire—hence the permit.[14]

Without her armband, Ruth felt freer to leave the old foreign areas in search of food and fuel, which had grown harder to find with each passing month. Of course, she always started close to home, clutching her puppet-government-issued ration stamps for sugar and butter (which by 1944 became margarine) and joining the long queue at Van Shing. She remembered the shop from before the war, when its name—which translated to "great prosperity"—seemed apt enough. Now the store's empty shelves turned its boastful moniker into a cruel joke. Hopefully Loring would have more luck at Yu Loong Shing, the only place where the two of them could redeem their coal briquette stamps. If none of the approved shops had any stock, Ruth and Loring would then range more widely, dipping deeper into their monthly loan from the Swiss government and trying to purchase what they needed on the black market.[15]

She felt increasingly grateful for Pete. When the Japanese canceled the third exchange voyage, Ruth continued the affair she had assumed would end with her repatriation. Loring was in denial, not wanting to accept that the man who lived with them and slept in his mother's bedroom was anything more than a close friend with valuable connections to the Swiss Consulate and the American Association. Was it willful ignorance? Ruth wasn't sure, though the difference in the lovers' ages fooled most of the people they knew—even her, she realized, after Pete had told her he loved her. She was unconvinced she felt the same, aware that much of her deep fondness for him reflected his attempts to get her and her son whatever they needed to survive in occupied Shanghai.[16]

Before dawn one October morning, Pete was still sleeping next to Ruth when the phone rang in the Moys' apartment. She quickly grabbed the handset before the sound woke Loring. "Hello, wai?" she said in a mix of English and Chinese. Then she gasped. The voice on the other end was Pete's brother

David, who had snuck out of the Kims' apartment and was calling from a neighbor's house. Several members of the Kempetai, the Japanese military police, were at the Kims' flat looking for Pete. His mother and siblings had stalled the officers by saying that he was out buying bread, but David told his brother to get home fast. Throwing on his coat and shoes, Pete sprinted out the door and down the street. Ruth felt a wave of nausea as she watched him from her window.[17]

The Kempetai men took Pete away and threw him in jail, where they interrogated him about his connections to the United States, the American Association, and the Swiss Consulate. The beatings began soon after, because Pete refused to accept the Japanese "suggestion" that he work for them as an English-language broadcaster. Ten days later, the Kempetai men finally released the battered and shaken young man. He now knew just how much information the Japanese had gathered about him, his family, and his friends. To his horror, he also discovered that while he was in jail, the military police had visited his mother several times to see if she would contradict his answers to their questions.[18]

The Kempetai men warned Pete not to leave the city, but as the weeks passed, he began to think about fleeing Shanghai. Of course, doing so would not be easy, since he had noticed the Japanese agents who routinely tailed him. Then, in early 1944, local authorities announced a draft of all men over sixteen who were not heads of household. That meant Dick, Pete knew, so the two brothers decided to make a break for it. Pete bade Ruth farewell but told her little else, not wanting to endanger her and Loring. The moment the weather grew warm enough to travel safely into the interior, Pete and Dick donned Chinese clothing and boarded a southbound night train toward Hangzhou.[19]

One humid June night just weeks after Pete's departure, Ruth heard a gentle tap at the front door. Her heart skipped a beat—she was not expecting visitors—but she forced herself to walk in an obviously unhurried manner to the front of the apartment. Before he left, Pete had warned her that the Japanese were watching him, and possibly her. Had occupiers discovered Pete's disappearance? Would the Kempetai arrest Ruth and torture her to find out what she knew? Taking a deep breath, she opened the door just a crack and peeked out. There stood a man dressed in Chinese clothing, his ruddy face eerily familiar and yet completely out of context. Then he grinned, and she realized she was looking at Jack Young.[20]

• • •

Ruth often teased Loring about his serious face, but the teen smiled broadly as Jack told them that Ernest was safe and well in Kunming. He had news about Pete, too, though Ruth tried to remain impassive as she listened to the story. Jack said that he and his mission partner had been sitting in the backroom of a teahouse in Kukong, the capital of unoccupied Guangdong, plotting how they would enter occupied China and reach Shanghai. Glancing through the doorway, he recognized Pete and Dick at a table in the outer room and discreetly summoned the two. Before the brothers left Kukong, they gave their identity cards, ration stamps, and other documents to Jack and his partner, enabling the men to get train tickets and food in the occupied areas. The Kims also briefed the American spies on the best way to slip into Shanghai; without their assistance and documents, Jack said, he and his partner might have made the entire trip on foot, and at much greater peril.[21]

Now, though, he needed Ruth and Loring's help. He had to find a place to stay, a safe base of operations for carrying out his Shanghai mission. He had already linked up with the remaining Kim brothers, who agreed to help him gather intelligence, but the Japanese were watching the Korean family's apartment and movements closely. Since the Kempetai had not visited the Moys, the occupiers had likely not noticed their involvement with Pete. Could Jack stay with Ruth and Loring? Mother and son looked at each other, knowing that the Japanese would likely torture and kill them if their involvement came to light. Turning to Jack, Ruth nodded. He could share her sons' room with Loring and sleep in Ken's old bed.[22]

Over the next four months, the apartment became the hub of a spy network that eventually included mother and son. Ruth initially assumed that her main task would be scavenging enough food for Jack, but by midsummer she found herself managing the web of Chinese women who evaded Japanese notice to pass on vital information to him. Ruth also took delivery of the newspapers that Pete's younger brother Art purchased in Shanghai's heavily Japanese neighborhood and then handed to older brother David, who brought them to her. Loring, still an avid photographer, quietly began snapping pictures of anything he felt might be useful for the American war effort, from Japanese broadsheet announcements to the faces and official seals of new senior officers. He also delivered messages for his cousin's spy network, unobtrusively slipping in and out of the French Concession. Meanwhile, Jack ranged across the city, gathering intelligence, taking detailed notes, and sending his coded findings to his contacts in Free China.[23]

During the months they shared a home, Ruth and Jack occasionally discussed the Lees, whom Loring still visited on occasion. Jack avoided getting in touch with his wife's aunt and uncle—the fewer people who knew he was in Shanghai, the better—but he soon came to share Ruth's disgust with their activities. In her eyes, they were little better than traitors: Alfred was working for the turncoat Kwoks at Wing On, Alice was socializing with Herbert, and Ruth knew from Pete that the Lees had removed their names from the repatriation list. Loring also told her that Alson and his friends sometimes went with Herbert to the German embassy to watch war films. Hearing such reports, Jack came to assume the worst about Alfred and Alice.[24]

He left the Moys' apartment in October 1944 after sensing that the Japanese were closing in. Jack could easily see the signs: the growing number of enemy agents loitering near the Moys' block of Rue Lafayette and the radio cars patrolling the area to determine who was transmitting illicit wireless signals. Before Jack disappeared, he promised Loring and Ruth that if he got out of occupied China, he would let Ernest know they were alive and well. Ruth asked Jack to tell Pete, too.[25]

THIRTY-THREE

Alice and Alfred

SHANGHAI, 1944–1945

THE JAPANESE CUT AND CUT AND CUT. They cut Shanghai into pieces with barbed wire and checkpoints and guards. They cut the hours of electricity that city residents received each day. They cut the number of trams that ran along the streets. They cut the amount of food available, so that the Lees' servants now waited in long lines to buy staples for the family, and the rice usually had pebbles in it. They cut the supply of butter altogether—oh, how Alice missed butter!—and replaced it with cheap, rancid margarine. By spring 1943, they even cut most of the remaining foreign community, placing many of Alfred and Alice's friends in internment camps.[1]

Yet amid all of this upheaval, the family's routines remained strangely unchanged. Alfred still went to work each morning, though he now rode a bicycle to an office in the New Wing On building on Nanking Road. Alice and Lenore still played mahjong every week, though now they sat at a table positioned under a window for more light. Alson still spent most of his waking hours thinking about sports, talking about sports, and playing sports, though many of his classmates quit the track and rugby teams to conserve precious calories. And Alice and her son still visited Han Ying and Moy Sing almost daily, though both were in failing health.[2]

When Alice saw Lenore or her parents by herself, she usually rode her bicycle, which Alfred bought for her on the black market after the Japanese confiscated the family car. The older Moys and Billy and Lenore Chang all lived at the Pax Apartments, too far to walk from the Lees' place, and Alice felt safer when moving through the streets as quickly as possible. In Shanghai, the worsening food shortages and the growing desperation of many residents made the already yawning gap between the wealthy and the poor even worse. She and Alfred had enough to eat, marking them as extremely privileged.

Alice always denied that she and her husband were rich—in her mind, that word described people like the Kwoks—but few of Shanghai's destitute would have agreed. The Lees lived and ate far better than the vast majority of wartime residents, and Alice knew that beggars, passersby, and rickshaw pullers alike could see it in her clothing and complexion.[3]

Herbert's princely salary meant that his parents wanted for nothing—his Nazi bosses made sure of that—but the news from Europe was starting to make him jittery. Most days, he spent his off-air time in his spacious office on Great Western Road, working on scripts and listening to enemy radio stations for material. On June 6, he was jotting down ideas for a new attack on President Roosevelt when he heard the first reports of the Allied landing at Normandy. Herbert frantically began dialing around on his set, eventually intercepting a broadcast that quoted General Dwight D. Eisenhower's stunning announcement: "People of Western Europe: A landing was made this morning on the coast of France by troops of the Allied Expeditionary Force. This landing is part of the concerted United Nations plan for the liberation of Europe. . . . Although the initial assault may not have been made in your own country, the hour of your liberation is approaching."[4]

Despite the early summer heat, Herbert began to tremble, and his breath came in short gasps. Rummaging around in the bottom drawer of his desk, he pulled out the bottle of whiskey he kept there and took a quick slug of it. The alcohol's heat hit him in the back of the throat, and he began to breathe normally again. Maybe the Wehrmacht would pin down the Allied forces on the beaches and push them into the English Channel, just like in 1940.

The August day that the Allies liberated Paris, Herbert poured himself a full glass. At least, he reasoned, the Japanese seemed to be making progress in Operation Ichigo. Ever since starting at XGRS, Herbert had cast himself as a Chinese patriot who hated any kind of foreign imperialism. While he knew better than to ridicule the occupiers directly, he sometimes made snide comments on the air about the spiraling prices of food, coal, and other necessities in occupied Shanghai. Now, though, he decided to change his tune, and increasingly he heaped praise on Japan and the conduct of its soldiers.[5]

True, he needed a few more stiff drinks before crossing that line the first time. The Nationalists in Chongqing have "a misunderstanding of Japan's aim in China," he intoned, taking a slug from his glass. The United States and Britain want "to conquer the whole of Asia and to suck the blood of the Asiatic people," and "if by any chance Japan should be conquered . . . the people of China will become the slaves of the Anglo-Americans." Writing and then reading such statements finally became easier when American bombers regularly began to appear over Shanghai late that fall.[6]

• • •

The same aircraft that terrified Herbert entranced his nephew. When the bombers started coming, Alson and some of the neighbor boys ran up to the roof of their building to get a closer look at the massive Superfortresses. Later, he compared notes with his school friends, though not when their Japanese instructors could hear them. They excitedly debated the exact number of planes and the extent of the destruction, including the way explosions broke plates, cups, and windows in people's homes. On November 12, when the collaborationist Chinese government announced the death of Wang Jingwei, Alson noted in his diary that "the Chinese government's president (?) is now Chen Gongbo," his question mark a subtle comment on the actual lack of power that puppet Chen exercised under the Japanese.[7]

Like their son, Alfred and Alice hoped that the arrival of the B-29s indicated American progress in the conflict, though they knew enough to fear what could happen before war's end. When a wave of planes bombed Shanghai's power plant, the hit left the Lees' building in darkness and disabled the pumps that brought water to their building. As the servants pulled out the Lees' kerosene lamps, Alice could not help but think about the film *Oil for the Lamps of China*, which she and Alfred had seen at the Capitol Theatre in 1938. Those days seemed so long ago.[8]

By December, the situation with Herbert had grown increasingly awkward and even uncomfortable. Whenever Alson saw his uncle, he had to remind himself not to talk about the war—not the US and Chinese P-40s that flew over the city on Christmas Eve, not the Superfortresses, and definitely not the articles he was reading in the copies of *Life* magazine that circulated on the black market. On the occasions that the Lees or Billy and Lenore socialized with Herbert, both couples took pains to avoid bringing up Allied progress in the conflict. Sometimes, though, he raised the issue himself while drunk and morose.[9]

When Alice saw Herbert by himself, she mainly stuck to a safe topic, their parents. Such discussions grew increasingly frequent and fraught by early 1945, since both Han Ying and Moy Sing were not just in poor health but actually dying. Alice now visited daily and often slept over at her parents' apartment. On January 21, when Han Ying passed away, Herbert initially joined his sister to sit with the body and greet the small groups of acquaintances and distant relatives who came to pay their respects. But soon he told her he could not take so much time away from work, and for the rest of the traditional three days and nights before burial, friends came to be with her instead.[10]

Herbert reappeared on the morning of day three to help his sister hire a horse-drawn carriage. From the Moys' apartment, the siblings took their mother's body to a funeral hall for encoffining and then to the Hungjao International Cemetery for burial. As the two walked the last part of the journey behind the carriage, each felt the inherent strangeness of trying to observe the traditional rites. This duty supposedly belonged to the oldest son, yet here they were, the youngest daughter and youngest son of a family scattered by war.[11]

• • •

Less than three weeks after Han Ying's death, Alice turned forty, and for the first time in her life, she felt old. Not adult—she ruefully recalled how *grown-up* marrying K. S. Lo had seemed, and how immature it had actually been—but *old*. Her mother was gone, her father blind, bedridden, and dying, and her son on the cusp of eighteen. She missed her family in America and longed for the prewar life she and Alfred had enjoyed so much. Of course, she knew that her husband would never see her the way she saw herself, but when she looked in the mirror these days, she noticed the bags under her eyes, the fine wrinkles, and the fatigue of the last four weeks—and four years. The white clothing that mourning families customarily wore did not help much, she decided, shaking her head at her reflection. She glanced longingly at the lovely red cloth that Alson, completely forgetting about mourning customs, had given her as a birthday gift.[12]

Late that afternoon, she heard voices in the hallway and a sudden, hearty knock at the door. Opening it just a crack—a wartime habit—she saw at least a dozen of her good friends crowded into the hallway. She gasped and then laughed as they smiled and yelled, "Surprise!" in a mix of Chinese and English. Her face lit up, and she turned to see her husband beaming behind her. Alfred never noticed her age, but he could tell she was depressed and had secretly planned the birthday gathering to raise her spirits. As the servants brought out the food they had quietly prepared, he could tell the plan was working. Alice still loved to be the center of attention, and he still loved seeing her so happy. War or no war, nothing would ever change that.[13]

THIRTY-FOUR

Kay and Ming Tai

NEW YORK, 1944–1945

IN THE WEEKS AFTER HELEN'S interview at the FBI office, she told herself over and over that she had not *really* lied about anything, or at least anything important. Bill had last seen Herbert in 1937, and of course Kay spoke perfect English, but were those details so crucial? There was no reason to involve Kay in Herbert's troubles, or to cost Bill a job that challenged and interested him. Helen was a faithful churchgoer, a staunch believer in not bearing false witness, and an ardent patriot, but she had also grown up in New York's Chinatown, where long experience taught residents to expect little fairness from the government. Since Herbert was out of its reach, the FBI might try to find big and small ways to punish his family instead.

Fortunately, her performance, and the siblings' larger strategy, had succeeded. They had worked it out carefully with Newark Chinatown leader Harry Lee Sooey. FBI agents with a copy of Herbert's old passport application had contacted Harry to find out if the XGRS broadcaster still had family in the area. Harry played dumb, claiming he did not know the answer, but he promised to make discreet inquiries and report back. Of course, Harry did not need to make "inquiries," since he had known the Moys and Chins since their days in Newark—when he, his wife, Lillian, and their children lived across the street from the Victoria.[1]

So Kay, Bill, Helen, and Harry crafted a plan to deal with the FBI. Harry would vouch for the siblings' patriotism and loyalty in his report to the Bureau. But he would claim to have located contact information only for Helen, to whom the FBI would likely reach out first. She had insisted on this, since she had the least to lose. The Typonds did not depend on her job, nor did they have any paper sons in their family, unlike Bill's father-in-law Wong Soon, or Ming Tai himself. Herbert's choices had broken Helen's heart, but she could do nothing to help him now. What she could do was cooperate as fully as possible with the authorities while deflecting interest away from Bill and Kay.[2]

• • •

To Kay's relief, no FBI agent showed up at the Chinatown Inn to ask uncomfortable questions. Ming Tai hoped to expand the business, but Herbert's situation would create some complications. *Expansion* did not mean new locations or a bigger footprint, however. The Palais's bankruptcy still haunted Ming Tai, whose old flamboyance had turned into caution. He no longer dreamed of rebuilding the restaurant empire he had created in the 1920s; instead, he simply hoped to restore his family to comfort and security. Now on the cusp of sixty-five, he was feeling his age, especially since Shau Hong's death. Though Ming Tai was still trim and energetic, Kay suddenly noticed his receding hairline and the way he always wore his glasses nowadays. She felt older too, though she was more than a decade younger than he. At some point, people even stopped expressing surprise that Jacqueline was her granddaughter rather than her daughter.[3]

The Palais had thrived during Prohibition, but what expansion meant these days was serving wine and liquor, which Ming Tai could tell was the key to real profits. Since late 1941, new licenses had been almost as hard to get as liquor itself: Defense plants greedily lapped up alcohol for industrial use and wanted sober workers. In late 1944, though, the end of the war in Europe finally seemed possible, and the War Production Board and the Office of Price Administration hinted at the end of rationing and shortages. Jim Typond heard through his political connections that the State Liquor Authority's informal limit on licenses would probably loosen up soon.[4]

The Chins knew from other friends in the business that getting a liquor license was not particularly easy even in ordinary times. Only citizens could apply, though if Herbert's actions prompted federal authorities to look into Ming Tai's status, Kay knew that a liquor license would be the least of their concerns. Any obvious connection to her baby brother could imperil the Chins. Theoretically, Herbert should have no bearing on their application, but who would approve a license for a traitor's family? Agent Johnson could easily squash their hopes.[5]

Luckily, the restaurant received its liquor license early in 1945, and the Chins leapt into action. Plans in hand, they closed the Chinatown Inn and started ripping out the paneling and banquettes. Partitioning the space into thirds, they mapped out how to install a bar on the far left side of the building, with a separate glass entrance door. Wartime shortages of labor and materials inevitably slowed the renovations and also dictated some décor choices. While the Palais had leaned imaginary French, with heavy blue velvet and yards of gold glitz, the Chins this time chose a minimalism they called "modernist." The lack of ornamentation allowed them to save money and avoid some of the worst supply bottlenecks. To give the place more curb appeal, they tore out the red siding on the front and replaced it with glass blocks, which seemed much more up-to-date.[6]

As the new space took shape, Ming Tai and Kay decided to transform their reopening into a grand opening by completely shedding the old Chinatown Inn identity. After all, the name had originally been a money-saving gambit, allowing them to reuse the sign from the failed Chinatown Casino. The Inn's popularity had enabled the couple to achieve genuine financial stability for the first time since the Depression, but they envisioned the renovated space as a new restaurant with a distinct identity, and they finally had enough money to splash out for a fresh sign, too. After considerable discussion, they decided to call the place the Pacific Restaurant, after the ocean that touched both the United States and China. The new name also reflected their hopes for a peaceful future for the two nations—and, by extension, for their own family.

· · ·

Like Kay, Bill also worried that Agent Johnson would show up at Sperry and ask his bosses if they knew that their employee's brother was a suspected traitor. Bill's work was hardly top secret, but the place was a *defense plant*, for God's sake, and he imagined his supervisors telling him to leave and never come back. He already suspected that Sperry would happily replace him the moment the white veterans returned. Still, Bill had started to let himself dream about the future, something he had rarely done in his life. Before the war, almost every Chinese American man of his generation worked in a restaurant or a laundry. If they wanted something different, they usually had to emigrate to China, as he, Herbert, Ernest, and so many of their other friends had done. George Wong, whose sister Bill had married, was still trapped in occupied Shanghai because of that.

But the Sperry job had given Bill a taste of freedom from waiting tables and from the customers who treated him like a stereotype. As the months passed, he felt more and more determined that after the war, he would figure out some way to hold on to that freedom. When Bill read that Brooklyn Polytechnic was running classes for defense-sector employees who wanted to improve their skills and knowledge, he did not have to think twice before enrolling. He knew that if he wanted to keep working in electronics, he would need to be far more qualified than his white competitors. That meant getting all the education he could.[7]

. . .

Helen never said so, but even she worried that Agent Johnson would show up at the Tag Building any minute, accuse her of lying, and convince her supervisor to fire her. Really, she knew she should feel lucky that she did not need her job, which was just her way of contributing to the nation's war effort. George made a fairly good living, certainly enough to support the four of them and his parents. Yet Helen loved the work she did and loved the first real paying job she had ever had. Running a lathe took concentration and skill, and she was very good at it. Although Helen kept her own home neat as a pin, she did not mind that at the end of her shift, her overalls were flecked with iron shavings and smelled of machine oil. And she took great pride in the fact that the lathe required a degree of physical strength many of the workers at Sperry lacked. To her delight, she could even feel her biceps hardening the way they had back at the Savage School of Physical Education. George was not an athletic father, leaving it to his wife and brother to play ball with the kids. So Donald whooped with surprise and delight when, after work one day, Helen flung a hard, cracking fastball into his catcher's mitt.[8]

She earned an award from plant leaders impressed by her work, but the real reward was the welcome fatigue she felt at the end of the day, a fatigue that made sleep possible. Because—like Kay, Ming Tai, Bill, and May, as well as much of the rest of the Chinese American population—Helen had to find a way to live with the nagging fears about the fate of her family members in occupied China. The siblings at least knew that Herbert was still alive, but they had no idea about anyone else.[9]

THIRTY-FIVE

Ernest and Ruth

KUNMING AND SHANGHAI, 1945

AS ERNEST'S JEEP APPROACHED the gate, he admired the way the mossy tiled roofs peeked above the walls of Kunming's WASC hostel. The compound, his home for the past year, still looked like the quiet, leafy college campus it had been before the war. After several days in the field, Ernest was always glad to be back, and today he was especially ready for a change of clothes and a shower. At Building B, he climbed the stairs to his second-floor quarters, which served as both bedroom and office. Flipping on the light, he stared around the room in stunned disbelief: Where were his uniforms, his papers, his books? Suddenly he heard footsteps and turned to see his deputy, Y. D. Wong, looking both apologetic and angry. McDonald, one of the American lieutenants, had demanded the room for his unit's use, and Wong had patiently explained why he could not have it. But as soon as Wong left, the American got someone to remove Ernest's belongings and office files and dump them downstairs. Even worse, Wong sputtered, McDonald had just disrupted the weekly memorial service for Sun Yat-sen.[1]

Ernest shook his head in disgust. He could easily imagine the sneering, arrogant white man berating poor Wong. So many US soldiers smugly believed that every Chinese they met was beneath them. Since joining the WASC, Ernest had arranged numerous cultural events and handed out countless English-language pamphlets to American soldiers to teach them about Chinese culture. He would have told anyone who asked that his goal was education, but really, it was respect—to push these white men to see the Chinese as allies and fellow humans, not racial inferiors. (That he tried to bond with the US officers by telling the occasional racist joke about Black people did not strike him as problematic.)[2]

Supposedly the American military wanted to foster such respect as well. During Ernest's first month in Kunming, he found and flipped through a copy of the US Army's *Pocket Guide to China*. As he read the very first pages, he found himself nodding vigorously. "Japan will harp on the color question first, last, and all the time. She will tell the Chinese . . . that Americans look down on nonwhite peoples," it said. "To counteract this propaganda you have to show the Chinese that the Americans treat the Chinese as we treat any of our allies, and that we respect them as human beings on an equality with ourselves." A year later, Ernest wondered at his own naivete. The pamphlet had been abandoned, left at the hostel by an American soldier who probably never even bothered to read it.[3]

Now Ernest drafted a complaint letter to the US Army's WASC liaison. As he described McDonald's actions, Ernest felt a surge of anger that made him abandon his usual diplomatic tone and deliver an uncharacteristic rebuke about the memorial ceremony disruption: "In China today such intrusions, especially by a national of another country, upon an official and mandatory memorial service is a serious affront, intolerable to the national sense of the Chinese people." Ernest knew that China desperately needed American support to fight Japan, but on days like this, he could almost understand Herbert's disillusionment. *Almost.* After all, Ernest knew the horrors of what the Japanese were doing in China, both from what he had seen with his own eyes and what he heard from friends and colleagues.[4]

One of those friends had lived with Ernest until just recently. Before the war, Ernest had known seventeen-year-old Dick Kim only slightly as one of Loring's many friends. But in summer 1944, Dick and his older brother Pete escaped from occupied Shanghai and arrived in Guilin, a major center of US Army operations. American officials whisked Pete away to Chongqing for weeks of interviews about the situation in Japanese-controlled areas, while Dick continued on to Kunming, where someone tipped Ernest off about the teen's imminent arrival. Since refugees from the Japanese Ichigo campaign were flooding into the city, Ernest insisted that Dick stay with him. He also made sure the youngster had access to food and even found him a job at the US Army Post Office. The young man deeply appreciated such generosity and tactfully said nothing about Pete and Ruth's relationship. Dick had just moved out after joining the army the previous December.[5]

Ernest missed the young man, who reminded him of his own sons, but he had little time to dwell on such feelings. To the relief of almost everyone in Kunming, by January 1945, Chinese and US forces seemed to have finally halted the Ichigo campaign. With the Nazis retreating across Europe, the Allies were also starting to shift resources to the Asia theater, and scores of US troops now arrived in Kunming every week. Although Ernest found many of the men as arrogant as McDonald, he was happy that the tide was finally turning. And when Jack Young dropped by after his return from Shanghai, Ernest felt lighter and happier than he had in months. Jack assured him that Wang Jingwei was dead as a doornail; he had seen the traitor's body himself before leaving occupied China. But to Ernest, Jack's most important news was that Ruth and Loring were safe and well, as were Moy Sing and Han Ying.[6]

• • •

That January, they celebrated Ken's twenty-fourth birthday with the guest of honor absent. Ruth baked a cake, though it was a short, flat thing with only token amounts of eggs, sugar, and flour. Loring set his camera timer while Ruth placed Ken's framed high school graduation photo—the last picture they had of him—on an end table behind the cake. Then she lit the candles and Loring rushed around to sit next to her for the picture. They had posed like this before—the previous Christmas, they even set up Ken's photo under their tree—playing a game intended to bolster their spirits.[7]

Each photo was a poignant expression of the hope that the three would see each other again. In the darkest days of the occupation, Ruth and Loring worked hard to reassure each other of that likelihood, especially once the third repatriation voyage fell through. Neither knew how long the conflict in China would drag on or what the Japanese would do to Shanghai in the meantime. By early 1945, the regular sight of American aircraft over the city was deeply encouraging, and Ruth and Loring easily read the truth between the lines of Japanese news bulletins. When Domei blasted the "barbaric enemy" for daring to "defile the objectives of Japanese reverence and veneration," mother and son celebrated the fact that American bombers had struck Tokyo and probably even the imperial palace. Reports that US troops were fighting to cross the Rhine but faced "stubborn resistance" from Nazis blowing up the bridges told them that retreating enemy units were desperate to slow the American advance into Germany. Even XGRS could not hide this truth.[8]

Ruth still tuned in occasionally, since it was the safest choice these days. Many people in occupied Shanghai covertly listened to Allied stations despite

Japanese prohibitions, but she and Loring had grown more cautious since Jack's departure. Mother and son knew that the Japanese had been closing in on their apartment, so for now they scrupulously followed the rules. That's how they heard the news of President Roosevelt's death, which a scornful Herbert announced in his April 13 program. "Only the tyrannical will of Franklin Delano Roosevelt forced the American people to shoulder the burden of a ghastly, costly, and totally unnecessary war," he claimed. "Roosevelt was a victim of his own insensate ambitions. He set out to conquer the world. He succeeded only in destroying himself."[9]

Roosevelt's death saddened Ruth, but not as much as what Herbert had become. After D-Day, with his paymasters retreating across Europe, XGRS's star broadcaster suddenly stopped making his snide asides about the Japanese. Since January 1945, the shift had become even clearer. Herbert completely toed the Japanese line, parroting their claims to be fighting against white supremacy and Anglo-American domination of China. Ruth had loathed Herbert's decision to work for the Nazis, but she was completely sickened by his willingness to serve the Japanese. He had once accused them of having "flooded the world with false allegations and propaganda," but now he was doing it for them.[10]

Ruth still remembered Herbert as a sweet and clever child whose parents and siblings doted on him. During one of her first winters in New York, she and Ernest took Bill and Herbert ice skating at the Van Cortlandt Park lake, twirling them while a light snow fell. At thirteen, Bill already struck her as slightly beaten down by the bigoted slights that Chinese Americans of his generation so often encountered; his baby brother, on the other hand, was a cheerful chatterbox who seemed impervious to scorn. Of course, Ruth knew that Herbert had grappled with racism as a teen and young man, but only now did she see what it had done to him.[11]

Still, she could never forgive him for the choices he had made. For now, Herbert was safe, comfortable, and well fed, while Ruth was not sure if she and Loring could survive another year of war. By early 1945, coal and food had grown increasingly scarce, while raging inflation sapped the value of the loans the Swiss consulate disbursed each month. The staff there tried to find ways to increase the monthly allowances, but the Japanese refused to consider the idea. So when Herbert speculated about what would happen if American troops landed on the China coast—"Shanghai citizens are used to wars around them and they have managed to weather them so far and are ready for whatever may come"—Ruth just had to laugh. Yes, she was ready for the much-anticipated US landing that would lead to the end of the war. It could not come too soon for her.[12]

But it did not happen that way at all. One August afternoon, Ruth and Loring heard the first hazy rumors about a terrible new weapon the United States had just used against Japan. No one in Shanghai knew exactly what had happened, since the Japanese government initially said nothing. In his next broadcast, Herbert seemed to confirm that something immense had indeed occurred, commenting that "the new atomic bomb which the Allies claim to have used in their raid on Hiroshima last Sunday open[s] up new possibilities in inhuman and barbaric warfare." Ruth knew what an atom was, but now she wracked her brain. What was an atomic bomb?[13]

THIRTY-SIX

Alice and Alfred

SHANGHAI, 1945

ON THE MORNING OF AUGUST 16, the Lees' phone rang just after breakfast. From down the hall, seventeen-year-old Alson heard his mother pick up the receiver and then, seconds later, begin to sob. He jumped up and ran out to Alice, who started to scream, "Herbert! Herbert!"—so loudly that people on the sidewalk outside looked up in alarm. Seeing his mother's stricken face, Alson knew without a doubt that his uncle must be dead. He picked up the telephone and attempted to call Alfred at the office, but he heard no tone. As Alice wept inconsolably, her desperate son looked in vain for the family's servants. Finally, he ran upstairs and used a neighbor's phone to reach Alfred, who said he would meet Alson and Alice at Herbert's radio station.[1]

The broadcaster's death was a shock but not a complete surprise. A few days earlier, Herbert had called the Lees to tell them that peace was imminent. The United States had dropped a second atomic bomb, this time on Nagasaki, and rumor had it that Japan was about to surrender. Excited but skeptical, Alfred phoned some of his friends, and all had heard similar news. Late that night, a few of them even brought over a precious bottle of hoarded champagne to share with the Lees. Outside, they could hear other people holding their own impromptu celebrations, including a group that sang and whooped in the middle of the street. Everyone felt both joy and relief that the war was almost over and that Shanghai had escaped further bombing.[2]

Almost everyone, that is. Herbert was the only sour face among the many people who stopped by the Lees' place the next day to discuss the latest news. Most of the visitors spoke excitedly of the unknown patriot who had strung up a Chinese national flag on Nanking Road, or of the Shanghai residents who were supposedly beating up Japanese soldiers in alleyways. Herbert grimaced at such reports and then informed his sister and brother-in-law that he was planning to kill himself to avoid punishment for his actions; since the Japanese had confiscated his German-issued pistol, he just needed to figure out how to take his own life. Horrified, the Lees attempted to talk him out of his plan, but to no avail.[3]

The next morning, Alice was still deeply shaken by her brother's declaration—so shaken that Alfred decided he must try again to change Herbert's mind. If he could just speak to his brother-in-law alone, man-to-man, surely he could get Herbert to give up this crazy idea. That afternoon, he slipped out of the house and beckoned Alson to come with him, knowing how much Herbert adored his nephew. The two hopped on their bicycles, bound for the apartment that the broadcaster had previously shared with his parents. Herbert had moved Marquita Kwan in that spring, right after Moy Sing's death, and now the once familiar flat felt strange and uncomfortable. Fortunately, Herbert's mistress was out when they arrived, and Alfred, seeing his chance, launched right into the speech he had already prepared in his head.[4]

He did not get very far before Herbert stopped him. "I know you mean well," the younger man said, "but I am determined to kill myself if we are defeated, and you will not change my mind." He explained to Alfred and Alson that his years at XGRS had been the happiest of his life. "I don't have a family, so this is the best choice," he concluded. And though he intended to leave all his money and valuables to Marquita, Herbert told Alson to come by and take his clothes after it was all over. Then Herbert asked to borrow Alfred's bike so that he could visit his parents' graves one last time. Riding away, he waved goodbye to his brother-in-law and nephew, who left the Pax Apartments carrying a garment bag full of suits that Herbert insisted they take home. Alson could never bring himself to actually wear any of them.[5]

• • •

Four days later, Alson replayed the scene in his mind as he and Alice approached the imposing modern structure that housed the radio station and German community center. As mother and son neared the building, they saw police detectives gathered around the low wall enclosing the small front yard. Then Alice gasped, having just noticed a body sprawled across the grass. Alson caught his mother's arm to keep her from going any farther, fearing she would faint if she saw Herbert's battered corpse up close.[6]

Suddenly, Alfred rushed up, having just arrived from his office on Nanking Road. After helping Alson steady Alice, he took a deep breath and approached the building, presenting himself to the policemen. Just as he had anticipated, the officers asked him to identify the body, and Alfred finally made himself look down at the corpse in the yard. Herbert lay face up, his eyes lifeless, his glasses broken, his swollen head covered with dried blood. Alfred noticed a deep slash, about five inches long, running across his brother-in-law's neck, as well as gashes on both his wrists. When one of the officers asked if the corpse was Herbert, Alfred just nodded, trying not to vomit.[7]

While Alice watched her husband from afar, Alson ran up the stairs to his uncle's old office on the third floor. Several policemen were photographing the scene, but when they finished, they allowed him to glance inside. From the doorway, he could see an empty whiskey bottle, a large puddle of dried blood on the floor, and Moy Sing's old straight razor, which Herbert had kept as a memento. Alson then realized that his uncle had first tried to kill himself by slashing his own wrists and throat with the razor, but it had not worked. Overcome by pain, Herbert had jumped out the window to hasten the end. As Alson descended the stairs, he felt overwhelmed by sadness at his uncle's wasted life and terrible death.[8]

In the days that followed, Alice swung between profound grief and white-hot anger at Marquita Kwan. Having never approved of her brother's relationship, Alice now claimed that the woman had encouraged Herbert to commit suicide. After all, Marquita stood to gain from his death, which both enriched her and freed her from a suddenly inconvenient connection to an accused traitor. Alfred tried to console Alice as she raged about that harlot's shameless behavior. Then he quietly explained to a confused Alson that Alice's fury was simply displaced sorrow.[9]

Alfred understood because he felt sorrow too. As he made arrangements for the burial, he remembered all the times over the previous months that he and Alice had urged Herbert to flee and just lie low for a while. Each time, the younger man had refused, and in spite of himself, Alfred knew why. Herbert had struggled to find a place both in America and in China, and that was *before* he betrayed both. Alfred still recalled his own days as a New York scoutmaster whose charges included little Herbie Moy, a bright-eyed, cheerful eight-year-old. As Herbie and the other Chinese American boys grew into adulthood, the Scout Law's morality and patriotism clashed with their lived experiences, whether as racial outsiders in America or as cultural outsiders in China. Herbert had made terrible choices, to be sure, but how many good options had he ever had?[10]

Three days after Herbert's death, the Lees buried him at the Hungjao International Cemetery, near the plot where the family had interred Han Ying and Moy Sing a few months earlier. Back then, Herbert performed the rites with the satisfaction that came from being the most filial Moy son. He and his siblings grew up knowing that the paramount duty of the oldest boy was to live with and care for his parents until death. However, even in New York, Ernest and his family kept their own apartment uptown; later, when Ernest told Bill and Herbert he would find them jobs in Shanghai, he had done so on the condition that *they* live with Moy Sing and Han Ying. And they had kept their end of the bargain, all while the jobs that Ernest promised them never materialized. When Ernest finally fled to Hong Kong, he had the gall to instruct Herbert to take care of Han Ying and Moy Sing, as if the younger man had not been doing so all along! But when Alice said her final goodbyes, she felt that Herbert's personal filiality could not make up for his larger crimes.

. . .

Late that same afternoon, a pair of C-46 Curtiss Commandos flew low and slow over the cemetery. Looking down from the lead plane, Pete Kim barely noticed the astonished Chinese workers staring up at him or the fresh dirt on Herbert's grave. Instead, he made a mental note of the burial ground, a key landmark indicating that the two aircraft were in the right place. A few minutes earlier, the copilot had given his seat to Pete, who was now directing the pilot to each of Shanghai's airfields in the hope that the planes could land at one of them. Hungjao Airfield had been a bust, a rutted dirt strip that looked like the Japanese had laced it with mines. So Pete told the pilot to fly east over the cemetery and then follow the line of Jordan Avenue into the French Concession. Before the planes tried the next possible airfield, Pete asked the willing pilot to buzz Ruth's apartment on Rue Lafayette and then the Kim family home on Route Pere Robert. He wanted his loved ones to know he was back in town.[11]

Around 5 p.m., the pilots finally landed successfully at Dachang airfield, a small strip northwest of the city center. Then they began negotiating with a low-ranking Japanese officer whose senior commander was drunk, a not uncommon situation in these post-surrender days. The defeated enemies were wary and suspicious, but too smart to use force against the small US team—especially when the Americans warned them of the dire consequences of any violence. Several hours later, after much back-and-forth, both sides came to an agreement: Escorted by Japanese troops and diplomats, the members of Pete's mission arrived late that night at the Swiss Consulate. Emile Fontanel and his staff greeted them with outward formality and barely suppressed smiles. The Swiss had spent almost four years trying to care for Allied civilians and POWs in their work as the neutral "protective power" in Shanghai. Now that Fontanel and his staff no longer needed to pretend to be impartial, they broke out their last bottle of champagne to drink with the Americans. They were particularly delighted to see their old friend and colleague Pete, not only safe but wearing a US Army lieutenant's bars.[12]

These were the borrowed insignia of a fake lieutenant, however. Pete had lobbied hard to join the mission, which used the crucial intelligence he had provided; the colonel overseeing the operation agreed that Pete's knowledge of Shanghai was important for the team's success. But since Pete was basically a corporal, and a noncitizen to boot, the officer gave him a rather unorthodox temporary promotion, while army friends provided pieces of uniform and insignia to make him look impressive. He needed these trappings because, as his beribboned credentials explained, "Peter Kim, United States Army, is the Official Representative of the Supreme Allied Commander, China Theater, for the purpose of establishing liaison between Allied Prisoners of War and Civilian Internees in the Shanghai area, and Allied Headquarters, China Theater."[13]

In the days after they arrived in Shanghai, Pete and the other mission members visited the city's Allied civilian and POW internment camps, where crowds of thin, weary, but jubilant prisoners cheered them as they spoke. The American soldiers pressed the Japanese to start releasing foreign nationals and then moved on to their next goal: locating the interned technicians and specialists who had once helped run the power plant and other key parts of Shanghai's mostly foreign-owned infrastructure. After US consular staff began returning to the city, the army lent them Pete, who worked long hours reuniting former internees with property that the enemy had taken, as well as assisting in the repatriation of Americans who wanted to leave China.[14]

Along the way, Pete heard more than his share of grumbling from US citizens struggling to come to grips with the new power dynamics in Shanghai. During the war, the Nationalists had successfully pushed their allies to end extraterritoriality and dismantle the foreign concessions once and for all. Now, Chinese authorities took control of the entire city for the first time in a hundred years, prompting many old foreign residents to complain about what they perceived as disrespectful Chinese police and officials. They also carped about the new Chinese names for the streets, and they blamed the spotty electrical service and terrible infrastructure on the municipal government, even though the city had endured eight years of war and occupation.[15]

Alfred and Alice did not join the chorus of naysayers, nor did many of their foreign-born Chinese friends. They had their fair share of problems, of course, from lost property and livelihoods to hard choices made under the duress of occupation. Unlike some of the Kwoks, the Lees had not thrown in their lot with the enemy, though the line was often blurry—at least in the eyes of some. The Lees occasionally saw white friends whom the Japanese had imprisoned during the war, and though most greeted the couple warmly, others accused Alfred and Alice of disloyalty. And then there was Herbert, whose infamy outlasted his death. When Chinese officials arrested Don Chisholm, an American who had broadcast for the Japanese in Shanghai, reporters inevitably compared him to Herbert. Some people also spread the claim that Herbert had not actually died by suicide but had been killed by Japanese who hated him.[16]

Alice felt a stab of pain at each new rumor and insinuation, but she tried her best to ignore the spiteful talk and instead look to the future. When the US Consulate reopened, she immediately sent messages to her family back in the States to let them know the Lees had survived the war. She also learned that the US Army was desperate for competent translators, and she easily landed a job with the Shanghai Port Command. Each morning, she biked up to the SPC offices at the Astor House Hotel, where in prewar days she and Alfred had attended club meetings and danced at society balls. Alice's work gave her an outlet for her energy and grief, as well as coveted access to beloved staples like coffee, butter, and chocolate—products she had not tasted since 1942.[17]

Alice was not the only one in the family with an army job. Alson wanted to enter college, but Chinese universities had not fully resumed operations in the formerly occupied areas. So he decided to wait on school for a year and instead work as a clerk and translator at the US Army Post Office. One day, he even sweet-talked a motor pool officer into lending him a lumbering Dodge station wagon, which he drove over rutted roads to the Lees' country house in Kiangwan. Several of the bungalow's casement windows were broken, and someone—either Japanese soldiers or ordinary looters—had broken into the place and carted off most of its contents. But at least it was still standing, and after returning the borrowed car, Alson called his father to report the good news.[18]

Alfred was jubilant, determined to repair the Kiangwan house and rebuild the life they had enjoyed before the war. Already, he and Alice were welcoming a stream of old friends returning to Shanghai, including Alson's godfather, H. C. Mei, who had been trapped in the Philippines when the Japanese invaded and spent three years in the Baguio Internment Camp. Now he came back to Shanghai to rebuild his law practice, and he and Alfred made plans to revive the Amity Lodge Masons. They talked for hours about H.C.'s side job promoting American products in China and Alfred's new position at the Kwoks' import-export and development firm. Of course, hyperinflation was rocking Shanghai's economy, but Alfred had always had a golden touch, and he was certain that the authorities would get the money situation under control very soon. Once that happened, he, H.C., and other bilingual and bicultural people were sure to become key players in the new Sino-American economic partnership that would undoubtedly define the postwar era.[19]

PART THREE

Revolution

1945–1961

WHEN JAPAN SURRENDERED IN AUGUST 1945, people across China celebrated. Not only was the war finally over after eight long years, but in 1943 the Allies had also renounced extraterritoriality and their last concessions, while the United States had repealed Chinese exclusion. Yet the cost of the conflict had been unimaginably awful: During the war, close to twenty million Chinese perished, and much of the country lay in ruins. Nor did the future seem all that bright. The anti-Japanese alliance that the Nationalists and the Chinese Communist Party (CCP) forged in 1937 after years of civil war had long since broken down, and almost everyone believed that a renewed civil war was now imminent.[1]

Across the Pacific, the United States emerged from World War II as the most powerful nation on earth. Insulated by oceans, the country largely escaped the physical devastation of war. Its economic strength was unprecedented, its citizens well fed, and its military unchallenged. This prosperity reached a broader swath of the population than ever before, with many people of color gaining access to jobs in the mainstream economy for the first time.[2]

However, the Cold War began even before the hot one ended. By early 1945, the United States and the Soviet Union were already jockeying for position, with leaders in Washington worried about Soviet attempts to dominate much of the postwar world. President Harry Truman hoped the Chinese Nationalists would become America's primary ally in East Asia but feared that a renewed civil war in China would undermine this goal. In late 1945, he sent General George C. Marshall to Nanjing to negotiate between the KMT and the CCP. Not only did the Marshall Mission fail to stop the civil war, but the continued presence of US troops made many non-Communist Chinese skeptical about the sincerity of American motives.[3]

The Chinese civil war, which broke out again in 1946, showed the continued impact of the recent Sino-Japanese conflict. During the Japanese occupation, the CCP used land reform to win over large segments of the rural population, recruited hundreds of thousands of peasant soldiers, and built a strong, well-trained, and relatively uncorrupt army and bureaucracy. By contrast, the Nationalist military never recovered from the first year of the war, when it lost many of its best officers and units. KMT weakness went beyond the battlefield and the aftereffects of the anti-Japanese struggle. Official corruption angered ordinary citizens, as did years of runaway inflation caused by the Nationalist regime's decision to print unbacked currency to cover its bills. Despite American aid and equipment, Chiang Kai-shek and his forces lost the civil war in 1949 and retreated to the island of Taiwan, also known as Formosa.[4]

Growing Soviet influence in Eastern Europe, together with the China situation, deeply influenced US domestic politics in the late 1940s. The Republican-controlled House Un-American Activities Committee began to accuse whole industries and the Truman administration of tolerating communist subversion. In early 1950, following the founding of the People's Republic of China (PRC), Senator Joseph McCarthy made his infamous claims that communist subversion in the State Department had led to the "loss of China."[5]

Initially, President Truman indicated that the United States would not intervene to stop an anticipated CCP invasion of Taiwan. This changed in mid-1950, when Soviet-backed North Korean forces invaded US-aligned South Korea. Truman not only sent US troops to Korea as part of a combined United Nations force, but also dispatched the US Seventh Fleet to patrol the Taiwan Strait and thwart the invasion of Formosa. The Korean War eventually transformed US-China relations more directly, too. In late 1950, PRC forces entered the conflict on the North Korean side, a move that prompted US authorities to surveil and even harass Chinese American communities. At the same time, the US gradually reengaged with the Nationalist government, recognizing the Republic of China on Taiwan as the legitimate government of China and signing the 1954 Mutual Defense Treaty with the KMT regime. The United States did not officially establish diplomatic relations with the PRC and recognize it as the sole legitimate government of China until January 1, 1979.[6]

THIRTY-SEVEN

Kay and Ming Tai

NEW YORK, 1945–1947

THE PACIFIC RESTAURANT OPENED in late spring 1945 with a neatly framed liquor license by the door and a newly installed air-conditioning machine. Except for these two innovations, the Chins used the tried-and-true techniques they had perfected at the Chinatown Inn: a skilled chef, moderate prices, and catering to lunch as well as dinner crowds. Kay knew they had a hit on their hands the first time one of her mahjong games ran late. Instead of heading uptown, she slept at the apartment the Chins kept over the restaurant, and when she left for home the next morning, hungry lunch customers were already crowding the sidewalk.[1]

The Pell Street apartment hosted a larger sleepover a few weeks later. On August 15, 1945, President Truman announced Japan's surrender, and the city erupted in a massive celebration. The cacophony of ringing church bells, honking cars, and drunken singing and dancing in the streets lasted into the early morning hours. No neighborhood celebrated more enthusiastically than Chinatown, where residents lit strings of firecrackers and held impromptu dragon dances with pounding drums and the large, snaking frames usually reserved for Chinese New Year. The Chins joined in the fun; for them and much of the community, the war had been going on since 1937, and almost everyone counted friends and loved ones both in the military and in Japanese-occupied China.[2]

By early September, Kay, Helen, and Bill had another reason to celebrate: They finally heard from Alice for the first time since Pearl Harbor. The siblings were overjoyed that the Lees had survived the war, though devastated to hear about the deaths of Moy Sing and Han Ying. Kay, Bill, and Helen had already learned about their youngest sibling from a ghastly wire service report in late August: "Herbert Moy was found with his throat and wrists slashed."[3]

None of them expected a happy ending for him, yet the news still came as a gut punch. Kay remembered Herbert like a favorite nephew: Spoiled yet utterly charming, he was one of Adelaide's first sidekicks and spent countless weekends in Glen Ridge. Helen felt his death more directly, for she helped raise Herbert and fruitlessly pushed him to make good choices. Faced with the horrible details of his death, she instead clung to the image of her youngest brother in 1932: smiling and funny, his lack of direction not yet verging into self-destruction. Realistic Bill had known it was over in 1943 when the FBI first started investigating Herbert, yet he quietly mourned the man to whom he had once been close, and whose decisions he both deplored and understood. When Ken sent all of them photos of the family graves at Hungjao International Cemetery, Bill was the only one who kept the picture of Herbert's.[4]

In spring 1946, Alice arrived in New York to visit her family and shared with them the details of Han Ying and Moy Sing's last days and Herbert's terrible suicide. Kay and Helen could see the toll these events had taken on her: Alice was more subdued than the free-spirited life of the party they remembered, and though Alfred was determined to rebuild their lives in China, she seemed less sure about the prospect. Still, after a few weeks crowded into the Chins' Morningside Heights apartment, she headed back to Shanghai.[5]

Her departure was part of a general exodus from the Chins' place that year. Alwin had found work as a research chemist, the kind of job that Ming Tai and Kay could never imagine a Chinese American getting before the war, and he moved to New Jersey to be closer to his company. Ronald departed for college up in the Finger Lakes, and Meme and her girls left for Seattle once the army discharged Henry. Gloria stayed with the Chins while her new husband—George Huang, a United Nations employee—was in London on a temporary assignment, but the young couple intended to find their own place when he returned.[6]

The apartment was hardly empty, yet Ming Tai and Kay knew that day was coming, and soon. Beah, who had just finished her physical therapy course at Columbia, was applying for jobs outside the city, Gloria was scouring the "apartments for rent" section, and Jack Young had just sent for Adelaide, Jacqueline, and little Chialing (whom everyone called Jolly). During the war, Jack decided to make the US Army his career; now officially an aide-de-camp in north China, he had become a crucial informal intermediary between the

Nationalists and Communists. He finally managed to arrange for his wife and daughters to join him in Beijing, too.[7]

As usual, Kay and Ming Tai said nothing to dissuade Adelaide, though they secretly wished her husband had a job like George Huang's. If Jack had to work abroad, did it always have to be in a war zone? To lessen her parents' concerns, Adelaide sent them a series of amusing, newsy letters from the Youngs' temporary home in Beijing, where the girls' playmates included the daughter of a top Communist general, Ye Jianying. Among other tidbits, the Chins learned that General Ye insisted the Youngs bring ten-year-old Jacqueline along to dinner one night so he could practice his English with her.[8]

The Chins appreciated such cheerful stories that winter. One of their first notes to Adelaide contained the terrible news that doctors had summoned Gloria to London in late November. For weeks, George suffered from a mysterious ailment that suddenly became debilitating, and he died within days of Gloria's arrival in Britain. After burying her twenty-seven-year-old husband, she boarded a flight back to New York, struggling all the while to understand how the future she had imagined for herself could have dissolved this way.[9]

• • •

Following Japan's surrender, defense contractor Sperry started cutting its workforce, and since Helen did not need her war job, she gave notice before the dreaded pink slip arrived. Everyone knew they would lay off the women first, and of course she still had plenty to keep her busy—cleaning the house, shopping, cooking, and church work took up much of her time. Still, life seemed much less interesting now, though her aging in-laws suddenly needed her in new ways. In his mid-eighties, Yip Typond was very slow and frail, and even fiercely independent Grace accepted help more often. Helen assisted both of them willingly and gratefully, remembering all the times during the war when Grace picked Donald up from school or cooked dinner for the whole family. Some of the big plants on Long Island offered daycare, but Sperry did not, and many of the women who worked with Helen depended on family or friends for childcare. When the war ended, those arrangements often unraveled, forcing out many who had been determined to keep their jobs.[10]

Now on the cusp of middle school, Donald was essentially a miniature version of George, thick glasses and all. When the Typond clan got together, Jim was still the one who roughhoused and played catch with the kids, but Donald and George were bonding more and more over their love of science and tinkering. Certainly, no one smiled more broadly when Donald's model airplanes won prizes. Helen was proud of him and equally proud of Jeanne, who entered Adelphi University in 1946 and took her Uncle Jim's advice to study business. Jeanne lived at home but did not spend much time there, except on weekends. Helen missed her, but the prospect that her daughter would earn the degree she herself had never attained delighted her.[11]

• • •

Bill managed to keep his job at Sperry through the first rounds of layoffs. Perhaps his extra training at Brooklyn Poly made the difference, but he wondered how long he could hang on once the white veterans started returning—especially those who used their GI benefits to get a degree. In the evenings, he continued to teach himself electrical engineering from books borrowed from friends and local libraries.[12]

Despite Bill's long nights, the Moys always made time to see his sisters, and they spent even more time with May's large and close-knit family, whose members gathered for every birthday and holiday at the Wongs' apartment in Harlem. Each time he walked through the door, Bill still shuddered a tiny bit, for he never forgot the humiliation of having to live with his in-laws and wait tables at Wong Soon's restaurant after returning from Shanghai. May's brother George and his family, recently repatriated from China themselves, now slept in that same bedroom and looked like they might be there for a while, since an influx of returning veterans had worsened the existing housing crisis in New York.[13]

Like Bill, George had originally emigrated to China for work, but he remained in Shanghai because his China-born wife could not stay in the United States permanently. Postwar legislation finally changed that, and though George did not know what kind of job he would find in America, he was definitely done with China. On weekends—the only time George was not looking for employment—Bill and May made sure to invite him and his wife, Sally, along with their kids, to outings in Central Park or camping trips up the Hudson. Their children were similar ages, but that was not the only reason. Having spent close to five years in the Wongs' spare bedroom, the

Moys understood George and Sally's situation more than anyone else in the family.[14]

Bill did not tell his brother-in-law that he, too, was looking for work. After all, he had a decent job while George had nothing, and he knew the kind of desperation the other man felt. But after months of studying electronics at night, Bill wanted something more challenging than his work at Sperry. And he wanted a better paycheck, too, now that he and May had decided to have another baby.[15]

THIRTY-EIGHT

Ernest and Ruth

SHANGHAI, 1945–1949

WHEN ERNEST WAS A BOY in New York, he often heard old Chinese men talk about "returning home in glory." It seemed to be the dream of every laundryman, waiter, and cook, and most of the merchants too. Maybe that's why there were so many ways to say it, like *wing guai gu li* (to gloriously go back to the native place) or *ji gam wan heung* (to return to your village in splendid garments of brocade). Arriving in Shanghai, Ernest realized that he had now achieved some semblance of *ji gam wan heung*. He wore a general's uniform and drew the official salary he had craved in the prewar years—a salary that could have made Ruth feel secure at last. As the city's new WASC head, Ernest wielded the power to assign rooms to Allied personnel regardless of the acute housing shortage. Despite spiraling inflation, he also enjoyed easy access to decent food and imported goods.[1]

Yet Ernest had always assumed that *ji gam wan heung* would be different than this—better than this. Instead, his marriage was over, his younger son hardly knew him, and he felt much older than his fifty years. He was disappointed to find little comfort at the Hungjao International Cemetery, where he went on his first free afternoon to pay his respects to his parents. Nor could he avoid seeing Herbert's grave nearby, so he walked over and looked at the stone. What on earth could Alfred and Alice have been thinking? In beautifully carved Chinese characters, the inscription read, "Entombed here is Herbert Moy, who was dedicated to filial piety and noble sacrifice." A man who had betrayed two countries, rendered in stone as if he were some sort of hero![2]

It was just another disturbing development in a long line of them. Ernest had noticed right away how profoundly different Shanghai felt when he returned from Kunming that autumn. Gone were most of the autos that once clogged the streets and lanes; luckier residents rode bicycles or crowded onto the dilapidated trams, but far more just walked, or really, shuffled. After years of shrinking food rations, most people looked thin and haggard. The gap between the wealthy and the poor, already wide in the 1930s, had grown under Japanese rule, and if Ernest was honest with himself, the arrival of the Nationalists had not improved the situation. Instead, the rising inflation of the postwar months gave Shanghai a growing air of menace and desperation.[3]

And then there was his own family—or what was left of it. When Ernest fled to Hong Kong in 1940, Loring had been a short, round-faced fifteen-year-old. Now twenty-one, he stood a head taller than his father and regarded the older man with a watchful shyness. Ernest soon realized that the war years had left Loring unusually mature in some ways but oddly naive in others. The naivete helped him block out some of the awfulness of the Japanese occupation, but it also blinded him to the obvious disintegration of his parents' marriage. Pete had lived in the Moys' apartment from early 1942 until he fled Shanghai in 1944, and yet, long after the war, Loring confessed to his brother Ken that he still hoped Ruth and Ernest would reconcile.[4]

His father had no similar illusions. Days after Ernest's arrival in Shanghai, Ruth asked for a divorce, and he did not try to talk her out of it. Pete had already moved back into the Moys' apartment, while Ernest was living in a room at the New Royal Hotel, the WASC headquarters out on Nanking Road West. Accepting the inevitable, Ernest helped pay for the attorney who drew up the divorce agreement. He did not really mind that much, especially after running into Elaine Hsieh on the street one day. To his tremendous relief, she had not just survived the Japanese occupation but was living in Shanghai now, and they soon resumed the relationship that the war had cut short.[5]

By the time Ken visited the city that fall, his parents had agreed to be civil for their sons' sake. Instead of dwelling on their divorce, they focused on the seemingly safe topic of the young men's futures. The two parents readily agreed to support Loring's college ambitions, but Ruth openly expressed her dismay at Ken's marriage. Ernest, who could not wait to meet his daughter-in-law and granddaughter, prudently waited to convey his enthusiasm to Ken until he was alone with his son. After all these years, he still had no desire to provoke Ruth's wrath.[6]

• • •

When Loring and Ken finally had a chance to talk privately, they shared their disappointment at Pete's continued presence in the family home and their mother's life. Ruth's sons were not the only ones who opposed the relationship. Most of Pete's old Shanghai friends thought the match a mistake, and his family had little good to say, either. Dick, now back in Shanghai with the US Army, was openly unhappy with Pete's choice, as were his mother and his brother Dave. Only Ruth and Pete's friend Jennie Chen, who had once been married to Chiang Kai-shek, offered any support, but even she gently pointed out the imbalances in their relationship.[7]

Ruth knew that Pete wanted to marry her, but she didn't know whether it was what *she* wanted. Some of her hesitation was practical: She had spent most of her adult life with a man who had more idealism than business sense, so Pete's uncertain finances and noncitizen status concerned her. In addition, C. C. Chang had come back into her life for the first time since his 1935 marriage. Now head of a government-backed food corporation, he was living part-time in Shanghai with his wife, the respected economist Djang Siaomei. Secretly, C.C. began to drop by Ruth's place, though both knew they had no real future together. Pete found out and came to see C.C. as a rival for Ruth's affections, years later recalling her deep "love for another" and confessing, "I knew from the beginning that I was not the one she should have married. But . . . I sought to make myself as indispensable to her as I could, hoping thereby she might eventually consent to a life with me." If he could get citizenship, he thought he could convince her to marry him.[8]

Because of the bar on Korean naturalization, some of Pete's army buddies started to work with a congressman stateside to pass a private bill to give him US citizenship in recognition of his extraordinary military service. In late 1946, he finally took the oath and naturalized, and the next year, Ruth at last agreed to marry him. Pete applied to his superior officer for the required permission (he parried any questions by listing Ruth's birth date as 1909), and the couple departed Shanghai for good, marrying in Honolulu in March 1948.[9]

• • •

By early 1946, US military and civilian personnel were flowing into Shanghai, where hyperinflation and the housing shortage complicated the WASC's work. In the midst of this, Ernest received a notice that the US Army had awarded him and a number of Chinese Army generals the new Medal of

Freedom for contributions to the US war effort. As Ernest examined the red-ribboned, bronze-colored medal—about the size of a fifty-cent piece but with a more satisfying heft—he felt a surge of pride in what he had accomplished during the war. Then he smiled ruefully: His job in Kunming had been a walk in the park compared to what he was doing in Shanghai.[10]

Secretary of State George C. Marshall and his entourage were frequently in town, having recently relocated to nearby Nanjing from Chongqing, where Marshall had been trying to mediate between the ruling KMT and the Communists. Marshall's staff and those working with them arrived in and left Shanghai often, especially once full civil war broke out in June 1946. The American visitors, and the wider conflict, made aspects of Ernest's job both more difficult and, at times, strangely trivial. In addition to assigning quarters to US officials, he arranged tourist jaunts for American GIs who wanted to see more of China. This also involved distributing scores of copies of *Places of Interest in Hangchow, Places of Interest in Nanking*, and other booklets in the WASC-produced tourist series, and he hoped that the newly arrived US servicemen and civilians appreciated China more than their wartime predecessors had.[11]

Ernest took the opportunity to travel a little himself in late summer, touring government facilities in other cities and bringing Loring along as his assistant. His younger son wanted to attend college in the United States the next year, so Ernest knew that this trip was likely their last chance for concentrated time together. After Loring departed Shanghai in summer 1947, Ernest fondly recalled their visit to the scenic palaces and temples of Beijing and the restored national capital of Nanjing.[12]

At least Ken came back to China in 1948, thanks to Ernest's ability to work his connections. Donald Gilpatric at the US Economic Cooperation Administration (ECA) promised to hire Ken for a few months, which would at least cover the young man's airfare and expenses. Beyond that, no one really knew. The Communists were making headway in the civil war, thanks to Chiang Kai-shek's bungling of the campaign to oust them from the Northeast. In 1947, President Truman recalled the last members of the Marshall Mission; like much of China's population, he saw the Nationalists as hopelessly incompetent and corrupt. Continued hyperinflation also meant that companies and ministries paid their employees in large bundles of bills, which lost value so quickly that workers literally ran to exchange their salaries for anything—food, durable goods, or foreign currency—before the stacks became worthless. Even the value of Ernest's salary was dwindling fast.[13]

So when Claire Lee Chennault offered him a job, Ernest jumped at the chance. After the war, the former Flying Tigers commander ran China Air Transport, a United Nations Relief and Rehabilitation Administration–connected air service. In 1948, Chennault and a partner purchased much of the company outright, with the KMT government owning the rest. The old general had seen Ernest's administrative abilities during the war and now asked him to join the newly renamed Civil Air Transport (CAT).[14]

At CAT, Ernest initially fell into a rhythm that recalled his days in prewar Hong Kong. When not at his office on the Bund or spending time with Elaine, he played volleyball for a local American team and softball for Chennault's CAT Pandas. As the months passed, though, the job grew more and more complex, since the pilots with whom Ernest worked now spent much of their time evacuating Nationalist officials and soldiers trapped in cities the Communists had overrun. Weixian, Taiyuan, Jinan, Luanxian—each week the KMT seemed to lose someplace else. Though Shanghai remained in Nationalist hands, the situation reminded Ernest of 1940, when so many people were fleeing to safety elsewhere.[15]

• • •

By January 1949, Ernest was spending whole weeks in Guangzhou, preparing to relocate CAT's staff there. Returning to Shanghai from one brief trip, he learned that the Communists had just taken Beijing, and in his diary, he described the "widespread deterioration of the Government" everywhere. Ken had more bad news when they next dined at their favorite spot, the Press Club, high up in Broadway Mansions. Meals there were reasonably priced, especially with inflation worse than ever (Ernest's salary now converted into less than US$30 a month). Over lunch, the younger man said that he was thinking about sending his wife and daughter home to the States, though they had joined him in Shanghai just a few months earlier. Ernest agreed that Ken was probably right, but he felt deeply depressed at the thought of this newest departure.[16]

In fact, Ernest left first, relocating to Guangzhou with the rest of the local CAT staff less than a week later. It was just as well, he knew, since he could no longer get any work done in Shanghai. Thousands of hungry, fearful refugees were pouring into the city each week from the Communist-occupied Northeast, and now the KMT military cordoned off the entire block around Ernest's office to prevent rioting. From Guangzhou, Ernest still kept a close eye on the worsening situation up north, eventually arranging for Elaine and her niece Kitty to leave Shanghai on a CAT plane. He also radioed his son with an offer to fly him and his family out, but Ken responded that the ECA was evacuating all of them imminently.[17]

Ernest asked one last favor, which is why Ken drove out to the Hungjao International Cemetery that April day for the traditional Qingming grave-cleaning festival. Despite the civil war, people all around the grounds were polishing and tidying their family graves. Ken got to work himself, scrubbing Han Ying and Moy Sing's headstone and weeding their plot before taking photos of his work to share with his father. On a whim, he also snapped a picture of Herbert's forlorn, overgrown grave nearby. Days later, Ken and his family left Shanghai for the last time, joining Ernest in Guangzhou. None of them ever visited the cemetery again.[18]

THIRTY-NINE

Alice and Alfred

SHANGHAI AND NEW YORK, 1946–1949

WITH ANGRY CRIES, THE MOB of Sichuanese students entered the Hangzhou University dorm, prompting Alson and his friends to scatter for safety. The frenzied group was looking for the leader of the campus's Shanghai Cantonese Club—that was Alson—and now they forced open the door of the room he shared with two other students. Rushing in, the group's leader flashed a knife and thrust it at Alson's chest. But the attacker gravely miscalculated, for Alson quickly pushed the other man's arm down, causing the student to slash himself across his own left wrist. By then, Alson's friends were emerging from hiding to join the melee in the room and the hall, though in the dark they could not always tell whom they were fighting. Suddenly someone else screamed in pain—one of the students had stabbed another one in the head—and the shock prompted both groups to disperse. As the Sichuanese youths fled, Alson noticed a pool of his attacker's blood on the dorm room floor.[1]

Access to electricity had prompted this battle, but the conflict went much deeper than that. When Hangzhou University finally reopened its home campus in fall 1946, the school's war-damaged power system struggled to keep up with student demand, especially in the evenings. One night in late November, Alson and his friends wanted to play basketball and turned on the lights at the court. The Sichuanese students, many of them poorer youths who entered the college when it relocated to Chongqing during the war, were studying in the library when their overhead lighting suddenly dimmed. Unable to see their books, they quickly figured out who the culprits were: the pampered Shanghai boys, most of them so wealthy and privileged that they did not really think about studying much. Why bother, when they did not need to keep scholarships or worry about getting jobs after college?[2]

The school administration fanned the flames by openly favoring the well-off. In August 1946, the college's president expelled scores of students who had taken part in political activism, a decision that affected poorer and more radical youths but few if any of the Shanghai boys. They—actually, their parents—paid their tuition bills promptly and showed little interest in politics. In the same vein, school administrators now tried to hush up the stabbing incident, but the story was too juicy for the Shanghai papers to ignore. Supposedly about electricity, this conflict was really about larger definitions of power: The Cantonese Club members were the scions of Shanghai's long-established Cantonese-origin business class, who owned some of the city's biggest department stores, trading firms, and hotels.[3]

At Tai On Development, the lurid story caught the eye of an amused clerk. He was thoroughly enjoying the reporter's account, which made the incident sound like a martial arts face-off from an opera, until he noticed where the violence had occurred. Alarmed, he rushed in to show the newspaper to his assistant general manager. Alfred thanked the man, closed the door to his private office, and immediately phoned Alice at home. After some quick discussion, he placed a second call, this one to the university, to summon his son back to Shanghai. The Lees were less concerned about Alson's involvement in the fight than in the rumors about his wounded attacker's ties to the Chinese Communist Party.[4]

When Alson returned to Shanghai, Alfred and Alice told him they would be sending him to the United States, where he could attend university safe from the civil war. He quickly agreed, and though he gained admission to schools in Los Angeles and New York, he chose Pennsylvania Military College on the outskirts of Philadelphia. The knife fight had shaken him deeply, and he decided that he needed some discipline and a break from the temptations of a big city. Alson left Shanghai in the spring of 1947, just a few weeks before his cousin Loring.[5]

Alice and Alfred had long avoided politics, yet Alson's situation reminded them that politics was increasingly unavoidable in postwar China. On campuses, police and KMT loyalists brutally suppressed growing student demonstrations against government policies and the civil war. KMT actions, such as demanding products at artificially low prices, alienated many factory owners and other businesspeople. Roaring inflation decimated the salaries of the middle class. And with each new KMT stumble in the civil war, another wave of foreign and Chinese companies moved their operations to Hong Kong, which the British had reoccupied in 1945.[6]

As conditions worsened, many of Alice and Alfred's friends and family were finally leaving China for good, despite their desire to stay. The famous architect Poy Gum Lee, whom Alfred had met as a New York Boy Scout years earlier, had given up trying to reestablish his practice in Shanghai. The Lees' close friend H. C. Mei departed in 1947, after the export firm he represented finally shuttered. Even Alfred's brother Chiu Hung and sister-in-law Suey Ping left China for Hong Kong's New Territories, where they bought a farm to run.[7]

Alfred still held out hope that China's economic and political outlook would improve, though his keen business sense told him otherwise. The truth was that he could not imagine leaving the city in which he had spent twenty years building the kind of life he could never have in the United States. Alice understood but felt increasingly uneasy about remaining in Shanghai. When the Lees traveled to New York to spend Christmas 1947 with Alson and the Chins, she gently suggested they consider moving back for good. Alfred disagreed, as Alice confessed to her old friend Anna Mei: "I wish he would get a job . . . in the good old U.S.A., but somehow I just can't persuade him."[8]

Even his son's legal problems could not keep Alfred in the United States. Just before Christmas, Alson applied for a routine extension of his student visa, which was set to expire the next June. The official who interviewed him learned that he had settled into life at PMC, declared accounting as his major, and hoped to graduate in the class of 1950. The man then told Alson that because he was under twenty-one and the child of US citizen parents, he could apply for a change of status that would allow him to stay in the United States permanently. This made sense to Alson, so instead of completing the form to extend his student visa, he filed one that stated: "I do not intend to leave the United States when my studies are completed and I desire to make this country my home." A delighted Alice promised that after Christmas, she would get to work on the list of documents he needed to support his application.[9]

She had barely gotten started when the INS served Alson with a warrant for his deportation. Was it entrapment? As angry as she felt, Alice did not have the time to dwell on the question. A new group of INS officials were now claiming that Alson's statement indicated he had not maintained his student status, or that he had entered as an immigrant, not a student—Alice was not quite sure, perhaps because the government seemed to be using any argument, however contradictory, that might stick. At least Alson would get a hearing in early February 1948, with Alice as his main witness. So, while

Alfred headed out to the West Coast on business, she stayed put in New York and started gathering any evidence she could find to make the case for allowing Alson to remain in the United States. To her great relief, the presiding inspector at the hearing recommended suspension of deportation. He forwarded his recommendation to the INS central office, where Alson's file remained in limbo for more than a year. With the immediate emergency past, Alice joined Alfred in San Francisco, and the two sailed back to Shanghai.[10]

• • •

The Lees' ship left California on August 20, 1948. The same day, Chiang Kai-shek introduced the "gold yuan," sending his son Chiang Ching-kuo to Shanghai to manage the transition from the old fabi to this new currency. Alfred first read about the switch when the steamer reached Honolulu, where local newspapers carried some vague stories about a measure intended to stop the hyperinflation that had hobbled China's economy. He felt a flicker of hope; maybe the plan would work and blunt the Communists' appeal. When the ship dropped anchor at Kobe in early September, he remained positive, despite growing reports of problems with the gold yuan's rollout. Once the Lees reached Shanghai, however, Alfred realized that the much-heralded reform was a disaster.[11]

Despite its name, the gold yuan had no gold backing. Just like with the old currency, the government simply printed money to cover its expenses; the one change this time was the harsh enforcement of exchange requirements and price ceilings. Chiang Ching-kuo used draconian methods to force local people, including many business leaders, to hand over their gold, silver, and foreign currency and accept the new notes. Authorities even arrested a number of Alfred's friends, including one of the Kwok brothers, for violating the law. A reporter described the results: "Shanghai to-day is a city of fear and dread. . . . [T]he Economic Police are hunting everybody who handled a foreign exchange transaction for the past several months." Far from saving the economic situation, the gold yuan turned even more Chinese against the Nationalist government.[12]

Alfred and Alice tried to soldier on, but their Shanghai world was shrinking by the day. Tai On Development's business ground to a halt, yet another casualty of Nationalist economic policies. By October 1948, the government's refusal to lift price ceilings created food shortages, since neither farmers nor manufacturers would sell their products at the required rates. Within weeks, rice riots broke out in the city. Meanwhile, most of the Lees' friends were quietly making contingency plans and shifting money to the safety of Hong Kong; many men sent their wives and children there, just in case. After all, Alice and Alfred's circle read like a who's who of what the Communists called "capitalists and imperialist running dogs": Billy Chang, the sharebroker; Percy Kwok, the exchange broker and investor; David Au, the banker and exporter; and, of course, Alfred Lee the businessman with US citizenship.[13]

Through Ernest, Alfred and Alice learned that the US Army had just evacuated Adelaide and her three daughters from Nanjing. (Jack Young had not told the Lees himself because he refused to speak to them, considering them traitors.) Even Marquita Kwan, possibly Alice's least favorite human being, left Shanghai. At least this meant the Lees would no longer see her parading along Nanking Road with her latest army officer boyfriend. On the other hand, Alice wondered if Kwan's departure was some kind of canary-in-a-coalmine moment.[14]

• • •

In early November 1948, with Nationalist forces on the brink of losing all of North China, the US Embassy began to advise Shanghai's Americans that "unless you have compelling reason to remain, you consider the desirability of evacuation while normal transportation facilities remain available." Foreign businesspeople increasingly discussed the risk of becoming Communist prisoners, and those with the money began booking passage on every available ship and plane. US citizens unable to pay high fares signed up for one of the three US Navy transports that arrived to evacuate Americans from the city. Unnerved, Alfred suggested that Alice go to Hong Kong, but she initially refused to consider leaving without him.[15]

Throughout early December, she held fast, though the various rumors—that the Communists had reached the Yangzi River, that the Nationalists had stopped the PLA's progress, that ordinary residents were fleeing Nanjing—rattled everyone's nerves. One day she was sure she would relent, only to hear contradictory news the next morning that made staying seem safe. Then, right before Christmas, a group of soldiers broke into the Shanghai home of a European and ransacked it, while Chinese military police stood by. Shaken by the tale, Alice agreed to go if Alfred accompanied her as far as Hong Kong. Getting a berth on a ship proved difficult, but Alfred asked around and managed to book them on a southbound steamer leaving right after the holiday. As much as he loved to lavish Alice with gifts, they did not exchange presents that year; instead, they spent their last Christmas in Shanghai hastily gathering and packing their most important possessions, including personal papers and photo albums.[16]

Alice had first seen Hong Kong more than two decades earlier, and, in many ways, she could measure the changes in her life by her visits to the colony: in 1926, with K. S. Lo; in 1937, as a refugee from wartorn Shanghai; in 1938, about to return to Shanghai with Alson; and now, fleeing from yet another conflict. In the 1920s, the place had seemed like such a backwater compared to Manhattan, though by the time she and Alson arrived there in 1937, tall buildings were starting to rise along the waterfront. She had grown familiar enough with Hong Kong that she could see both its recovery from the war and the occasional glaring gaps between structures, the blackened stones, even an empty pedestal where she vaguely remembered a statue in prewar days. The harbor was clogged, with ships of all descriptions entering or sitting at anchor, many of them carrying refugees from the civil war. The new arrivals found everything expensive, from food to housing, which only those with gold could secure.[17]

The Lees had discussed the possibility of Alice waiting in Hong Kong, but the crush of desperate people there and the spiraling prices convinced them to shift gears. Alice sailed on to San Francisco while Alfred returned to Shanghai—just for a little longer, he promised. In the end he remained well into the spring of 1949, unable to let go. When fighting threatened outlying areas of the city, he slowly and lovingly shut up the country home where he and Alice had lived since restoring it after the war. He was staying with Billy and Lenore Chang when well-connected friends advised him to leave while he still could. By then, PLA troops were starting to encircle the city, so the one way out was to fly, and airplane tickets were difficult to come by. Only on May 17, with the Communists closing in, was he able to reserve a seat on a Hong Kong–bound flight.[18]

As the plane took off from Lungwha Airfield, Alfred looked out to the south and saw long lines of PLA soldiers waiting to cross the Huangpu by boat. Another passenger pointed out an eerily related sight to the north: columns of Nationalist troops massing by the city's central waterfront, preparing to board a large evacuation ship bound for Taiwan. But the plane climbed quickly and steeply in order to evade possible gunfire, so the city below quickly faded from view. A few hours later, the flight landed safely at

Kai Tak, which was crowded with refugees arriving from Shanghai. Alfred even recognized a few people as he waited patiently to purchase another ticket, this one to San Francisco. When he finally arrived in the city of his birth a week later, the first thing he noticed was the newsstands' blazing headlines: Shanghai had fallen to the Communists the day before.[19]

FORTY

Kay and Ming Tai

NEW YORK, 1949–1950

CLUTCHING PLATES AND CHILDREN'S HANDS, the hungry guests descended on the long buffet that ran all the way down the side of the spacious room. After opening in mid-1945, the Pacific Restaurant had become so successful that within four years, Ming Tai and Kay were about to pay off the mortgage on the building and had also expanded the dining area to seat three hundred people. None of the guests tonight were paying customers, though. Earlier that day, Beah had married a young architect named Wayman Wing at the Riverside Church, and the Chins held the wedding dinner at the Pacific. Kay, who swapped her gray satin mother-of-the-bride suit for a Chinese silk dress that night, beamed at the newlyweds and her other children and grandchildren, all of whom had assembled for the event. Little Jolly served as flower girl for the aunt she had come to know during Beah's brief stint with the Economic Cooperation Administration in China. They had even evacuated on the same ship back to the States when the Communists closed in.[1]

All of Kay's siblings were there, too, except for Ernest—and Herbert, of course, though no one felt much like talking about him. Sitting at the Moy family table, Helen fiddled with her corsage and avoided the subject altogether. She had no desire to dredge up yet another painful memory in a year full of them. Helen, George, and their children were still reeling from the death of George's parents in swift succession: Yip Typond in August 1948 and Grace in July 1949. Alfred and Alice also did their best to be cheerful, despite the fact that they expected a decision any day on Alson's INS deportation appeal. In a strange inversion of the usual order of things, only Bill seemed particularly upbeat. He had recently started a job at the ITT radar and electronics facility in Nutley, New Jersey, and he, May, Patricia, and baby

Christopher had moved out of the city to a garden apartment in Belleville, New Jersey.[2]

Of course, the China situation remained the elephant in the room for all of them, just as it did for so many Chinese Americans that year. Almost everyone toasting to Beah and Wayman's health and happiness had relatives in Guangdong—and, increasingly, in Hong Kong, to which many Chinese fearful of the Communists had fled. Ernest was still in Guangzhou, but he and his remaining Civil Air Transport colleagues were preparing to evacuate to the British colony. Alfred knew the China situation firsthand, too, since he had escaped from Shanghai just a few months earlier. As for Alice, she often lay awake at night wondering what she would do if the INS deported Alson to Communist China, where some of his old college classmates probably remembered the battle that prompted his departure in the first place. Even Helen's husband George, who had no close relatives in the old country, seemed so preoccupied that he just picked at the delicious food on his plate.

• • •

A civil engineer with Gifford Construction, George had spent his career laying out roads and sewers. His in-laws and even his brother Jim viewed his job as mind-numbingly dull, yet he found it engrossing and challenging. Looking around the table that evening, he particularly appreciated his good fortune. George had begun his career in the booming early 1920s, when he was just out of college. In those days, a few companies were so desperate for good civil engineers that they overlooked his race, and by working longer and harder than his white colleagues, he had managed to stay employed even during the Depression. By contrast, Bill had been in his early thirties when he got his war job at Sperry; now forty, he was happy to have an entry-level electronics technician position, working alongside men fifteen years younger than he. Alfred, who was George's age, had seemed adrift since his return from China. He and Alice were living off their savings and her secretarial salary while he searched for some kind of steady work. And even though the Pacific was doing well, all the Moy siblings and spouses remembered the spectacular collapse of Ming Tai's restaurant empire in the early 1930s.[3]

Helen glanced at George and guessed what he was thinking. His job was steady and reliable, just like he was, and it had enabled him to give the Typonds the kind of middle-class life that many in Chinatown envied. Yet she worried about her quiet, serious husband, who fought the pressures he faced at work with cigarettes and copious amounts of antacid. When they dressed for the wedding that morning, she noticed that his suit was hanging rather loosely from his shoulders. Oblivious to her concerned look, he knotted his paisley tie and carefully inserted a folded pocket square into his double-breasted gray jacket. Then they hurried out to the car with Jeanne and Donald, not wanting to be late.[4]

. . .

As George pushed his food around his plate, Bill dug in with gusto. His brother-in-law's job sounded tedious, though it had some advantages. Unlike ITT, Gifford was not a major defense contractor with a security clearance program modeled on the federal government's own. Bill felt fortunate that he had gotten his new job before the situation in China really deteriorated. The Moy siblings had been appalled at Herbert's choices, but the fact that he aligned himself with fascists instead of communists was a bit of a lucky break. Given the way politicians were talking about communism these days, the other Moys might be much worse off now if their youngest brother had favored Mao instead of Hitler.[5]

Bill wondered if the Communist victory on the mainland would threaten his family's recent, hard-won financial security. Back in 1937, when the Moys returned from Shanghai, Bill had contemplated with dread a future waiting tables and washing dishes at his father-in-law's Chinese restaurant. The most he could hope for seemed to be the chance to manage a chop suey joint one day, or perhaps to own one, as Wong Soon did. Neither option appealed to him at all. Now, Bill was a research engineer helping develop microwave and radar technology, and he and May were saving up for a house in the suburbs.

All these gains could slip away, though. Bill knew that white people often treated their Chinese American acquaintances as surrogates for China. This had been beneficial, if belittling, when China was an ally: Congress finally repealed Chinese exclusion in 1943 (though the token quota of 105 immigrants a year suggested that legislators' racial views had not changed much). At Sperry, well-meaning coworkers had sometimes given Bill, Helen, and other Chinese American workers a thumbs up and a cheerful "ding ho," a Chinese phrase meaning "very good!" It was often the only bit of the language that US soldiers in the China theater knew, and people on the home front soon learned it, too. Bill tried to be gracious at such moments, even as he bristled inside at the awkward gesture. But given the current national frenzy about communism, the sudden emergence of a Communist China might be really, really bad for all of them.[6]

Unable to do much about such giant issues, Bill took his feelings of powerlessness to the local pistol range—usually the one in Wood Ridge, or sometimes Teaneck. As a teenager, he had tried target shooting a few times but quit when he left for China. He returned to the sport when he, May, and the kids moved to New Jersey, since he found that pistol shooting gave him a sense of control and confidence, feelings he often lacked. To his deep satisfaction, shooting also won him the respect and admiration of the white men, frequently police officers, who lined up next to him at the range. He soon became accustomed to the inevitable transformation, having seen it so many times: his fellow shooter's sideways glance, the surprised arch of the eyebrow, the derisive smile tugging at the edge of the mouth. And then the inevitable slack-jawed look of amazement when the shooting started. Because Bill was not just good—he was *superb*.[7]

• • •

Days after Beah's wedding, Mao Zedong announced the founding of the People's Republic of China (PRC). In New York, the local papers noted with alarm Mao's promise that "new China" would ally "first of all (with) the Soviet Union" and its satellites. Even eight thousand miles away, Kay could imagine Ernest's despair at this turn of events. He would certainly be livid if he knew that some younger Chinese in the community were celebrating the inauguration of the new government. Of course, few in the Chins' circle felt much pleasure in the Communists' victory, but they had all seen it coming for months. Anyone with family members in the old country knew about the roaring inflation, corruption, and incompetence of the Nationalists.[8]

Kay felt sorriest for friends and family who were directly affected by the advent of the new regime. Ming Tai wondered which of his nieces and nephews had managed to slip into Hong Kong from the mainland. Alice was beside herself with fear about Alson's future, and Alfred walked around in a daze, unable to come to grips with the fact that he would almost certainly never see Shanghai again. Adelaide's in-laws remained in Guangdong, while B. A. Liu, who had met the Chins while a student in the 1930s, had a wife and three children in Shanghai. Now a UN employee, he had seen Kay and Ming Tai often after resuming his friendship with the widowed Gloria, the last of their children still living at home. Posted to Paris for a new assignment, he seemed fated to wander from place to place, unable to return to China.[9]

B.A., a statistician at the United Nations, had spent two years at the organization's temporary headquarters in the old Sperry plant out in Lake Success—the very same building where Helen worked during the war. Despite the distance from Manhattan, it was generally crowded with tourists. On Monday, June 26, throngs of reporters and even more visitors than usual buzzed about the place: The day before, communist North Korean armies had crossed the 38th parallel, invading noncommunist South Korea. Now the UN Security Council was deliberating about how to respond, and it soon voted to "recommend . . . that the Members of the United Nations furnish such assistance to the Republic of Korea as may be necessary to repel the armed attack and to restore international peace and security in the area."[10]

. . .

In 1949, Ming Tai and Kay had finally breathed easier when Adelaide and her daughters, and eventually Jack, returned to the United States from China. The Youngs now lived in San Francisco, just a short drive from Jack's new posting at the Presidio. After the Security Council voted, though, President Truman immediately dispatched US forces to Korea, and Jack, an active-duty major, shipped out in July 1950. For the Chins, the gnawing fear returned.[11]

The war quickly made an even larger impact on the family, and on the Chinese American community as a whole. Previously, Truman had maintained that he would not intervene to protect the Nationalists on Taiwan from a predicted Chinese Communist invasion. Now, though, the president worried about such a move further destabilizing the region, and he ordered the US Seventh Fleet to patrol the Taiwan Strait. Truman's decision marked a reengagement, however reluctant, with the Chiang regime. It also alarmed PRC leaders, as did UN forces' movement north of the 38th parallel. In November 1950, as those troops advanced toward the Yalu River, the PRC entered the Korean War to support North Korea.[12]

Across the US, people of Chinese ancestry wondered if they would end up in concentration camps the way Japanese Americans had back in 1942. Until November 1950, a small but vocal number of local Chinese leftists had supported the PRC quite publicly, but now the local Chinese Consolidated Benevolent Association (CCBA) and other Chinese New Yorkers scrambled to drown them out. The CCBA leaders held most of their meetings at the Pacific Restaurant, so that was where they made their widely reported statement of support for the US/UN effort in Korea and their claim that all Chinese New Yorkers backed the Chiang regime.[13]

The truth was much more complicated. Most residents felt deeply ambivalent about both the Communists and the Nationalists, but few dared say that out loud. Jim Typond's business partner Shavey Lee, whom reporters had started calling the "Mayor of Chinatown," told anyone who would listen that "at least 99.9 percent" of Chinese New Yorkers were anti-Communist, and "many of those who do not like Chiang Kai-shek personally prefer him to Mao." To prove it, several dozen Chinatown groups rented a bus and sent one hundred protestors to Lake Success to demonstrate against the Chinese Communist representatives attending a UN meeting there.[14]

. . .

As community members rushed about trying to prove their patriotism, B. A. Liu arrived in town after several months in Paris. B.A. had not seen his family in China since 1937, and long before then he had grown distant from his wife. One night back in 1938, he had confessed to his friend Vivian Chen Dai what she and Kay both suspected: B.A. loved Gloria, despite the difference in their ages and the fact that he was already married. "He says he's waiting for Gloria to find herself and hopes someday he may have a chance to court her, but right now he's tied by family considerations," Vivian wrote to her husband Bingham. Gloria was fond of B.A. too, but Vivian thought she deserved better and was relieved when her sister moved on.[15]

More than a decade later, though, B.A.'s feelings had not changed, while Gloria's had returned. Now that the US and the PRC were at war, B.A. decided it was unlikely he would see his family in China again, so he persuaded Nationalist representatives in New York to grant him a divorce from his wife. Days later, he married Gloria, and the newlyweds sailed for Paris in early January 1951. After forty years and seven children, Ming Tai and Kay were empty nesters at last.[16]

FORTY-ONE

Ernest

HONG KONG AND NEW YORK, 1950–1953

REFUGEES POURED INTO HONG KONG by the thousands each week. They walked across the border at Lo Wu, traveled by train from Guangzhou, and arrived on the ships dropping anchor off Kowloon. The newcomers thronged the narrow streets, lived in shantytowns on hillsides, and sometimes begged for money on the sidewalks. Ernest could tell from their clothes, faces, and manners that the vast majority were city people fleeing Mao's peasant army. A good number were old friends, too, including Billy and Lenore Chang and Henry Joe Young, a boyhood pal from New York. Of course, Ernest was also a refugee of sorts. In mid-October 1949, he evacuated Guangzhou with the last of the city's CAT employees; by year's end, the company had no more bases on the mainland, while Nationalist China seemed likely to disappear once the People's Liberation Army invaded Taiwan.[1]

Almost everyone Ernest knew in Hong Kong now seemed to exist in a strange holding pattern, and he was no exception. He, Elaine, and Kitty lived together in a tiny Causeway Bay flat, where a rotating cast of mainland evacuees slept on their floor. Ernest and Elaine still enjoyed each other's company, but as always, their relationship had no definite future, just like so much of life in Hong Kong these days. Her tolerant husband, diplomat Wei-lin "Willy" Hsieh, continued to remit some money for her support, but he could not fund her indefinitely; Sweden had officially recognized the PRC as China's legitimate government, forcing Willy, the Republic of China's last ambassador to that Scandinavian country, to step down. The Swedes let him stay for now, but he was not sure what to do next.[2]

As for Ernest, he planned to return to the United States, though that was much easier said than done. After all, he had destroyed his US passport before leaving Japanese-occupied Hong Kong in 1942. Now he joined the crush of Chinese Americans and their dependents besieging the US Consulate in Hong Kong to get needed travel documents. In January 1950, he submitted the required paperwork, hoping to leave that March, but by June he had resigned himself to a very long wait indeed.[3]

Through it all, he continued working at CAT in Kowloon, though he sometimes avoided his office to dodge the many people who dropped by to ask for loans and favors. Even then, he still gave out more money than he could really spare to friends and acquaintances who were marooned and broke in Hong Kong. Needing a break from the stress, he often took drives to Repulse Bay to swim with Elaine, and he joined the reconstituted Shanghai Senior Pandas, now an exile group competing in Hong Kong's softball league.[4]

By spring 1950, he increasingly found himself trying to dream up solutions for the problems he saw all around him. That May, he helped organize the American University Club with other recent arrivals from the mainland, and he soon pushed the group to create an employment service for members. When President Truman sent the Seventh Fleet to the Taiwan Strait in July, Ernest began to dream much bigger. He wrote to the ambassador to China, John Leighton Stuart, now in Washington, to propose a new university in Hong Kong to accommodate displaced high school graduates from the mainland. Their services, he wrote, would eventually "be needed to liberate and rebuild China." In August, when he finally received the documents required to book passage to the United States, he decided that he must find a way to continue his anticommunist refugee advocacy there.[5]

. . .

Ken and Charlotte's apartment was a convenient streetcar ride to Capitol Hill. Within days of Ernest's arrival, he had already started making the rounds to present his *Hong Kong Tiger Standard* credentials. The "tiger" referred to newspaper founder Aw Boon Haw's cash cow, Tiger Balm, a medicinal ointment popular across Southeast Asia and with Ernest's own sister Kay. The *Standard* was a new paper that opposed communism, and fortunately Ernest knew editor L. Z. Yuan from their Shanghai days. When he offered to work for almost nothing, L.Z. was delighted to name him the paper's official Washington correspondent.[6]

Ernest attended the usual press conferences and filed his pieces with the *Standard*'s editors, who nevertheless seemed to prefer cheaper wire service stories to his. No matter: He viewed his correspondent gig as far less important than finding ways to help and resettle Hong Kong's educated Chinese refugees, whom he believed were crucial to a future noncommunist China. As soon as he could get an appointment, he went down to the State Department to discuss his idea, armed with memos, statistics, and dozens of employment service forms from the American University Club. Ernest explained how the American government could take real steps to not only "preserve the . . . usefulness" of educated refugees for the liberation of the mainland, but also "win the hearts and minds of the intellectuals and professionals." The officials who met with him seemed vaguely sympathetic and promised to get back to him—at some point.[7]

Regardless, the refugee project quickly became Ernest's driving passion, consuming more and more of his energy and attention. The letters he sent to Elaine and to other friends in Hong Kong often contained requests for refugee-related information, names, and other data, and he used his connections from WASC and CAT days to try to drum up interest at the Pentagon. Ernest also waited until mid-November to go up to New York, though he had not seen Helen and Kay since 1934 and Bill since 1937. He was simply too busy lobbying the State Department to visit his family before then. Still, seeing his siblings again after so long touched him deeply. "This family reunion was the first time I had seen Katie and Helen . . . in 16 years," he wrote in his diary. "It was indeed a happy occasion. It seemed like a dream." Then he woke up and jumped back into the project, scheduling a raft of meetings in Manhattan with people who might be able to help him.[8]

By 1951, he had enlisted some allies but no actual funding, so he spent weeks at a time and then the entire summer in New York trying to convince the China Institute, the International Rescue Committee, and other NGOs to adopt his plan. Working from Gloria's old bedroom in Ming Tai and Kay's Morningside Heights apartment, he finally talked a liberal anticommunist publicist named Harold L. Oram into taking up the cause. Ambassador Stuart also agreed to act as honorary chairman of a committee to raise funds for what Ernest now called "Emergency Aid to Chinese Intellectuals." Still brimming with this initial triumph, he set out for San Francisco that September to cover for the *Standard* the signing of the official Allied peace treaty with Japan.[9]

After he arrived in the Bay Area, though, he found a cable from Oram reporting that Stuart had backed out under pressure from officials in Washington. "The State Dept. must not appear to have anything to do with the project since it does not wish directly or indirectly to be associated with it," Ernest groused in a letter to friend and fellow anticommunist activist Geraldine Fitch. "What do you think of that?" It was not a rhetorical question. He had started to hear rumors that someone, maybe at State, was actively disparaging him and his plans. As Ernest sat listening to the delegates' speeches, he could not stop wondering who was trying to stop him, and why.[10]

Still, he tried his best to enjoy the rest of his trip, staying with Adelaide and her girls and visiting with the Lees and Loring, who had just graduated from the University of California, Berkeley. Then his son surprised him with the news that Ruth was about to receive a Medal of Freedom for her intelligence work in Shanghai. Since getting his own Medal of Freedom in 1946, Ernest had learned that recipients were almost always civilians, not soldiers, a fact that diminished some of the decoration's appeal; after all, he took great pride in calling himself a retired general. While a bit vexed by Loring's news, he agreed to accompany his son to the event, especially since Pete, who had made the army his career, was still in Korea. Ernest congratulated his ex-wife after the ceremony, and they even took a drive down the coast, chatting more easily than he had assumed was possible about their boys, his siblings, and her niece Ruth Ann's recent performance in a ballet he had seen in New York. But while the afternoon was pleasant enough, the ceremony had wounded his vanity; always prone to embellishing his résumé, Ernest almost completely stopped mentioning his Medal of Freedom to anyone after Ruth got hers.[11]

• • •

Late that year, Ernest relocated permanently to Kay and Ming Tai's place. He could just as easily work for the *Standard* from there as from Washington, given the concentration of Chinese Nationalist officials and lobbyists in New York. More to the point, he would soon lose his Washington home anyway, since Ken had taken a job in the Marshall Islands and was planning to move his family there. Mainly, though, Ernest believed he could promote his Chinese intellectual aid project most effectively in New York, near Oram.[12]

All winter, Ernest also tried to get to the bottom of the negative rumors about him, asking around the State Department but failing to get a straight answer. First he heard that officials there were "questioning my motives." Then Oram told him that the government thought he was a paid agent of the Nationalist government. Behind the scenes, the State Department's intelligence bureau offered a whole grab bag of sometimes contradictory information to discredit Ernest. Investigators raised the issue of Herbert's wartime activities before suggesting that Ernest might also be the son of Eugene Moy, the managing editor of the *China Daily News*—New York's last pro-PRC paper. The fact that Ernest was actually older than his supposed father did nothing to dispel this bizarre rumor. The most damning contention came from "a high ranking military officer" who called Ernest a "rank opportunist," a "dangerous character," and "a 'stinker' with whom no one should associate." Ernest knew nothing of these charges. Convinced that he just needed to quash the paid-foreign-agent rumor, he responded in characteristic fashion with a multi-point memo that denied it.[13]

He believed he had been successful when, just before Christmas, Oram snagged a meeting with Minnesota congressman Walter Judd. The fiercely anticommunist former China missionary agreed to lead Ernest's project as long as he did not actually have to run it. For that, Oram tapped Christopher Emmet, a seasoned organization leader who became executive vice-chair of what the men now officially named Aid Refugee Chinese Intellectuals (ARCI). Judd's name attracted an array of prominent founding members, from Bertrand Russell, Rebecca West, and Thornton Wilder to Dean Rusk, General Chennault, and Henry Luce. Geraldine Fitch also promised to join. With the member list growing, Emmet began to plan a glittering inaugural gala, while the State Department and the CIA agreed to provide secret financial backing for the group.[14]

So Ernest felt vindicated on the January 1952 day when ARCI's executive board held its inaugural meeting. The board elected officers, passed a resolution of gratitude for Ernest's work, and discussed the foundation and government support ARCI now expected. Yet as Ernest later wrote, "Today has been, personally, a historic one—a day of unprecedented personal victory and great disappointment. . . . The great disappointment is that the federal government gives its blessing and support on condition that I do not participate in the operations! What a menace I must be to the land of my birth—the country that I have served with all my heart and energy! I am a suspected foreign agent!! And a 'splinter' influence!!"[15]

Outraged, he sent a stream of letters to Representative Judd and State Department officials to protest the vague charges against him. At the same time, he was growing increasingly impatient with progress on the ground in Hong Kong, drafting a series of "TOP SECRET" memoranda that pressed Emmet and Judd to move faster and to beware of Communist sabotage in the colony. Finally, Ernest begged Emmet for a ticket to Hong Kong, arguing that only he could get things moving outside of the organizational structure. "Unless I go in a private capacity to Hongkong [*sic*], I dread to think what may happen to ARCI," he pleaded. No ticket materialized, nor did the government change its position. And though Ernest's name remained on ARCI's long list of sponsors, Oram and Emmet quietly eased him out of any real role in the group, while relegating his frustrated, insistent memos to the wastebasket.[16]

FORTY-TWO

Alice and Alfred

SAN FRANCISCO AND NEW YORK, 1952–1955

ALFRED COULD STILL BE CHATTY and charismatic at parties and club meetings, but he increasingly retreated into a depressed silence at home. After all, he had spent his entire adulthood trying to avoid the life he now had. The Lees rented a smallish apartment only blocks from Alfred's childhood home in San Francisco's Chinatown. The successful career he had built in Shanghai was just a memory; these days, he was a fifty-year-old insurance salesman whose clients were mostly friends and family who pitied him. Once upon a time, he had been Alice's knight in shining armor, saving her from an unhappy marriage and giving her the life of luxury she craved. These days, her job kept them afloat, though she never complained and instead did her best to cheer him up.[1]

Alice understood his depression, having experienced something similar when she first returned from Shanghai. Waiting for Alfred to get out of China, she desperately missed their old life there, from the country house to the servants to the social whirl they had loved so much. But then the INS located Alson's dormant case file, rejected his initial appeal, and restarted deportation proceedings against him, and she pulled herself together because her son needed her. She would do anything she could to keep the government from sending him back to China.

In Chinatown, those in the know said to talk to Albert Chow, who could use his political connections and knowledge of the immigration system to solve Alson's problem—for the right price. But Alice and Alfred had lost most of their savings when they fled Shanghai, so the "right price" proved far too high. Instead, Alice got a secretarial job at an import-export firm—teaching shorthand for fun in Shanghai had kept her sharp—and began shopping for an attorney they could afford. She eventually found Samuel E. Yee, a 1948 law school graduate who had just started his own practice. Though green, he was smart, inexpensive, and happy for her business, and he quickly appealed the deportation order. Convinced by Yee's argument, the INS restored Alson's student status and suspended the deportation proceedings in November 1949. That meant Alson could stay in the United States until he graduated, which bought him seven more months. Given the tiny Chinese quota for immigrants, Yee and officials at the INS advised Alson to convince a congressperson to sponsor a private bill giving him permanent residence. Alice got right to work, and in March 1950, San Francisco representative Franck Havenner introduced H.R. 7960, "a bill for the relief of Ai-shen Miles Lee."[2]

Though the measure soon stalled in the Judiciary Committee, the INS quietly shifted its position as the months wore on. In April 1950, immigration officials used a provision from the Displaced Persons Act of 1948 to grant Alson a visa extension based on the persecution he might anticipate in the newly communist PRC. Havenner's private bill was still sitting in committee when Alson graduated from Pennsylvania Military College, so he moved in with his parents in San Francisco and got a job as an entry-level accountant. By the time he needed to extend his visa again, the PRC had been fighting in the Korean War for several months. Now immigration officials were even more open to Alson's argument that his "military training at the Pennsylvania Military College, together with service in the United States Army R.O.T.C.... would, no doubt, be an added cause for fear of persecution or discrimination." They granted yet another extension.[3]

• • •

In the midst of all this, Alice received Ernest's brief telegram with the terrible news that Helen's fifty-two-year-old husband George had died suddenly of an erupted ulcer and internal bleeding. Alice could not attend George's funeral on such short notice, so she arranged instead to take time off later that spring and come east. Alson had just been accepted into Columbia's graduate accounting program, so she helped him settle into his New York apartment and then spent some much-needed time with Helen. Even three months after George's death, Alice noticed how worn and tired her middle sister looked. Helen's once round cheeks were strangely thin, and she struggled to smile. Jeanne, though obviously sad, greeted the Lees warmly, but Donald seemed surly, almost hostile. Alice could hardly blame him—he was just seventeen and probably still in shock.[4]

A few days after Alice's arrival, Bill and May invited everyone out to Pompton Plains, New Jersey, the first time all the living siblings had been together in more than twenty years. The couple had just bought a little Cape Cod–style house, the first home they ever owned, and they were immensely proud of it. Bill was steadily rising up the ranks at nearby ITT, no longer a technician but a researcher whom his colleagues respected. Though never a joiner, he had even started a pistol club with a handful of local target-shooting enthusiasts.[5]

Everyone knew that Alice could do more harm than good in the kitchen, so she pitched in by keeping four-year-old Chris out of the way while May put the finishing touches on dinner. After Ernest joined her, she tried her best to feign interest in his newest enthusiasm: drafting John Foster Dulles to run for president. Suddenly, she noticed something very strange: Chris was the only small child at their gathering. There had always been crowds of kids and grandkids at these events, but nowadays they all lived in distant parts of the country. Ernest's sons were even farther away, with Ken and his family in Micronesia and Loring working on an American President Lines ship in East Asia. And the Chins were finally empty nesters, at least if you didn't count Ernest, who slept in their front bedroom.[6]

• • •

Back in San Francisco, she found herself missing both Alson and her sisters and thinking about how much she had enjoyed being in New York and seeing so many friends from the old days in China. Many of their Shanghai crowd were on the East Coast now, including Billy and Lenore's daughter Joyce, Leon and Dora Kwok, and Harriett Lee Ho. Sure, a few seemed lost, even desperate, like Ernest's old boss Loy Chang; a Harvard graduate and former bigshot in the Ministry of Finance, Loy was now so impoverished he often showed up at the Chins' apartment uninvited for dinner. Still, most of the others had adjusted fairly well, and maybe Alfred would too. If they moved back to New York, perhaps he could find a better job, and since Alice had been working at the Social Security Administration for a couple years, she could easily transfer offices.[7]

All that summer and fall, Alfred resisted the idea. Then, right before Thanksgiving, he got a letter from Billy in Hong Kong reporting that Lenore had died of cancer on board the SS *President Cleveland* en route to a US-run hospital in Japan. The one comforting detail was the presence of junior purser

Loring Moy, who helped care for her in her last hours. Shortly after the new year, the Lees' old friend H. C. Mei also died suddenly in Berkeley. His death shook something loose in Alfred, who quietly agreed to the move east.[8]

The Lees made plans to invest their modest savings in a home near the Chins. For a time, Ming Tai had sunk the profits from the Pacific Restaurant into commercial real estate, even as he and Kay rented their own apartment in Harlem. But twenty years after losing their Glen Ridge Victorian to foreclosure, they had decided to buy again. Once the Lees arrived in New York, Kay, Alfred, and Alice started house hunting, often with Alson and Ernest in tow. They drove out to Queens one day and Long Island the next, carefully searching for the developers who were willing to sell to Chinese. It was a relatively small number, and most of those companies still drew the line at Blacks. After a few days of looking, the two couples came up with a new idea: buying a two-family home of some type. In late April 1953, they signed a contract for two attached brick units in the Mayfield Terrace tract of Flushing, Queens.[9]

Alice thrived in New York, working to cheer Helen, making up for lost time with Kay, and beaming with pride at Alson, now an accounting professor at his alma mater, Pennsylvania Military College. She enjoyed her job and her popularity with her new colleagues and supervisors at the Social Security office, too. In her free time she liked to entertain family, friends, and even her boss at the new Flushing house. True, she could not cook well, but she knew how to lay out canapes and make a tasty cocktail.[10]

Although he always perked up on such occasions, Alfred seemed as lost in New York as he had in San Francisco. Officially, he continued to sell insurance, but on most days he sat at the family dining table and kept busy managing the couple's shrinking savings or corresponding with friends and Masonic Lodge brothers. That fall, worried about the family's finances, he finally started working as a waiter at the King Yum Chinese tiki restaurant on Union Turnpike, about a mile from home. It was the job that many American-born men of his generation feared and loathed, but what choice did he have? On days when Alfred felt too depressed to go in, Ernest, who needed the money too, subbed for him at $12.50 a shift.[11]

. . .

By the time Alson got engaged in late 1954, Alice knew that Alfred wanted to go back to the West Coast. Maybe it was the reminder that everyone else's life was moving forward. Maybe he just wanted to be closer to China—even if he knew, deep down, that he would never go back. Alson was planning to leave the PMC faculty and look for a job at one of the big Manhattan accounting firms; since he and his soon-to-be wife would need a place to live, Alice suggested that the young couple take over the Flushing unit when the older Lees returned to San Francisco.[12]

Just weeks before the June 1955 wedding, Alson finally became an American citizen. Although the private bill for his citizenship had stalled, he was now able to naturalize with "displaced person" status, a category Congress had created after the war for people who could not return to their homelands. After taking the oath, Alson laughingly explained to his fiancée, Lillian Yick, that now she knew he was marrying her for love and not citizenship. Alice chuckled at the joke and slept better than she had in months.[13]

The wedding took place in Boston, where Lillian had grown up. Since she lived in New York now, her sister Mary planned the entire event, from the church ceremony to the post-wedding dinner at King Wah Low in Boston's Chinatown. Alwin, the Chins' oldest son, served as his cousin's best man, while Donald Typond stood as an usher. Although Kay and Ming Tai couldn't make it, the other siblings trekked north for the June affair and discovered, as always, that they already knew half the "strangers" in attendance. The number of second- and third-generation Chinese Americans on the East Coast was still quite small, and the twenty-somethings among them all socialized on weekends—just as their parents had done during their Chinese Students Alliance days decades before.[14]

At the wedding dinner, Helen, Jeanne, and Bill sat at Alice and Alfred's table, watching in amusement as Bill's young son Chris struggled with his chopsticks. The group chatted about Jeanne's clerical job, Bill's winning pistol team, and everyone's summer plans—from the Lees' move back to San Francisco to Helen's visit to her niece in Seattle. The whole time, they were secretly wondering if Lillian would go through the traditional Chinese wedding ritual the way so many brides in their circle still did: holding a cup in both hands, bowing her head, and offering ceremonial tea to her in-laws. Everyone held their breath as Alson brought Lillian to the table, and then the entire group burst out laughing when the newlyweds produced a bottle of whiskey. As Alice and Alfred drank a glass with the newlyweds, the mother of the groom had a twinkle in her eye. Neither she nor Lillian cared much for the old rituals, so the two had agreed beforehand to dispense with all of them. They were going to get along just fine.[15]

As the evening continued, Alice watched her husband chatting with various Chins, Moys, Yicks, and friends who had come up to Boston for the big event. Alfred still enjoyed occasions like these, yet Alice could see the way his feelings of failure weighed on him. For as long as she could remember, her sisters, brothers, in-laws, nieces, and nephews had all agreed that Alice was the spoiled one, the pampered one, the luxury-loving party girl whom Alfred had rescued from genteel poverty. That had been true to a point, but when the Lees lost almost everything and the INS came after Alson, she found a new strength to fight for her son, to find a steady job, and to build a new life for her family in a country they barely knew anymore. Looking across the table at Alfred, Alice saw a broken man whom she still loved despite his struggles. He had saved her when she needed saving. Now, she promised herself, she would save him.

. . .

In the years that followed, Helen looked back on that night with tremendous affection. She still missed George, but she had started moving forward again and thinking about the future, making travel plans and watching her children grow into adults. Donald looked so handsome in his suit, with his ROTC buzzcut and a carnation in his buttonhole. She remembered Jeanne most vividly: healthy and vibrant, smiling at her mother, repinning her favorite red hat as they chatted. The young woman had not yet noticed the slight lump on her neck or felt the fatigue that indicated the presence of thyroid cancer.[16]

FORTY-THREE

Kay, Ming Tai, and Ernest

NEW YORK AND TAIPEI, 1955–1958

LILLIAN AND ERNEST QUICKLY PERFECTED their evening ritual: She washed and rinsed each plate, then handed it to him to dry and put away. After Alice and Alfred's return to the West Coast, Kay often invited Alson and his new wife over for dinner. The couple commuted to jobs in Manhattan, a considerable distance from Flushing, and Kay's legendarily excellent cooking was better than what Lillian could whip up on the fly after work. Ernest almost always ate with them and then helped clean up, since he still lived in the Chins' guest bedroom.[1]

Kay never pushed Ernest to pay rent or move out, though he had been staying with the Chins for more than three years now. After all, he always did some of the chores, weeding the garden, dusting the furniture, and vacuuming the house for hours. But even if he had done nothing to help out, he was still her brother, and he had already faced so much rejection since his return to New York, including the *Hongkong Tiger Standard* almost never publishing his pieces and ARCI's leadership sidelining him. Of course, such setbacks could not stop Ernest's political work. In addition to sending a steady stream of letters about US-China policy to American newspapers and officials, he also headed the Chinatown American Legion's "Committee on Americanism" and helped Chinese sailors fight deportation.[2]

Despite such frenetic activity, though, he did not really seem to have a *job*. After Ernest joined the 1952 Chinese Americans for Eisenhower Committee—John Foster Dulles had not run, after all—the head of the local Chinese American Republican organization encouraged him to apply for jobs in the new administration, but none ever materialized. Then he agreed to act as New York representative for a Hong Kong magazine and film distributor, yet this did not seem to pay much, if anything. Nevertheless, he constantly came up with new ways to try to make money, such as selling mutual funds, representing a Hawaiian orchid company, or creating a marriage bureau to match lonely Chinese American bachelors with Hong Kong refugee women. Though he quietly depended on money from his sons and siblings, his idealism had not changed since his boyhood a half century earlier. It was a well that never ran dry.[3]

Still, when Kay looked across the dinner table, she could not help noticing just how old her brother seemed. His new hearing aids helped some, but he increasingly struggled during family conversations, and his cataracts made him fear that he might lose his eyesight. Sometimes he fought depression, trying to shake it off by throwing himself into some new project or other, from developing soy protein for hungry refugees to helping run a friend's frozen food business. Kay realized that what kept both Chins feeling young were the visits from their children and ever-expanding throng of grandchildren, so she was pleased when Ken and Charlotte invited Ernest to live with them in California—and had to bite her tongue when he turned them down. Kay knew that her brother would never be content to rest, at least while Sun Yat-sen's revolution remained unfinished.[4]

That's why, rather than California, Ernest was seriously thinking about going to Taiwan. For quite a while, J. L. Huang, his old WASC boss, had been urging Ernest to travel to the island on an inspection tour of sorts and see for himself the good work the Nationalist government was doing there. All Ernest needed to do was come up with the money for his plane ticket. That was a pretty big ask, yet J.L. assured Ernest that if he could get to Formosa, he could stay as long as he wanted at an official hostel, meet with government leaders, and visit the offices involved in overseas Chinese work.[5]

The cost was not the only reason Ernest hesitated to take such a big step, though. He and Elaine had exchanged scores of letters since his move to the United States, and he had remitted thousands of dollars he could not really spare to help support her. He always imagined that she was waiting for him, despite being married to Willy. So, in fall 1955, he told her about J.L.'s idea and proposed that she join him in Taiwan. He was stunned and dismayed when she gently but firmly rejected the plan. "This has been the darkest day, mentally, that I have ever spent in my life," he wrote in his diary.[6]

• • •

In early 1956, the INS and the Justice Department launched a nationwide crackdown on unlawful Chinese immigrants, sending waves of panic through Chinatowns across the country. The main targets were the thousands of "paper sons" now labeled "potential communist agents" by overzealous State Department officials. Ming Tai knew that the INS was not really looking for people like him; after all, he had come to the United States before the fall of the Qing dynasty, and all his living children were unquestionably US citizens. Yet he, Kay, and everyone in their community felt the psychological and economic impact of the dragnet. In New York, mixed-status families like the Chins were more common than fully "legitimate" ones like the Typonds. Every legal immigrant and US-born Chinese in the city knew someone—usually many someones—who had entered the country unlawfully. Now such people started avoiding Chinatown altogether, especially after the Chinese-language press reported that police in San Francisco were stopping Chinese on the street to check their papers.[7]

Eager to defend the community and desperately needing a distraction, Ernest attended a CCBA emergency meeting to help formulate a response to the crackdown. The room was filled with important Chinatown men (only men, as usual), including many old friends and acquaintances. The former Palais manager C.M. Joe, now head of the On Leongs, was there, as was immigration lawyer Tommy Lee, still reeling from his brother Shavey's death a few months earlier. Given all the egos in the room, the meeting quickly grew heated: After just a few minutes, the American Legion post commander stormed out with a large number of his comrades. Ernest stayed put, but he suddenly felt tired and worn, his depression back with full force. Maybe now *was* the time to go see Taiwan.[8]

• • •

Neither Kay nor Helen expressed much surprise at Ernest's sudden departure that summer. They had seen it before, many times—moving apartments, changing jobs (always changing jobs), chasing dreams—all while oblivious to what was under his nose, especially his family. Kay helped him pack, and Helen used her Abraham & Straus employee discount to buy him a going-away gift.[9]

She had worked at the famous Brooklyn department store's downtown flagship for about two years now, the first paid job she had held since running a lathe at Sperry during the war. After all, George's life insurance and their savings could not last forever, and certainly the $15 monthly check from his old bosses at Gifford did not buy much more than some groceries. Luckily, Helen enjoyed both the work and her colleagues, a diverse bunch of mainly widowed and divorced women. Together with her New York siblings, these new friends helped support her in the months after Jeanne's thyroid surgery. Still, Helen worried about Donald's departure. Her son had just graduated from college, paid for in part by an ROTC scholarship, and now the army was sending Lieutenant Typond to South Korea. At least the war there had ended, but given Jeanne's precarious health, Helen wished her son was closer.[10]

Despite growing fatigue, Jeanne wanted desperately to return to France, where the Typonds had sent her after her 1950 graduation from Adelphi. Helen could not refuse this wish, so she helped her daughter arrange the trip; after Jeanne's ship sailed, Helen lay awake nights worrying about what would happen if the young woman's condition worsened. Then the telegram came, summoning Helen to Idlewild Airport to meet Jeanne, who returned from Paris by plane looking pale and drawn. She died less than two weeks later as Donald rushed home from Korea on an army transport flight. He arrived in time for her funeral, held at the same place as George's five years earlier. Mother and son stood flanked by Jim and Lonnie Typond and their daughters, Kay and Bill and their families, Helen's many church friends, and some of the Abraham & Straus women. Everyone's face wore some version of sadness mixed with disbelief, and none more than Helen's. George's death had been excruciating, but she had always expected to outlive him. Burying her twenty-eight-year-old child was an unimaginable horror.[11]

• • •

Ernest arrived in the hottest, rainiest part of Taiwan's torrid summer and moved into the Number 9 Hostel in central Taipei. Built by the Japanese, Number 9 was spare but comfortable enough, reminding him of the WASC facilities he had once overseen in Kunming. There was even a Kunming Street nearby, though that novelty quickly wore off. After the end of Japanese rule, the Nationalist government renamed all of Taipei's streets after mainland cities and provinces, meaning that local maps read like a catalog of everything the Chiang regime had lost. Still, Ernest was initially impressed by what he saw on the island. He had first visited Taiwan in the late 1940s, when a combination of wartime bombing damage and postwar KMT looting left widespread destruction. Now he noted with approval the improvements in island infrastructure and living standards.[12]

Ernest enjoyed much about those first months in Taiwan, with friends, local organizations, and the press extending a warm, flattering welcome. He received invitations to make speeches at the Taipei Rotary Club and to a visiting delegation of Chinese Americans, and KMT journalists portrayed him as a stellar example of a loyal, anticommunist "overseas Chinese leader." What he found particularly delightful were the political nods after so many years. Foreign Minister George K. C. Yeh met with him for a "long talk," Ernest boasted to his sons, and he almost burst with pride when he got an invitation from Chiang Kai-shek to share with the leader his impressions of Taiwan.[13]

Ernest also caught up with Geraldine Fitch, whose husband now ran the local office of ARCI. The Chiang regime, despite protestations of support, deeply feared the potential political and economic impact of educated refugees and threw up many roadblocks to ARCI's plans. The group did eventually manage to help resettle fourteen thousand people in Taiwan, work ARCI was wrapping up by the time Ernest arrived. With no more funding on the line, ARCI leaders welcomed Ernest's help, so he served as a local troubleshooter once the Fitches departed. After years of lauding Congressman Judd's leadership, reporters began to acknowledge that Ernest had actually proposed ARCI in the first place.[14]

. . .

Seeing Elaine took some of the wind out of his sails, of course. He knew she would be at Kitty's wedding, which took place in Hong Kong in May 1957, yet he was surprised at just how raw her rejection remained. So he was already depressed when he returned to Taiwan just days before rioters in Taipei attacked and burned the US Embassy and the US Information Service office there. The mob of twenty-five thousand initially gathered to protest an American military court's acquittal of a US Army sergeant who had killed a Chinese man, an outcome that inflamed simmering resentment of American arrogance and cultural imperialism. Chiang's regime routinely stifled the press and suppressed popular discontent, yet the police this time could somehow not manage to stop the mob's seven-hour rampage. The US government quickly determined that Nationalist officials had encouraged the riot to obliquely express KMT leaders' dissatisfaction with US policies—especially American unwillingness to support an invasion of the mainland.[15]

Now US supporters of Taiwan struggled to understand the ingratitude of the Free Chinese, and Ernest had no good answer for them. In the past, he had publicly flayed the arrogance of America's representatives abroad, but he was now horrified by the rumors that top KMT officials had encouraged the mob. Local resentment of American soldiers, the lack of trust between the US and its Chinese partners, the Chiang regime's manipulation—all of it reminded him too much of wartime Kunming, although back then victory had seemed likely, even imminent. He realized with sudden dismay that the current situation actually recalled postwar Shanghai, when everything was falling apart.[16]

A few days after the riot, Ernest flew back to Hong Kong on business. He had planned the trip weeks earlier, after deciding to settle permanently in Taiwan and start a company there. He would represent American products, a prospect that initially seemed exciting. He even came up with a name, the American United Sales Agency. But now he just felt old, tired, and depressed, his once rosy view of Taiwan's future greatly altered.[17]

Walking through the busy streets of Hong Kong's Central district, he caught a glimpse of his own squinting reflection in a shop window: balding, stooped, almost emaciated. Ernest knew there was something wrong—he had been losing weight, feeling unwell, and fighting insomnia for months—and his trusted regimen of homeopathic mixtures, vitamins, and the occasional dose of synthetic hormones did not seem to be doing much. Putting out his cigarette, he stepped into a chemist's shop and picked out several different medications, which were cheap and lightly regulated in the colony: sleeping pills, two kinds of anti-anxiety medications, and more testosterone.[18]

Yet after his return to Taipei, his gloom only deepened. The new business did not make enough money to pay for the office he leased, his eyesight and hearing continued to deteriorate, and his appetite did not return. Despite having many local friends, he felt achingly lonely for his family in the United States, as well as for the companionship he had once imagined he would share in Taipei with Elaine. In the past, his sense of serving something larger would have buoyed him, but ever since the riot, he found himself struggling to sustain his faith in the KMT. As ARCI's troubleshooter, he had glimpsed the party's problems over and over but tried to ignore their larger meaning. Now he could no longer do that. Writing to Adelaide in mid-January 1958, he referred to an exchange he had with her sister after he made up his mind to stay permanently in Formosa. "When Glor asked me whether I would be happy in Taiwan, I replied that I would be only 'less unhappy,'" he noted.

"Experience reveals discoveries. Try to read between the lines. Forgive this depressing report. I have to be truthful with my own people." Was it fatigue and illness, or had his idealism finally dried up?[19]

The hostel clerk could not answer these questions. He knew only that General Huang was on the phone, and the general was a very important man. So the attendant knocked on Ernest's door with growing urgency before finally entering the room. He saw the sleeping man fully clothed and lying on the bed, an almost empty pill bottle on the nightstand next to him. There was also a handwritten note in English, which the clerk picked up but could not really decipher. Addressed to General Huang, it said: "I am completely exhausted and am no longer useful. . . . I deeply regret the trouble I am causing you. I can only beg your forgiveness. Your friendship has been one of the treasures of my life. May God bless America and China, the two countries I love and have given my all to serve." When the attendant reached out to shake the sleeping man's arm, he recoiled at its rigidity. Backing out of the room, he closed the door and ran to the phone to inform General Huang that his friend was dead.[20]

FORTY-FOUR

Siblings

SAN FRANCISCO, NEW YORK, TAIPEI, AND HONG KONG, 1958–1961

ALICE SMILED AS SHE WATCHED Alfred hastily finish his breakfast and rise to leave for his office at the airport. He would never be quite the same as he was in Shanghai, but he no longer felt like a failure. When they moved back to San Francisco after Alson's wedding, Alice had gently and continuously encouraged her husband to apply for a federal job. Yes, he was much older than the usual candidates, but the rapid expansion of government agencies in the Bay Area meant new opportunities for all of them. Finally, Alfred had relented. After a brief period as a clerk, he had advanced to his current position as a Customs Service inspector. It was not his dream job—that existed in another time and place—but it paid decently, included a pension, and allowed him to draw on his import-export experience. He stuck with it until his retirement.[1]

Alice felt profound relief at her husband's relative contentment. He had just started at the Customs Service when they heard the news about Ernest, yet another casualty of 1949 and the end of their Shanghai world. Alice didn't think her husband would ever take his own life, but she hadn't believed that her oldest brother would, either—until he did. Of course, the party line was that ill health and financial setbacks pushed Ernest to suicide; in fact, that was the *literal* party line, the conclusion that J. L. Huang and his Nationalist friends reached in Taiwan. But Ernest's family knew that his loss of faith in the future of the KMT had helped push him over the edge.[2]

Like her siblings, Alice felt particularly sorry for Loring. After Ernest arrived in Taipei, he registered at the US Embassy and listed Kay as his next of kin, yet for some reason his suicide note instructed J.L. to inform only his younger son of his death. So it was Loring who received the general's brief, regretful telegram from Taiwan and the more specific follow-up letter. After consulting his brother Ken, Loring scrambled to make decisions about his father's body, belongings, and debts, all from thousands of miles away. At the same time, the poor kid was not just working a full-time job but trying to plan his own wedding, too. Unlike Ruth, Ernest had supported his son's relationship with Moyra, so while Alice and Alfred could not get to New York for the ceremony, Kay and Helen made sure to attend.[3]

. . .

Kay saw Helen more frequently these days. Ever since Jeanne's death, the Chins made a point of inviting her over as often as possible. Helen had finally sold the family home in Flatbush, which she declared too large and too expensive, though the ghosts that haunted it didn't help either. Fortunately, Jim and Lonnie Typond had a neighbor on their street with an apartment to rent, so Helen moved to their block of Parkside. It was a convenient commute both to her church and to Abraham & Straus, where she now helped manage the sixth-floor beauty salon and optometry shop.[4]

Although Helen found a second family at A&S, nothing could replace her sisters. With Alice in California, the three valued their infrequent reunions more than ever. In November 1960, the Lees came east to see Alson, Lillian, and their little son Douglas Alfred, as well as to attend the Chins' fiftieth anniversary party. Kay and Ming Tai sat at the center of the long head table, with their two sons on one side, their five daughters on the other, and all their grandchildren arrayed in front of them. A somewhat faded and tattered double happiness banner hung on the wall behind them—an original decoration from their wedding banquet fifty years earlier—and Kay, Alice, Helen, and all the Chin daughters wore festive silk Chinese cheongsam.[5]

The banner, the dresses, and many of the toasts were very Chinese, which is how Kay's children still thought of her, yet at sixty-seven she had never left the United States. True, she longed to see China, but under the circumstances, she had given up hope of even getting close. While she could probably travel to Taiwan, which they all called "Free China" now, nobody really thought of it as the real thing. Instead, Hong Kong was the closest they could get to the mainland, but at eighty, Ming Tai felt too frail to make such a trip, while Alice, Alfred, Bill, and May showed little interest in returning to a place that held so many painful memories.[6]

Then Josephine Hong announced her plan at the monthly Chinese Women's Association meeting, which Kay and Helen always attended. Under

Josephine's leadership, the CWA raised money each year for the Hua Hsing Children's Home, a Taipei orphanage founded by Madame Chiang Kai-shek. In October, Josephine would lead a delegation of CWA members to Taipei, where they would deliver their annual gift in person to the orphanage. She and her husband, both active in the New York KMT branch, never encountered any difficulties traveling to Taiwan, but ordinary tourists didn't always fare so well. Fortunately, Taiwan had recently relaxed its visa regulations after more than a decade, so travelers could now stop there if they were transiting between other places. The CWA group planned to travel from New York to Japan, then to Taiwan, finishing in Hong Kong.[7]

Kay locked eyes with her sister. If not now, when? She knew that Helen wanted to see Asia, too, and planning such a trip alone seemed a bit overwhelming. If they went with the CWA, they just needed to get passports and make sure Helen could take some vacation time. Ming Tai encouraged Kay, sending his Hong Kong niece Mary the sisters' itinerary. The Chins' daughter-in-law Emily had grown up in the colony, so she contacted her parents, who insisted Kay and Helen bunk with them. The two sisters now had a place to stay and a set of enthusiastic tour guides, and Helen's A&S colleagues even threw her a surprise party to celebrate her departure. For the first time in years, she felt excitement at the prospect of a new adventure.[8]

• • •

At Taipei's Sungshan Airport, an efficient minder from the Women's Federation met the New York group members and shepherded them onto a bus for the quick trip to the city center. Kay and Helen peered out the window, fascinated by the pedicabs, low concrete buildings, and palm trees. Even before they crossed the Keelung River, they caught sight of the large, luxurious Grand Hotel atop a hill. Modeled after Beijing's Hall of Supreme Harmony, it was located at the center of a large, walled preserve accessible only through well-guarded gates. The whole setup worked to deter foreign-local interactions, an unsurprising goal in what remained a repressive state.[9]

When the CWA members left the compound, they did so with a Women's Federation member, riding together in a bus that took them to the destinations on their prearranged itinerary. The only glimpses Kay and Helen had of ordinary people came from the windows. At the orphanage, Madame Chiang greeted the group in English, thanking Josephine for the gift as the government photographer snapped away. Both Helen and Kay thought about the official picture from Ernest's meeting with Chiang Kai-shek; their brother had been so proud that he made copies to send to all his siblings. His sisters would not have a similar experience, it seemed. The Women's Federation handlers gestured for them to stand out of the way while the photographer posed only the group's leaders with Madame Chiang, who then left the building with her entourage.[10]

By the time the CWA reached Sun Moon Lake, the island's most famous beauty spot, the two sisters had become skilled at stepping aside as local dignitaries and party officials greeted Josephine and her husband and snapped the customary photos. So Kay and Helen were surprised to find two straw baskets of vividly purple flowers awaiting them at the Evergreen Hostel. Yes, the manager said, the gifts were for them, not Josephine or the more prominent women in the group. Kay opened the envelope attached to her basket and got a lump in her throat at the sight of General J. L. Huang's business card, on which he had written: "To Dr. Moy's sisters." The Evergreen's manager had also known Ernest right after the war, and he gushed to the women about their brother's patriotism and love for the party. Kay briefly caught Helen's eye. Both knew of Ernest's ultimate disillusionment, but they appreciated the kind gesture.[11]

Despite being crowded, humid, and overwhelming, Hong Kong was something of a relief for Kay and Helen after their busy days in Taiwan. The CWA members went their separate ways, meaning no more gated compounds, set itineraries, or stuffy dinners together in hotel dining rooms. Instead, the sisters stayed with the Wongs, Emily's parents, while Ming Tai's niece Mary and her husband, Norman, took them to all the big sights on Hong Kong Island. They rode up the Peak Tram, caught a bus to Repulse Bay, and giggled at tacky Tiger Balm Gardens, which Ernest had never mentioned in his year as *Hong Kong Tiger Standard* correspondent. For Kay, the highlight was definitely the Star Ferry to Kowloon. Not only did she spy her first real rickshaw at the Tsimshatsui pier, but the sight of Hong Kong's skyline and the harbor clogged with ships, tugs, and little "walla-walla" boats enthralled her. On the ride back, she rushed down the aisle like an excited child to snag a rail-side seat for a better view.[12]

For Kay and Helen's last night in the colony, the Wongs planned a going-away dinner at the Golden City restaurant in Central, but first they took advantage of the lovely weather to drive their guests out to the lush and rural New Territories. Now the women saw a completely different colony from the concrete precincts of Hong Kong Island. Their first stop was the Greenville

Amusement Park; just like Taipei's Grand Hotel or the tourist trap rickshaws at the Tsimshatsui ferry pier, Greenville exuded nostalgia for a lost China, right down to the classical archway entrance and a teahouse modeled on the famous marble Summer Palace boat in Beijing. After exploring the place, the group motored on through Yuen Long before pulling over near Deep Water Bay, gazing across the water, and admiring the remarkably clear blue sky. Then the Wongs pointed toward a green strip of land on the other side of the bay: China, the country that had so deeply shaped the Moy siblings' lives and identities. It was as close as the two sisters would ever get, so they lingered a while, savoring the sight.[13]

Epilogue

THE FAMILY MEMBERS MILLED ABOUT the casket, still struggling to believe the day had really come. Given the severity of Ming Tai's stroke, no one expected Kay to die before he did. But then she exhausted herself caring for him, finally suffering a massive, fatal heart attack of her own, and now the cheerful, steady matriarch of the family was gone.[1]

Suddenly the wailing started, and all heads swiveled toward the source of the horrible noise. No one knew this howling woman, whose heartrending cries set everyone's teeth on edge. Then the funeral director discretely whispered that *he* recognized her: One of the last professional mourners in Chinatown, she had probably been sent by some well-meaning friend of the family. Jack Young, who had come to the funeral in full dress uniform despite his recent divorce from Adelaide, now nodded at Beah's husband, Wayman. The two men walked over to the mourner, picked her up in her chair, and carried both outside to the curb. After setting her down gently on the sidewalk, they thanked her for her excellent work and then returned inside, pulling the door firmly shut behind them.[2]

Ten months later, Ming Tai passed away. Now the Chins' children finally sold off their parents' real estate holdings, including the Pell Street building Ming Tai had purchased half a century earlier. None of them could see keeping it, its tiny rooms and cramped floor plan so very different than their own comfortable suburban homes. Instead, the Chins' children and grandchildren—a huge tribe of cousins—began to gather at other places, their reunions featuring huge spreads of food and corny talent shows. Dedicated to her home and family, Kay would have approved. And she would have been pleased at how close her children remained; four of the seven eventually settled in the small North Carolina town where Vivian and Bingham first moved after his retirement from Duke University.[3]

. . .

In spring 1965, an FBI clerk retrieved a dusty old file that contained hundreds of pages of reports about a long-forgotten treason suspect from the war years. Authorities from NASA's security division had requested the dossier as part of an employment background check. The job applicant did appear to be the dead traitor's brother, but officials decided that Bill Moy himself was neither a Communist nor sympathetic to the party. Having cleared this hurdle, Bill landed his dream job at Grumman Aerospace, joining the team that developed a lunar lander for the proposed moon mission.[4]

When he got the Grumman offer, Bill was working in Virginia, and now he and May moved to Long Island. In order to keep target shooting legally, Bill discovered that he needed to take a required New York State novice course at a local pistol club. The instructor could not hit a target nearly as well as Bill, who found the class so intolerable that he finally quit his longtime hobby. He did not miss it much, however; a respected and successful engineer, he no longer needed the pastime that had once given him such a sense of control and competence.[5]

On July 16, 1969, Bill watched the Apollo 11 launch while at work, since Grumman had installed television monitors for its employees. But the moon landing date was a Sunday, so he and his son were at home in Dix Hills, glued to the TV in the small room off the kitchen. Walter Cronkite had been broadcasting for hours, describing the lunar module's undocking from the command module and its progress toward the moon's surface. May used most of the afternoon to work on Chinese calligraphy and brush painting, which had become her passion over the previous decade, but she came in to watch the last few minutes of the lunar module's descent.[6]

CBS showed a simulation of the landing and broadcast a live feed of the radio communications between astronauts Buzz Aldrin and Neil Armstrong and Mission Control. Bill leaned forward intently, listening to the beeps and static as the module hovered just feet from the lunar surface. Then it touched down. "Man on the moon!" Cronkite gasped. Bill felt a mix of triumph, relief, and awe, then smiled when Armstrong's voice crackled: "The Eagle has landed!" Cronkite teared up, momentarily dumbstruck, as were the Moys and millions of other Americans. The next day, the lunar module lifted off from the moon's surface using radar Bill had helped develop, and then it delivered the two astronauts safely back to the command module. Although he lived another twenty-three years, it was the proudest moment of Bill's life.[7]

. . .

Helen watched the moon landing from her new apartment in Oakland. A year earlier, she had retired from Abraham & Straus and moved to the Bay Area to be closer to the Lees in Richmond. By the time she arrived in California, Alfred was in increasingly poor health, a stroke having forced his early retirement from the civil service. Alice worked at Social Security for a few more years while caring for her ailing husband, lovingly buttoning his shirts, tying his shoes, and helping him eat his meals. When Alfred's condition became more than she could manage, she moved him to a nearby nursing home where he could receive around-the-clock care. Still, she visited him every day, and while he rarely spoke anymore, he always lit up when she walked into his room. After Alfred's death in 1978, Alice got only a little respite from grief: Helen developed pancreatic cancer and died in 1981.[8]

Alice took solace in her many friends and the hobby the Kwok sisters had failed to interest her in so many years before: bowling. In Shanghai, she had seen no reason to bother with it, but now she came to enjoy the comradery of her league, developing a wicked armswing that helped her rack up the senior trophies. She proudly showed them to her grandchildren, who knew better than to expect their "Gallopin' Granny" to bake their favorite treats. After all these years, she still hated to cook, so instead she took them bowling and then out to eat.[9]

Alson, Lillian, and the kids always visited her during their summer home leaves in the United States. By the mid-1960s, Alson had left his big accounting firm and joined Singer Sewing Machine, which eventually sent him to Taiwan to run its operations there. The family stayed in Taipei for eight years, and the entire time, C. Y. Lin—probably the only person besides Alice with any memory of Alson's birth father—lived nearby. But since Alson had no idea C.Y. even existed, K.S. Lo remained as much a mystery to his son as he had always been.[10]

. . .

Alice's grandchildren grew up in a very different America than the one she and her siblings had known. Racial discrimination persisted, but it was not as brutal and open as it had been when Bill waited tables at a chop suey restaurant or when Herbert had to leave school for dating a white girl. Nor did it carry the kind of legal sanction that had cost Alice her citizenship for marrying a China-born student. By the late 1960s, a new wave of Chinese immigrants—first from Hong Kong and Taiwan and eventually from the mainland—were also transforming the Chinatowns in which the six Moys had grown up. Their children and grandchildren watched these changes from the comfort of the suburbs, part of the first generation of Asian Americans to gain access to such places.

The Moy descendants had a very different relationship with China, too. In the 1920s and 1930s, four of the six siblings and their spouses moved to that country, a very common choice for Chinese Americans of their generation. In the postwar decades, none of their children or grandchildren could imagine doing the same. The 1970s thaw in US-China relations occurred after most of the siblings had died, and the remaining ones expressed no interest in visiting their old home. Some of the more curious grandchildren did eventually make the trip, but while a few worked there for brief periods or helped relatives emigrate to the United States, none envisioned a future on the mainland the way their grandparents had.[11]

• • •

A month after Alfred's death, Alson returned to mainland China for the first time since leaving Shanghai more than thirty years earlier. Now fifty, he traveled to Guangzhou as one of the Singer representatives to the big Canton Trade Fair. At the monthlong event, he joined hundreds of other foreign businesspeople deeply curious about recent political and economic shifts in the PRC. After Mao Zedong's 1976 death, Hua Guofeng, the chairman's handpicked successor, became the official premier and leader. But within a year or so, observers could see that the real power belonged to Vice Premier Deng Xiaoping, supported by Marshall Ye Jianying, who had once practiced his English with Adelaide's daughter Jacqueline. In 1978, Deng was just starting to launch his "reform and opening policies," so the development that transformed China so dramatically in the next few decades had not yet begun.[12]

The Singer executives did sense potential there, but when they offered Alson the chance to lead the company's new PRC operations, he turned them down. He opted instead for early retirement and the opportunity to travel as much as possible with Lillian. During one of their trips in 1995, Alice, now in a nursing home, passed away at age ninety, having outlived all her siblings. Her granddaughters, unwilling to disrupt their parents' vacation, waited to tell Alson and Lillian until the couple's return to the US. Alice had wanted it that way: The woman who, in life, loved being the center of attention specified that her family make as little fuss as possible after her death.[13]

Alson and Lillian's travel destinations eventually included China, which they visited several times as it reopened to US tourists. In 1999, unable to suppress his curiosity any longer, Alson arranged for a car and driver to take him and his family to the Kiangwan country home Alfred had loved so much. The house remained standing, but it was in poor condition; squatters lived in some of the rooms, and buildings occupied the former yard and tennis court. Alson knew from Shanghai officials that he could reclaim the property if he found the deed, but his parents had lost the document at some point after fleeing China. And really, what would he do with such a home now? After his family explored the place a little more, they all climbed back into their car and drove away, returning to their lives elsewhere.[14]

ACKNOWLEDGMENTS

The Moys of New York and Shanghai would not exist without the assistance and encouragement of many people and institutions across the country, as well as in Europe and Asia.

I started working on the book during the COVID-19 pandemic, so I depended on a wide range of archivists and librarians who either located and scanned material I couldn't access directly or answered follow-up questions about collections I had visited years earlier. My thanks to the staff at the Academia Sinica, Appalachian State University Special Collections Research Center, East Carolina University Joyner Library, Harvard-Yenching Library, Hoover Institution, George C. Marshall Foundation, Maryknoll Mission Archive, National Taiwan University, New York Public Library, Northfield Mount Hermon School, San Francisco Maritime Museum, Shanghai Municipal Archives, Stanford University Special Collections, Swiss Federal Archives, and University of Miami Archives and Special Collections. Yue Ma at the Museum of Chinese in America offered crucial research materials. Peerless federal employees at the National Archives and Records Administration facilities in College Park, Seattle, San Bruno, New York, Boston, and Chicago made this project (and all of my past work) possible.

A sabbatical from Baruch College and a Weissman School of Arts and Sciences Dean's Office research grant enabled me to finish the manuscript.

At CUNY, Ava Chin, Eva Chou, Vince DiGirolamo, Elizabeth Heath, Thomas Heinrich, Martina Ngyuen, Mark Rice, and Ky Woltering gave advice, feedback, and assistance. My thanks as well to student research assistants Yuan Zhou, Linda Abramson, and Justin Lee. Outside CUNY, Bryan Hayashi, Alison Hinderliter, Robert Kim, Sue Kriete, Heather Lee, Sophie Loy-Wilson, Scott Seligman, and K. Ian Shin shared helpful archival materials, while Stella Dong, Katherine Marino, and Ellen Wu offered enthusiastic encouragement for the book. Cindy Broholm, Rona Vail, and Bob Yee advised me on the impact of Moy family ailments. I deeply appreciate Mae Ngai's early and consistent support and feedback, which was crucial to this project's success. And I am honored that Helen Zia, whose work and activism I greatly admire, generously agreed to write the foreword.

Over the past few years, I interviewed or corresponded with numerous Moy descendants, as well as other people who knew the siblings and their spouses. Many shared not just memories but photos and documents. My thanks to Stephen Chang, Alan Chen, Ming Kay Chen, Doug Chu, Steve Hance, Art Kim, Dick Kim, Deborah Lau, Jennifer Lau, Bert Lee, Eileen Lee, Isabell Chin Leong, Chris Moy, Fred Moy, Sara Moy, and Tamra Moy, as well as the late Alson Lee and Sherman Chen. I am particularly grateful to Jolly Young King for sending me copies of her mother's letters, family history documents, and Ernest Moy's diaries and papers from the late 1940s and 1950s. Lillian Lee recounted her husband's stories, patiently answered my many questions, and welcomed me into her home to meet and talk with her children and other Moy relatives. Special thanks to Douglas Lee, an early and ardent supporter of this book, who connected me to other relatives and family friends, provided photos and documents, and helped make this project possible.

My agent, Elise Capron, took a chance on a manuscript about the most extraordinary family she'd never heard of. Editor Niels Hooper, Nora Becker, and the team at the University of California Press embraced the Moys, while comments from readers Erika Lee and K. Scott Wong made the book better.

I am also tremendously grateful for the love and support of my family, especially Marlene and Jim Bentzien, Nancy Bowman, Joy Brooks, Lisa Brooks, Jill Brooks-Garnett, Charles and Norma Griffith, Dara Griffith, Michelle Purrington, and Jennifer Tucker. Theo and Olive Brooks-Griffith offered the comfort that only wagging tails can provide.

Finally, I would never have dared to start this project had Pam Griffith not urged me to write the kind of book she knew I wanted to do all along, and then gently reminded me: "Don't postpone Moy." She read multiple drafts of the manuscript, gave honest and valuable feedback, and never stopped believing in the worthiness of this project, or of me. Words are inadequate to express my gratitude for her love, encouragement, and partnership.

ABBREVIATIONS FOR FREQUENTLY USED SOURCES

AML	Alson M. Lee personal papers (private)
AMLD	Alson M. Lee diary (private)
ARCI	Aid Refugee Chinese Intellectuals collections, Hoover Institution
AU	Archives Unbound database, Gale
BC	*The Brooklyn Citizen* newspaper
BE	*The Brooklyn Daily Eagle* newspaper
BFO	British Foreign Office Files for China, AM/Archives Direct database
BSU	*Brooklyn Standard Union* newspaper
BTU	*Brooklyn Times-Union* newspaper
CP	*China Press* newspaper, Shanghai
CSM	*Chinese Students Monthly* (journal of the Chinese Students' Alliance of America)
CT	*Chicago Tribune* newspaper
CWR	*China Weekly Review* newspaper, Shanghai
DJC	Douglas J. Chu collection, Museum of Chinese in America, New York
EAP	*Editor and Publisher* magazine, New York
EKMD	Ernest K. Moy diaries (in possession of the author)
EKMP	Ernest K. Moy papers (in possession of the author)
FM	Frederic Moy papers (private)
FRUS	Foreign Relations of the United States series, US Government Publishing Office
GF	Papers of George A. Fitch and Geraldine T. Fitch, Harvard-Yenching Library, Harvard University

HEM	FBI file of Herbert Erasmus Moy, Classification 100, RG 65, National Archives, College Park, Maryland
JTY	Jack T. Young, *Yinshuisiyuan* (Never forget where you came from) (Taipei: Central Daily News, 1989)
JYK	Jolly Young King collection (private)
LAT	*Los Angeles Times* newspaper
LCY	Chi-yung Lin, *Lin jiyong xiansheng fangwen jilu* (Record of Mr. Chi-yung Lin's oral histories) (Taipei: Institute of Modern History, Academia Sinica, 1983)
MFHR	Eugenia "Beah" Chen Wing, "My Family History Record," February 1981, Jolly Young King collection
MH	Northfield Mount Hermon School archives
ML	Alson M. Lee, "My Life" memoir, 2014 (private)
NARA-BOS	National Archives and Records Administration facility, Boston
NARA-CHI	National Archives and Records Administration facility, Chicago
NARA-CP	National Archives and Records Administration facility, College Park
NARA-DC	National Archives and Records Administration facility, Washington, DC
NARA-NY	National Archives and Records Administration facility, New York City
NARA-SB	National Archives and Records Administration facility, San Bruno
NARA-SEA	National Archives and Records Administration facility, Seattle
NCDHL	*North China Desk Hong List*, various years, published by *North China Daily News*, Shanghai
NCH	*North China Herald* newspaper, Shanghai
NFA	Norwood Francis Allman papers, Hoover Institution
NYCMA	New York City Municipal Archives
NYDN	*New York Daily News* newspaper
NYHT	*New York Tribune/New York Herald-Tribune* newspaper
NYS	*New York Sun* newspaper
NYT	*New York Times* newspaper
PK	Peter Kim Papers, George C. Marshall Foundation Library and Archives, Lexington, Virginia

RGR	Victoria Chen Luke, "Recollections of Glen Ridge," Jolly Young King collection
SCMP	*South China Morning Post* newspaper, Hong Kong
SEPM	*Shanghai Evening Post and Mercury* newspaper, Shanghai and New York
SFA	Swiss Federal Archives, Bern, Switzerland
SMP	"Policing the Shanghai International Settlement, 1894–1949" database, Gale Archives Unbound
VCD	Vivian Chen Dai letters to Bingham Dai, Bingham Dai Papers Collection, Special Collections, Appalachian State University, Boone, North Carolina
WTM	William T. Moy family scrapbooks (private)
WWCNY	Warner M. Van Norden, *Who's Who of the Chinese in New York* (New York: Warner M. Van Norden, 1918)

NOTES

PROLOGUE

1. Madeline Y. Hsu, *Dreaming of Gold, Dreaming of Home: Transnationalism and Migration Between the United States and South China, 1882–1943* (Stanford University Press, 2000), 2–3; Adam McKeown, *Chinese Migrant Networks and Cultural Change: Peru, Chicago, Hawaii, 1900–1936* (University of Chicago Press, 2001), 44; Melissa Macauley, *Distant Shores: Colonial Encounters on China's Maritime Frontier* (Princeton University Press, 2021), 59–61; Scott Seligman, *Three Tough Chinamen* (Earnshaw, 2012), 13–14.

2. MFHR, 19; Moy Sing testimony, May 23, 1911, p. 17, file 2500/141, NARA-BOS; Erika Lee, *At America's Gates: Chinese Immigration During the Exclusion Era, 1882–1943* (University of North Carolina Press, 2003), 25–30; Charlotte Brooks, *Alien Neighbors, Foreign Friends: Asian Americans, Housing, and the Transformation of Urban California* (University of Chicago Press, 2009), 21–24; Beth Lew Williams, *The Chinese Must Go: Violence, Exclusion, and the Making of the Alien in America* (Harvard University Press, 2018), 55–62.

3. Lew Williams, *The Chinese Must Go*, 55–62.

4. Huping Ling, *Chinese Chicago: Race, Transnationalism, Migration, and Community Since 1870* (Stanford University Press, 2012), 31–37.

5. Ling, *Chinese Chicago*, 100–107; Judy Yung, *Unbound Feet: A Social History of Chinese Women in San Francisco* (University of California Press, 1995), 24–25.

6. MFHR, 19; Moy Sing testimony, May 23, 1911, pp. 17–18, and May 24, 1911, p. 26, and Horn She testimony, May 23, 1911, pp. 9, 12, file 2500/141.

7. Michelle T. King, *Between Birth and Death: Female Infanticide in Nineteenth-Century China* (Stanford University Press, 2014), 5; MFHR, 19–20; Cook County Birth Certificates Index, 1287951 and 1287739, Ancestry.com; "The Chinese New Year," *Philadelphia Times*, January 26, 1895.

8. "Chinatown in Great Glory," *Philadelphia Times*, May 26, 1895.

9. "Chinatown in Great Glory."

10. "Some Spicy Testimony," *Philadelphia Inquirer*, December 13, 1895; "More Light on Police Abuses," *Philadelphia Times*, December 13, 1895; "Tales of Low Blackmail," *Philadelphia Times*, December 19, 1895.

11. Edwin G. Burrows and Mike Wallace, *Gotham: A History of New York City to 1898* (Oxford University Press, 1898), 1204–6; MFHR, 19–20; Charlotte Brooks, *Between Mao and McCarthy: Chinese American Politics in the Cold War Years* (University of Chicago Press, 2015), 16; *Twelfth Census of the United States, Vol. 1: Population, Part 1* (USGPO, 1901), 568.

12. Horn Ying testimony, May 23, 1911, p. 9; MFHR, 20–21.

13. "Woman Doctors Chinese," *Topeka Daily Capital*, December 6, 1903; "Dr. Esther Bok," *Buffalo Commercial*, August 5, 1907. My thanks to Cindy Broholm, professor of nursing at Long Island University, for explaining the likely impact of so many pregnancies so close together.

14. Mary Ting Yi Lui, *The Chinatown Trunk Mystery: Murder, Miscegenation, and Other Dangerous Encounters in Turn-of-the-Century New York City* (Princeton University Press, 2005), 172; "New York City," *Journal of Education* 53, no. 20 (May 16, 1901), 321; "A Chinese Kindergarten," *NYS*, March 23, 1910.

15. Moy Kie Gooie testimony, May 23, 1911, p. 15, file 2500/141; MFHR, 20, 49; Edmond Yee, *The Soaring Crane: Stories of Asian Lutherans in North America* (Augsburg Fortress, 2002), 21–22; "New York City," *Journal of Education* 55, no. 19 (May 8, 1902), 305; "Sun Yat-sen One of Three," *NYS*, October 15, 1911.

PART ONE: FAMILY

1. Him Mark Lai, *Chinese American Transnational Politics*, ed. Madeline Y. Hsu (University of Illinois Press, 2010), 10–13; Kathryn Edgerton-Tarpley, *Tears from Iron: Cultural Responses to Famine in Nineteenth-Century China* (University of California Press, 2008), 1–4; Tobie Meyer-Fong, *What Remains: Coming to Terms with Civil War in 19th Century China* (Stanford University Press, 2013), 7–11.

2. McKeown, *Chinese Migrant Networks and Cultural Change*, 86–90; Paul A. Cohen, *History in Three Keys: The Boxers as Event, Experience, and Myth* (Columbia University Press, 1997), 83–105.

3. Lai, *Chinese American Transnational Politics*, 10–13; Charlotte Brooks, *American Exodus: Second-Generation Chinese Americans in China, 1901–1949* (University of California Press, 2019), 46–50, 70; Weili Ye, *Seeking Modernity in China's Name: Chinese Students in the United States, 1900–1927* (Stanford University Press, 2002), 83–84.

4. Brooks, *American Exodus*, 2–6, 11, 38–40, 76, 174.

CHAPTER ONE: KAY

1. MFHR, 49–51; "Weather," *NYT*, November 21, 1910.

2. MFHR, 49; Sucheng Chan, "The Exclusion of Chinese Women," in Sucheng Chan, ed., *Entry Denied: Exclusion and the Chinese Community in America, 1882–1943* (Temple University Press, 1991), 105–17; *Thirteenth Census of the United States, 1910, Vol. 1: Population* (Washington: USGPO, 1913), 630–32.

3. MFHR, 49; Lui, *The Chinatown Trunk Mystery*, 1–5, 8–15.

4. MFHR, 49; *WWCNY*, 26; *1910 United States Federal Census*, Manhattan Ward 6, ED 45, p. 9b, Ancestry.com. Ming Tai's surname in most sources is romanized as *Chin*, as is Kay's until the 1940s, when she began to use *Chen*. The couple's children tended to use *Chen*, but not always, so I have stuck with *Chin* for simplicity and to reflect most of my sources.

5. RGR, 5; MFHR, 49; "Police Reserves Must Be Called," *Meadville Daily Republican* (Pennsylvania), November 22, 1910.

6. MFHR, 49.

7. MFHR, 49.

8. MFHR, 50–51; "Big Day in Chinatown," *Times-Democrat* (New Orleans), December 23, 1910.

9. MFHR, 1–3; Chin Mow (Chin Ming Tai) testimony, January 17, 1908, pp. 1–2, file 96/942, and Chin Ming Tai testimony, March 30, 1922, p. 1, file 6/1235, NARA-NY.

10. Kathleen López, *Chinese Cubans: A Transnational History* (University of North Carolina Press, 2013), 149.

11. MFHR, 54.

12. Isabell Chin Leong interview with the author, June 27, 2022.

13. "Bride and Bridegroom at City Hall's Chinese Wedding Yesterday," *NYHT*, November 22, 1910; MFHR, 51.

14. "Chinese Wed in City Hall," *NYHT*, November 22, 1910; "Picturesque Chinese Wedding," *Salt Lake Telegram*, November 30, 1910; "Big Day in Chinatown."

15. "Big Day in Chinatown"; "New Marriage Law," *NYHT*, August 4, 1907; "Police Reserves Must Be Called."

16. "Bride and Bridegroom at City Hall's Chinese Wedding Yesterday"; "Police Reserves Must Be Called."

17. MFHR, 51.

18. MFHR, 51; "Big Day in Chinatown."

19. "Big Day in Chinatown."

CHAPTER TWO: ERNEST

1. "Chinatown in Great Glory: The Baby Boy of Mr. and Mrs. Moy Sing Given a Name," *Philadelphia Times*, May 26, 1895; photograph, file 2500/141, NARA-BOS.

2. New York State Certificate and Record of Birth, "Moy Kee," December 7, 1896, and "Moy Kee" testimony, May 13, 1911, pp. 1–5, file 2500/141; Moy K. Gooie, "Meaning of Chinese Reform," *Chicago Sunday Examiner*, April 23, 1911.

3. Lee, *At America's Gates*, 42; Hsu, *Dreaming of Gold, Dreaming of Home*, 86–87; Chin Jin Gow affidavit, September 30, 1958, p. 1, file 2500/141.

4. Horn She testimony, May 23, 1911, pp. 9–13, and Moy Kie Gooie testimony, May 23, 1911, pp. 14–16, file 2500/141.

5. Moy Kie Gooie testimony, 15–16; Lucy E. Salyer, *Laws Harsh as Tigers: Chinese Immigrants and the Shaping of Modern Immigration Law* (University of North Carolina Press, 1995), 59; Lee, *At America's Gates*, 100–109; Lui, *The Chinatown Trunk Mystery*, 204–10.

6. Moy Kay Sum testimony, May 24, 1911, pp. 30–31, and Jeremiah J. Hurley to Inspector in Charge, Vancouver, June 12, 1911, p. 1, file 2500/141.

7. ML, 7; Lawrence Downs, "Word for Word: The 1910 Boy Scout Manual," *NYT*, July 9, 2000; "Chinese Lads Organize Troop of Boy Scouts," *BC*, June 25, 1911.

8. "Chinatown Clean, Dives Wiped Out, Its Horrors Gone," *New York Evening World*, December 10, 1912; "Exile Fair Ah Fong, Beauty for Whom Tongs Waged War," *New York Evening World*, March 5, 1913; "Claws of the Dragon Losing Grip on New York's Famous Chinatown," *NYS*, June 15, 1913.

9. Brooks, *American Exodus*, 89–91; *WWCNY*, 35; "Sun Yat Sen One of Three," *NYS*, October 15, 1911; "The Chinese Revolution Was Born and Nourished in the United States," *NYHT*, January 7, 1912.

10. "No Dragon on Flag of China Republic," *NYT*, October 15, 1911; Ernest K. Moy, "Sun Yat-sen to Me," EKMP; L. Eve Armentrout Ma, *Revolutionaries, Monarchists, and Chinatowns: Chinese Politics in the Americas and the 1911 Revolution* (University of Hawai'i Press, 1990), 122–24.

11. Moy, "Sun Yat-sen to Me," 2–3; "Personalities: Serving Chinatown—Judy Yung," *American Libraries* 4, no. 5 (May 1973), 273.

12. Moy, "Sun Yat-sen to Me," 4; Moy, "Meaning of Chinese Reform."

13. Edward J. M. Rhoads, *Manchus and Han: Ethnic Relations and Political Power in Late Qing and Early Republican China, 1861–1928* (University of Washington Press, 2000), 173–74; "Insurgents Here Elated," *NYHT*, October 24, 1911; Meyer-Fong, *What Remains*, 4–7.

14. "No Dragon on Flag of Chinese Republic."

15. *NYT*, "War Spirit Fills All Chinatown," October 23, 1911; *NYHT*, "For Chinese Air Squad," December 1, 1911.

16. Photo 2012.037.615, ca. 1912, DJC.

17. Brooks, *American Exodus*, 54–55.

18. Louis J. Beck, *New York's Chinatown: An Historical Presentation of Its People and Places* (Bohemia Publishing, 1898), 28–29; *BC*, "Chinese Lads Organize Troop of Boy Scouts"

19. Brooks, *Between Mao and McCarthy*, 20–21, 36–37.

20. I have found no mention or photo of Ernest in the Dewitt Clinton High School 1913 *Clintonian* yearbook, nor have I found any mention in the newspapers of him competing on the track team (as he claimed).

21. Advertisement for National School of Chiropractic, *McClure's Magazine*, February 1914.

22. Advertisement for National School of Chiropractic in Robert T. Morris, *Doctors Versus Folks* (Doubleday Page, 1915), 204; Marie-Claire Bergere, *Sun Yat-sen*, trans. Janet Lloyd (Stanford University Press, 1998), 27–28.

23. 1915 New York State Census, "Enumeration of the Inhabitants of Block 4, ED 2, AD 3," June 1, 1915, Ancestry.com.

CHAPTER THREE: ALICE

1. "Police Reserves Must Be Called," *Meadville Daily Republican* (Pennsylvania), November 22, 1910; MFHR, 49; RGR, 11.

2. Deborah Lau interview with the author, August 24, 2020; Bert Lee interview with the author, September 23, 2020; Chris Moy conversation with the author, March 25, 2023; Douglas Chu YouTube channel, "Typond Home Movies 3," ca. 1939, https://www.youtube.com/watch?v = PEEutWkxIjw (accessed April 13, 2024).

3. Photos 2015.037.608–1 and 2015.037.629, 1914–1922, DJC; "New Men to Run New York Club," *CSM*, November 1910, 93.

4. "Asbury Park, NJ," 1923 and 1926, "Glen Ridge, NJ," 1919 and 1922, unlabeled Glen Ridge ca. 1920, beach photos ca. 1921, WTM.

5. MFHR, 19; "Tong Fights, Opium and Chop Suey Do Not Epitomize Chinese Life Here," *NYHT*, September 29, 1912; photo 2015.037.614–2, June 1916, DJC.

6. "A Chinese Kindergarten," *NYS*, March 23, 1910; "Chinatown Awakens: Women of Chop Suey District Want English Teaching, Moving Pictures and Votes," *NYHT*, April 14, 1912; "Suffrage Meeting for Chinese Women," *BE*, April 8, 1912; "Personal Notes," *CSM*, January 1915, 254; Florence Thom testimony, June 27, 1914, pp. 1–2, file 6/1906, NARA-NYC; photos 2015.037.607–2, 2015.037.610, 2015.037.615, and 2015.037.635, 1917–1926, DJC.

7. Zhitian Luo, "National Humiliation and National Assertion: The Chinese Response to the Twenty-One Demands," *Modern Asian Studies* 27, no. 2 (1993): 299–303; S.N.D. North, "The Negotiations Between Japan and China in 1915," *American Journal of International Law* 10, no. 2 (1916): 222–37; "New York Chinese Students' Club," *CSM*, April 1915, 465; "Japan Defied by Chinese Here," *NYHT*, February 24, 1915; *NYHT*, "Chinese Students Send Protest," February 23, 1915; "Chinese Students Stirred by Danger," *BE*, May 2, 1915.

8. Bert Lee interview with the author; *WWCNY*, 57, 88; Brooks, *American Exodus*, 6–7.

9. Lillian Lee email to the author, May 30, 2020; Stephen Chang interview with the author, September 8, 2022; "Rainbow Division Advances," *NYHT*, April 28, 1918.

10. Elene Foster, "Liberty's Daughters of All Lands Sell Bonds," *NYHT*, April 14, 1918; "Daughters of China Ask American Women for Aid Against Republic's Foes," *China Review*, October 1921, 235; H.C. Chen, "The Chinese Boy Scouts in New York," *CSM*, March 1918, 271; Chloe Arnold, "Americans All: Glimpses of War and the Red Cross on the Great East Side of New York," *Red Cross Magazine* 13, no. 6 (June 1918), 13, 15; Susan L. Glosser, *Chinese Visions of Family and State, 1915–1953* (University of California Press, 2003), 37–52.

11. Mabel Lee, "The Meaning of Woman Suffrage," *CSM*, May 1914, 526.

12. Xiaohuang Yin, "Writing a Place in American Life: The Sensibilities of American-Born Chinese as Reflected in Life Stories from the Exclusion Era," in Sucheng Chan, ed., *Chinese American Transnationalism* (Temple University Press, 2006), 212–14.

CHAPTER FOUR: KAY AND MING TAI

1. Michael Wilson, "What New York Looked Like During the 1918 Flu Pandemic," *NYT*, April 2, 2020; "The Quality of Women's Service," *The Woman Citizen*, September 28, 1918, 352; Julian A. Navarro, "Influenza in 1918: An Epidemic in Images," *Public Health Reports* 125, sup. 3 (April 2010), 13; RGR, 1.

2. Brooks, *Between Mao and McCarthy*, 213–14; Albert M. Camarillo, "Navigating Segregated Life in America's Racial Borderhoods, 1910s–1950s," *Journal of American History* 100, no. 3 (2013): 646–54.

3. "James Vaughan Storey Dies," *NYHT*, March 25, 1927; Shirley J. Yee, *An Immigrant Neighborhood: Interethnic and Interracial Encounters in New York Before 1930* (Temple University Press, 2012), 70.

4. Allen S. Hilborn draft card, Glen Ridge, NJ, September 12, 1918, Ancestry.com; *Directory of Montclair, Bloomfield, Caldwell, Essex Fells, Glen Ridge and Verona* (Price and Lee, 1916), 810, 826. William Brown, owner of the brokerage, knew Edwin Rayner through the Amherst Club of New York. "Edwin A. Rayner," *NYHT*, January, 18, 1934; "Amherst Men at Dinner," *NYHT*, December 21, 1895.

5. RGR, 1–3; *Newark Evening News*, "Real Estate and Building," October 18, 1919; US Department of the Interior, "National Registry of Historic Places Inventory—Nomination Form for Glen Ridge, NJ," June 25, 1982, pp. 1, 8.

6. Glen Ridge High School, *Senior Annual 1920* (Glen Ridge High School, 1920), 27.

7. RGR, 1–2, 7, 13.

8. "In the Real Estate Field," *NYT*, December 24, 1919; City of New York, *City Record: Annual Record of Assessed Valuation of Real Estate in the City of New York. Borough of Manhattan, 1921*, XLIX, Supplement Vol. 1, 21; photo and records in file 25/1251, NARA-NYC; *Polk's (Trow's) New York City Directory, 1922–1923: Manhattan* (Polk's, 1922), 1709.

9. Chin Mow testimony, January 17, 1908, pp. 1–5, file 96/942, NARA-NYC.

10. Leo Bergholz, "Precis in re Chan Shau Hong," July 6, 1921, p. 1, in file 7032/2034, NARA-SEA; SS *Princess Charlotte/Empress of Asia*, passenger manifest, July 21, 1921, Ancestry.com.

11. SS *Princess Charlotte/Empress of Asia*, passenger manifest.

12. Leo Bergholz, "Precis in re Chau Chai Ching," July 6, 1921, p. 1, in file 7031/449, NARA-SEA.

13. Lee, *At America's Gates*, 92–100; Bergholz, "Precis in re Chau Chai Ching."

14. Columbia University, *Directory of Officers and Students, 1921–1922* (Columbia University, 1921), 99; Isabell Chin Leong interview with the author, June 27, 2022.

15. Leong interview.

16. Leong interview; MFHR, 4.

CHAPTER FIVE: ERNEST

1. Advertisement for National School of Chiropractic, *Business*, October 1914, 157; Ernest K. Moy draft card, June 5, 1917, Ancestry.com; "Stiff Exams for Those Who Heal Without Drugs," *CT*, August 6, 1916; Gordon W. Rice, "Pseudomedicine," *Journal of the American Medical Association* 58, no. 5 (February 1912), 560–62; Arthur J. Cramp, *Nostrums and Quackery and Pseudo-Medicine, Vol. 3* (Chicago: American Medical Association, 1936), 59–60; Cuthbert Powell, "Modern Pseudomedical Cults," 78, and n.a., "News Items," 68, in *Monthly Bulletin of the Federation of State Medical Boards of the United States* 1, no. 6 (September 1915); George Creel, "Mail Order Miracle Men," 87–92, in *Monthly Bulletin of the Federation of State Medical Boards of the United States* 1, no. 7 (October 1915).

2. Illinois State Board of Health, *Official Register of Legally Qualified Other Practitioners* (Board of Health, 1917), 29; Lizabeth Cohen, *Making a New Deal: Industrial Workers in Chicago, 1919–1939* (Cambridge University Press, 1990), 33–36; Moy draft card.

3. Moy draft card; Ernest Moy to editor, *Day Book* (Chicago), October 24, 1916; "This Is How U.S. Classifies Men for Draft," *CT*, November 15, 1917; "Exempted Men Called Upon for Special Service," *CT*, December 9, 1917; "Slackers and Seditious Meet with Bad Luck," *CT*, March 31, 1918; Arthur Sears Harding, "Loopholes for Draft Escape Shut by U.S.," *CT*, August 1, 1917; *Final Report of the State Council of Defense of Illinois* (State of Illinois, 1919), 194; "Committee at Large," *Chicago Commerce*, May 9, 1918, 25; "Find Farm Laborers Now," *Orange Judd Farmer* (Illinois), April 27, 1918.

4. "Find Farm Laborers Now"; "Application for Farm Help," *Orange Judd Farmer* (Illinois), April 13, 1918; *Who's Who in China*, 5th edition (China Weekly Review, 1936), 187.

5. *Chicago Central Business and Office Building Directory* (Winter, 1919), 185; Cohen, *Making a New Deal*, 36.

6. Woodrow Wilson speech to US Congress, January 8, 1918; Erez Manela, *The Wilsonian Moment: Self-Determination and the International Origins of Anticolonial Nationalism* (Oxford University Press, 2009), 42–43, 52–53, 99–100.

7. "Northwestern," *CSM*, March 1919, 349–50.

8. "Northwestern"; Paul Z. and Ruth Koesun photos, ca. 1910s–1920s, FM.

9. "Graduates from Other Departments," *The Citizen* (Berea, Kentucky), June 6, 1917; Frances E. Willard National Temperance Hospital, *Thirty-Fourth Annual Report, 1918–1919* (Frances E. Willard National Temperance Hospital, 1919), 19–20, 25; *Fourteenth Census of the United States, 1920*, Chicago Ward 1, ED 22, Sheet 1, Ancestry.com; "Kill 1 Chinese, Wound 2 in New Tong Outbreak," *CT*, October 21, 1924.

10. Emma Pease affidavit, March 8, 1904, A. W. Swift affidavit, September 14, 1903, and Louisa M. Scofield affidavit, November 14, 1903, in file 2005/2695, NARA-CHI.

11. Untitled item, *Belvidere Standard*, February 14, 1894; "Baby Girl," *Belvidere Daily Republican*, November 28, 1900; Tamra Moy interview with the author, February 1, 2020.

12. "In Dire Distress," *Belvidere Daily Republican*, January 18, 1902; *Thirteenth Census*, Chicago Ward 1, ED 145, sheet 1B, Ancestry.com; Ling, *Chinese Chicago*, 49–53; Immigrant and Chinese Inspector to East Boston Commissioner of Immigration, February 25, 1925, p. 1, file 60/128, NARA-NYC. My thanks to Heather Lee for providing a copy of this file.

13. "Chinese Children to Speak," *CT*, May 30, 1907; "Chinese to Join Crusade on South Chicago Levee," *CT*, June 1, 1907; "Must Send Chinese Child to School," *Spokane Press*, February 6, 1909; *Lewis Annual* (Lewis Institute, 1917), 44.

14. Manela, *The Wilsonian Moment*, 177–96; Ernest K. Moy and Ruth Koesun marriage license, Cook County, Illinois, June 25, 1919.

15. Cohen, *Making a New Deal*, 36–38.

16. *Fourteenth Census*, Manhattan AD 1, ED 73, sheet 130B, Ancestry.com; "Leaders of Boy Scout Drive for $1,000,000 and Chinese Lads Helping to 'Put It Over,'" *New York Evening World*, June 10, 1919.

17. *WWCNY*, 48, 57; William G. Jordan, *Black Newspapers and America's War for Democracy* (University of North Carolina Press, 2001), 59.

18. "Suffragists Win Pledge of Aid by Chinese Alliance," *NYHT*, November 5, 1917; "On Leong, Hip Sing Tongs Sign National Peace Pact," *NYHT*, September 18, 1925; "Contribute to Representative Government," *The Alliance Advocate* 1, no. 1 (January 1920): 1–2; "*Tushenghui tongren zhuyi*" (CACA members, take note), *Chinese Republic News* (New York), August 7, 1920; *Polk's (Trow's) New York City Directory, 1922–1923: Manhattan* (Polk's, 1922), 1292.

19. "Kill 1 Chinese, Wound 2 in New Tong Outbreak"; Brooks, *American Exodus*, 25–26; "Reactions to the Attack by Knox," *NYHT*, September 7, 1919.

20. "Fourth Anniversary Celebration," *The Alliance Advocate* 1, no. 1 (January 1920): 3; *Millard's Review of the Far East*, "Who's Who in China: Mr. Ma Soo," December 4, 1920.

21. "Chinese Urge US Invite South China to Parley," *NYHT*, September 17, 1921; Ernest K. Moy testimony, September 9, 1920, p. 2, file 9270/2–4, NARA-SEA; John B. Powell, *My Twenty-Five Years in China* (Macmillan, 1945), 65–68.

22. "Canton Government Asks Share in Conference," *China Review*, August 1921, 88; "Chinese Mass-Meeting in New York Urges South China Participation in Washington Conference," *China Review*, October 1921, 198–200; "Claims of South China Are Urged," *Christian Science Monitor*, September 17, 1921; "China and Her Needs Told to Flatbush 12:45 Members," *Chat* (Brooklyn), January 13, 1923; "Addresses Kiwanis Club," *BE*, March 1, 1922; "Editor Moy Asks America to Co-operate with China," *BSU*, December 15, 1922.

CHAPTER SIX: ALICE

1. Alice Lee to Rep. Franck R. Havenner, February 25, 1950, p. 1, AML.

2. Bill Moy photos, ca. 1923–1927, WTM; photo 2015.037.617–1, 1924, DJC; Savage School for Physical Education, 1922 yearbook (in possession of the author).

3. Photos 2015.037.612, 2015.037.614–1, 2015.037.617–1, and 2015.037.609, 1920, 1923, 1924, DJC.

4. Photos 2015.037.629, 1922, DJC; "Girls' Events," (CSA Eastern Section) *Conference Daily*, September 12, 1921, 1–3; "Souvenir List," *Conference Daily*, September 7–14, 1921, 1–4; CSA Eastern Section, *Nineteenth Annual Conference of the Eastern Section* (CSA, 1923), 38–39.

5. *China Review*, "Nanyang Brothers, Expanding Import-Export Business," March 1924, 78; Sherman Cochran, *Big Business in China: Sino–Foreign Rivalry in the Cigarette Industry, 1890–1930* (Harvard University Press, 1980), 55–61.

6. Columbia University, *Catalogue, 1923–1924* (Columbia University, 1923), 286; Elsie Borg Goldsmith, compiler, *Opportunities for Vocational Training in New York City* (Vocational Service for Juniors, 1922), 6.

7. Columbia University, *Catalogue, 1923–1924*.

8. Photos 2015.037.609, 1924, and 2015.037.611, 1922, DJC; CSA, *The Handbook of the Chinese Students in the U.S.A.* (CSA, 1922), 72; oral history interview with Mary Monduluk Koesun, November 27, 1965, p. 12, file 7, box 13, Ruth Ann Koesun Collection, Jerome Robbins Dance Division, New York Public Library; *China Review*, "Chinese Physician in the New York Health Department," September 1924, 191; "Seize Tong Chief Here for Chinese Terrorist Plot," *CT*, July 25, 1924; "Murder Plot Bared by Chinese on Stand," *NYT*, November 11, 1924.

9. "Chinese Revolt Against Raid on Mah Jong," *NYHT*, January 7, 1924; "Magnet on a String Hoists $5000 in Opium in Raid on Chinese," November 5, 1923; "White Woman and 2 Chinese Are Arrested in Opium Raid," March 3, 1924; "Drug Den Raiders Round Up 23 Men and Three Women," *BE*, February 14, 1924; *BE*, "Chinatown 'Queen' and Six Men in Drug Raid," March 19, 1924; Michael A. Lerner, *Dry Manhattan: Prohibition in New York City* (Harvard University Press, 2007), 72–76.

10. Photo 2015.037.636–2, 1926, DJC; *NYS*, "New York's Chinatown Annexed to the United States," February 8, 1914; Lillian Lee email to the author, June 6, 2020.

11. Lee to Havenner, p. 1; Yoland Skete-Laessig, *When Newark Had a Chinatown: My Own Personal Journey* (Dorrance, 2016), 148–62; Chih Meng, "The Chinese of Newark, New Jersey: A Social Survey," MA thesis, Columbia University, 1924, 13, 19–20; *Newark Directory 1930* (Price & Lee, 1930), 1383.

12. Photo 2015.037.608–2, DJC; adverstisement for John Mullins and Sons, *Newark Evening News*, Nov. 17, 1924.

13. Photos 2015.037.629, 2015.037.630, 2015.037.635, 2015.037.638–1, 2015.037.638–2, and 2015.037.639–1, 1924–1926, DJC; Stephen Chang interview with the author, September 8, 2022; University of Pennsylvania, *Bulletin for the Session of 1922–1923* (University of Pennsylvania, 1922), 568; Herbert E. Moy, "Application for Admission to Mount Hermon School," September 1927, p. 3, Schauffler Library, Northfield Mount Hermon School.

CHAPTER SEVEN: KAY AND MING TAI

1. Advertisement for Palais D'Or, *NYT*, September 17, 1924; "Glory Enough for All," *NYHT*, January 1, 1925.

2. "9 Cafes Padlocked in Broadway Drive," *NYT*, May 15, 1924; "Want Dry Ban off 2 Broadway Cafes," *NYT*, August 19, 1924; "Palais Royal May Reopen but Under Drastic Rules," *BTU*, July 20, 1924; "Palais D'Or," *Variety*, September 24, 1924; "Chinese Restaurant on B'Way Doing $25,000 Weekly Trade," *BTU*, May 12, 1924; Charles G. Shaw, "11:30 to 3:00," *Smart Set* 71, no. 2 (June 1923), 76.

3. "Chop Suey May Be Palais Royal Dish, If Padlock Is Lifted," *NYHT*, June 11, 1924; "New Incorporations," *NYT*, June 11, 1924; "Palais Royal May Reopen but Under Drastic Rules"; "Palais D'Or"; Chew Mon Joe testimony, May 8, 1928, p. 1, file 125/349; John E. Safran to A. W. Brough, file 61/65, NARA-NYC; Chew Mon Joe, affidavit, October 28, 1919, Chew Mon Joe passport application, Ancestry.com.

4. Shaw, "11:30 to 3:00," 76; "Orchestra Reviews," *Billboard*, January 14, 1926; C. A. Fowler and C. H. Stewart to "To Whom It May Concern," March 26, 1918, file 61/65, NARA-NYC; postcard of Palais D'Or interior, ca. 1925, in possession of the author; photo of Palais D'Or exterior, December 28, 1925, in Drucker & Baltes Co. Billboard Collection, New York Historical digital collections, https://digitalcollections.nyhistory.org/islandora/object/islandora%3A51137 (accessed April 15, 2024).

5. "Strickland at Palais D'Or," *Variety*, September 10, 1924; "Brass Bands Growing More Common in Radio's Mistaken 'Entertainment,'" *Variety*, July 23, 1924; Untitled item, *Billboard*, October 18, 1924; "Drive Your Hay Fever Away," and "Station WJV," *Chat*, June 28, 1924; "WHN, New York," *Bayonne Times*, October 21, 1924.

6. "At the Key," *Galveston Daily News*, July 21, 1925. Based on 1924 radio schedules from newspapers in the New York metropolitan region.

7. "Tau Gamma Phi Sorority to Honor President," *BSU*, May 3, 1925; "Friendship League to Fete Heads," *BTU*, April 27, 1927; "Palais D'Or."

8. "Irwin Abrams on WEAF," *Variety*, April 24, 1926; "Rolfe's Own Orchestra in B'way Restaurant," May 12, 1926; Huseyin Leblebici, Gerald R. Salancik, Anne

Copay, and Tom King, "Institutional Change and the Transformation of Interorganizational Fields: An Organizational History of the US Radio Broadcasting Industry," *Administrative Science Quarterly* 36, no. 3 (1991): 346–47; Mark Lloyd, *Prologue to a Farce: Communication and Democracy in America* (University of Illinois Press, 2006), 107. Radio times based on 1926 schedules from the New York metropolitan newspapers.

9. Charles Metz, "Attack on New York," *Harper's* 153 (June 1, 1926), 87; advertisement for La Touraine Coffee, *Rochester Democrat and Chronicle*, March 7, 1927; Howard Thain, "Palais D'Or, New York City," https://digitalcollections.nyhistory.org/islandora/object/nyhs%3A2257 (accessed April 15, 2024).

10. "Yellow Lights," *New Yorker*, March 24, 1928, 17; Ming, Sherman, and Alan Chen interview with the author, June 13, 2022; Lillian Lee and Chris Moy conversation with the author, March 25, 2023; VCD, November 22, 1938, 35.7/23.

11. VCD, September 1, 1936, 35.4/2; RGR, 11; JTY, 81.

12. RGR, 1–5, 7–10, 12–13; photos 2015.037.621–2, 2015.037.622, 2015.037.630, ca. 1920s, DJC.

13. Photo, Chin family car with chauffeur, ca. 1922, JYK; RGR, 9.

14. RGR, 4, 11.

15. Henry H. Franklin, "Herbert Erasmus Moy, with aliases," April 1, 1943, p. 1, file 100155291 sec. 1, 2 of 3, box 72, HEM.

16. "Refused Right to Wed Chinese, Girl Tries to Die," *NYDN*, October 10, 1932; "Girl, 19, Recovering from Effects of Poison," *Plainfield Courier* (New Jersey), October 10, 1932; Moy, "Application for Admission to Mount Hermon School," p. 3; advertisement for Eagle Restaurant, *Newark Evening News*, December 30, 1926.

17. Northfield Mount Hermon School, "Our History," https://www.nmhschool.org/about-us/our-history (accessed April 15, 2024); Moy, "Application for Admission."

18. Moy, "Application for Admission," 3, 6.

19. H. F. Cutler to Lee W. Beattie, September 13, 1927, p. 1, in Moy, "Application for Admission."

CHAPTER EIGHT: ERNEST AND RUTH

1. Dorothy Wong, "Student World: Greater New York," *CSM* 20, no. 6 (1925), 71; "Many Races Honor Dr. Sun's Memory," *NYT*, March 23, 1925, 3; "Peking and Dr. Sun," *SCMP*, November 24, 1924; "Bolshevism in China," *SCMP*, December 19, 1924; John Fitzgerald, *Awakening China: Politics, Culture, and Class in the Nationalist Revolution* (Stanford University Press, 1996), 169–70.

2. "Chinese and Whites Honor Sun Yat-sen," *NYT*, March 14, 1927; "Black Sees Cantonese as 'Red Democrats,'" *BE*, April 8, 1927.

3. See, for example, Ernest Moy, "Zai shengming benbao wei qiaobao fuwu gai bu suofei" (to reiterate, this newspaper serves overseas compatriots at no cost)," *China Monitor*, December 1925, 1, box 371, Chinese American Citizens Alliance

collection, Special Collections, Stanford University; "New Chinese Paper," *EAP*, November 21, 1925.

4. Photos of John Y. Lee, Ruth K. Moy, Ernest Moy, Kenneth Moy, and Loring Moy, 1924–1926, FM; Frederic Moy conversation with the author, March 27, 2023.

5. "New Chinese Paper"; "Exchange Club to Hold Important June Meeting," *Chat*, May 30, 1925; Ernest K. Moy, "Review of Standardized Mahjong," *Saturday Review of Literature*, October 4, 1924, 164; Annelise Heinz, *Mahjong: A Chinese Game and the Making of Modern American Culture* (Oxford University Press, 2021), 30–39, 124.

6. "Flatbush to Clamp Lid on Ultra-Modern Dances," *BSU*, November 28, 1924; "No Reason to Worry about China's Future," *BSU*, February 6, 1925; "Recall Days 50 Years Ago," *BTU*, October 12, 1926; "Exchange Club to Hold Important June Meeting"; "Problems of China Told Rotary Club," *BE*, February 6, 1925. Food descriptions from the Buttolph collection of menus at the New York Public Library.

7. Wong, "Student World: Greater New York"; "Peking and Dr. Sun"; "Bolshevism in China"; Fitzgerald, *Awakening China*, 250–59; "Coup Splits Canton Reds," *NYT*, March 26, 1926; Thomas F. Millard, "Shanghai Alarmed over China Chaos," *NYT*, September 10, 1926; Lewis S. Gannett, "New Strong Man Holds Half of China," *NYT*, November 14, 1926.

8. Lloyd E. Eastman, *The Abortive Revolution: China Under Nationalist Rule, 1927–1937* (Harvard Council on East Asian Studies, 1974), 94; Parks M. Coble, *The Shanghai Capitalists and the Nationalist Government, 1927–1937* (Council on East Asian Studies, 1980), 31–38.

9. "Soaring Values of Midtown Sites," *NYT*, January 7, 1926; "Many Leases Made in Midtown Section," *NYT*, December 19, 1926. For Ernest's neighbors, see *Poor's Register of Directors of the United States* (Poor's, 1928), *passim*, and 1928 issues of *Hardware Age*, *Motor Age*, and *The Jobber's Salesman*.

10. "Lists Four New Ministers," *NYT*, March 17, 1927; "Cantonese Start News Agency Here," *NYT*, March 18, 1927; "Says Reports from China Are Garbled," *BSU*, April 14, 1926; Hallett Abend, *My Life in China, 1926–1941* (Harcourt, Brace, 1943), 125–26; FRUS 1927 (vol. 2, no. 6).

11. "Says Reports from China Are Garbled"; Wen-hsin Yeh, *Provincial Passages: Culture, Space, and the Origins of Chinese Communism* (University of California Press, 1996), 252–54.

12. Suisheng Zhao, *Power by Design: Constitution-Making in Nationalist China* (University of Hawai'i Press, 1996), 101–5; "Madame Sun Yat-sen at Moscow with Eugene Chen Says Masses of Chinese Are Revolutionists," *CP*, September 9, 1927.

13. Stamp on rear of Form 430, January 16, 1928, file 9270/2–4, NARA-SEA; "Weather" and "Shipping Notes," *CP*, February 2, 1928.

14. Untitled item, *Minguo Ribao* (Shanghai), May 16, 1928; "American Players Criticized," *NCH*, March 10, 1928; Zhao, *Power by Design*, 104–5; "Passengers Departed," *CP*, July 16, 1928.

15. *NCDHL* 1928, 179; "Ling-Tong," *NCH*, April 7, 1928.

CHAPTER NINE: ALICE AND K.S.

1. "Sunday Pictorial Section," *CP*, April 8, 1928.

2. Brooks, *American Exodus*, 35–36.

3. *1924 Bomb* (Iowa A&M, 1924), 388, 521; *Iowa State College of Agriculture 1924 Catalog* (Iowa A&M, 1924), 334; Alice Moy Lee testimony, January 15, 1938, p. 4, file 170/452, NARA-NYC; photo of K. S. Lo, ca. 1926, AML; Dorothy Wong, "Student World," *CSM* 20, no. 3 (1925): 65–66.

4. Deborah Lau interview with the author, Aug. 24, 2020.

5. State of New York, "Certificate and Record of Marriage," September 5, 1925, NYCMA; "Student World," *CSM* 21, no. 1 (1925): 74.

6. LCY, 1–12; Joseph C. Nardini, "Precis in re Lo King Shiu, also Lo Gwai Chee," July 19, 1920, file 19380-2-25, NARA-SB.

7. Alice Moy Lee testimony, p. 4.

8. Seung-joon Lee, *Gourmets in the Land of Famine: The Culture and Politics of Rice in Modern Canton* (Stanford University Press, 2011), 25, 88; Brooks, *American Exodus*, 26.

9. Brooks, *American Exodus*, 34–39; Lau interview with the author.

10. "Passengers: Departed," *SCMP*, November 3, 1926.

11. LCY, 11–13.

12. LCY; Donald A. Jordan, *The Northern Expedition: China's National Revolution of 1926–1928* (University of Hawai'i Press, 1976), 123–26.

13. LCY, 12–13; Hanchao Lu, *Beyond the Neon Lights: Everyday Shanghai in the Early Twentieth Century* (University of California Press, 1999), 249; Timothy B. Weston, *The Power of Position: Beijing University, Intellectuals, and Chinese Political Culture, 1898–1929* (University of California Press, 2004), 244; "Fudan daxue: yanxi junshi huaxueji" (Fudan University: Chemistry studies put on military footing), *Shishixinbao* (Shanghai), December 30, 1929.

14. Lau interview.

15. Lee, *At America's Gates*, 95.

CHAPTER TEN: KAY AND MING TAI

1. Photos 2015.037.637–1, May 1926, and 2015.037.636–2, August 1926, DJC; photo "Asbury Park, 1923," WTM.

2. Item 2015.037.533, 1928, DJC; marriage certificate 5539, 1928, NYCMA; Huie Kin, *Reminiscences* (San Yu Press, 1932), 111.

3. MFHR, 4–6.

4. Douglas Chu email to author, January 19, 2021; MFHR, 49; "Over a Hundred Elementary Schools Have Honor Rolls," *BE*, October 11, 1912; "Stiff Schedule in N.Y.U. Team," *BE*, January 15, 1923; *Polywog* (Polytechnic Institute Junior Class, 1920); *Yearbook* (American Society of Civil Engineers, 1924), 289.

5. MFHR, 6; RGR, 5; Chris Moy interview with the author, March 25, 2023; Typond family photo, ca. 1906, Douglas J Chu collection. Grace and Yip Typond testified in 1929 and 1930 before her trip to China. Unusually for Chinese immigrants of this generation, both used English. File 134/96, NARA-NY.

6. RGR, 11–12.

7. Photos 2015.037.622, 2015.037.624, and 2015.037.630, 1924–1926, DJC; Glen Ridge photos, 1920–1925, WTM.

8. Photo 2015.037.643–2, DJC; Herbert Moy to Thomas Elder, July 24, 1928, MH.

9. MFHR, 9; Leong interview.

10. "Chinese Restaurant on B'Way Starts with $200,000 Investment," *Variety*, November 30, 1927, 1, 56; *Polk's (Trows) New York City Copartnership and Corporation Directory, 1929* (R. L. Polk, 1929); "Restaurant Will Pay $2,000,000 Broadway Rental," *NYHT*, September 7, 1929.

11. "Jardin Royal," *Variety*, December 21, 1927, 54; "Cabaret Bills," *Variety*, April 4, 1928, 56; Jardin Royal postcard, Cooper Union "Broadway's Restaurants," https://cooper.edu/gallery/broadways-restaurants, accessed Nov. 12, 2023.

12. Chew Mon Joe testimony, May 8, 1928, pp. 1–2, file 125/349, NARA-NY; "Business Records," *NYT*, December 28, 1928; Leong interview.

13. "Restaurant Will Pay $2,000,000 Broadway Rental."

CHAPTER ELEVEN: ERNEST AND RUTH

1. FRUS 1928, Vol. 2, 192; photos from Purdys, July 1928, FM; MFHR, 11–12; photo 2015.037.586–1, DJC; Cook County, Illinois Birth Index, Ancestry.com; Leong interview.

2. "Foreign Correspondents in the United States," *EAP*, January 26, 1929, 250.

3. "Flatbush Affairs Crowding Each Other for Public Attention," *Chat*, January 12, 1929; Untitled item, *Newark Evening News*, March 7, 1929; Ruth Moy photo at Harkness Pavilion, 1929, FM; "Moy Heads Correspondents," *EAP*, May 18, 1929, 65.

4. Ch'en Chieh-ju, *Chiang Kai-shek's Secret Past: The Memoir of His Second Wife, Ch'en Chieh-ju*, ed. Lloyd Eastman (Westview, 1993), 254–62; Ruth and Ernest Moy photo with John Y. Lee, ca. 1928, Ruth Moy photo with Frank Lee, ca. 1929, and Jennie Chen photos and name card, undated, FM; Brooks, *American Exodus*, 45, 54, 106; "Obituaries," *NCH*, April 26, 1939.

5. Chih Meng, *Chinese American Understanding: A Sixty Year Search* (China Institute, 1981), 150–56; *China Institute in America* (China Institute, 1930), 6; *Who's Who in China*, 4th edition (China Weekly Review, 1931), 315.

6. "Mei Lan-fang," *Variety*, March 5, 1930, 53; "Mei Lan-fang Arrives Tomorrow," *NYT*, February 7, 1930; "Mei Lan-fang Gives a New Program," *NYT*, March 10, 1930; Nancy Guy, "Brokering Glory for the Chinese Nation: Peking Opera's 1930

American Tour," *Comparative Drama* 35, nos. 3–4 (2001–2), 377; Tian Xu communication with the author, August 2021.

7. See, for example, the following *NYT* articles from 1930: "Mei Lan-fang Here with His Actors," February 9; "Reception for Mei Lan-fang," February 17; "Mei Lan-fang Guest at Tea Party Here," February 19; "To Greet Mei Lan-fang," February 20; "To Honor Mei Lan-fang," March 3; "Reception for Mei Lan-fang," March 4; "Tea for Mei Lan-fang," March 18; "Mrs. Campbell Honors Mei Lan-fang," March 19; "Guests of Theatre Club Luncheon," March 20.

8. Alluded to in two letters: C. C. Chang to Ruth Moy, ca. May 1947, p. 2, and C. C. Chang to Ruth Moy, 1933, FM.

9. Pang-Mei Natasha Chang, *Bound Feet and Western Dress* (Knopf, 2011), 39, 94; Chang to Moy, May 1947, and typed lyrics to "Dark Night," n.d., FM.

10. *Who's Who in China*, 314.

11. "Honorary Star Will Play Here," *LAT*, April 27, 1930; Myra Nye, "Society of Cinemaland," *LAT*, May 18, 1930; Mei Lanfang tour photos, April–June 1930, and Ruth Moy parking ticket, May 10, 1930, FM.

12. "East Meets West in Studio," *LAT*, May 14, 1930; "Mei Lan-fang Address Lauded," *LAT*, May 31, 1930; Nye, "Society of Cinemaland"; Mei Lanfang tour photos; Alma Whitaker, "Chinese Peace Gesture Made," *LAT*, May 8, 1930.

13. Moy parking ticket; Mei Lanfang tour photos; program for "Song O' My Heart," Grauman's Chinese Theatre, ca. May 1930, C. C. Chang to Ruth Moy, January 11, 1949, and C. C. Chang to Ruth Moy, July 10, 1948, FM.

14. C. C. Chang scrapbook, FM.

15. C. C. Chang scrapbook; Chang to Moy, July 10, 1948.

16. "Press Association Notes," *EAP*, September 6, 1930, 36; untitled item, *Newark Evening News*, February 26, 1929.

17. "Press Association Notes," 36.

18. Photos of Ernest, Loring, and Kenneth Moy, 1930 AML; Ernest Moy testimony, June 26, 1934, p. 1, file 4382/4848, NARA-SB.

CHAPTER TWELVE: ALICE

1. Photo of Honolulu reunion, 1930, AML; US Department of Labor, *Treaty, Laws, and Rules Governing the Admission of Chinese* (USGPO, 1926), 33–34, 75–76.

2. Lim "Luke" Young and Kau En "Ella" Young testimony, February 21, 1930, pp. 1–5, file 4382/3985, NARA-SB; Edward Y. Kau testimony, April 28, 1926, pp. 1–4, file 34/831, NARA-NY; Board of Special Inquiry, "In the matter of Alice Lo," August 7, 1930, pp. 2–3, file 4387/390, NARA-SB.

3. Lillian Lee email to the author, May 30, 2020; photo, *CP*, April 5, 1928.

4. Board of Special Inquiry, "In the matter of Alice Lo," p. 1; LCY, 12; *Shishixinbao* (Shanghai), "Fudan daxue: yanxi junshi huaxueji" (Fudan University: Report on launch of military-affairs-related chemistry program), December 30, 1929; Deborah Lau interview with the author, August 24, 2020.

5. Lau interview; Board of Special Inquiry, "In the matter of Alice Lo," p. 1; LCY, 12.

6. Miles Lo, "Declaration of Non-immigrant Alien about to Depart for the United States," June 4, 1930, p. 1, and Miles Lo photos with car, May 25, 1930, AML; classified ads, *CP*, August 4, 1930.

7. Alice Moy Lo, "Form of Chinese Certificate," June 1930, AML.

8. "Deaths," *CP*, July 18, 1930; "List of Manifest of Alien Passengers for the United States: S. S. Taiyo Maru," July 24, 1930, Honolulu Arriving and Departing Passenger and Crew Lists, Ancestry.com; "List of Manifest of Alien Passengers for the United States: S. S. Shinyo Maru," August 29, 1930, California Arriving Passenger and Crew Lists, 1882–1959, Ancestry.com.

9. A. C. Monk to George V. Monk, November 22, 1930, p. 2, file 1285.10.c2, A. C. Monk and Co./A. C. Monk Family Collection, J. Y. Joyner Library, Eastern Carolina University.

10. William M. Wright, "White City to White Elephant: Washington's Union Station Since World War II," *Washington History* 10, no. 2 (Fall–Winter 1998–1999), 27; *Segregation Scholarships, Episode 2: Traveling While Black* (WNET, September 15, 2023); Mary Bo Tze Lee, "Problems of the Segregated School for Asiatics in San Francisco" (MA thesis, University of California, Berkeley, 1920), 29–40; Brooks, *Alien Neighbors, Foreign Friends*, 11–38; "Alumni Plan Minstrel Show for Nov. 26," *CP*, November 6, 1926; "Shanghai Boy Scouts Plan Lyceum Program," *CP*, February 27, 1936.

11. Photo of Ronald Chin and Miles Lo, December 1930, AML; photo 2015.037.586–8, 1930, DJC.

12. A. C. Monk to George V. Monk, p. 2; MFHR, 2–5; Douglas Lee email to the author, August 10, 2020.

13. Chu Ming to District Director, January 17, 1931, p. 1; copy of Vancouver manifest, January 17, 1931; Douglas Jenkins to Secretary of State, February 25, 1931, pp. 1–2, in file 4387/390; Alfred S. Lee testimony, November 28, 1930, p. 1, file 132/672, NARA-NYC.

14. Alice Lee to Anna Kong Mei, ca. January 1948, p. 1; Alice M. Lo and K. S. Lo divorce agreement, February 12, 1931, AML; ML, 2; photographs ca. March 1931, AML; *NCDHL* 1931, 99.

15. Alice Moy and Alfred Lee marriage certificate, March 28, 1931, "Consular Reports of Marriages, 1910–1949," Ancestry.com; petition in re adoption of Miles Lo, April 30, 1931, AML.

16. Lau interview; LCY, 12; Guangxi Zhuang Autonomous Region Committee of the Chinese People's Political Consultative Conference, Cultural and Historical Materials Research Committee, *Guangxi wenshi ziliao xuanji, 1* (Selected compilation of material on Guangxi literature and history, vol. 1) (Cultural and Historical Materials Research Committee, 1981), 97; *Zhongguo gongcheng renming lu* (Who's who of Chinese engineers) (Society of Chinese Engineers, 1941), 130.

PART TWO: WAR

1. Meg Jacobs, *Pocketbook Politics: Economic Citizenship in Twentieth-Century America* (Princeton University Press, 2004), 95–99; Ella Howard, *Homeless: Poverty and Place in Urban America* (University of Pennsylvania Press, 2013), 23–42; Touré F. Reed, *Not Alms but Opportunity: The Urban League and the Politics of Racial Uplift, 1910–1950* (University of North Carolina Press, 2008), 107–8; Brooks, *American Exodus*, 116.

2. Austin Dean, *China and the End of Global Silver, 1873–1937* (Cornell University Press, 2020), 136; Joseph W. Esherick, *Accidental Holy Land: The Communist Revolution in Northwest China* (University of California Press, 2022), 91–93; Jeffrey N. Wasserstrom, *Student Protests in Twentieth-Century China: The View from Shanghai* (Stanford University Press, 1991), 173–98.

3. Lu, *Beyond the Neon Lights*, 28–36; Brooks, *American Exodus*, 12.

4. Rana Mitter, *Forgotten Ally: China's World War II, 1937–1945* (Mariner, 2013), 99–169, 175–78, 251.

5. Wen-hsin Yeh, "Prologue: Shanghai Besieged," in Wen-hsin Yeh, ed., *Wartime Shanghai* (Routledge, 1998), 2–11.

CHAPTER THIRTEEN: KAY AND MING TAI

1. RGR, 9–12; *The 1930 Veterropt* (Georgia Wesleyan College, 1930), 237; "Restaurant Will Pay $2,000,000 Broadway Rental," *NYHT*, September 7, 1929; "Largest Chink Eatery on B'way; Seats 2,500," *Variety*, August 28, 1929, 47.

2. "Largest Chink Eatery on B'way"; "Rolfe Solely with Lucky Strike Concern," *Variety*, May 21, 1930, 56; Cohen, *Making a New Deal*, 139–40.

3. "Tex in Chink Joint?," *Variety*, July 16, 1930, 59; "Palais D'Or Owners Trying to Break Morgan's Contract," *Billboard*, March 28, 1931, 40; "Chinese Eateries Launch a Revival of Floor Shows," *Variety*, November 24, 1931, 35.

4. "Business Records," *NYT*, February 7, 1932, and February 19, 1932; "Assignments," *NYHT*, February 8, 1932; "Judgements Filed," *NYHT*, February 12, 1932; "Assignee Notices," *BC*, April 15, 1932.

5. James Typond diploma, 1923, DJC; James Typond testimony, January 8, 1930, p. 3, file 134/96, NARA-NY; "Assignee Notices," *BC*, April 15, 1932; "Auction Sale," *BTU*, June 6, 1932; "Auction Sale," *BTU*, February 24, 1933.

6. "Sheriff's Sale," *Jewish Chronicle* (Newark), April 1, 1932; population schedule, Newark City enumeration district no. 756, sheet 15B, 1930 United States Federal Census, Ancestry.com; MFHR, 49.

7. Population schedule, Brooklyn enumeration district 24469, sheet 12A, 1930 United States Federal Census.

8. Leong interview.

9. William Taft Moy testimony, October 19, 1932, pp. 2–3, file 166/137, NARA-NY; "Court Would 'Lock' Newark Chinatown," *Newark Evening News*, October 15, 1930; "Federal Raiders Get 145 Chinese Opium Smokers," *NYHT*, February 3, 1931; "29 Seized in Narcotic Raid," *NYHT*, February 16, 1931.

10. William Taft Moy testimony; Shau Hong Chin testimony, September 28, 1932, pp. 3–4, file 165/916, NARA-NY.

11. Leong interview; William and May Wong Moy photos, ca. 1932, WTM; Sara and Chris Moy email to the author, April 4, 2021; William Taft Moy and May F. Wong, Certificate and Record of Marriage, November 4, 1932, NYCMA.

12. Population schedule, Syracuse, enumeration district 34–208, sheet 5B, 1930 United States Federal Census; "Girl, 19, Recovering from Effects of Poison," *Plainfield Courier-News*, October 10, 1932.

13. "Girl, 19, Recovering from Effects of Poison"; "Refused Right to Wed Chinese, Girl Tries to Die," *New York Daily News*, October 10, 1932.

14. "Refused Right to Wed Chinese"; State of New York, Affidavit for License to Marry and Marriage License, October 26, 1932, New York Municipal Archives; Henry H. Franklin, "Herbert Erasmus Moy, with aliases," April 1, 1943, p. 1, file 100–155291-sec 1, 1 of 3, Box 72, HEM.

15. MFHR, 4; SS *Manhattan*, "List or Manifest of Aliens Employed on the Vessel as Crew," October 27, 1932, sheet 7, and SS Manhattan, "Crew List," September 7, 1932, sheet 13, in "New York, U.S., Arriving Passenger and Crew Lists," Ancestry.com.

16. Jack Young testimony, September 19, 1931, pp. 1–2, file 132/993, NARA-NY; Ruth Harkness, *The Lady and the Panda* (Carrick and Evans, 1937), 52; Michael Kiefer, *Chasing the Panda: How an Unlikely Pair of Adventurers Won the Race to Capture the Mythical "White Bear"* (Da Capo Press, 2002), 17–19.

17. Jolly Young King email to the author, June 16, 2020; VCD, March 12, 1935, p. 1, 35.3; VCD, December 6, 1938, p. 7, 35.7/25.

18. *Sixteenth Census of the United States, 1940: Population Vol. 2, Characteristics of the Population* (USGPO, 1943), 925.

CHAPTER FOURTEEN: ERNEST AND RUTH

1. Arriving ship photos, August 1930, Savoy Apartments, ca. 1931, and C.C. Chang to Ruth Moy, Chengdu, 1933, p. 4, FM.

2. *Who's Who in China*, 4th edition, 314; Bruce J. Dickson, "The Lessons of Defeat: The Reorganization of the Kuomintang on Taiwan, 1950–52," *China Quarterly* 133 (March 1993), 58–59; Frederic Wakeman Jr., *Spymaster: Dai Li and the Chinese Secret Service* (University of California Press, 2003), 27, 67.

3. Ernest K. Moy to Paul Linebarger, October 17, 1930, p. 1, file 38, box 11, P.M.W. Linebarger papers, Hoover Institution; "Men and Events," *CWR*, April 11, 1931.

4. "E.K. Moy to Direct Nan Mow Brokerage Co.," *CP*, February 26, 1933.

5. "Fairbanks Pays Glowing Tribute to Shanghai at Cathay Hotel Reception," *CP*, February 12, 1931; "Reception," *NCH*, February 17, 1931; "Fashions for the Chinese Lady," *NCH*, February 24, 1931; Fairbanks invitation, February 1931, FM.

6. Mitter, *Forgotten Ally*, 56; Wen-hsin Yeh, *Shanghai Splendor: Economic Sentiments and the Making of Modern China, 1843–1949* (University of California Press, 2007), 124–25.

7. Wakeman, *Spymaster*, 41, 47–52; Thomas W. Burkman, *Japan and the League of Nations: Empire and World Order, 1914–1938* (University of Hawai'i Press, 2008), 167–68; Wang Kewen, "Wang Jingwei and the Policy Origins of the 'Peace Movement,' 1932–1937," in David P. Barrett and Larry N. Shyu, eds., *Chinese Collaboration with Japan, 1932–1945: The Limits of Accommodation* (Stanford University Press, 2002), 22; Rana Mitter, *The Manchurian Myth: Nationalism, Resistance, and Collaboration in Modern China* (University of California Press, 2000), 140.

8. "Has Kuomintang Collapsed? Asks Veteran Member," *CP*, January 29, 1932.

9. "Y.W.C.A. Opens Quarters for War Refugees," *CP*, February 6, 1932; "Red Cross Asks Donations for Victims of War," *CP*, February 9, 1932; "Volunteer Work Growing Among Local Chinese," *CP*, February 27, 1932; "Foreign Women Organize to Aid Chinese Troops," *CP*, February 5, 1932, "Wounded Being Given Treatment by 54 Hospitals," March 8, 1932; "Many Foreign Women Busy Sewing for Chinese Troops," *CP*, February 10, 1932; "Foreign and Chinese Women Ask More Aid for Wounded Soldiers," *CP*, February 18, 1932.

10. "Story of a Shanghai War Hospital Told as Doctor and Organizer Is Praised," *CP*, May 27, 1932; Ruth Moy hospital photos, February–March 1932, FM.

11. "Story of a Shanghai War Hospital."

12. "Story of a Shanghai War Hospital"; Ruth Moy hospital photos; George A. Fitch, *My Eighty Years in China* (Mei Ya International Edition, 1987), 423.

13. Fitch, *My Eighty Years in China*, 423; Ruth Moy hospital photos.

14. "Moy Appointed Head Of Shun Shih News Agency," *CP*, May 2, 1932; "Moy Resigns from China Press to Resume Private Business," *CP*, January 29, 1933.

15. William Taft Moy testimony; Herbert Erasmus Moy passport application, October 14, 1932, p. 1, file 100–155291-sec. 1, 1 of 3, box 72, HEM; conversation with Chris Moy, March 23, 2023; Brooks, *American Exodus*, 132.

CHAPTER FIFTEEN: ALICE AND ALFRED

1. SS *Mariposa*, "List or Manifest of Inbound Passengers, Los Angeles Harbor," March 29, 1938, Ancestry.com; "To Entertain at Tea Dance," *CP*, March 31, 1929; "Foreign Women Organize to Aid Chinese Troops," *CP*, February 5, 1932; "Men and Events," *CWR*, September 24, 1932.

2. "Moy Appointed Head of Shun Shih News Agency," *CP*, May 2, 1932; "School Of Commerce To Expand Work," *CP*, January 20, 1933; "Moy Resigns from China Press to Resume Private Business," *CP*, January 29, 1933; "Standard Dairy Farm

Formally Organized," *CP*, December 14, 1932; *Rosenstock's Business Directory of China 1933* (Millington, 1933), 211.

3. William Taft Moy testimony; Herbert Erasmus Moy passport application; SS *President Coolidge* photos, December 1932, WTM; "Bryan Returns From 8-Months Home Leave," *CP*, December 24, 1932; "Moy Resigns from China Press to Resume Private Business"; *Who's Who in China*, 5th edition, 65.

4. VCD, March 12, 1935, 35.3; Lee to Havenner.

5. 1930s photographs, AML; Brooks, *American Exodus*, 142–47.

6. *Rosenstocks 1933 Business Directory of China*, 127; Bryna Goodman, *Native Place, City, and Nation: Regional Networks and Identities in Shanghai, 1853–1937* (University of California Press, 1995), 287–89, 315.

7. 1930s photos, AML; Lillian Lee conversation with the author, March 25, 2023; Stephen Chang interview with the author, September 8, 2022; "W.C.T.U. to Sponsor Luncheon," *CP*, May 23, 1935.

8. Photos, January 1934, and unknown newspaper, "*Guijuhui daibiao meihuaquan lishiheng jiang zai fei gouliu batian*" (Masonic representatives H.C. Mei and Alfred Lee will spend eight days in the Philippines), ca. February 1934, AML; Richard T. Chu, *Chinese and Chinese Mestizos of Manila: Family, Identity, and Culture, 1860s–1930s* (Brill, 2010), 292–97.

9. Chang interview with the author; Shanghai American School, *Columbian 1933* (SAS, 1933), 62, 66, box 8, Shanghai American School papers, Yale Divinity School Special Collections; class photo, June 1937, AML.

10. *Zhongguo gongcheng xuehui huiyuan tongxunlu* (China Engineering Society member directory) (China Engineering Society, 1930), 52; Alice Moy Lo and King Shiu Lo, divorce agreement, February 12, 1931, p. 1, AML.

11. Alson Miles Lee, "Certificate of Baptism," American Community Church, Shanghai, October 28, 1934, AML.

CHAPTER SIXTEEN: KAY AND MING TAI

1. VCD, March 12, 1935, 35.3, and July 22, 1938, 35.7/6; MFHR, 4; Kiefer, *Chasing the Panda*, 23–27.

2. MFHR, 4; Kiefer, *Chasing the Panda*, 55.

3. MFHR, 5–6; Kiefer, *Chasing the Panda*, 2; VCD, "Summer in Chicago—1934," and December 2, 1937, 35.5/6.

4. Photos 2015.037.586–12, 1932–1933, 2015.037.586–13, July 1934, 2015.037.586–17, 1936, 2015.037.586–20, 1938, and 2015.037.543, DJC; Bruce Edward Hall, *Tea That Burns: A Family Memoir of Chinatown* (Free Press, 1998), 241–42.

5. George Y. Typond draft registration card, February 15, 1942, Ancestry.com; "200 Idle Listed for Sewer Work," *BTU*, September 10, 1934; "PWA Approves Award to Weston Company," *BTU*, September 25, 1934; "Strike Ties Up Relief Project in Island Park," *BTU*, September 26, 1935.

6. Photos 2015.037.586–04, 1928, 2015.037.586–12, 1932, 2015.037.586–16, 1935, 2015.037.586–20, DJC.

7. Kevin Mumford, *Newark: A History of Race, Rights, and Riots in America* (New York University Press, 2007), 30–49; *Fifteenth Census of the United States, 1930*, Newark ED 7–56, SD 5, sheet 5B, and *Sixteenth Census of the United States, 1940*, Newark SD 10, ED 25–85, sheet 2A (both 203 Mulberry); *Sixteenth Census of the United States, 1940: Population, Vol. 2: Characteristics of the Population, Part 4* (USGPO, 1940), 925.

8. Leong interview.

CHAPTER SEVENTEEN: ERNEST AND RUTH

1. Photos from May–June 1930 scrapbook, FM.

2. "Successful Operation Performed on Mrs. Moy," *CP*, January 29, 1933; "Obstretric and Gynecological Section," *China Medical Journal* 37, no. 2 (February 1923), 176.

3. "Moy Resigns from China Press to Resume Private Business," *CP*, January 29, 1933.

4. "Trust Company for Overseas Chinese Meets," *CP*, July 2, 1933.

5. *Columbian 1933*, 62, 66; College Sainte Jeanne d'Arc, "Programme of events," pp. 1, 3, October 1936, FM.

6. *NCDHL 1934*, 210; "Legal Notice," *BE*, April 24, 1933; *Shishixinbao* (Shanghai), "*Ying weihu qiaoshang liyi*" (Need to safeguard the interests of overseas merchants), March 24, 1934.

7. "Trust Company for Overseas Chinese Meets," *CP*, July 2, 1933; "Treasurer of Trust Company Faces Charge," *CP*, October 27, 1934; Niv Horesh, *Shanghai's Bund and Beyond: British Banks, Banknote Issuance, and Monetary Policy in China, 1842–1937* (Yale University Press, 2009), 115.

8. Ernest K. Moy testimony, June 26, 1934, pp. 1–2, file 4383/4848, NARA-SB; "*Yundong gaishan yimin li zhuanyuan*" (Lobby commissioner to improve immigration regulations) and "*Shanghai huaqiao xintuo gongsi hanlu*" (Shanghai Overseas Trust Company correspondence), *Sanminchenbao* (Chicago), July 25, 1934; "Overseas Trust Company to Be Liquidated," *CP*, September 27, 1934.

9. *Sanminchenbao*, "*Meiqiju qishi*" (notice from Ernest K. Moy), July 28, 1934; VCD, "Summer in Chicago—1934"; Port Arthur Cafe envelope labeled "7–26–34," July 1934, FM.

10. "Local News Brevities," *CP*, October 24, 1934; "Liquidators Named for Overseas Trust," *CP*, October 1, 1934; "Chen Trial Concluded in First Court," *CP*, December 11, 1934; *Shishixinbao*, "*Kong chenzipei qinzhan*" (Thomas P. Chan accused of embezzlement), October 27, 1934.

11. "Standard Dairy Farm Formally Organized," *CP*, December 11, 1934; "Loy Chang Is Named New Customs Director Succeeding Shen Shu-yu," *CP*, January 31,

1935; "Men and Events," *CWR*, February 1, 1936; *Who's Who in China*, 5th edition, 187; Douglas Lee email to the author, November 18, 2023; Chihyun Chang, *Government, Imperialism and Nationalism in China: The Maritime Customs Service and Its Chinese Staff* (Routledge, 2013), 62–71.

12. Chang, *Government, Imperialism and Nationalism in China*, 1–2, 95–96; Hsiu Shu-Cheng to editor, *CWR*, September 14, 1940.

13. *American University Men in China* (American University Club of Shanghai, 1936), 202, 220; Edward J. Brundage, *Illinois Attorney General's Report for the Biennium 1919–1920* (State of Illinois, 1920), 226–27.

CHAPTER EIGHTEEN: ALICE AND ALFRED

1. *NCDHL 1934*, 529; Mrs. Jack Young, "Last School in China," *CP*, April 12, 1934; "Expedition to Sikong Pushes West over Pass," *CP*, April 13, 1934; "Youngs Trek to Lifting in State of Real Mobilization," *CP*, June 29, 1934; "Young Expedition Returns to Shanghai with New Specimens," *CP*, November 2, 1934; "Explorations on Border of Tibet Traced: Jack Young Tells R.A.S. Meeting of Last Trip into Sikong Country," *CP*, November 23, 1934; "Wife of Chinese Explorer Tells of Trials on Border," *CP*, December 7, 1934; "Hunting on the Tibetan Border: Adventurous Young Couple Describe Experiences," *NCH*, December 12, 1934; "Jack Young Delivers Lecture on Recent Exploration Trip," *CWR*, December 1, 1934; VCD, March 12, 1935, 35.3.

2. "Here and There," *NCH*, July 31, 1935; Ford photo, ca. 1934, and Mokanshan photos, July 1934–August 1935, AML.

3. A Correspondent, "Mokanshan in New Guise," *NCH*, May 6, 1930; "If You're Considering the Mountains This Summer, Mokanshan Offers Plenty of Room in Which to Ramble," *CP*, June 29, 1931; "Opening of New Roads Is Big Boon," *CP*, April 23, 1933; "Mokanshan Has Plenty of Room and Fresh Air," *CP*, May 27, 1934; Sherman Cochran and Andrew Hsieh, eds., with Janis Cochran, *One Day in China: May 21, 1936* (Yale University Press, 1983), 98–104; Wakeman, *Spymaster*, 111–21, 139–56; Frances Wood, *No Dogs and Not Many Chinese: Treaty Port Life in China, 1843–1943* (John Murray, 1998), 181.

4. Mokanshan photos; *NCH*, "Mokanshan Notes," August 30, 1933; "If You're Considering the Mountains This Summer"; "Mrs. Wu, Mrs. Chang Leave for Peiping," *CP*, August 27, 1936.

5. Photo 2015.037.046, May 1934, DJC; May Wong Moy testimony, January 29, 1935, p. 5, file 168/119, NARA-NYC.

6. VCD, March 12, 1935, 35.3; "Mrs. Young Entertains at Tea Party Today," *CP*, September 25, 1935.

7. May Wong testimony, 4–5.

8. Peter Rand, *China Hands: The Adventures and Ordeals of the American Journalists Who Joined Forces with the Great Chinese Revolution* (Simon and Schuster,

1995), 82; Herbert E. Moy, "Gala Fall Dance of Ex-Collegians Planned," *CP*, September 25, 1933; Herbert E. Moy, "Shanghai Show World," *CP*, January 25, 1935.

9. Herbert Erasmus Moy, "Application for Registration," October 31, 1934, p. 1, file 100155291-sec 1, 1 of 3, box 72, HEM.

10. ML, 6; William James Burke, "Herbert Erasmus Moy, with Aliases," March 5, 1943, p. 2, file 100155291-sec 1, 2 of 3, box 72, HEM.

11. "International Club in I.R.C. Quarters," *NCH*, December 4, 1935; Hal P. Mills, "Sidelights from the Press Row," *CP*, October 2, 1936; Tobit Vandamme, "The Rise of Nationalism in a Cosmopolitan Port City," *Journal of World History* 29, no. 1 (2018), 42–46; Sophie Loy-Wilson, "Daisy Kwok's Shanghai: Life in China Before and After 1949," in Kate Bagnall and Julia T. Martínez, eds., *Locating Chinese Women: Historical Mobility Between China and Australia* (Hong Kong University Press, 2021), 242–43.

12. "New Social Club to Make Bow Today," *CP*, December 1, 1935; "New Social Club to Open December 12," *CP*, December 3, 1935; "International Club to Make Bow at 5:30 P.M.," *CP*, December 18, 1935; "Large Inaugural Party," *CP*, December 2, 1935; "Anna May Wong Will Be Guest of I.C. Soon," *CP*, April 5, 1936; "Brilliant Gathering at I. C. Tea Dance," *CP*, April 9, 1936."

13. E. A. Westlake, "Strays," *QST: The Official Organ of the ARRL* 13, no. 9 (September 1929), 8; "Shanghai Municipal Police (Specials)," *Shanghai Municipal Gazette*, December 30, 1932, 577; *All About Shanghai and Environs: A Standard Guide Book* (University Press, 1934), 84; *Shibao* (Shanghai), "*Quanguo guangbo wuxian diantai*" (All the radio broadcasters in China), January 29, 1934; "Station XMHC Will Be 'at Home' Today: Fourth Anniversary to Be Celebrated Here," *CP*, January 21, 1937; "Novel Radio Skit to Be Broadcast by XMHC," *CP*, November 27, 1936; "More Artists Added to Overseas Program," *CP*, December 10, 1936; D. S. I. Laurier, "Summons No. 2884 Issued by Judge Foo of the Shanghai First Special District Court at the Request of the Ministry of Communications," July 21, 1937, p. 1, file D681308, SMP.

14. "Radio Programmes to Be Censored," *NCH*, May 6, 1936; "Censors to Watch Radio More Closely," *CP*, July 1, 1936; "New Bill of Fare Served over Ether," *CP*, July 3, 1936; "Radio Artists File Protest Against Ban," *CP*, November 13, 1936.

15. Peter S. Li, "The Social Construction of Chinese in Canada," in Huping Ling, ed., *Asian America: Forming New Communities, Expanding Boundaries* (Rutgers University Press, 2009), 224–25; D. S. Larby, "Summons No. 2884," July 31, 1937, p. 1, file D681305, SMP; Laurier, "Summons," 2.

16. Hal P. Mills, "Sidelights," *CP*, October 9, 1936, and January 24, 1937.

CHAPTER NINETEEN: KAY AND MING TAI

1. *Sixteenth Census of the United States, 1940: Population, Vol. 2*, 925.

2. Advertisement for Lucky Palace, *Daily Worker*, June 29, 1934; *New York City Guide* (Federal Writers Project, 1939), 106; "Business Records," *NYHT*, July 30, 1935;

"Sunshine Bow for New Luna," *Billboard*, June 8, 1935; "Bankruptcy Notices," *BC*, August 24, 1937.

3. VCD, November 22, 1938, 35.7/23, and December 14, 1938, 35.7/26.

4. VCD, October 21, 1938, 35.7/18, and January 29, 1939, 35.8/4; Ming Kay, Alan, and Sherman Chen interview with the author, June 13, 2022.

5. *Sixteenth Census of the United States, 1940*, Manhattan SD 21, ED 31–1831, sheet 63A; Chris Moy conversation with the author, March 25, 2023; Leong interview.

6. Leong interview.

7. Advertisement, *BTU*, October 22, 1930; Douglas J. Chu's photos of the Chinese Whoopee Revue in Paris, scans in possession of the author; "Surprise Party," *Fall River Daily Globe*, May 26, 1915; "Marriage Intentions," *Fall River Evening Herald*, May 15, 1911.

8. Douglas J. Chu, "Typond Old Home Movies" 1–6, https://www.youtube.com/@douglaschu2000 (accessed April 29, 2024).

9. "Moran Concedes He Got Taxi Cash," *NYT*, June 4, 1939; David Porter, "Along City Streets," *Spectator*, September 3, 1936.

10. Photos 2015.037.586–14 through 2015.037.586–18, 1935–1937, DJC; "Yee Yoke Poy, 3, Is Baby Queen of Chinatown," *NYHT*, June 13, 1937.

11. MFHR, 6.

12. "Chinese Defy Jap Ultimatum," *Asbury Park Evening Press*, July 8, 1937.

13. VCD, September 1936, 35.4/1, and September 20, 1936, 35.4/3; "Jack Young Uses Plane to Return from Sikong," *CP*, March 28, 1937; US Consulate, Tientsin, "Report of Birth: Jacqueline Lita Young," June 21, 1937 (DOB May 30, 1937), Ancestry.com; Mitter, *Forgotten Ally*, 79–85.

14. See, for example, Alexander Alland, *Manhattan: Pell Street—Mott St*, 1939, https://digitalcollections.nypl.org/items/510d47dd-50ab-a3d9-e040-e00a18064a99, Irma and Paul Milstein Division of United States History, Local History and Genealogy, The New York Public Library Digital Collections (accessed April 29, 2024).

15. Ira Wolfert, "Gotham Chinese Are Sure Japan Will Be Beaten," *Nebraska State Journal* (Lincoln), August 13, 1937.

CHAPTER TWENTY: ERNEST AND RUTH

1. "Has Kuomintang Collapsed?"; Mitter, *Forgotten Ally*, 64–75, 85–89, 98–99.

2. *NCDHL 1937*, 109, 296; Yeh, "Prologue," 4; *CP*, "All Japanese to Have Left Hankow Today," August 11, 1937; "Defense Forces and S. V. C. Take Up Settlement Positions" and "Hongkew Bristling with Armed Activity," August 13, 1937.

3. *NCDHL 1937*, 296; "RKO-Radio Chief," *CP*, November 17, 1934.

4. *NCDHL 1934*, 135; William Taft Moy testimony, "In the Matter of the Application of Moy, Patricia," October 16, 1937, p. 1, file 7030/10430, NARA-SEA.

5. Sara and Chris Moy email to the author, February 28, 2021; "50,000 Flock into Concessions from Suburban Districts," *CP*, August 6, 1937; "U.S. Consulate

Takes Census for Emergency," *CP*, August 8, 1937; "Foreigners of City Lay Plans for Emergency," *CP*, August 13, 1937; *FRUS 1937, Vol. 4*, 259–60, 286.

6. Chris and Sara Moy email to the author, April 4, 2021.

7. "Defense Forces and S.V.C. Take Up Settlement Positions," *CP*, August 13, 1937, "S.M.C. Moves to Alleviate Food Shortage" and "City's Amusement Places Are Closed," *CP*, August 16, 1937; "Most Central Area Firms Close Doors," *CP*, August 17, 1937; Brooks, *American Exodus*, 152.

8. Mitter, *Forgotten Ally*, 100–108; "4000 Refugees Taken Care Of," *NCH*, August 18, 1937; "590 Killed, 898 Wounded as Planes Drop Bombs in Downtown Sections; Casualties Include Many Foreigners," *NCH*, August 15, 1937; "Food Problem Facing Refugees Now Acute," *NCH*, August 18, 1937; Abend, *My Life in China*, 254; Christian Henriot with Nicolas Bozon, map of Shanghai refugee camps in 1937, created in 2006, at https://www.virtualshanghai.net/Maps/eAtlas?ID = 303 (accessed May 1, 2024).

9. William T. Moy, "Last Morning, August 20, 1937," WTM; "First Batch of Foreign Men Evacuated," *CP*, August 21, 1937.

10. Photos of "Bloody Sunday," August 14, 1937, and "Red Cross No. 17 Shanghai, China," November 9, 1937, FM; *FRUS 1937, Vol. 4*, 266–67.

11. Ruth Moy, "Application for Financial Assistance," August 1937, pp. 1–2, and Ernest K. Moy to American Consulate General, August 28, 1937, p. 1, in Shanghai Vol. 2668, RG 84, NARA-CP.

12. James B. Pilcher to National City Bank of New York, August 30, 1937, p. 1, Shanghai Vol. 2668; "Planes Bomb S. S. Hoover by Mistake," *CP*, August 31, 1937; "President Hoover Is Bombed," *NCH*, September 1, 1937.

13. "U.S.S. Sacramento Will Take Americans South," *CP*, September 7, 1937; Ernest K. Moy to Clarence E. Gauss, October 4, 1937, and J. B. Pilcher, "Re: Complaint of Mr. Ernest K. Moy," October 4, 1937, in Shanghai Vol. 2668; J. B. Pilcher, "Final List of American Citizens Sailing on Board U.S.S. Sacramento," September 13, 1937, Shanghai Vol. 2665, RG 84; Bert Lee interview with the author, September 23, 2020.

14. Ernest K. Moy to Clarence E. Gauss, October 4, 1937.

15. "Few Americans Leave," *NCH*, September 15, 1937; "U.S.S. Sacramento Takes 1st Americans Evacuated by Navy," *CP*, September 14, 1937.

16. All in Shanghai Vol. 2668: Moy to Gauss, October 4, 1937; Moy to Gauss, October 7, 1937; Moy to Gauss, October 12, 1937; Moy to Gauss, October 23, 1937; "Sez Me" to editor, October 4, 1937, and "Anti-Tinpots" to editor, October 8, 1937, *SEPM*; J. B. Pilcher memo re: Ernest K. Moy, October 11, 1937; Leighton Shields to Gauss, October 20, 1937; Shields to Moy, October 20, 1937; Gauss to Shields, October 20, 1937; Pilcher to Moy, October 26, 1937; Ruth Moy to Gauss, October 29, 1937; Pilcher to Ruth Moy, November 1, 1937; Ruth Moy, "Application for Transportation on U.S. Government Vessel," November 1937.

17. All in FM: Ruth Moy to Gauss; Pilcher to Ruth Moy; "Chaumont, Bound for Manila, Calls at Woosung Today," *CP*, November 9, 1937; USS *Chaumont* mess

receipt, November 9–12, 1937; USS *Chaumont*, "Tender Schedule," November 11, 1937; St. Francis Hotel, Hong Kong, receipts, November 14, 1937.

CHAPTER TWENTY-ONE: ALICE AND ALFRED

1. ML, 1–2; photos of Kiangwan house, 1935–1937, and "Kwok family garden" photo, 1936, AML.

2. Bert Lee interview with the author; ML, 1–2.

3. Lee family photos, 1935–1937, AML; ML, 1–2; "Three Killed in Affray Near Aerodrome," *NCH*, August 11, 1937; "Down Woosung Way," *CP*, August 9, 1937 and "Japanese Get Old Airdrome into Condition," August 13, 1937.

4. ML, 2.

5. Christian Henriot with Nicolas Bozon, map of Shanghai refugee camps in 1937, created in 2006, at https://www.virtualshanghai.net/Maps/eAtlas?ID = 303 (accessed May 1, 2024); Christian Henriot with Nicolas Bozon, map of Shanghai's bombed and destroyed areas, August–October 1937, created in 2006, https://www.virtualshanghai.net/Maps/eAtlas?ID = 294 (accessed May 1, 2024); "800 British Troops Off for Shanghai," *CP*, August 15, 1937; "Wide Areas in Hongkew, Yangtszepoo Burnt Out," *CP*, August 22, 1937; "Foreign Forces Mobilized in Shanghai," *NCH*, August 18, 1937.

6. *NCDHL 1937*, 203; "Japanese Held Back as Reinforcements Arrive at Woosung," *CP*, September 2, 1937; "Volunteers and Foreign Troops Called Out," *NCH*, August 18, 1937; ML 2.

7. Bert Lee interview; "British Women, Kids Leaving," *CP*, August 17, 1937; "Cocktail Party on Liner Big Success," *CP*, May 14, 1937; "More Foreigners Evacuate," *NCH*, August 20, 1937.

8. Bert Lee interview; "Press Gang Active," *CP*, July 29, 1937; "Conscription to Be Enforced Immediately," *CP*, August 1, 1937; "Weather Monday," September 13, 1937; "Farmers Suffer Big Losses in War Areas," *CP*, October 13, 1937.

9. "As Shanghailanders Continue to Evacuate," *NCH*, September 22, 1937; "Foreign Sailings," *CP*, April 2, 1937; "C.S.M.N. Scores Seizure of Lower Wharf," *CP*, August 20, 1937; "More Refugees," *SCMP*, September 18, 1937.

10. "More Refugees," *SCMP*, September 18, 1937; "As Shanghailanders Continue to Evacuate," *NCH*, September 22, 1937.

11. Brooks, *American Exodus*, 160; "Crowds Flock to Hongkong," *SCMP*, August 21, 1937; "Central British School," *SCMP*, August 26, 1937

12. Bert Lee email to the author, June 18, 2023; Bert Lee interview with the author; *SCMP*, "Conte Biancamano," September 9, 1937; advertisement for Lloyd Triestino ships, *SCMP*, September 15, 1937; "Shipping Movements," *SCMP*, September 18, 1937; "Canton Schools," *SCMP*, September 21, 1937; Irving Linnell telegrams to US Secretary of State, September 4 and September 24, 1937, file "Canton, 1937, 800 (August–September)," box 1, "US Consulate, Canton, Classified General Records," UD entry 2286, RG 84, NARA-CP.

13. Bert Lee interview.

14. *Hong Kong Telegraph*, President Liner Travel Service ad, August 21, 1937; advertisement for Canadian Pacific travel, *SCMP*, July 1, 1937.

15. Advertisement for Jimmy's Kitchen, *SCMP*, February 10, 1937.

16. Bert Lee email; Alson and Lillian Lee interview with the author, May 14, 2020; S.S. *President Coolidge*, "List or Manifest of Alien Passengers for the United States," October 6, 1937, Ancestry.com; Lee Moy Kee-ging, Republic of China passport, August 30, 1937, and "Chinese Certificate," August 30, 1937, AML.

17. Bert Lee interview; ML, 2.

18. Bert Lee interview; *Napa Journal*, "Mrs. Hong to Visit Here," March 26, 1932.

CHAPTER TWENTY-TWO: KAY AND MING TAI

1. VCD, November 13, 1937, 35.5/5.

2. David Porter, "Along City Streets," *The Spectator*, September 3, 1936.

3. Emily Lee Shek, Petition for Naturalization, March 18, 1935, New York State and Federal Naturalization Records, Ancestry.com.

4. Brooks, *American Exodus*, 174; Moy Kee Ging Lee, Petition for Naturalization, November 9, 1937, New York State and Federal Naturalization Records.

5. Handwritten note, ca. January 1938 and Haff telegram to INS Ellis Island, December 17, 1937, file 132/672, NARA-NYC.

6. VCD, October 22–23, 1937, 35.5/2; October 28, 1937, 35.5/3; November 3–9, 1937, 35.5/4; November 13, 1937, 35.5/5; and December 2, 1937, 35.5/6.

7. VCD, December 2, 1937, and December 31, 1937; VCD, March 28, 1938, 35.6/8; J. L. Huang, *Memoirs of J. L. Huang* (Yingzhong Publishing, 1984), 111.

8. VCD, December 31, 1937; VCD, January 5, 1938, 35.6/2.

9. VCD, December 2, 1937, January 5, 1938, and July 3, 1938, 35.7/2.

10. VCD, April 3, 1938, 35.6/1; VCD, December 2, 1937.

11. VCD, November 22, 1938, 35.7/23; June 5, 1938, 35.6/12; June 30, 1938, 35.6/13; VCD, July 3, p. 5; "Hines Jury Turns to Gambling Raids," *NYT*, June 16, 1938; "Valentine Squad Raids Betting Ring," *NYT*, July 21, 1938; "Records of Tammany Police Heads Subpoenaed by Dewey for Trial," *NYT*, August 26, 1938; "94 Chinese Fined for Gambling," *NYT*, October 10, 1938.

12. VCD, July 22, 1938, 35.7/6, and December 8, 1938, 35.7/7; SS AP54, "List of United States Citizens," December 31, 1943, sheet no. 1, Ancestry.com.

13. VCD, August 26, 1938, 35.7/10, and September 3, 1938, 35.7/11.

14. VCD, February 8, 1939, 35.8/5, and January 29, 1939, 35.8/4; "Manhattan Transfers," *NYT*, January 30, 1939; "Sale in Chinatown a Prelude to the Fair," *NYT*, February 2, 1939; "Bank Disposes of Two Flats on Amsterdam Av.," *NYHT*, January 31, 1939.

15. William Taft Moy, INS Seattle entry application, October 14, 1937, p. 1, file 7030/10429; *Sixteenth Census of the United States, 1940*, Manhattan SD no. 21, ED

31–1831, sheet 63A; transcript, "In the Matter of the Application of Moy, Patricia," October 16, 1937, pp. 1–3, file 7030/10430, NARA-SEA; "Manila to House More from China," *NYT*, August 23, 1937; "Americans Quit China War Zones," *NYT*, September 4, 1937.

16. Chris and Sara Moy email to the author, April 4, 2021; William Taft Moy draft card, October 16, 1940, Ancestry.com.

17. Leong interview; Chris and Sara Moy email to the author.

18. Moy family photos, 1939, WTM; photos 2015.037.392, 2015.037.397, and 2015.037.399, 1939, DJC.

CHAPTER TWENTY-THREE: ERNEST AND RUTH

1. SS *President Coolidge*, "List or Manifest of Alien Passengers for the United States: List 7," November 16, 1937, Ancestry.com. Description of third-class travel based on 1930s photos from collections in Calisphere, as well as my own May 2023 tour of the NYK steamship *Hikawamaru* in Yokohama, Japan.

2. "Assassin Kills Rich Chinese; Called Tyrant," *CT*, November 2, 1937; "Investigate Slaying of Chicago Chinatown Leader," *Logansport Pharos-Tribune* (Indiana), November 2, 1937; "Chicago Chinatown Asked to Solve Chin Murder," *Decatur Herald* (Illinois), November 3, 1937.

3. *South Bend News-Times*, "Mother Loses in Fight for Child," April 21, 1922; "Conversation #1 with Mary Mandulick Koesun," November 27, 1965, pp. 7–8, 21, 32–35, file "Personal: Interview with Mary Mandulick Koesun, 1965," box 13, Ruth Ann Koesun Collection; Frederic Moy interview with the author, December 7, 2022.

4. "Conversation #2 with Mary Mandulick Koesun," December 11, 1965, pp. 4–8, file "Personal: Interview with Mary Mandulick Koesun, 1965"; photos of the Moys and Koesuns, December 1937, FM.

5. *The Williston Log 1938* (Williston Academy, 1938), 56, 94; Anna Koesun Koe testimony, May 5, 1938, p. 1, file 170/676, NARA-NYC; Loring Moy testimony, February 17, 1938, pp. 1–2, file 25/226, NARA-NYC.

6. VCD, June 5, 1938, 35.6/12; C. R. Lewis, "Radiophone Amateur Gives Vital Service in Troubled Times," *CP*, October 13, 1937; "New Hospital Opened by Local Business Group," *CP*, November 8, 1937.

7. "Shanghai Bane," *NCH*, November 3, 1937; "Fires Still Burning All Over Nantao," *NCH*, December 1, 1937; Parks M. Coble, *Chinese Capitalists in Japan's New Order: The Occupied Lower Yangtze, 1937–1945* (University of California Press, 2003), 12–13; Diana Lary and Stephen MacKinnon, *Scars of War: The Impact of Warfare on Modern China* (UBC Press, 2001), 123.

8. Coble, *Chinese Capitalists in Japan's New Order*, 20–25; *NCDHL 1938*, 99.

9. Frederic Wakeman Jr., *The Shanghai Badlands: Wartime Terrorism and Urban Crime, 1937–1941* (Cambridge University Press, 2002), 23–52; "Head of Chinese Found on Route Dufour; Note Warns Anti-Japan Acts," *SEPM*, February 11, 1938, clipping, FM.

10. Brooks, *American Exodus*, 101–3, 168–70; "Herman Liu Shot Dead By Assassin," *CP*, April 8, 1938; "Many Attend Last Rites for Dr. Liu," *CP*, April 10, 1938; "Konomi 'Brains' of Terrorists," *NCH*, September 14, 1938; Percy Finch, *Shanghai and Beyond* (Charles Scribner's Sons, 1953), 310.

11. "Head of Chinese Found": Wakeman, *Shanghai Badlands*, 53–55; Loring Moy photo, December 1937, FM; Kenneth Philander Moy testimony, August 20, 1941, p. 1, file 4382/4849, NARA-SB.

CHAPTER TWENTY-FOUR: ALICE AND ALFRED

1. *NCDHL 1937*, 203; "Local Auto Service Man Fails to Return from Trip to Pootung," *CP*, November 6, 1937; "Fires Sweep East War Area; Chinese Air Raiders Active," *CP*, August 21, 1937; "Chinese and American Tobacco Companies Lose Heavily as Result of War," *CWR*, October 30, 1937; George V. Monk to A. C. Monk & Co., June 20, 1938, p. 1, file KIC Doc. 0005.1285.10b, ECU.

2. "Grads of N.Y.U. Organize New Alumni Group," *CP*, June 16, 1936; "American University Club Plans Tea Dance," *CP*, November 26, 1936; Wu Ai-lien, "Chinese Social Notes," *NCH*, March 3, 1937.

3. George V. Monk to A. C. Monk & Co.; Alfred S. Lee, form SF2602, December 21, 1937, file 12017/52098, NARA-SB; VCD, May 12, 1939, 35.8/8, and November 3, 1937, 35.5/4; Alfred S. Lee testimony, January 15, 1938, p. 1, file 132/672, NARA-NYC.

4. Brooks, *American Exodus*, 190–91.

5. Summons no. 2884, July 29, 1937, p. 1, file D68139, SMP.

6. DSI Laurier, "Report: Search Warrant No. 2441 Issued by Judge Feng at the Request of the Shanghai Telegraph Office," July 21, 1937, pp. 1–2, and N. White to Commissioner of Police, August 12, 1937, p. 1, in file D6813, SMP.

7. N. White to Commissioner of Police, p. 1; D.S. Larby, "Report: Overseas Broadcasting Company," October 5, 1937, p. 1, file D68139.

8. D. S. Pitts, "Report: Emergency Orders Delivered to Wireless Stations in the Settlement," August 17, 1937, p. 1, file D68139, and G. Godfrey Phillips, "Shanghai Municipal Council Emergency Order," August 16, 1937, file D681313, SMP.

9. Pitts, "Report," p. 1; Wen-hsin Yeh, "Urban Warfare and Underground Resistance," in *Wartime Shanghai*, 111.

10. D.S. Larby, "Report: Mr. F.L. Kernan," October 6, 1937, pp. 1–2; Larby, "Report: Overseas Broadcasting Company," October 19, 1937, p. 1; Laurier, "Report: Improper Method of Broadcasting by the Overseas Broadcasting Station," November 1, 1937, p. 1; Herbert E. Moy to Deputy Commissioner, November 26, 1937; all the preceding in file DS 8113, SMP; "Further Details Are Published of Japanese Massacre of Chinese Civilians," *CWR*, October 9, 1937; Addison E. Southard to Secretary of State, December 15, 1937, Central Decimal File 893.20246G, Records of the US Department of State, China, 1930–1939, part 1, AU.

11. "Police Working on Theory Sunday Night Bombings Work of Pro-Japan Group," *CP*, June 14, 1938; Wakeman, *Shanghai Badlands*, 115–17; DSI Logan,

"Report: Overseas Broadcasting Company," May 11, 1938, p. 1, file D8113, SMP; Glenn W. Wilson, "Herbert Erasmus Moy," March 3, 1943, p. 1, file 100155291, sec-1, 3 of 3, box 72, HEM.

12. Alfred S. Lee testimony, January 15, 1938, p. 1, in file 132/672; *NCDHL 1937*, 49, 203; *NCDHL 1938*, 45. Such positions were not nearly as powerful or lucrative in the 1930s as they had been a half century earlier, but they were still quite desirable. Many companies, including Monk and Carolina, stopped using the term *comprador*, but Shanghai foreigners colloquially referred to Alfred as the comprador of Carolina Leaf.

13. *FRUS 1938, Vol. 4: The Far East*, 366–67.

14. "Passengers," *CP*, March 8, 1938, and April 21, 1938; photos from Empress of Canada voyage, April 1938, AML; Alson M. Lee, "Application by Displaced Person Residing in the United States to Adjust Immigration Status," ca. 1950, p. 2, AML; "Officers Named for Chinese Women's Club," *CP*, May 11, 1938; "American University Club Annual Meeting Slated For Wednesday," *CP*, June 11, 1938; "Local Alumni of N. Y. School Entertained," *CP*, December 2, 1938.

15. "Local Alumni of N. Y. School Entertained"; advertisement for Jimmy's Kitchen, *CP*, December 4, 1938.

CHAPTER TWENTY-FIVE: KAY AND MING TAI

1. "'Miss Shanghai' Is Baby Winner in Chinatown," *NYHT*, June 18, 1939; "Chinese Children Vie in Field Games," *NYT*, June 19, 1938, "Chinese Children Vie on Play Day," and untitled weather report, June 18, 1939; Chris Moy conversation with the author, March 25, 2023.

2. "'Miss Shanghai' Is Baby Winner in Chinatown."

3. "Moran Concedes He Got Taxi Cash," *NYT*, June 4, 1939; William Eng Hong and Rose Vivian Wong, marriage license, September 5, 1939, NYCMA; VCD, May 19, 1939, 35.8/17; MFHR, 5, 10.

4. VCD, January 29, 1939, 35.8/4; "Bank Disposes of Two Flats on Amsterdam Av.," *NYHT*, January 31, 1939; "Mechanics Liens," *NYHT*, November 10, 1939.

5. Chinatown Casino photo, 1939, item 2015.043.072, Eric Y. Ng Collection, MOCA; "Business Records," *NYT*, March 21, 1940.

6. Dan Yee Chin draft card, April 25, 1942, Ancestry.com.

7. T.J. Molloy to Inspector in Charge, August 27, 1940, pp. 1–2, file 6/1235, NARA-NYC.

8. John T. Cahill to District Director of Immigration, August 27, 1940, p. 1, file 6/1235.

9. Chinatown Inn menu, ca. 1942, item 2007.072.022, Ng collection; "Dining and Dancing," *NYHT*, December 7, 1940.

10. MFHR, 5–6; *NYHT*, "China Relief Will Honor Heads of Women's Clubs," September 28, 1941; Alwin B. Chen draft card, October 16, 1940, Ancestry.com;

Chinatown Inn ad, *China Monthly* 2, no. 10 (October 1941), 21; VCD, March 30, 1939, 35.8/11.

11. VCD, February 8, 1939, 35.8/5; Young Jack Tai testimony, July 22, 1940, pp. 1–2, file 132/993, NARA-NYC; Richard J. H. Johnston, "Explorer Offers Vital Aid in War," *NYT*, November 5, 1950.

12. VCD, December 6, 1938, 35.7/25; MFHR, 4; SS *President Cleveland*, "List or Manifest of Alien Passengers for the United States," June 27, 1940, Ancestry.com; W. Langhorne Bond, *Wings for an Embattled China* (Lehigh University Press, 2001), 287; Mitter, *Forgotten Ally*, 3.

13. Huang, *Memoirs of J. L. Huang*, 111; Young Jack Tai testimony, 2; John P. Roche, "The Loss of American Nationality: The Development of Statutory Expatriation," *University of Pennsylvania Law Review* 99, no. 1 (1950): 33–36.

14. Bond, *Wings for an Embattled China*, 287.

CHAPTER TWENTY-SIX: ERNEST AND RUTH

1. Ruth Koe and Ernest Moy, Agreement of Divorce by Mutual Consent, October 3, 1945, FM.

2. Loring Moy to New Brunswick Local Board No. 31, August 21, 1950, p. 1, FM; "Inter-Scholastic Sports Meeting," *NCH*, April 26, 1939; "Shanghai Schools Beat Chinese," *NCH*, May 24, 1939; "Marine Athletes Defeat S.A.S.," *NCH*, April 24, 1940; "League Baseball," *NCH*, July 3, 1940; "Censorship of Press at 'Y' Debate," *CP*, February 5, 1938; "Marriage Is Boring, Says Speaker at 'Y,'" *CP*, November 12, 1938; E. K. Moy to editor, *CP*, August 28, 1938.

3. "US Court for China," *NCH*, May 13, 1936; "News Brevities," *CP*, July 10, 1937; photo of Moy apartment, ca. 1940, FM.

4. Burke, "Herbert Erasmus Moy," p. 2; John Sterling Adams, "Hebert Erasmus Moy," March 4, 1943, p. 2, file 100155291 sec-1, 1 of 3, box 72, HEM; ML, 7.

5. Carroll Duard Alcott, *My War with Japan* (Henry Holt, 1943), 309–26.

6. Mitter, *Forgotten Ally*, 202–10; Wai Chor So, "Race, Culture, and the Anglo-American Powers: The Views of Chinese Collaborators," *Modern China* 37, no. 1 (2011), 70, 75–77; Marcia Reynders Ristaino, *Port of Last Resort: The Diaspora Communities of Shanghai* (Stanford University Press, 2001), 100–116.

7. "War in Europe Disrupts Normal Life of Shanghai and Entire Far East," *CWR*, September 9, 1940; "Central Fund," *NCH*, October 25, 1939; "Shanghai French Women Thanked," *NCH*, December 13, 1939; "Polish Fund Sends Money, Clothing," *NCH*, March 20, 1940; "More Britons Here Respond to the Call," *NCH*, September 18, 1940; Mitter, *Forgotten Ally*, 287.

8. Yeh, "Prologue," 2.

9. *Dagongbao*, "*Hu shuiwuxuexiao*" (Shanghai Customs College), August 7, 1940; "Nanking Official Takes Over Customs College," *CWR*, August 10, 1940; Shanghai Municipal Council, "Licence to Drive a Motor Vehicle," July 30, 1940, FM.

10. "Coming and Going," *SCMP*, September 2, 1940; Timothy Brook, *Collaboration: Japanese Agents and Local Elites in Wartime China* (Harvard University Press, 2005) 228–39.

11. "Coming and Going"; "House-Boy Fined," *SCMP*, September 5, 1941; *Dagongbao*, "*Shuiwuzhuanmen*" (Customs College), January 21, 1941; Hsiu Shu-cheng to editor, *CWR*, September 14, 1940, and September 28, 1940; Su-chow Ho to editor, *CWR*, September 21, 1940, and October 12, 1940; C. Y. Hwang to editor, *CWR*, November 23, 1940; "Customs College Not Open in Hong Kong," *NCH*, November 20, 1940; Kwong Chi Man and Tsoi Yiu Lun, *Eastern Fortress: A Military History of Hong Kong, 1840–1970* (Hong Kong University Press, 2014), 148–50; Chang, *Government, Imperialism and Nationalism in China*, 153.

12. "Chinese Consular Invoice Office Notification," *SCMP*, December 9, 1938; Ruth and Loring Moy passport, September 2, 1940, FM; Brooks, *American Exodus*, 141, 191.

13. Ruth and Loring Moy passport.

14. "Baseball Corner," *SCMP*, May 20, 1941; Directeur des Services de Police to R. W. Campbell, March 29, 1941, FM.

15. "Recovery of the Piano Trade," *NCH*, July 15, 1936.

16. "Camp Proposed as Solution to Shanghai's Beggar Problem to Be Opened Shortly," *CWR*, November 23, 1940; E. Petersen to Editor, *NCH*, October 23, 1940; *NCDHL 1941*, *passim*.

17. *NCDHL 1941*, 141, 217; Peter Kim, "Personal Qualifications Questionnaire," August 15, 1945, pp. 1–2, B1 F1 201 File 1945–46a, PK; S. Moutrie & Co. piano receipt, October 30, 1940, FM.

18. "Baseball Corner," *SCMP*, May 20, 1941, and August 30, 1941.

19. Yeh, *Shanghai Splendor*, 155–56; "Shanghai in Trim for Xmas," *NCH*, December 25, 1940; EKMD, August 24, 1952.

20. Alcott, *My War with Japan*, 309, 325–30.

21. "Radio XMHA Jam," *SCMP*, December 18, 1940; "Propaganda War," *SCMP*, December 16, 1940; "German Propaganda," *SCMP*, March 4, 1941; sign-off from FBI transcripts of Herbert Moy broadcasts in file 100155291 sec-3, 2 of 3, box 73, HEM; "Overseas S.W. Stations Received Easily in Eastern Australia," *The Wireless Weekly* (Sydney, Australia), January 4, 1941, 30.

CHAPTER TWENTY-SEVEN: ALICE AND ALFRED

1. Richard P. Butrick telegram to Secretary of State, October 14, 1940, American Consulate General Shanghai, Vol. 2881, RG 84, NARA-CP; Secretary of State telegram to consulates in East Asia, February 11, 1941, pp. 1–2, and US Consul General Canton, "Circular to American Citizens in the Canton Consular District," February 14, 1941, p. 1, American Consulate General Canton, Vol. 689, RG 84, NARA-CP; *FRUS 1940, Vol. 4*, 931–40.

2. Wakeman, *The Shanghai Badlands*, 54, 128–35.

3. "Sound and Fury of the War in Shanghai," *CWR*, February 8, 1941; *NCDHL 1941*, 256, 521; Astrid Freyeisen, *Shanghai und die Politik des Dritten Reiches* (Konigshausen & Neumann, 2000), 346–48. My appreciation to Ky Woltering for translating parts of this book for me from the German.

4. Carter Gleysteen, "Herbert Erasmus Moy," March 26, 1943, pp. 2–4, file 100155291 sec-1, 2 of 3; Wilson, "Herbert Erasmus Moy," 2; Adams, "Herbert Erasmus Moy," 2; "Bill and Mac" program description based on transcripts in file 100155291 sec-2, 2 of 2, box 72, HEM.

5. Alcott, *My War with Japan*, 298, 309–29, 343.

6. Freyeisen, *Shanghai und die Politik des Dritten Reiches*, 382–83; Wilson, "Herbert Erasmus Moy," p. 2; James Burke, "Herbert Erasmus Moy," 3.

7. Freyeisen, *Shanghai und die Politik des Dritten Reiches*, 340; John P. Ansley, "Herbert Erasmus Moy," November 22, 1943, p. 2, file 100155291 sec-2, 2 of 2, box 72, HEM; "Is 'Lord Haw-Haw a Renegade American?," *CWR*, April 5, 1941.

8. Frank Lockhart to Secretary of State, September 24, 1941, p. 2, Decimal File 893.74, China: Records of the Department of State, 1940–1949, AU; Burke, "Herbert Erasmus Moy," p. 3; Herbert Moy, "Roosevelt Wants War," *Shanghai Calling!* II:7 (November 25, 1941), 9–24.

9. Based on Erik Watts, "Note on Conditions in Shanghai December 8th, to December 19th, 1941," April 4, 1942, pp. 1–5, BFO371/31651.

10. "Shanghai Action" and "Radio Closes Down," *SCMP*, December 9, 1941; Watts, "Note on Conditions," p. 1; Brooks, *American Exodus*, 173–75.

11. Powell, *My Twenty-Five Years in China*, 356–58.

12. I.K.W. to editor, *NCH*, October 15, 1941; "Conditions in Shanghai," ca. February 1942, p. 1, file FO371/31651; Watts, "Note on Conditions," p. 1; *NCDHL 1941*, 49.

13. "How the World Heard Grim News of Japan's Attacks," *Daily Mirror* (Sydney), December 8, 1941.

14. Herbert Moy, "War in the Pacific," *Shanghai Calling!* 2, no. 11 (December 23, 1941): 3–7.

15. Moy, "War in the Pacific," 3–7; Watts, "Note on Conditions," p. 1; Burke, "Herbert Erasmus Moy," 3.

CHAPTER TWENTY-EIGHT: KAY AND MING TAI

1. Michael E. Ruane, "'WAR!' How a Stunned Media Broke the Pearl Harbor News," *Washington Post*, December 6, 2011; clips of radio bulletins from December 7, 1941, https://archive.org/details/194112072230NBCRSherlockHolmes/1941-12-07; "Hull Brands Japanese Answer to Terms 'Infamous Falsehood,'" *NYHT*, December 8, 1941.

2. Franklin D. Roosevelt address to Congress, December 8, 1941, Library of Congress, https://www.loc.gov/resource/afc1986022.afc1986022_ms2201/?st = text (accessed May 9, 2024); Steven M. Gillon, *Pearl Harbor: FDR Leads the Nation into War* (Basic Books, 2011), 177.

3. "Japanese Bomb Towns, Bases in Philippines," *NYHT*, December 8, 1941; "Hongkong Sees Land Assaults Due After Raids," *NYHT*, December 9, 1941.

4. Jeremy Black, *World War Two: A Military History* (Routledge, 2003), 92–97; "Siege Is Defied by US Pilots at Hongkong," *NYHT*, December 15, 1941; "Mother Writes of Hongkong Escape by Air," *NYHT*, February 19, 1942.

5. "Mother Writes of Hongkong Escape by Air"; Bond, *Wings for an Embattled China*, 287.

6. Leong interview; MFHR, 9.

7. Leong interview

8. "Factories Ease Race-Religion Discrimination," *NYHT*, August 23, 1941; "Mayor Assails Unions Which Shut Out Negro," *NYHT*, February 17, 1942; "Racial Job Ban Ordered Ended at 8 War Plants," *NYHT*, May 27, 1942; "NAACP Charge Bias at Sperry's," *New York Amsterdam Star News*, August 22, 1942; Nelson Lichtenstein, *Labor's War at Home: The CIO in World War II* (Temple University Press, 2003), 92–93; Reed, *Not Alms but Opportunity*, 156–57.

9. Chris and Sara Moy email to the author, April 4, 2021; Advertisement for Sperry Gyroscope, *NYHT*, January 29, 1942; advertisement for Sperry Gyroscope, *NYHT*, December 13, 1942; "Workers as Warriors," *BE*, March 4, 1942; William T. Moy draft card, October 16, 1940, 1942, Ancestry.com.

10. "Chinese Women Organize," *NYT*, March 19, 1942; Katherine Blanck, "Organizes Chinese Women Here," *BE*, July 28, 1942; MFHR, 6.

11. Blanck, "Organizes Chinese Women Here"; "Mrs. Jack Young Takes Respite from Hunting—Helps New Life Movement," *CWR*, June 16, 1934; photo 2012.021.004, ca. 1942, Carole Wong collection, MOCA.

12. *NYHT*, "'Grandma' Low Aids A.W.V.S. in Chinatown Unit," December 9, 1942, "Chinatown Opens Center for All Allied Fighters," April 25, 1943, and "War Bond Drive Off with a Rush in Chinatown," January 24, 1944; photo 2015.037.168, ca. 1942, DJC.

13. Brooks, *Between Mao and McCarthy*, 58; Kenneth P. Moy reconstructed military record, 1942–1946, p. 1, National Personnel Records Center; photo 2015.037.006, August 1943, DJC.

14. Photo 2012.021.004 and photo 2015.037.283, April 1944, DJC; "Chinese WAAC Had to Increase Weight to Enlist," *NYHT*, September 19, 1942.

15. "Chinese WAAC Had to Increase Weight to Enlist."

16. "Workers as Warriors," *BE*, March 4, 1942; "Gas Rationing Based on Five Types of Cards," *NYHT*, May 7, 1942; photo 2015.037.541, June 1943, DJC.

17. Item 2015.037.530, February 25, 1943, DJC; "A Guest of the Nation," *NYHT*, February 18, 1943; "Weather" and "City Extends Welcome Today to Mrs. Chiang," *NYHT*, March 1, 1943; items 2015.037.540 and 2015.037.542, June 1943, DJC; "China's First Lady Visits Sperry," *Sperryscope* 9, no. 12 (July 1943), 7.

1. EKMD, April 13, 1952. Occupied Hong Kong description based on Jun Ke Choy, *My China Years, 1911–1945: Practical Politics in China after the 1911 Revolution* (Eastwest), 185–86; Irma Tam Soong, *Chinese American Refugee: A World War II Memoir* (Hawaii Chinese History Center, 1984), 20–37; Gwen Dew, *Prisoner of the Japs* (Knopf, 1943), 145–46; Gordon King, "Brief Report on Conditions Prevailing in Hongkong During the Period 25th December, 1941 to 17th February, 1942," March 18, 1942, pp. 4, 8, BFO371/31671; "Escape from Hongkong," *SCMP*, April 4, 1946.

2. Soong, *Chinese American Refugee*, 28–29; E. T. Williams to C. H. B. Joly, ca. August 1942, p. 1, file "Inspector General's Confidential Correspondence with Kuan-wu Shu, 1942–1943 (call no. 1239, RMCSC, SHAC), Chinese Maritime Customs Service database, AU.

3. Ming, "Hongkong Under Japanese Occupation," 4; Chang, *Government, Imperialism and Nationalism in China*, 153–54; Charles Knaggs, "Information about Macau and the Macau Area," June 11, 1942, pp. 1–4, and G. A. MacCaskie, "Report on Conditions in Macau," May 1942, pp. 6–10, BFO371/31630. C. S. Archer's novel *China Servant* (Collins, 1946), 16, affirms that few Customs employees saw a Wuzhou posting as desirable.

4. "River Shipping," *SCMP*, January 1, 1937.

5. Jean-Paul Wiest, *Maryknoll in China: A History, 1918–1955* (M. E. Sharpe, 1988), 363–66; Meagan Cairns email to the author, August 4, 2023; Fr. Lavin, "The Mission at Luoding, 1935," Catholic Foreign Mission Society of America/Maryknoll Mission Archive, https://doi.org/10.25549/impa-m4361 (accessed May 11, 2024).

6. KYKX, "Herbert Moy, Active Collaborator," November 3, 1944, p. 1, CIA FOIA OSS Collection, https://www.cia.gov/readingroom/document/0000112811 (accessed May 11, 2024).

7. Williams to Joly, 1.

8. Williams to Joly, 1.

9. "Baseball Corner," *SCMP*, June 9, June 16, and September 1, 1941.

10. Loring Moy to New Brunswick Local Board no. 31, August 21, 1950, p. 1, FM; Grace Cook, "Out Where We Live," *SEPM*, September 10, 1943; Arthur Kim interview with the author, February 10, 2024; "Conditions in Shanghai," ca. February 1942, p. 2, BFO371/31651.

11. Brooks, *American Exodus*, 179; Richard Kim interview by Terry Shima, June 21, 2006, and Peter Kim, "Carter's One Man Army," n.d., Veterans' Oral History Program, Library of Congress, https://www.loc.gov/item/afc2001001.53062/?ID = mv0001 (accessed May 11, 2024); Peter Kim, "Personal Qualifications Questionnaire," 1–2.

12. Arthur Kim interview with the author; "The Chinatown Crier," *Chinese Digest* (San Francisco), April 1938, 3.

13. Swiss Consulate General Shanghai, "Report of the Swiss Consulate General in Charge of British, American, and Netherlands Interests During the Pacific War,

1941–1945," February 1946, section VIII, dokument 1, reference code E2001–02#1968/218#478*, SFA.

14. Kim, "Carter's One Man Army"; Peter Kim to Paul J. B. Murphy, August 11, 1945, pp. 2–3, file B1 F19 "Correspondence 1943–1946," PK; Arthur Kim interview with the author.

15. Kim to Murphy, 3; Swiss Consulate General Shanghai, Section for Protection of American Interests, "Accounts as of June 30th, 1942," June 30, 1942, p. 14, subdossier 10: dokument 24, reference code E2001–02#1968/218#478*, SFA.

CHAPTER THIRTY: ALICE AND ALFRED

1. ML, 3; photos from the Kadoorie School, 1942–1945, AML; A.H. George, "Intelligence Report on the Situation in the Shanghai Area," September 25, 1942, p. 9, BFO371/31651; John W. Dower, *War Without Mercy: Race and Power in the Pacific War* (Pantheon, 1986), 241–50.

2. George, "Intelligence Report on the Situation in the Shanghai Area," pp. 3–6; "Conditions in Shanghai," May 1942, p. 1, BFO371/31651.

3. Brooks, *American Exodus*, 179; George, "Intelligence Report on the Situation in the Shanghai Area," pp. 4–5; A. P. Finch to Undersecretary of State for Foreign Affairs, November 18, 1942, pp. 1–6, BFO371/31651; Powell, *My Twenty-Five Years in China*, 370–91; Burke, "Herbert Erasmus Moy," 1–2.

4. George, "Intelligence Report on the Situation in the Shanghai Area," pp. 19–22; J.M. Hardie, "Notes on the Occupation of Shanghai," April 1942, pp. 1–2, file 371/31651; ration card and ration coupons for butter, margarine, coal briquettes, and matches and soap, ca. 1944, FM.

5. Max Haefeli, "Report on Repatriation of American Nationals from Occupied China after Outbreak of Hostilities on December 8, 1941," October 24, 1945, pp. 2–4, dokument 2, reference code E2200.290A#1970/121#115*, Swiss Consulate General Shanghai, Section for Protection of American Interests, "Accounts as of June 30th, 1942," June 30, 1942, p. 11, subdossier 10: dokument 24, reference code E2001–02#1968/218#478*, and American Association, "Statement of Account as of March 31st, 1942," pp. 1–9, subdossier 10: dokument 12, SFA.

6. Haefeli, "Report on Repatriation," 1–2; Heern Hans Degen, "Bericht von Heern Hans Degen ueber die Evakuationsreise per T/S Conte Verde am 29, Juni ab Shanghai mit Bestimmung Lourenço-Marques mit Kommandant Ugo Chinca" (Report of Heern Hans Degan on the SS *Conte Verde*'s evacuation voyage of June 29 from Shanghai to Lourenço-Marques with Captain Ugo China), July 3, 1942, pp. 1–4, and "Passenger List, S.S. Conte Verde," pp. 1–40, Unterlagen 2, reference code E2200.136–02#1000/183#48*, SFA.

7. Powell, *My Twenty-Five Years in China*, 403–4; Robert P. Martin, "Japs Convert Shanghai into Concentration Camp for Foes," *Oakland Tribune*, May 17, 1942; American Legation, Bern, No. 2348, July 25, 1942, p. 1, subdossier 5: dokument 7,

and No. 2495, August 12, 1942, pp. 1–2, subdossier 1: dokument 3, reference code E2001–02#1000/113#248*, SFA.

8. Emile Fontanel telegram to US State Department, July 24, 1942, subdossier 1: dokument 3, reference code E2001–02#1000/113#248*; Haefeli, "Report on Repatriation," 4.

9. Fontanel telegram.

10. Haefeli, "Report on Repatriation," 2, 4.

11. Gleysteen, "Herbert Erasmus Moy," 2; Anne Allison, "Review of Radio Listening in China, 1937–1945," June 11, 1945, pp. 9–10, file "Propaganda—Foreign," in "The Chinese Civil War and U.S.-China Relations: Records of the US State Department's Office of Chinese Affairs, 1945–1955" database, AU; Herbert Moy, "Roosevelt—'Man of Peace,'" *Shanghai Calling!* 3, no. 4 (March 31, 1942); Herbert Moy, "The End of the Road'" *Shanghai Calling!* 2, no. 12 (December 30, 1941).

12. Burke, "Herbert Erasmus Moy," March 5, 1943, p. 3; Astrid Freyeisen, *Shanghai und die Politik des Dritten Reiches*, 383.

13. "People in the News," *CWR*, November 3, 1945.

14. YKX-902, "Espionage," January 12, 1945, p. 1, CIA FOIA OSS Collection, https://www.cia.gov/readingroom/docs/DOC_0000112812.pdf (accessed May 12, 2024).

15. Robert Bickers, *Empire Made Me: An Englishman Adrift in Shanghai* (Penguin, 2004), 145; Gordon Fortin, "Shanghai General Report No. 1," October 12, 1945, p. 4, BFO371/46246.

16. Wellington K. K. Chan, "Personal Styles, Cultural Values and Management: The Sincere and Wing On Companies in Shanghai and Hong Kong, 1900–1941," *Business History Review* 70, no. 2 (1996), 150–54; Chen Danyan, *Shanghai Princess: Her Survival with Pride and Dignity* (Better Link Press, 2010), 21–22; Yeh, *Shanghai Splendor*, 56–61; Coble, *Chinese Capitalists in Japan's New Order*, 142; "New Social Club to Make Bow Today," *CP*, December 1, 1935; "Amity Lodge to Have Round of Socials," *CP*, September 27, 1935; "Grads Of N.Y.U. Organize New Alumni Group," *CP*, June 16, 1936.

17. Moira M. W. ChanYeung, *Lam Woo: Master Builder, Revolutionary, and Philanthropist* (CUHK Press, 2017), 29–30.

18. Coble, *Chinese Capitalists in Japan's New Order*, 146–47.

19. "Conditions in Shanghai," 1; Hardie, "Notes on the Occupation of Shanghai," 1; "Questionnaire on North and Central China," ca. October 1942, p. 16, and R. J. E. Price, "Conditions in Shanghai from Outbreak of Pacific War to 19th March 1942," p. 3, BFO371/31651.

20. Coble, *Chinese Capitalists in Japan's New Order*, 145–46.

21. Brooks, *American Exodus*, 4.

22. Swiss Consulate Shanghai, "Report of the Swiss Consulate General in Charge of British, American, and Netherlands Interests During the Pacific War, 1941–1945," February 1946, section XI, dokument 2, reference code E2200 .290A#1970/121#90*, SFA.

23. Swiss Consulate General, "Statement of American Civilian Relief Loans Paid Out in Shanghai as of December 31st, 1942," p. 19, subdossier 10: dokument 26, reference code E2001–02#1968/218#478*, SFA.

CHAPTER THIRTY-ONE: KAY AND MING TAI

1. Clarence L. Johnson, "Herbert Erasmus Moy, with aliases," July 13, 1943, p. 3, file 100–155291-sec 2, 2 of 2, box 72, HEM.

2. Johnson, "Herbert Erasmus Moy," 3–4.

3. Johnson, "Herbert Erasmus Moy," 3–4.

4. "U.S. Probes 11 Named as Jap Propagandists," *Washington Post*, August 4, 1943.

5. Zach Fredman, *The Tormented Alliance: American Servicemen and the Occupation of China, 1941–1949* (University of North Carolina Press, 2022), 112; "Chinese Parry 1st Chungking Raid in 2 Years," *NYHT*, August 24, 1943; "Two Repatriates Describe Life in Internment Camp," *NYHT*, December 5, 1943; "35 from Brooklyn on Jap Exchange Ship," *BE*, October 14, 1943; "Eager Relatives Here Await the Gripsholm," *BE*, November 30, 1943.

6. MFHR, 5–6, 13; S.S. *AP 54*, "List of United States Citizens," December 31, 1943, no. 1, "California, Arriving Passenger and Crew Lists," and Henry S. Luke record, Department of Veterans Affairs BIRLS Death File, Ancestry.com.

7. Leong interview; Leong email.

8. Leong email; Hong Chan death certificate, August 16, 1944, NYCMA.

9. MFHR, 9–10; Leong interview.

10. Leong email; Hong Chan death certificate.

11. Leong email; Leong interview.

CHAPTER THIRTY-TWO: ERNEST AND RUTH

1. Parks M. Coble, *The Collapse of Nationalist China: How Chiang Kai-shek Lost China's Civil War* (Cambridge University Press, 2023), 15–27; *The Chinese Journals of L.K. Little, 1943–1954, Vol. 1*, ed. Chihyun Chang (Routledge, 2018), 47–48; Danke Li, *Echoes of Chongqing: Women in Wartime China* (University of Illinois Press, 2010), 173; Vincent K.L. Chang and Yong Zhou, "Redefining Wartime Chongqing: International Capital of a Global Power in the Making, 1938–46," *Modern Asian Studies* 51, no. 3 (2017): 578–83.

2. Fredman, *The Tormented Alliance*, 21–23, 32–36.

3. Brooks Atkinson, "Chungking Raided After Two-Year Lull," *NYT*, August 24, 1943; Mitter, *Forgotten* Ally, 251, 315–34.

4. *L.K. Little, Vol. 1*, 12; Mitter, *Forgotten Ally*, 175–76.

5. JTY, 179–80; Huang, *Memoirs of J. L. Huang*, 111; S.S. *AP 54*, "List of United States Citizens," December 31, 1943, no. 1, "California, Arriving Passenger and Crew Lists," Ancestry.com; Fredman, *The Tormented Alliance*, 27–28.

6. Huang, *Memoirs*, 118; *Laws (Abstract) and Board Rulings Regulating the Practice of Medicine in the United States and Brief Statements Regarding Medical Registration Abroad* (American Medical Association, 1929) offers state-by-state explanations of the ban on all but medical doctors using the title "Dr."

7. Ernest Moy photos, ca. 1944–1945, FM.

8. Fredman, *The Tormented Alliance*, 67.

9. Ernest Moy correspondence, March–July 1944, and Ernest Moy to George Ross, March 15, 1944, file "201—WASC Correspondence 1943–1945," container 14, RG 493, NARA-CP.

10. Mitter, *Forgotten Ally*, 315–34; Coble, *The Collapse of Nationalist China*, 18–22.

11. Tamra Moy interview with the author, February 1, 2020; "Marriages," *Harrisburg Telegraph*, June 3, 1943; untitled item, *SEPM*, March 17, 1943.

12. Kenneth P. Moy service photo, ca. 1943, FM; photo 2015.037.003, 1944, DJC; Kenneth P. Moy reconstructed military record.

13. Inspector Tanaka to Ruth Moy, May 4, 1943, and "Permit to Dispense with Armband" #370, May 1943, FM.

14. Sir H. Seymour to Anthony Eden, February 4, 1943, p. 4, BFO371/35799.

15. Ration stamps, ca. 1943–44, FM; *NCDHL 1941*, 319.

16. Richard Kim email to the author, June 6, 2020; Peter Kim to Loring and Kenneth Moy, March 23, 1978, p. 3, FM.

17. Shima interview with Richard Kim; Kim, "Carter's One Man Army," 1.

18. Shima interview with Richard Kim; Kim, "Carter's One Man Army," 1.

19. Shima interview with Richard Kim.

20. JTY, 258.

21. Shima interview with Richard Kim; Chialing "Jolly" Young King email to Richard Kim, Sara Moy, and Alson M. Lee, March 18, 2010, AML.

22. JTY, 258.

23. JTY, 258; King email to Kim, Moy, and Lee.

24. Stephen Chang interview with the author, September 8, 2022; "Herbert Moy, Espionage," 2.

25. JTY, 258.

CHAPTER THIRTY-THREE: ALICE AND ALFRED

1. Yeh, "Prologue," 11–12; British Embassy, Chungking, "News Summary," May 1943, p. 6, BFO371/35800; Chang interview.

2. AMLD, August 1944; Chang interview; Wang Jishen, ed., *Zhanshi Shanghai jingji* (Shanghai's wartime economy) (Shanghai Economic Research Institute, 1945), 184; Xu Wancheng, *Shanghai bai ye rencai xiaoshi* (Biographies of leading Shanghai businesspeople) (Longwen Bookstore, 1945), 289.

3. Chang interview; photo of Alice M. Lee, ca. 1945, AML; Yeh, "Prologue," 11–13; Frederic Wakeman Jr., "Urban Controls in Wartime Shanghai," in *Wartime Shanghai*, 146–47.

4. Tom van der Voort, "The Sounds of D-Day," Miller Center, University of Virginia, https://millercenter.org/the-presidency/educational-resources/listen-sounds-d-day (accessed January 10, 2024); Office of Strategic Services, report YKX-466, November 3, 1945, p. 1, box 22, OSS Classified Sources and Methods Files "Withdrawn Records," RG 226, NARA-CP.

5. "Two-Faced Diplomacy," *Melbourne Herald*, April 5, 1944; document 113198, ca. 1944, p. 2, originally CIA FOIA OSS collection, preserved at Archive.org, https://ia600307.us.archive.org/10/items/cia-readingroom-document-0000113198/0000113198.pdf (accessed June 26, 2025).

6. Wesley Frank Craven and James Lea Cate, eds., *The Army Air Forces in World War II, Vol. 5* (USGPO, 1983), 111, 141–45; OSS, report YKX-466, pp. 1, 3; Bernard Wasserstein, *Secret War in Shanghai* (Houghton Mifflin, 1998), 250; YKX-902, "Espionage," January 12, 1945, p. 1.

7. AMLD, November 13, 1944.

8. AMLD, November 21–23, 1944; Jennifer Lau, "The Life of a Chinese-American Born in Shanghai," December 3, 2007, in possession of the author; Chang interview; advertisement, *CP*, July 22, 1938.

9. AMLD, December 24, 1944.

10. Chang interview; AMLD, December 24, 1944, and February 12, 1945.

11. AMLD, January 22–23, 1945; photo 2015.037.433, January 1945, DJC.

12. AMLD, February 12, 1945.

13. AMLD, February 12, 1945.

CHAPTER THIRTY-FOUR: KAY AND MING TAI

1. Henry H. Franklin, "Herbert Erasmus Moy, with aliases," May 12, 1943, p. 1, file 100–155291-sec 1, 1 of 3, box 72, HEM.

2. Franklin, "Herbert Erasmus Moy, with aliases," 1.

3. VCD, June 5, 1938, p. 3, 35.6/12.

4. Harvey E. Runner, "State of Business," *NYHT*, September 17, 1944; "Byrnes Predicts Food Rationing End by July 1," *NYHT*, September 10, 1944; "Halved Supply in '43 Forecast for Nation's Liquor Retailers," *NYHT*, January 27, 1943; "Liquor Dealers Urge Limit on State Licenses," *NYHT*, October 20, 1944.

5. WPA Marketing Laws Survey, *State Liquor Legislation* (USGPO, 1941), 664–71.

6. Pacific Restaurant postcard, ca. 1948, in possession of the author; photo 2017.037.196, ca. 1949, DJC.

7. "Brooklyn Polytechnic Gives Ten Free Courses," *BE*, March 5, 1944; MFHR, 21.

8. Item 2015.037.514, 1943 and photo 2015.037.183, ca. 1942, DJC; Joseph W. Roe and Charles W. Lytle, *Factory Equipment, Second Edition* (International Textbook, 1937), 46–47; 18–19; Mary Elizabeth Pidgeon, *Women's Work and the War* (Science Research Associates, 1943), 27–28.

9. Item 2015.037.535, May 1, 1944, DJC.

CHAPTER THIRTY-FIVE: ERNEST AND RUTH

1. Photos of Kunming WASC Hostel #1, October 1945, RG 342, NARA-CP, https://catalog.archives.gov/id/204830830 and https://catalog.archives.gov/id/204830870 (accessed January 21, 2024); Ernest Moy to Joseph DiPietro, January 9, 1945, pp. 1–2, file "WASC Correspondence 1945," container 13, RG 493, NARA-CP.

2. Fredman, *The Tormented Alliance*, 5, 73–74; Ernest Moy, "Speech at Veterans' Dinner to Commemorate the 5th Anniversary of the 14th U.S. Air Force," March 10, 1948, p. 2, subject folder 25, box 20, NFA.

3. US Army Special Service Division, Army Service Forces, *A Pocket Guide to China* (War and Navy Departments, 1942), 2–3.

4. Moy to DiPietro, 2.

5. Richard Kim email; Shima interview with Richard Kim; Kim, "Carter's One Man Army," 1; Fredman, *The Tormented Alliance*, 44, 56; FRUS, Vol. 4, 1944, 98.

6. Coble, *The Collapse of Nationalist China*, 21–22; JTY, 265–66; Mitter, *Forgotten Ally*, 352; Fredman, *Tormented Alliance*, 21, 56.

7. Photo of Ruth and Loring Moy, January 1945, FM.

8. American Information Service, "Domei News," March 7, 1945, p. 1, and April 16, 1945, p. 7, AU; Ruth and Loring Moy photos, December 1944 and January 1945, FM.

9. JTY, 258; Foreign Broadcast Information Service, "Herbert Moy, Broadcasts by, Since 1 January 1945," ca. August 1945, file 100–155291-sec 3, 1 of 3, box 72, HEM.

10. "Nanking Denounces Cutting of Wires," *NYT*, September 20, 1931.

11. "Weather," *NYT*, January 15, 1922, 1; Ruth, Bill, and Herbert Moy, January 15, 1922, WTM.

12. Foreign Broadcast Information Service, "Herbert Moy, Broadcasts by, since 1 January 1945"; Emile Fontanel telegraph to Swiss government political interest section, January 6, 1945, unterlagen 34, subdossier 24, file E2001–02#1000–110#426_5451224, SFA; US Office of Information, "Chinese Press Review," May 16, 1945, p. 6, Records of the US Information Service in China, Chinese Press Reviews and Summaries, 1944–1950, AU; Coble, *The Collapse of Nationalist China*, 80.

13. "Herbert Moy, Broadcasts by, Since 1 January 1945."

CHAPTER THIRTY-SIX: ALICE AND ALFRED

1. AMLD, August 16, 1945.

2. AMLD, August 10, 1945.

3. AMLD, Aug 11, 12, and 13, 1945.

4. AMLD, August 11, 1945; Huashan Road Police Substation, "*Riyu shanghai difangfayuan jianchashu guanyu Mei Qiquan deng tiaolouzisha*" (Japanese puppet Shanghai District Court investigation of Herbert Moy's jump from a building to his death), August 16, 1945, pp. 1–2, file R44–2-6104, code 431001, no. 1300100285804, files of the Japanese Puppet Shanghai District Court, Shanghai Municipal Archives.

5. AMLD, August 11 and 17, 1945.

6. *Shanghai Calling!*, drawing of building, March 31, 1942, 2; AMLD, August 16, 1945; Huashan Road Police Substation, "*Mei Qiquan deng tiaolouzisha*"; "Tokyo's Regular Commentators and Commentaries," August 4, 1943, p. 9, Central File: Decimal File 894.76, U.S. State Department Records on the Internal Affairs of Japan, AU.

7. AMLD, August 16, 1945; "*Mei Qiquan deng tiaolouzisha.*"

8. AMLD, August 16, 1945; "*Mei Qiquan deng tiaolouzisha.*"

9. AMLD, August 17, 1945; KR/IS, "Information Concerning the Death of Herbert Moy," November 5, 1945, p. 2, #WN24213, box 22, Entry 211, RG 226, NARA-CP.

10. AMLD, August 11, 16, and 17, 1945; Downs, "Word for Word."

11. Shima interview with Richard Kim; Kim, "Carter's One Man Army," 1; Art Kim interview.

12. Kim, "Carter's One Man Army," 6–9.

13. Kim, "Carter's One Man Army," 3–5; Art Kim interview; "Credentials," August 15, 1945, pp. 1–2, file 1, box 1, US Army Personnel Files, PK.

14. Capt. Robert L. Peaslee to Sen. Richard Russell, October 30, 1945, pp. 1–2, and Peter Kim to P.R. Josselyn, September 28, 1945, pp. 1–4, in file 1, box 2, PK; photo of mission members at an internment camp, ca. August 1945, Preston Schoyer papers, in possession of Robert Kim.

15. US Information Service, "Chinese Press Review," January 7, 1946, p. 3, Records of the U.S. Information Service in China, AU; Randall Gould, "Hong Kong and Shanghai Vie for Place," *Christian Science Monitor*, September 29, 1945; *Christian Science Monitor*, "Foreign Trade Sees Shanghai Facing Change," October 24, 1945.

16. *SEPM*, "Don Chisholm Reported Held in Shanghai, Moy Found Dead," October 12, 1945; ML, 3; "Yanks Hailed in Shanghai," *Baltimore Sun*, August 30, 1945; "Japanese in Canton Get Surrender Terms," *NYT*, September 11, 1945; Clark Lee, *One Last Look Around* (Duell, Sloan and Pearce, 1947), 169.

17. Lee to Havenner, AML; Ernest J. Heppner, *Shanghai Refuge: A Memoir of the World War II Jewish Ghetto* (University of Nebraska Press, 1995), 135.

18. Lee to Havenner, 2; photo 2015.37.354, 1945, DJC.

19. "Cable from Dr. Mei," *SEPM*, July 13, 1945; "Trade Drive in China," *Hong Kong Sunday Herald*, December 2, 1945; Brooks, *American Exodus*, 195; Coble, *The Collapse of Nationalist China*, 84–85.

PART THREE: REVOLUTION

1. Mitter, *Forgotten Ally*, 362–367.

2. Susan A. Brewer, *To Win the Peace: British Propaganda in the United States During World War II* (Cornell University Press, 1997), 234; Richard B. Finn, *Winners in Peace: MacArthur, Yoshida, and Postwar Japan* (University of California

Press, 1992), 13; Suzanne Mettler, *Soldiers to Citizens: The G. I. Bill and the Making of the Greatest Generation* (Oxford University Press, 2005), 15, 74–76, 122–23; Zaragosa Vargas, *Labor Rights Are Civil Rights: Mexican American Workers in Twentieth-Century America* (Princeton University Press, 2004), 204–216; Brooks, *Alien Neighbors, Foreign Friends*, 144–53.

3. Michael Green, *By More Than Providence: Grand Strategy and American Power in the Asia Pacific Since 1783* (Columbia University Press, 2017), 254–59; Fredman, *The Tormented Alliance*, 18–20, 180.

4. Mitter, *Forgotten Ally*, 5–7, 106–7, 318–24, 363–70; Coble, *The Collapse of Nationalist China*, 19–34, 196.

5. Jonathan Bell, *The Liberal State on Trial: The Cold War and American Politics in the Truman Years* (Columbia University Press, 2004), 20–55; Nancy Bernkopf Tucker, *Taiwan, Hong Kong, and the United States, 1945–1992: Uncertain Friendships* (Twayne, 1994), 35; Ellen Schrecker, *Many Are the Crimes: McCarthyism in the United States* (Princeton University Press, 1998), 209.

6. Tucker, *Taiwan, Hong Kong, and the United States*, 29–36; Brooks, *Between Mao and McCarthy*, 105–7.

CHAPTER THIRTY-SEVEN: KAY AND MING TAI

1. Lillian Lee email to the author, February 12, 2024; "Cues to Dining," *Cue* (New York), June 2, 1945, 25; Ruth G. Davis, "Going Places," *BE*, March 22, 1946; Lew Sheaffer, "Night Life," *BE*, January 14, 1947; Al Salerno, "Night Life," *BE*, November 17, 1948.

2. John G. Rogers, "Second Holiday for City Today, Banks to Open," *NYHT*, August 16, 1945.

3. "Yanks Hailed in Shanghai," *Baltimore Sun*, August 30, 1945. The AP story was widely reported in late August and early September 1945.

4. Herbert Moy grave photo, April 1949, WTM. Photos of Moy Sing and Han Ying's graves, but not Herbert's, are in Helen's and Alice's photo books. Helen's book included no photos of Herbert after 1932.

5. Roche, "The Loss of American Nationality," 43–44; SS *Marine Phoenix*, "List of United States Citizens," number 1, April 7, 1946, "Washington, Arriving and Departing Passenger and Crew Lists," Ancestry.com; Alice M. Lee to Anna Kong Mei, ca. January 1948, p. 1, and Alice M. Lee photos from 1946–1947, AML.

6. MFHR, 5–7; Luke BIRLS Death File; Somerville township sheet 2, Somerset, NJ, 1950 US Federal Census, Ancestry.com; F. C. Sharpley to Adrian Pelt, November 30, 1946, p. 1, in file 8, box 50, S-0472, Central Registry (302–200–2), OSG, United Nations Archives and Records Management Section, New York, NY.

7. "Chinese Combat Command," *China Lantern* 3, no. 8 (May 30, 1945), https://www.cbi-theater.com/lantern/lantern053045.html (accessed March 2, 2024); "Record of Assignments," 1968, p. 2, Jack Young military record; George Huang record, August 20, 1945, in "Border Crossings from Canada to US," Ancestry.com;

"Class Notes," *Wesleyan Alumnae Magazine*, May 1946, 20; City of London, 1946 Death Register, Vol. 5D, p. 118.

8. Adelaide Young to US family members, January 5, 1947, p. 1, and February 27, 1947, p. 3, JYK.

9. City of London Death Register; Dr. Robert Yee email to the author, March 10, 2024; American Overseas Airlines, Air Passenger Manifest, December 9, 1946, p. 1, New York Arriving Passenger and Crew Lists, Ancestry.com.

10. "Aviation Industry Lays Off Workers," *NYT*, August 16, 1945.

11. Photos 2015.037.359–361, 366, 368, 1940s, DJC; Adelphi University, *1950 Oracle Yearbook* (Adelphi University, 1950), 111.

12. Sara and Chris Moy email to the author, April 4, 2021.

13. "State Plan Made for City Housing," *NYT*, January 18, 1946; S.S. *Lavaca*, "List or Manifest of Alien Passengers for the United States," October 1945, List 10, in California Arriving Passenger and Crew Lists, Ancestry.com; photos of Wong family gatherings, 1942–1950, WTM.

14. Photos of Moy family outings, 1940–1950, WTM.

15. Sara and Chris Moy email.

CHAPTER THIRTY-EIGHT: ERNEST AND RUTH

1. Ernest Moy appointment notification, September 14, 1945, FM. The two versions above—榮歸故里 and 衣錦還鄉—together with other variations, appeared in many Chinese American newspapers of the time. For more discussion of the idea, see Michael Williams, *Returning Home with Glory: Chinese Villagers around the Pacific, 1849 to 1949* (Hong Kong University Press, 2018), 15.

2. Kenneth Moy photo of Herbert Moy's gravestone, April 1949, WTM.

3. Coble, *The Collapse of Nationalist China*, 84–88; Suzanne Pepper, "The KMT-CCP Conflict, 1945–1949," in Lloyd E. Eastman et al., eds., *The Nationalist Era in China, 1927–1949* (Cambridge University Press, 1991), 305–11; Lu, *Beyond the Neon Lights*, 64–66. For views of postwar Shanghai, see, for example, Edward I. Matthews Jr. home movie of Shanghai in 1946, https://www.youtube.com/watch?v = NVSoCG71OQE&t = 741s (accessed March 25, 2024); Arthur Fiddament collection, Historical Photos of China, available at https://hpcbristol.net/collections /fiddament-arthur (accessed March 25, 2024).

4. Photos of Loring Moy in June 1941 and November 1945, and Loring Moy to Kenneth Moy, March 28, 1948, p. 1, FM; Arthur Kim interview with the author, February 10, 2024.

5. Peter Kim to Hoff, January 7, 1946 [misdated 1945], file B1 F19 correspondence 1943–46a, PK; Ernest Moy appointment notification; Flora Belle Jan, *Unbound Spirit: Letters of Flora Belle Jan*, ed. Fleur Yano and Saralyn Daly (University of Illinois Press, 2006), 224; EKMD April 13, 1952.

6. Photo, "Ken and Lo in a pedicab, Shanghai," November 1945, Loring Moy to Kenneth Moy, March 28, 1948, and Loring Moy to Selective Service Local Board 31,

August 21, 1950, pp. 1–2, FM; Kenneth Moy reconstructed military service record; Tamra Moy interview with the author, February 1, 2020.

7. Arthur Kim interview; Loring Moy to Kenneth Moy, March 28, 1948; Peter Kim to Loring and Kenneth Moy, March 23, 1978, p. 3, FM.

8. Peter Kim to Loring and Kenneth Moy, March 23, 1978, p. 3, and C. C. Chang to Ruth Moy, July 1948, FM; *1947 Shanghai Telephone Directory and Buyers' Guide* (Shanghai Telephone Co., 1947), 16; *Qingbao* (Qingdao), "*Guoda jinchen shou ci dahui*" (first meeting of the National Assembly this morning), November 25, 1946.

9. 79th US Congress, private law 808, August 2, 1946, in file B1F1 201 1945–46d, PK; "Request for Permission to Marry," March 1, 1948, p. 1, file B1F2 201 file 1947–49b, PK; Bob to Pete, Nov. 30, 1945, and Peter Kim to Lt. Col. W. A. Ohls, Feb. 4, 1946, file B1F19 correspondence 1943–46c, PK; Ruth and Peter Kim wedding photos, 1948, FM.

10. Fredman, *The Tormented Alliance*, 3; US Army Forces China, list of Medal of Freedom recipients, May 14, 1946, FM; *Federal Register*, Vol. 12, June 21, 1947, 4021; Coble. *The Collapse of Nationalist China*, 88–95.

11. FRUS, 1945 (*Vol. 7: The Far East, China*), 746; S. E. Shifrin, "Peiping a Much Militarized City: Hotel Accommodations Scarce," *CWR*, September 26, 1946; M. Taylor Fravel, *Active Defense: China's Military Strategy Since 1949* (Princeton University Press, 2019), 54; Huang, *Memoirs of J. L. Huang*, 158–59.

12. Photos of Loring and Ernest Moy, August–September 1946, and Loring Moy to Ruth Moy, September 25, 1948, FM.

13. Donald Gilpatric memo about Kenneth Moy, May 24, 1948, p. 1, in "Inter-Office Memos, 1947–1948," May 29, 1948, Economic Cooperation Administration's Relief Mission in Post-War China, 1946–1948, AU; Fravel, *Active Defense*, 55–56; Mitter, *Forgotten Ally*, 369; Coble, *The Collapse of Nationalist China*, 165–68.

14. "New Air Service," *SCMP*, January 8, 1948; "CAT denial," *SCMP*, May 1, 1948; "Success of C.A.T.," *SCMP*, July 25, 1948; "*Paiqiu daibiaodui jinxi lianxi*" (Volleyball teams practicing tonight), *Dongnanbao* (Shanghai), April 23, 1948; "*Bangqiu youyi sai*" (Friendly baseball competition), *Dongnanbao* (Shanghai), May 26, 1948; "*Xiongmao leiqiu zheng jing*" (Pandas softball team travels to Nanjing), *Shenbao*, October 9, 1948; Anna Chennault, *A Thousand Springs: The Biography of a Marriage* (Paul S. Eriksson, 1962), 199–200.

15. "Taiyuan Exodus," *SCMP*, July 21, 1948; "Tsinan's Fate," *SCMP*, September 26, 1948; "Airline Withdraws," *SCMP*, December 2, 1948; 79th US Congress, private law 808, August 2, 1946, in file B1F1 201 1945–46d, PK; "Request for Permission to Marry," March 1, 1948, p. 1, file B1F2 201 file 1947–49b, PK; Bob to Pete, November 30, 1945, p. 1, and Peter Kim to Lt. Col. W. A. Ohls, February 4, 1946, pp. 2–3, file B1F19 correspondence 1943–46c, PK; Ruth and Peter Kim wedding photos, 1948, FM.

16. EKMD, January 24, 1949; Ernest Moy to Loring Moy, February 7, 1949, p. 1, and Kenneth Moy to Loring Moy, November 17, 1948, FM; Coble, *The Collapse of Nationalist China*, 173–91.

17. EKMD, February 10–12 and April 26, 1949.

18. "E.C.A. Mission," *SCMP*, May 2, 1949; Ernest Moy to Loring Moy; Kenneth Moy photos of family graves ("Chinese Decoration Day"), April 1949, WTM.

CHAPTER THIRTY-NINE: ALICE AND ALFRED

1. ML, 4; newspaper clipping, "*Fasheng xiedou*" (armed fight breaks out), ca. November 1946, AML.

2. ML, 4–5.

3. ML, 4–5; Swhard Tung to editor, *CWR*, August 31, 1946; undated clipping of Alfred and Alice Lee, ca. 1947, AML; Wasserstrom, *Student Protests*, 250–61.

4. ML, 4–5; undated clipping of the Lees.

5. Alice Moy Lee to Anna Kong Mei, ca. January 1948, AML; ML 8; Marine Lynx, list of alien passengers for the United States, May 20, 1947, Ancestry.com.

6. Wasserstrom, *Student Protests*, 271–73; Lynn T. White, *Policies of Chaos: The Organizational Causes of Violence in China's Cultural Revolution* (Princeton University Press, 2016), 52–54; A. Doak Barnett, *China on the Eve of Communist Takeover* (Praeger, 1968), 18–20; Catherine R. Schenk, "Commercial Rivalry between Shanghai and Hong Kong during the Collapse of the Nationalist Regime in China, 1945–1949," *International History Review* 20, no. 1 (1998), 70.

7. "S'hai Lawyer Passes Away in America," *SCMP*, February 28, 1953; Brooks, *American Exodus*, 199; Bert Lee interview; *WWCNY*, 50.

8. Lee to Mei, 1; "Foreign Visitors," *Foreign Commerce Weekly* 29, No. 8, November 23, 1947, 8–34.

9. W. F. Watkins to Chief, Expulsion Section, Immigration and Naturalization Service, January 22, 1948, p. 1; "In re Ai-shen Miles Lee, file A-6712032," November 7, 1949, p. 2, AML.

10. Lee to Mei; "In re Ai-shen Miles Lee," p. 2; W. F. Watkins and P. A. Esperley to Ai-shen M. Lee, January 28, 1948, AML; SS America Transport, passenger manifest, Ventura, California, to Shanghai, August 20, 1948, Ancestry.com.

11. Coble, *The Collapse of Nationalist China*, 173–191; *Nippon Times*, "Party Aboard Ship," September 3, 1948; *Nippon Times*, "Prices Still Topsy Turvy 3 Days After Yuan Switch," August 26, 1948.

12. Coble, *The Collapse of Nationalist China*, 173–191; *SCMP*, "Finance Scandal," September 4, 1948, "S'Hai Economic Scandal," September 6, 1948, "Shanghai Arrests," September 10, 1948, "Anxiety in Shanghai," September 19, 1948.

13. "Retired Banker and Executive Dies," *SCMP*, March 5, 1959; *NYT*, "Percy Kwok Dead," July 9, 1974; Jolly Young email to the author, December 4, 2022.

14. "Shanghai Plight," *SCMP*, October 31, 1948; "Rice from Colony," *SCMP*, November 14, 1948; "Evacuation Begins," *SCMP*, November 21, 1948; S.S. *Dick Lykes*, passenger list, March 3, 1948, Ancestry.com; British Naval Office, "Shanghai General Report No. 1," October 12, 1945, p. 4, BFO371/46246.

15. FRUS 1948 (Vol. 3), 873, 890, 900–902; "Leaving China," *SCMP*, November 30, 1948; "U.S. Consul Warns," *SCMP*, December 2, 1948; "Xmas Shopping,"

SCMP, December 20, 1948; "Coming and Going," *SCMP*, December 29, 1948; "Personalia," *China Mail*, December 29, 1948; "*Chukou chuanqi yugao*" (Outward sailing times), *Ta Kung Pao*, December 22, 1948.

16. "Yangtse Stand," *SCMP*, December 5, 1948; "Evacuees Return," *SCMP*, December 11, 1948; "Evacuation: Panic Dying Down," *SCMP*, December 21, 1948; "Shanghai Robbery," *SCMP*, December 22, 1948; "Coming and Going," *SCMP*, December 29, 1948; *China Mail*, "Personalia," December 29, 1948; *Ta Kung Pao*, "*Chukou chuanqi yugao*"; Barnett, *China on the Eve of Communist Takeover*, 96–99.

17. I base my descriptions of the waterfront over time from the photos on Gwulo.com.

18. "Reds Tighten Squeeze," *SCMP*, May 17, 1949; Alfred Lee to "Ted," February 12, 1951, and Alson M. Lee, "Application by Displaced Person Residing in the United States to Adjust Immigration Status," ca. 1950, p. 2, AML; Douglas Lee email to the author, July 14, 2024.

19. "Reds Tighten Squeeze," *SCMP*, May 17, 1949; Alfred Lee to "Ted."

CHAPTER FORTY: KAY AND MING TAI

1. "Manhattan Transfers," *NYT*, August 31, 1949; "Eugenia Chen Is Married to Wayman C. Wing," *Ogden Standard Examiner*, September 25, 1949; Al Salerno, "Night Life," *BE*, November 17, 1948; photos 2015.037.008, 2015.037.050, 2015.037.087, 2015.037.129, September 17, 1949, DJC; USAT Simon B. Buckner, "List of In-bound Passengers," December 8, 1948, lists 110 and 116, Ancestry.com.

2. Photo 2015.037.127, 1949, DJC; Yip Typond death certificate, August 10, 1948, NYCMA; death notices, *BE*, July 10, 1949; *1950 Census of Population and Housing*, Belleville, Essex, NJ, ED 7–10, sheet 7, Ancestry.com; Thomas G. Finucane, Chair, Board of Immigration Appeals, "In re Ai-shen Miles Lee or Ai-Shen Miles"; Chris and Sara Moy email to the author, April 4, 2021.

3. Chris and Sara Moy email; Lillian Lee interview with the author, April 23, 2024; *1950 Census of Population and Housing*, San Francisco, CA, ED 38–251, sheet 77, Ancestry.com.

4. Photos 2015.37.127 and 2015.37.087, September 1949, DJC.

5. Benjamin O. Fordham, *Building the Cold War Consensus: The Political Economy of US National Security Policy, 1949–51* (University of Michigan Press, 1998), 137–40.

6. K. Scott Wong, *Americans First: Chinese Americans and the Second World War* (Harvard University Press, 2005), 187; Brooks, *Alien Neighbors, Foreign Friends*, 135–36.

7. William T. Moy shooting photo, ca. 1930, WTM; Chris and Sara Moy email to the author.

8. "New Republic Proclaimed for China by Reds," *NYHT*, September 22, 1949; Brooks, *Between Mao and McCarthy*, 78–81, 91.

9. Alexander V. Pantsov and Steven I. Levine, *Deng Xiaoping: A Revolutionary Life* (Oxford University Press, 2015), 146; T. Timothy Chen, "Conversations about Dr. Bangnee Alfred Liu," *Bulletin of the International Chinese Statistical Association*, July 1999, 24–25; Transcontinental and Western Air flight 45346, "Air Passenger Manifest," March 31, 1950, Ancestry.com.

10. Executive Office of the UN Secretary General, "Directory of the Specialized Agencies and the Office of the High Commissioner for Refugees," ca. 1950, p. 3, file "Specialized Agencies, General, January 1948–December 1954," item S-1555-0000-0049-00001, United Nations Archives online, https://search.archives.un.org/s-1555-0000-0049-00001 (accessed May 29, 2024); "U.N. Soon to Open Part of New Unit," *NYT*, June 25, 1950; "U.N. Secretariat Staff Gets Rush Call for Korea Talks," *NYT*, June 26, 1950; Harry Fox, "Visiting the U.N.," *NYT*, June 11, 1950; A. M. Rosenthal, "Red North 'Guilty,'" *NYT*, June 26, 1950; George Barrett, "Record U.N. Crowd at Korea Session," *NYT*, June 28, 1950; United Nations Security Council Resolution 82 (1950), https://digitallibrary.un.org/record/112025?ln = en&v = pdf (accessed May 29, 2024); Green, *By More Than Providence*, 275–78.

11. Jack T. Young army record; MFHR, 69.

12. Green, *By More Than Providence*, 277–78; Brooks, *Between Mao and McCarthy*, 105.

13. Brooks, *Between Mao and McCarthy*, 105–7; *Troy Record*, "Chinatown Youth to Fight Against Reds," December 8, 1950; "N.Y. Chinese Back Chiang," *NYHT*, December 3, 1950.

14. Brooks, *Between Mao and McCarthy*, 111; *Wilkes-Barre Times Leader*, "Against Red China," January 18, 1951; "Mott St. Chinese to Rally at U.N.," *BE*, December 12, 1950; Ralph Chapman, "Bamboo Curtain at Lake Success," *NYHT*, December 3, 1950.

15. VCD, October 11, 1938, pp. 6–7, 35.7/16.5; Chen, "Conversations," 24.

16. Chen, "Conversations," 24; SS *Liberte*, Manifest of Outward-Bound Passengers (Aliens), January 4, 1951, Ancestry.com; MFHR, 5–6; A. Kuckein to Honolulu District Director, September 11, 1950, p. 1, file 4382/4848, NARA-SB.

CHAPTER FORTY-ONE: ERNEST

1. Chi Kwan Mark, *Hong Kong and the Cold War: Anglo-American Relations 1949–1957* (Oxford University Press, 2004), 16–19; *SCMP*, "Air Traffic," October 14, 1949; *SCMP*, "The Refugee Beggar," August 3, 1952; EKMD, October 14 and December 11, 1949, and January 3, 1950.

2. EKMD, December 20 and December 30, 1949; Wei-lin Hsieh to Loring Moy, November 8, 1949, FM; FRUS 1949 (Vol. 4), 250.

3. EKMD, January 23, 1950, and March 28, 1950.

4. EKMD, March 27, April 3, April 24, April 28, May 2, May 19, and July 24, 1950; "Softball," *SCMP*, February 9, 1950.

5. EKMD, July 3, 1950; "New H.K. Club," *SCMP*, May 18, 1950; "Second University Need," *SCMP*, July 20, 1950; Ernest K. Moy, "Intellectuals and Professionals: From a Memorandum Submitted in a Conference at the State Department," October 10, 1950, p. 2, and "Facts Relating to Chinese Intellectuals in Hong Kong," August 11, 1951, pp. 1–2, file "Correspondence, 1951–1953," box 22, GF.

6. "Bombing Outrages," *SCMP*, February 26, 1938; "Chinese Clubs," *SCMP*, November 2, 1949; "Chinese Refugees' Aid," *SCMP*, November 26, 1956; Christopher Rea and Nicolai Volland, *The Business of Culture: Cultural Entrepreneurs in China and Southeast Asia, 1900–65* (University of British Columbia Press, 2014), 121–36; EKMD, September 11, September 25, October 22, November 21, and December 27, 1950.

7. Moy, "Intellectuals and Professionals," 2; Madeline Y. Hsu, *The Good Immigrants: How the Yellow Peril Became the Model Minority* (Princeton University Press, 2015), 138–39; Ernest K. Moy to Geraldine Fitch, March 13, 1951, p. 2, file "Correspondence, 1951–1953." 1950 numbers of the *Hong Kong Tiger Standard* contain almost none of Ernest's work but hundreds of DC stories from the standard wire services

8. EKMD, October 5, October 11, November 11, and November 28, 1950, and January 20, March 7, March 13, and March 30, 1951.

9. Ernest K. Moy to Geraldine Fitch, June 4, 1951, p. 1, August 9, 1951, p. 1, and September 6, 1951, all in file "Correspondence, 1951–1953"; Sutcliffe to Allman, 1; Hsu, *The Good Immigrants*, 139; Ernest K. Moy to Chih Meng, July 21, 1951, p. 1, file "Correspondence, 1951–1953"; Joseph G. Morgan, *The Vietnam Lobby: The American Friends of Vietnam, 1955–1975* (University of North Carolina Press, 1997), 19.

10. Ernest K. Moy to Geraldine Fitch, September 14, 1951, p. 1, and September 1, 1951, p. 1, file "Correspondence, 1951–1953."

11. EKMD, April 8 and September 3–16, 1951.

12. Brooks, *Between Mao and McCarthy*, 114–16; Marvin Liebman, *Coming Out Conservative: An Autobiography* (Chronicle Books, 1992), 81–83, 89–91; EKMD, October 25, 1951.

13. Ernest K. Moy to Geraldine Fitch, November 13, 1951, p. 1, file "Correspondence, 1951–1953"; Ernest K. Moy, untitled memo, December 11, 1951, p. 1, file 19, box 20, NFA; Anne B. Wheeler to Harrison M. Holland, May 24, 1951, p. 1, file SC5101258526 (350.4 Aid Refugee Chinese Intellectuals, Inc.), Records of the Office of Chinese Affairs, 1945–1955, AU.

14. Liebman, *Coming Out Conservative*, 91–97; ARCI press release, ca. May 1952, file "Chinese Consolidated Benevolent Association," box 7, ARCI; ARCI letterhead, in file "Correspondence," box 91, Christopher T. Emmet papers, Hoover Institution; Hsu, *The Good Immigrants*, 142.

15. Liebman, *Coming Out Conservative*, 97; EKMD, January 21, 1952.

16. Liebman, *Coming Out Conservative*, 92–94, 97; Ernest K. Moy, "NY Memo," March 18, 1952, Ernest K. Moy to Dr. Judd and Mr. Emmet, March 14, 1952, Ernest K. Moy to Walter Judd and Christopher Emmet, March 7, 1952, Ernest K. Moy to Christopher Emmet, April 24, 1952, and Ernest K. Moy to Christopher Emmet, May 13, 1952, p. 2, all in file "Correspondence," box 91; EKMD, March 22, 1952.

CHAPTER FORTY-TWO: ALICE AND ALFRED

1. Lillian Lee interview with the author, April 23, 2024; Lillian Lee email to the author, June 6, 2020; Deborah Lau interview with the author, August 24, 2020; *Polk's Crocker-Langley San Francisco City Directory 1951* (R. L. Polk, 1951), 759.

2. John Jacobs, *A Rage for Justice: The Passion and Politics of Phillip Burton* (University of California Press, 1995), 22; Hastings College of Law, *Announcement* (University of California, 1948), 24; Samuel E. Yee to Alice M. Lee, August 27, 1949, AML; Finucane to Samuel E. Yee; Lee to Havenner; US Congress, *Journal of the House of Representatives, Eighty-First Congress, 2nd Session* (USGPO, 1950), 281.

3. *In re Ai-shen Miles Lee*, 1–2; Hsu, *The Good Immigrants*, 104–26; Public Law 82–60, 1951; US Congress, *Journal of the House of Representatives*, 281; ML, 9.

4. EKMD, February 3–7, 1952; photo 2015.037.160, June 1952, DJC; Lee interview.

5. EKMD, May 8 and 31,1952; "Incorporations," *Paterson Morning Call*, May 2, 1952; ML, 9.

6. EKMD, April 18 and June 3, 1952.

7. EKMD, June 6–16, 1952.

8. Dr. Clara Raven, "Autopsy Report," November 1952, appended to "Report of the Death of an American Citizen," March 18, 1953, Ancestry.com; "Well-Known Chinese Dies in Berkeley," *Berkeley Gazette*, February 24, 1953.

9. EKMD, April 23, 24, and 29, 1953; Kenneth T. Jackson, *Crabgrass Frontier: The Suburbanization of the United States* (Oxford University Press, 1985), 241.

10. Lillian Lee interview; ML, 9.

11. EKMD, October 3–November 15, 1953.

12. Lillian Lee interview; ML, 9–10.

13. *United States Statutes at Large, 1954, Vol. 68, Part 2* (USGPO, 1955), B38–B48.

14. Lillian Lee text to the author, April 11, 2024; ML, 9; Lee-Yick wedding photos, June 5, 1955, AML.

15. Lillian Lee interview; *Paterson Morning Call*, "Police Score Ninth Straight Pistol Win," June 9, 1955; EKMD, September 6, 1955; Lillian Lee email to the author, June 6, 2020. For a description of what the ceremony looked like around this time, I have used Jade Snow Wong, *Fifth Chinese Daughter* (Harper & Bros., 1945), 140.

16. Yick-Lee wedding photo, June 5, 1955, AML; Douglas Chu, email to the author, January 19, 2021; item 2015.037.449, and photo 2015.037.546, ca. 1957, DJC; Robert S. Pollack, *Tumor Surgery of the Head and Neck* (Lea & Febiger, 1957), 16; "News of Brooklyn G.I.s," *BE*, March 29, 1954.

CHAPTER FORTY-THREE: KAY, MING TAI, AND ERNEST

1. Lillian Lee email to the author, June 6, 2020.

2. Ernest K. Moy to editor, *NYHT*, April 26, 1952; Ernest K. Moy to editor, *NYT*, March 4, 1955 and April 1, 1955; "Rotary Hears Speaker on 'Formosa,'" *Pater-*

son Morning Call, July 6, 1955; "*Meiqiju zhangyi wei qiaobao benzou jiaoshe*" (Out of a sense of justice for overseas compatriots, Ernest Moy reaches out), *Chinese Journal* (New York), March 14, 1955; EKMD, July 18, 1951, and May 12, 1952.

3. EKMD, January 30, February 10, July 28, and October 25, 1953; January 24, January 31, February 21, February 28, and April 1, 1954; November 13, 1955; and *passim*.

4. EKMD, February 17, April 3–May 31, June 21, and June 25, 1953; March 6 and December 15, 1954; and June 15, 1955; Ming Kay, Sherman, and Alan Chen conversation with the author, June 13, 2022; MFHR, 11–15.

5. Liu Yifu, "*Fangong laodoushi meiqiju*" (Old anti-communist friend Ernest K. Moy), *Zhongyang Ribao* (Taipei), September 29, 1956; Lillian Lee interview with the author, April 23, 2024; Loring Moy to Ruth Kim, September 22, 1955, p. 2, FM; EKMD, September 2 and 8 and October 7 and 8, 1955.

6. EKMD, September 2 and October 7, 1955 and *passim*.

7. Brooks, *Between Mao and McCarthy*, 157–59, 162, 167–68; "US Inquiry Hurts Chinatown Trade," *NYT*, March 17, 1956; D.E. Yarbrough, "Report of Investigation," March 9, 1956, p. 6, file 56364/51.6, box 598, RG 85, NARA-DC; JTY 81.

8. Yarbrough, "Report of Investigation," March 9, 1956, pp. 7–8; D.E. Yarbrough, "Report of Investigation," March 16, 1956, p. 4, file 56364/51.6.

9. EKMD, September 6 and 7, 1955; Tamra Moy interview.

10. EKMD, August 5, 1953; items 2015.037.581 and 2015.037.584–1/2, ca. early 1960s, DJC. I base my description of the A&S employees on directory and newspaper research on the women Helen Typond mentioned in items from this era.

11. Paul N. Kotakis, "Army ROTC at One Hundred," *Military Review* 96, no. 3 (2016), 107; "Balloons Vital to Artillery," *Stars and Stripes* (Pacific Edition), March 6, 1957; *Prattonia 1956* (Pratt Institute, 1956); "News of Brooklyn GIs," *BE*, March 29, 1954; MFHR, 22; "Deaths," *BE*, February 5, 1952; "Deaths," *NYHT*, May 24, 1957; Empress of Scotland passenger manifest, April 6, 1957, Pan-Am flight 115/12 passenger manifest, May 12, 1957, and army aircraft R7V-1 General Declaration, May 25, 1957, Ancestry.com. My description of thyroid cancer in the 1950s relies on Maurice M. Black and Francis D. Speer, *Human Cancer: A Manual for Students and Physicians* (Year Book Publishers, 1957), 130–32, and a series of June 2024 email conversations with Dr. Robert Yee.

12. Denny Roy, *Taiwan: A Political History* (Cornell University Press, 2003), 52–54, 58–60; Jane B. Young, "Report of the Death of an American Citizen: Ernest K. Moy," April 28, 1958, Ancestry.com; Liu, "*Fangong laodoushi meiqiju*"; Ernest K. Moy to Christopher Emmet, March 6, 1957, p. 1, Christopher Emmet papers, Hoover Institution. I have based my hostel description on the photos and details from the website taipeiairstation.blogspot.com.

13. Liu, "*Fangong laodoushi meiqiju*"; "*Xinji taipingyang liang an yi gongmin*" (One citizen connecting the two sides of the Pacific), *Shibao Zazhi* (Taipei) 17, no. 2 (February 23, 1957); "*Lumei laoqiaoling meiqiju fabiao tanhua*" (Venerable overseas leader Ernest K. Moy speaks), *Zhengqizhonghua* (Taipei), May 25, 1957;

"*Zongtong zuo jiejian meiqiju*" (President yesterday received Ernest K. Moy), *Zhengqizhonghua* (Taipei), May 1, 1957; Ernest Moy note on photo with George Yeh, May 21, 1957, FM.

14. Hsu, *The Good Immigrants*, 145–46; Geraldine Fitch to Christopher Emmet, August 26, 1956, p. 1, Fitch to Bill Howard, August 25, 1957, p. 1, Travis L. Fletcher to George Fitch, Feb. 25, 1957, p. 2, and Ernest K. Moy to B. A. Garside, April 3, 1957, in file "Correspondence, 1954–1959," Box 22, GF.

15. *SCMP*, photo, May 5, 1957; Tucker, *Taiwan, Hong Kong, and the United States, 1945–1992*, 90–91; Roy, *Taiwan*, 136; *FRUS 1955–1957, Vol. 3*, 530–44.

16. Alfred Kohlberg to Ernest Moy, June 10, 1957, p. 1, file "Ernest K. Moy," box 28, Alfred Kohlberg papers, Hoover Institution; Ernest K. Moy to Christopher Emmet, March 6, 1957, p. 1, file "Moy," box 91, Emmet papers; Tucker, *Taiwan, Hong Kong, and the United States, 1945–1992*, 92.

17. "Coming & Going," *SCMP*, June 5, 1957; "Personalities," *SCMP*, June 8, 1957; "Dr. Moy Commits Suicide at Hostel," *China Post*, February 2, 1958, file 19, Box 20, NFA.

18. Advertisement for Jiecheng (Jebsen's), *Wah Kiu Yat Po* (Hong Kong), July 8, 1957; "Inventory of Personal Effects of the late Ernest K. Moy," in "Report of the Death of an American Citizen: Ernest K. Moy"; Marjorie Topley, *Cantonese Society in Hong Kong and Singapore: Gender, Religion, Medicine and Money*, ed. Jean DeBernardi (Hong Kong University Press, 2011), 502–3.

19. A. A. E. Franklin to Selwyn Lloyd, November 5, 1957, p. 1, BFO371/127452; copy of Ernest K. Moy to Adelaide Chen Young, January 15, 1958, in possession of the author.

20. *China Post*, "Dr. Moy Commits Suicide at Hostel"; *Central Daily News* (Taipei), "*Qiaoling meiqiju zisha*"; Yeh Jih-sung and Li Pao-chu, "Coroner's Certificate of Examination," January 31, 1958, pp. 1–2, in "Report of the Death of an American Citizen: Ernest K. Moy."

CHAPTER FORTY-FOUR: SIBLINGS

1. *Polk's Crocker-Langley San Francisco City Directory 1957* (R. L. Polk, 1957), 779; *Polk's Crocker-Langley San Francisco City Directory 1958* (R. L. Polk, 1958), 812; Lillian Lee interview with the author, April 23, 2024; Margaret O'Mara, *Cities of Knowledge: Cold War Science and the Search for the Next Silicon Valley* (Princeton University Press, 2004), 54.

2. Tamra Moy interview; "Dr. Moy Commits Suicide at Hostel"; "*Qiaoling meiqiju zisha*."

3. Jane B. Young to Department of State, March 13, 1958, p. 1, in "Report of the Death of an American Citizen: Ernest K. Moy"; J. L. Huang telegram to Loring Moy, January 31, 1958, FM; Jack T. Young Army record; photo 2015.037.246, May 1958, DJC; EKMD, August 11, 1954 and October 2, 1955.

4. *Brooklyn Telephone Directory 1959* (New York Telephone Company, 1959), 1488; Helen Typond entry card, November 18, 1961, New York State Passenger and Crew Lists, Ancestry.com; items 2015.037.581 and 2015.037.584–1/2, DJC.

5. "Happiness Plus at Anniversary," *New York Daily News*, December 1, 1960; photo 2015.037.238, November 1960, DJC.

6. RGR, 5; "Happiness Plus at Anniversary."

7. Photos 2015.037.238 and 2015.037.456, October 1961, DJC; "See the Isle Beautiful," *Taiwan Today*, September 1, 1961, https://taiwantoday.tw/print.php?unit = 12,29,33,45&post = 23496 (accessed June 29, 2024).

8. Item 2015.037.584–1/2, DJC.

9. David Frazier, "Taiwan's Foundational Building Boom," *Taipei Times*, March 28, 2024, https://www.taipeitimes.com/News/feat/archives/2024/03/28/2003815572 (accessed June 30, 2024).

10. Photographs "*Songmeiling jiejian qiaoling*" (Madame Chiang meets with overseas leaders), October 24, 1961, items 002–050113–00016–101 and 002–050113–00016–103, President Chiang Kai-shek Cultural Materials, Academia Historica, Taipei, Taiwan.

11. Photos 2015.037.039 and 2015.037.57, and item 2015.037.603a, October 1961, DJC; Tamra Moy interview with the author, February 1, 2020.

12. MFHR, 2, 8–9; photos 2015.037.025, 2015.037.020, 2015.037.034, 2015.037.053, and 2015.037.054, 1961, DJC.

13. Photos 2015.037.144, 2015.037.159, and 2015.037.054, October-November 1961, DJC.

EPILOGUE

1. Ming Kay, Sherman, and Alan Chen interview with the author, June 13, 2022.

2. Jolly Young email to the author, August 1, 2024.

3. "Deaths," *NYT*, October 28, 1967; MFHR, 20; Chen interview.

4. Date stamps and handwritten pull notes on documents in box 72, HEM.

5. Chris Moy conversation with the author, March 25, 2023.

6. "Launching," *Farmingdale Observer*, July 17, 1969.

7. Chris Moy, "Lunar Landing," July 26, 2024, in the author's possession; National Air and Space Museum, "Apollo 11 timeline," https://airandspace.si.edu/explore/stories/apollo-missions/apollo-11-moon-landing/apollo-11-timeline (accessed July 28, 2024); "Tools and Technology from the Apollo Program," https://airandspace.si.edu/explore/stories/tools-and-technology-apollo-program#:~:text = The%20manned%20Apollo%20missions%20were,module%2C%20and%20a%20lunar%20module. (accessed July 28, 2024); CBS News, "From the Archives: Apollo 11 Moon Landing Leaves Walter Cronkite 'Speechless,'" https://www.youtube.com/watch?v = oMF58ZP681A (accessed July 28, 2024).

8. Item 2015.037.580, ca. 1968, DJC; Lillian Lee email to the author, January 12, 2024; Lillian Lee interview with the author, April 23, 2024.

9. Lau interview; Alice Lee photo with trophies, 1970s, AML; Douglas Lee text to the author, November 15, 2024

10. ML, 12–13.

11. MFHR, 12, 78; Chen, "Conversations about Dr. Bangnee Alfred Liu," 24.

12. ML, 7, 16; Victor Zorza, "De-Maoisation Under Way," *SCMP*, May 13, 1978; "All Eyes on the Canton Fair," *SCMP*, October 13, 1978; Yan Sun, *The Chinese Reassessment of Socialism, 1976–1992* (Princeton University Press, 1995), 23–41.

13. Lau interview.

14. Lillian Lee text to the author, July 28, 2024; ML, 7, 19, 23–25; Douglas Lee email to the author, July 28, 2024.

NOTE ON METHODOLOGY AND SOURCES

Over the past two decades, I have written three other books, each of which led me in different ways to this one. Researching *Alien Neighbors, Foreign Friends* taught me to think about the overt and covert discrimination that circumscribed Chinese Americans' ambitions long after World War II. *Between Mao and McCarthy* immersed me in the complicated and contradictory world of Chinese American politics in the midcentury years. And *American Exodus* helped me understand the lives of the thousands of Chinese Americans who emigrated to China in the prewar decades.

In writing these books, I also gained a deep familiarity with the first sizable cohort of second-generation Chinese American citizens. Indeed, it is a small enough group that the same people sometimes appear in more than one of my books. The Moys are no exception. I first encountered Ernest, as well as Jim Typond and Shavey Lee, while doing research for *Between Mao and McCarthy;* Alice, Alfred, Herbert, Ernest, and Ruth all appear in *American Exodus*—as do Henry Young and his brothers Nom Chu and Chu Su Gunn, Shavey Lee's sister Emily, architect Poy Gum Lee, Alson's godparents H.C. and Anna Mei, and many others. In some ways, *The Moys of New York and Shanghai* is like a sequel to *American Exodus,* because it takes one of that book's most intriguing stories, explores it in greater depth, and follows it to its end.

In this new book, I have tried to render the Moys and their world as vividly as possible while staying faithful to rigorous historical research standards. When I do not have direct accounts of events—for example, Ernest's arrival in 1928 Shanghai or escape from occupied Hong Kong—I have relied on others' contemporary and overlapping narratives of the same experiences. To create a sense of atmosphere, I have looked at scores of photos and watched numerous old films, many of them home movies, of prewar and midcentury New York, San Francisco, Kunming, Shanghai, Chongqing, Taipei, and Hong Kong. I am lucky as well to have visited, and in some cases to have lived in, just about every place I mention in this book, including Beijing, Chongqing, Hong Kong, Taipei, and Yokohama, as well as Brooklyn, Chicago, Evanston, Honolulu, Manhattan, and San Francisco.

Fortunately, the Moys corresponded frequently, enjoyed photography, and kept diaries and scrapbooks, and several of their children and grandchildren preserved family stories and genealogies for future generations. Since all of the siblings and spouses died more than thirty years ago, I never had the chance to meet any of them. To give readers a sense of this family as real people, I have used not just archival materials, letters, diaries, home movies, and photos, but also a series of interviews, emails, and follow-up questions with Moy descendants. In several cases I met these descendants in person. Unsurprisingly, their portrayals of the siblings varied by generation and relationship—the Moys' children and in-laws described them differently than their grandchildren did—but the divergence itself was valuable, and many of the accounts helped fill in details about Helen, George, and Herbert, who have no living direct descendants.

Moy family friends proved invaluable, too, providing additional information and background on Herbert, Pete, Ruth, Shau Hong, and Billy and Lenore, as well as on wartime and postwar Shanghai. As with all families, several descendants and friends repeated stories that turned out, upon further research, to be more myth than fact; still, the interviews, questions, meetings, and correspondence were crucial in helping me transform facts, dates, and names into living, breathing people. That said, all errors are mine alone.

Below, I describe in greater depth some of the more important sources that I used for each part of the book. Many of these sources, including family scrapbooks, photos, objects, and letters, remain in private hands, but Moy descendants generously allowed me access to them with no preconditions for their use or for the manuscript as a whole. After examining their incredible holdings, I am convinced that as intriguing as the Moys were, there are other Chinese American families whose past is likely just as extraordinary.

PART ONE: FAMILY

This section relies on contemporary English- and Chinese-language newspapers and magazines from every city in which the Moys lived or traveled; real estate, business, and city directories from New York and New Jersey; Chinese Student Alliance publications; high school and college yearbooks; and back issues of *Variety* and *Billboard*. It also uses the voluminous National Archives and Records Administration (NARA) files connected to Chinese exclusion—from Forms 430 ("Application of Alleged American Citizen of the Chinese Race for Preinvestigation of Status") to Chinese merchants' Section 6 (exempt class) testimony and certificates. For material on the family's daily life, I am indebted to Eugenia "Beah" Chen

Wing's extensive 1981 family history record and description of her parents' wedding; Victoria "Meme" Chen Luke's written account of the Chins' life in Glen Ridge; and Jack T. Young's memoir. I also rely extensively on the privately held photo scrapbooks of Bill and May Moy and Alfred and Alice Lee, as well as Helen Typond's photos and scrapbooks. Ruth Moy Kim not only kept detailed photo records of these years but also a scrapbook that C.C. Chang sent her, as well as numerous letters from him alluding to their relationship. For historical background, I draw especially on Erika Lee, *At America's Gates: Chinese Immigration During the Exclusion Era, 1882–1943* (University of North Carolina Press, 2003), Madeline Y. Hsu, *Dreaming of Gold, Dreaming of Home: Transnationalism and Migration Between the United States and South China, 1882–1943* (Stanford University Press, 2000), and Mary Ting Yi Lui, *The Chinatown Trunk Mystery: Murder, Miscegenation, and Other Dangerous Encounters in Turn-of-the-Century New York City* (Princeton University Press, 2005).

PART TWO: WAR

To describe the family's daily life in the 1930s and early 1940s, I use the scores of letters that Kay's daughter Vivian sent to her fiancé and then husband Bingham Dai between 1935 and 1939, almost all of them written from the Chins' home in New York; Alson Lee's wartime diary in Chinese and his postwar documents; the aforementioned photos and scrapbooks of Helen, Bill and May, and Alice and Alfred; Ruth's photos and collected letters and objects, including Japanese-issued ration coupons, identity documents, and other ephemera from occupied Shanghai; and Swiss consular records from Shanghai, which deal with the protection of American interests. Pete Kim's papers offer a fuller picture of his life in prewar and wartime Shanghai. The Shanghai police record of Herbert Moy's 1945 death provides crucial clues to his last hours and Marquita Kwan's identity, while C.Y. Lin's oral history, done in Taiwan in the early 1980s, dispels some of the mystery around K.S. Lo. NARA sources about the Moys at this time include Form 430 files; Herbert Moy's extensive FBI file; digitized copies of three of his XGRS broadcasts; Foreign Service volumes for Shanghai, Hong Kong, and Canton; and the WASC correspondence in the US Forces in the China-Burma-India Theater files. I also use English and Chinese-language newspapers, magazines, and directories from New York, Newark, Chicago, Shanghai, Hong Kong, and other cities; copies of Nazi-backed magazines *Shanghai Calling!* and *Twentieth Century;* Jack Young's memoir and Alson Lee's "My Life" memoir; and numerous accounts from 1930s and 1940s Shanghai residents, most notably Carroll Duard Alcott, *My War with Japan* (Henry Holt and Company, 1943) and John B. Powell, *My Twenty-Five Years in China* (Macmillan, 1945). Particularly useful primary-source databases for diving into Herbert's activities and the situation in occupied Shanghai in general are Shanghai Municipal Police records, British Foreign Office files, Australian shortwave radio magazines, and VirtualShanghai and Pastvu.com. Key secondary sources for this section include Hanchao Lu, *Beyond the Neon Lights: Everyday Shanghai in the Early Twentieth Century* (University of California Press, 1999) and Frederic Wakeman Jr., *The Shanghai Badlands: Wartime Terrorism and Urban Crime, 1937–1941* (Cambridge University Press, 2002) for life in Shanghai; Parks M. Coble, *Chinese Capitalists in Japan's New Order: The Occupied Lower Yangtze, 1937–1945* (University of California Press, 2003) for business conditions and the Kwok family; Chihyun Chang, *Government, Imperialism and Nationalism in China: The Maritime Customs Service and Its Chinese Staff* (Routledge, 2013) for the Customs College; and Rana Mitter, *Forgotten Ally: China's World War II, 1937–1945* (Mariner, 2013) for the larger war.

PART THREE: REVOLUTION

For details about the family's life in the postwar 1940s and 1950s, I rely on the detailed daily diaries that Ernest kept between 1949 and 1955 and that included both extraordinary events and mundane details, from his vacuuming to his snacks; Alson Lee's postwar documents and "My Life" memoir; the photos and scrapbooks of Helen, Bill and May, and Alice and Alfred; Ruth's photos, letters, and ephemera, including correspondence between Loring and Ken, Wei-lin "Willy" Hsieh, Pete, and others; Pete Kim's letters; and letters that Adelaide Chen Young sent her family from Beijing during the Chinese Civil War. I also use English- and Chinese-language newspapers, magazines, and directories from New York, Shanghai, Hong Kong, and the San Francisco Bay Area. I rely on the Gwulo.com site and VirtualShanghai to capture the feel of Hong Kong and Shanghai, and Ancestry.com to track family movements across the Pacific and the United States, as well as for Ernest's detailed death report. The digitized records of the United Nations offer information on both George Huang's early death and B. A. Liu's work, while Academia Sinica's Institute of Modern History archives document Ernest's visit to Taiwan and his sisters' later trip there. To describe Ernest's varied activities, I also use a trove of his letters, notebooks on soy protein, and photographs and documents, which, like his diaries, are in my possession; the files of ARCI, the papers of Christopher Emmet, and the papers of Ernest's friend Norwood F. Allman; and the letters he and Geraldine Fitch exchanged. Key secondary sources for this section include Zach Fredman, *The Tormented Alliance: American Servicemen and the Occupation of China, 1941–1949* (University of North Carolina Press, 2022); Parks M. Coble, *The Collapse of Nationalist China: How Chiang Kai-shek Lost China's Civil War* (Cambridge University Press, 2023); and Madeline Y. Hsu, *The Good Immigrants: How the Yellow Peril Became the Model Minority* (Princeton University Press, 2015).

INDEX